GUITAR AND VIHUELA
An Annotated Bibliography

Pablo Minguet E Yrol, *Academia Musical de los Instrumentos*...
(Madrid: Joaquin Ibarra, 1774), frontispiece.

GUITAR AND VIHUELA

An Annotated Bibliography

by

Meredith Alice McCutcheon

RILM RETROSPECTIVES No. 3

PENDRAGON PRESS

NEW YORK

Other titles in the series RILM Retrospectives:

No. 1 *Thematic Catalogues in Music: An annotated bibliography* by Barry S. Brook (1972) ISBN 0-918728-02-9

No. 2. *French Language Dissertations in Music: An annotated bibliography* by Jean Gribenski (1979) ISBN 0-918728-09-6 Out-of-Stock

Library of Congress Cataloging in Publication Data

McCutcheon, Meredith.
  Guitar and vihuela.

  (RILM Retrospectives; no. 3)
  Includes index.
    1. Guitar—Bibliography.   2. Vihuela—Bibliography.
  I. Title. II. Series.
  ML128.G8M45   1985   016.7876′1′09   85-17437

Copyright 1985 by Meredith Alice McCutcheon

ML
128
.G8
M45
1985

Table of Contents

List of Illustrations xiii

Introduction
- I. Guitar and Vihuela: A Historiography xv
- II. Identifying and Locating Music for Guitar and Vihuela xxii
- III. The Bibliography: Its Purpose, Contents, and Organization xxvi

Acknowledgments xxviii

How To Use The Bibliography xxix

Abbreviations

- General abbreviations xxx
- Abbreviations for periodicals and dictionaries indexed xxxii
- Sigla for library locations (Appendix I, II, and the main text) xxxvi
- Abbreviations for publishers of modern editions (Appendix II) xliv

The Bibliography

Chapter I: GENERAL HISTORIES AND DICTIONARIES			1
A. The Early Guitar: The Sixteenth through the Eighteenth Century (Including Studies of Tablature Notation in that Period)	1-5	vs.	3
B. General Surveys: The Sixteenth through the Twentieth Century	6-50		4
C. Dictionaries of Guitarists	51-55		13
Chapter II: NATIONAL HISTORIES			15
A. Argentina	56-62		17
B. Brazil	63-66		19
C. Czechoslovakia	67		19
D. Denmark	68-69		20
E. France			
F. Germany	70		20
G. Great Britain	71-72		20
H. Italy	73-76		21

260168

TABLE OF CONTENTS

I.	Latin America	77–78	21
J.	Mexico	79–84	22
K.	Paraguay	85	23
L.	Peru	86	23
M.	Poland	87–88	23
N.	Portugal	89	24
O.	Russia	90–108	24
P.	Spain	109–111	27
Q.	United States	112–151	27
	General	112–123	27
	The American Guild of Banjoists, Mandolinists, and Guitarists	124–129	29
	The American Guitar Society	130	30
	The Society of the Classic Guitar	131–133	30
	Blantchor, Francis	134	31
	Blessner, E.	135	31
	Carr, Benjamin	136	31
	Ferrer, Manuel Y.	137	31
	Foden, William	138–147	31
	Hayden, William	148	32
	Krick, George C.	149	33
	Pick, Richard	150	33
	Weiland, Francis	151	33
R.	Uruguay		33

Chapter III: HISTORIES OF THE RENAISSANCE PERIOD 35

A.	General Surveys	152–192	
	Guitar and Vihuela	152–159	37
	Guitar	160–166	38
	Vihuela	167–192	39
B.	Musical Forms	193–202	44
C.	Tablature Studies	203–207	46
D.	Individual Composers, Performers, Theorists, Publishers, and Authors	208–251	
	Ballard, Robert *See* Le Roy, Adrian		
	Barberis, Melchior de	208	47
	Bermudo, Juan	209–214	47
	Cabezón, Antonio de	215–216	49
	Cervantes, Miguel de	217–220	49
	Daza [Daça], Esteban	221–222	50
	Fuenllana, Miguel de	223–227	50
	Gorlier, Simon		51
	Guzman, Luis de	228	51
	Henestrosa, Luys Venegas de *See* Venegas de Henestrosa, Luys		
	Le Roy, Adrian; Ballard, Robert	229–230	52

vi

Milan, Luis	231–240	52
Morlaye, Guillaume		54
Mudarra, Alonso		54
Narváez, Luis	241–242	54
Phalèse, Pierre; Bellère, Jean		55
Pisador, Diego	243–247	55
Sancta María, Thomas de	248–249	57
Valderrábano, Enríquez de	250	57
Venegas de Henestrosa, Luys	251	57

Chapter IV: HISTORIES OF THE BAROQUE ERA			59
A.	General Surveys	252–266	61
B.	The Chitarra Battente	267–268	64
C.	Musical Forms	269–284	64
D.	Performance Practice and Tuning	285–294	68
E.	Individual Authors and Theorists	295–329	
	Bonanni [Buonanni], Filippo	295–296	70
	Brossard, Sébastien de	297–298	70
	Cerreto, Scipione	299–300	71
	Covarruvias Orozco [Horosco], Sebastien de	301–302	71
	Giustiniani, Vincenzo	303–307	72
	Grassineau, James	308–309	72
	Mersenne, Marin	310–314	73
	Nassarre [Nasarre], Pablo	315–317	74
	North, Roger	318	75
	Pepys, Samuel	319	75
	Praetorius, Michael	320–325	75
	Talbot, James	326–327	76
	Trichet, Pierre	328	76
	Turner, William	329	79
F.	Individual Composers and Performers	330–385	
	Abreu, Antonio; Prieto, P. F. Victor		79
	Amat, Juan Carlos [Joan Carles]	330–331	79
	Aranies, Juan		80
	Bailleux, Antoine		80
	Briceño, Luis de	332–334	80
	Campion, François		80
	Carré Sieur de la Grange, Anthoine		81
	Clementi, Orazio	335	81
	Colonna, Giovanni Ambrosio		81
	Corbetta, Francesco	336–348	81
	Diesel, Nathanael	349–351	84
	Doizi de Velasco, Nicolao		84
	Espinel, Vicente	352–353	84
	Fasolo		85
	Fiorillo, Tiberio ("Scaramouche")	354	85
	Foscarini, Giovanni Paolo	355–356	85

TABLE OF CONTENTS

Gallot, Henry François de	357–359	85
Gragnani, Filippo		86
Granata, Giovanni Battista	360	86
Grénerin, Henri		86
Guerau, Francisco	361	86
Kremberg, Jakob	362	86
Lemoine, A.		87
Matteis, Nicola	363–364	87
Médard, Remy		87
Milanuzzi, Carlo		87
Millioni, Pietro		87
Minguet Y Yrol, Pablo		88
Montesardo, Girolamo		88
Murcia, Santiago de	365–368	88
Pellegrini, Domenico	369	91
Pico, Foriano		91
Roncalli, Ludovico		91
Ruiz de Ribayaz, Lucas	370–371	91
San Severino, Benedetto		91
Santa Cruz, Antonio de		92
Sanz, Gaspar	372–376	92
Severi Perugino, Francesco		93
Sotos, Andrés de		93
Vargas Y Guzman, Juan Antonio	377–378	93
Visée, Robert de	379–385	93

Chapter V: HISTORIES OF THE EARLY SIX-STRING GUITAR			95
A.	Early Nineteenth-Century Sources	386–391	97
B.	General Studies	392–413	98
C.	Individual Composers and Performers	414–628	
	Aguado, Dionisio	414–423	102
	Arcas Lacal, Julián Gavino	424–426	104
	Basilio, Padre [né Miguel García]	427	104
	Berlioz, Hector	428–439	104
	Boccherini, Luigi	440–444	106
	Cano, Antonio		107
	Carcassi, Matteo	445–447	107
	Carulli, Fernando	448–453	107
	Call, Leonard von	454–456	108
	Coste, Napoleon	457–462	109
	Diabelli, Anton	463–465	109
	Ferandiere, Fernando	466	110
	Ferranti, Marco Aurelio Zani de	467	110
	Giuliani, Mauro	468–484	110
	Gragnani, Felipe		113
	Horetzky, Felix	485–487	113
	Huerta Y Katurla [Caturla], Don Trinidad		114
	Kreutzer, Joseph	488	114

viii

TABLE OF CONTENTS

Legnani, Rinaldo Luigi	489–492	114
Matiegka, Wenzelslaus Thomas	493	115
Mertz, Johann Kaspar	494–497	115
Molitor, Simon	498–499	116
Moretti, Federico	500–502	116
Paganini, Niccolò	503–517	117
Pelzer, Ferdinand and daughters Catherine Josepha (Madame Sidney Pratten) and Giulia	518–521	119
Regondi, Giulio	522–525	121
Scheidler, Christian Gottlieb	526–528	120
Schubert, Franz	529–540	121
Sor [Sors], Joseph Fernando Macari	541–583	123
Stoll, Franz de Paula		128
Thompson, General T. Perronet	584–585	128
Weber, Carl Maria von	586–589	129
Zani de Ferranti, Marc Aurelio *See* Ferranti, Marc Aurelio Zani de		
Miscellaneous Composers and Guitarists	590–628	129
D. The Terz Guitar	629–631	134

Chapter VI: FROM TÁRREGA TO THE PRESENT		137
A. General Surveys	632–645	139
B. Notation	646–648	141
C. Individual Composers, Performers, and Publishers	649–851	
Abreu, Sergio and Eduardo (Duo)		142
Almeida, Laurindo	649	142
Anido, Maria Luisa	650–653	142
Argento, Dominick	654–656	142
Athenian Guitar Duo (Liza Zoi and Evangelos Assimakopoulos)		143
Barrios Mangoré, Agustín Pio	657–661	143
Bellow, Alexander	662	144
Berg, Alban		144
Biberian, Gilbert		144
Bickford, Vahdah Olcott [née Ethel Lucretia Olcott]	663–664	144
Boulez, Pierre	665	144
Bream, Julian	666–670	144
Brindle, Reginald Smith		145
Britten, Benjamin	671–673	145
Cano, Antonio		146
Carrillo-Trujillo, Julián Antonio	674–677	146
Carlevaro, Abel	678	146
Castelnuovo-Tedesco, Mario	679–684	147
Chilesotti, Oscar	685	147
Company, Alvaro		148
Cuarteto, Dona-Dio		148

ix

TABLE OF CONTENTS

Dodgson, Stephen	686–688	148
Dorigny, Henry; Ito, Ako (Duo)		148
Falla, Manuel de	689–694	148
Falú, Eduardo	695	150
Fortea, Daniel		150
Henze, Hans Werner	696–699	150
Hindemith, Paul	700	150
Jeffery, Brian	701	151
Kagel, Mauricio		151
Leckie, Walter J.	702	151
Llobet, Miguel Soles	703–710	151
Lorca, Federico García	711–712	152
Martin, Frank	713	152
Mozzani, Luigi	714–715	153
Pedrell, Carlos		153
Pedrell, Felipe	716	153
Petrassi, Goffredo	717–719	153
Pomponio-Martinez Duo		154
Ponce, Manuel M.	720–737	154
Presti, Ida; Lagoya, Alexander (Duo)	738–746	156
Pujol, Emilio	747–759	157
Quine, Hector		159
Rodrigo, Joaquin	760–767	159
Rosetta, Giuseppe	768	160
Schönberg, Arnold	769	160
Sainz de la Maza, Regino		160
Segovia, Andrés	770–801	160
Stockhausen, Karlheinz		165
Stravinsky, Igor		165
Takemitsu, Toru	802–803	165
Tansman, Alexander	804–805	165
Tárrega, Francisco	806–829	166
Torroba, Federico Moreno	830–832	168
Turina, Joaquin	833	169
Villa-Lobos, Heitor	834–846	169
Webern, Anton		171
Williams, John		171
Yepes, Narciso	847–851	171
Zarate Duo		172

D. Selected Interviews of Performers and
Composers   852–870
(Interviews are also included under the
more extensive individual listings in
Section C.)

Artzt, Alice	852–854	172
Barrueco, Manuel	855	172
Boyd, Liona	856	172

TABLE OF CONTENTS

Brouwer, Leo	857	173
Chiesa, Ruggero	858	173
Diaz, Alirio	859–860	173
Duarte, John		173
Fisk, Eliot	861–862	173
Ghiglia, Oscar	863	174
Isbin, Sharon	864–865	174
Lauro, Antonio	866–867	174
The Romero Family (Celedonio [father], Celín, Pepe, Angel [sons])	868–869	175
Sainz de la Maza, Regino	870	

Chapter VII: ICONOGRAPHY ... 177

A. General Surveys	871–883	179
B. The Seventeenth Century	884	183
C. Nineteenth-Century Lithography	885–887	183
D. Individual Artists	888–894	
Goya Y Lucientes, Francisco José de	888–889	184
Picasso, Pablo	890–892	184
Watteau, Jean Antoine	893–894	185

Chapter VIII: DESIGN AND CONSTRUCTION ... 187

A. General Surveys	895–902	189
B. Dictionaries of Luthiers	903–905	190
C. The Sixteenth Century: Vihuela and Guitar	906–915	
Source Readings	906	191
Secondary Works	907–912	192
Modern Lutistry	913–915	193
D. From 1600 to 1900		
Source Readings, Including Construction Manuals	916–922	193
Secondary Works: Luthiers and Historical Instruments	923–931	195
Individual Luthiers	932–945	
Banks, Benjamin	932	196
Garcia Castillo, Enrique	933	196
Lacote, René François		196
Martin, Christian Frederick	934	196
Otto, Jakob August		196
Panormo, Louis	935	196
Staufer, Johann Georg	936	197
Stradivari, Antonio	937	197
Tielke, Joachim	938–939	197
Torres Jurado, Antonio de	940–945	198
E. National Histories	946–957	198
Argentina	946	199
Austria	947	199
France	948–949	199

xi

TABLE OF CONTENTS

	Germany	950	199
	Mexico	951–952	200
	Spain	953–957	201
F.	Individual Luthiers of the Twentieth Century	958–998	
	Barbero, Marcello	958	200
	Bernabé, Paulino	959	201
	Bouchet, Robert	960	201
	Caldersmith, Graham	961	201
	Cone, Michael	962	201
	Dickens, Fred T.	963	201
	Esteso Lopez, Domingo	964–966	201
	Fernandez, Francisco	967	202
	Fleta, Ignacio	968	202
	Fleta, Francisco Manuel	969	202
	Garcia, Enrique		202
	Haines, Daniel	970	203
	Hauser, Hermann	971–973	203
	Hernandez, Sobrinos de Santos	974–975	203
	Ibanez, Salvador	976	203
	Kasha, Michael	977	204
	Lorca, Antonio	978	204
	Oribe, José	979	204
	Orozco, Juan	980	204
	Pimentel, Lorenzo	981	204
	Ramirez, José and family	982–986	204
	Rodriguez, Manuel	987	205
	Romanillos, José	988–989	205
	Rubio, David	990–992	205
	Schneider, Richard	993–994	206
	Simplicio, Francisco		206
	Tatay, Vicente	995–996	206
	Velazquez, Manuel	997	207
	Vogl, Hans	998	207
G.	Construction Manuals	999–1015	207
H.	Studies of Acoustics and other Scientific Aspects of the Guitar's Construction	1016–1030	209
I.	Guitar Strings	1031–1033	212
J.	The Eight-String Guitar	1034	213
K.	The Ten-String Guitar	1035–1036	213
L.	The Microtonal Guitar	1037–1039	213

Appendix I:	Periodicals Devoted to the Guitar and Other Fretted Instruments	215
Appendix II:	Music for Guitar and Vihuela Printed before 1800 and Modern Editions	223
	Chronological List	307
How To Use The Index		313
Index		314

xii

List of Illustrations

I Pablo Minguet E Yrol, *Academia Musical de los Instrumentos . . .* (Madrid: Joaquin Ibarra, 1774), frontispiece. (Courtesy of the Music Division of the New York Public Library, Astor, Lenox and Tilden Foundations). frontispiece

II Etching. *Street Singer* by Edouard Manet. Reprinted, with permission from Sydney Beck and Elizabeth Roth, *Music in prints* (The New York Public Library, 1965). 2

III Etching. *Musicians in a Bistro* by Jacques Villon (pseud. of Gaston Duchamp). Reprinted, with permission from Sydney Beck and Elizabeth Roth, *Music in prints* (The New York Public Library, 1965). 18

IV Federico Moretti, *Principios para tocar la guitarra de seis ordenes* (Madrid: por Josef Rico, 1799), Tabla I, p. 9. (Courtesy of the Music Division of the New York Public Library, Astor, Lenox and Tilden Foundations). 58

Va Juan Carlos Amat, *Guitarra Espanola, y Vandola* (Gerona: Joseph Bro, [ca. 1765]), Title page. (Courtesy of the Music Division of the New York Public Library, Astor, Lenox and Tilden Foundations). 77

Vb Juan Carlos Amat, *Guitarra Espanola, y Vandola* (Gerona: Joseph Bro, [ca. 1765]), Chord chart. (Courtesy of the Music Division of the New York Public Library, Astor, Lenox and Tilden Foundations). 78

VIa Andres de Sotos, *Arte para aprendre con facilidad . . .* (Madrid: imprenta de Cruzada, 1764), "La Tabla Laberinto", p. 36. (Courtesy of the Music Division of the New York Public Library, Astor, Lenox and Tilden Foundations). 89

V.Ib Lucas Ruiz de Ribayaz, *Luz, y Norte Musical* (Madrid: Melchor Alvarez, 1677), Title page. (Courtesy of the Music Division of the New York Public Library, Astor, Lenox and Tilden Foundations). 90

LIST OF ILLUSTRATIONS

VII   Lucas Ruiz de Ribayaz, *Luz, y Norte Musical* (Madrid:
      Melchor Alvarez, 1677), Xacaras, Folias, and Pabanas in
      Alfabeto Tablature, p. 66. (Courtesy of the Music Division
      of the New York Public Library, Astor, Lenox and Tilden
      Foundations).   94

VIII Engraving. *Music Party with Guitar and Mandolins* by
      Vincent M. Langlois. Reprinted, with permission from
      Sydney Beck and Elizabeth Roth, *Music in prints*
      (The New York Public Library, 1965).   135

IX   Etching. *Blind Guitarist on the Horns of a Bull* by
      Francisco José de Goya Y Lucientes. Reprinted, with
      permission from Sydney Beck and Elizabeth Roth, *Music
      in prints* (The New York Public Library, 1965).   181

X   Lithograph. *The Clown Andreff with Guitar* by Hans
      Fischer. Reprinted, with permission from Sydney Beck
      and Elizabeth Roth, *Music in prints* (The New York
      Public Library, 1965).   182

IX   Etching. *Still Life* by Henri Laurens. Reprinted, with
      permission from Sydney Beck and Elizabeth Roth, *Music
      in prints* (The New York Public Library, 1965).   186

Introduction

I. Guitar and Vihuela: A Historiography

The guitar and vihuela each have their own distinctive characteristics, repertoire, and history. The vihuela (or vihuela de mano) is an instrument whose only extant repertoire dates from the sixteenth century and whose popularity was confined to Spain and Portugal. The changing definition of the guitar, from the four-course (double-strung) and five-course Renaissance guitars to the six-string classic guitar most commonly used today, includes many variant forms and various stringing and tuning practices. Yet the actual physical shape and the correlations made between the two instruments in early sources suggest that a study of one without the other would be inappropriate. Their histories are inseparable. The purpose of this essay is not to present a detailed survey of the treatment of the guitar and vihuela by historians but rather to expose some of the main problems, clarifying them with illustrative examples.

The attempt of some authors to formulate theories on the origins and the evolution of the guitar and vihuela before approximately 1500 without adequate documentation has resulted in the publication of much inaccurate information. The earliest known sources of music, literature, and instruments which clearly define the guitar and vihuela date from the sixteenth century. Studies of etymology and of iconography preceding this period should be judged in view of the present lacunae. Although many of the general and early histories listed in this bibliography do include history which precedes the sixteenth century, the first chapter devoted to a specific period, Chapter III: Histories of the Renaissance Period, is confined to the sixteenth century.

The relationship of the guitar and vihuela to other plucked stringed instruments whose histories can be traced back to as early as the thirteenth century has been confused. For this reason, I suggest some recent articles on the gittern, citole, lute, and mandora which contain research on literature and iconography before 1500. In addition to Lawrence Wright's detailed consideration of the gittern and citole in "The medieval gittern and citole: a case of mistaken identity," *Galpin Society Journal* XXX (May 1970) 8-42, which may be followed up by Daniel Heartz's "An Elizabethan tutor for the guitar," *Galpin Society Journal* XVI (May 1963) 3-21 (entry 229), the following articles are recommended:

INTRODUCTION

BAINES, Anthony, trans. "Fifteenth-century instruments in Tinctoris's *De inventione et usu musicae." Galpin Society Journal* III (March 1950) 19-26.

GILL, Donald. "Mandores and colachons." *Galpin Society Journal* XXXIV (March 1981) 13-41.

LOCKWOOD, Lewis. "Pietrobono and the instrumental tradition at Ferrara in the fifteenth century." *Rivista Italiana di Musicologia* X (1975) 115-23.

PAGE, Christopher. "The fifteenth-century lute: new and neglected sources." *Early Music* IX (January 1981) 11-31.

PAGE, Christopher. "Fourteenth-century instruments and tunings: a treatise by Jean Vaillant? (Berkeley MS 744)." *Galpin Society Journal* XXX (March 1980) 17-35.

Only seven composers published works for the vihuela in sixteenth-century Spain. Luis Milan's *Libro de musica de vihuela de mano, intitulado El maestro...* (Valencia, 1535 [colophon 1536]) is the first printed work for the instrument. This was followed by six other publications: Luis de Narváez's *Los seys libros del Delphín de música de cifras para tañer vihuela* (Valladolid, 1538), Alonso Mudarra's *Tres libros de musica en cifras para vihuela* (Sevilla, 1546), Enríquez de Valderrábano's *Libro de musica de vihuela, intitulado Silva de sirenas* (Valladolid, 1547), Diego Pisador's *Libro de música de vihuela* (Salamanca, 1552), Miguel de Fuenllana's *Libro de musica para vihuela, intitulado Orphenica lyra* (Sevilla, 1554), and Esteban Daza's *Libro de musica en cifras para vihuela, intitulado el Parnaso* (Valladolid, 1576). Four other composers of vihuela music are identified in a manuscript entitled "Ramillete de Flores, O Coleccion de Varias Cosas Curiosas," which is located in the Biblioteca Nacional in Madrid. These are Fabricio, Francisco Paez, Mendoza, and López. This manuscript is described in Cook 170 and Marcos 180. Only López is known to be mentioned elsewhere in a source. In Juan Bermudo's *Declaracion de Instrumentos* (Ossuna, 1555, entry 211), Libro segundo, capitulo XXXV, f. XXIX', Lopez musician of señor duque de arcos is included in a list of masters of the vihuela active in Spain. Also cited are [Luis de] Narvaez, Martin de jae[n], Hernando de jaen of Granada, [Miguel de] Fuenllana musician of señora marquesa de taripha, Mudarra canon of the yglesia major de Sevilla, and Anrrique [Enríquez de Valderrábano] musician of Señor conde de miranda.

Music for four-course guitar appears first in Mudarra's publication for vihuela. Fuenllana's work contains music for both four-course and five-course guitar. In this work, the five-course instrument is called "vihuela de cinco ordenes" [vihuela of five-courses] whereas the four-course instrument is called "vihuela de quatro ordenes, que dizen guitarra" [vihuela of four-courses, which is called guitar.] Between 1549 and 1578 only books for four-course guitar were printed in Venice by Melchior de Barberis, in Paris by Gregoire Brayssing, Simon Gorlier, Adrian Le Roy, and Guillaume Morlaye, and in Louvain and Antwerp by Pierre Phalèse and Jean Bellère.

xvi

INTRODUCTION

Authors of the sixteenth through the eighteenth centuries distinguished the guitar from the vihuela by its size, stringing, and tuning. In particular, texts by Juan Bermudo (entry 211), cited above, Sebastien de Covarrubias Orozco (entries 301–02), and Pablo Nassarre (entries 315–16) give descriptions of the instruments.

Juan Bermudo's *Declaracion de Instrumentos* (Ossuna, 1555) is the most detailed source on the tuning and the stringing of sixteenth-century vihuelas and guitars. Several instrument types are described in the text. In Libro segundo, "De la distancia que tiene la guitarra y bandurria," Capitulo XXXII, f. XXVIII', Bermudo cites two common tunings for the four-course guitar: *a los viejos* and *a los nuevos*. The old tuning, most suitable for old romances and strummed music, is described as the interval pattern 5-3-4. Bermudo's description of the *guitarra a los nuevos* (Libro quarto, "De las guitarras," Capitulo LXV, f. XCVI), quoted by John Ward (entry 191, p. 5) in English translation, clarifies one correlation made between the two instruments.

> . . . if you wish to make the vihuela into a guitarra *a los nuevos* [i.e., with four courses of strings tuned a fourth, a third, and a fourth apart],remove the first and sixth [strings], and the four strings that remain are those of the guitar. And if you wish to make the guitar into a vihuela, put on the sixth and the first [strings].

Bermudo also states that the five-course guitar was an instrument in use in Spain (Capitulo XXXII, f. XXVIII') and mentions [Luis de] Guzman as a player of the seven-course vihuela (Capitulo XXVIII', f. XXIX). It is only in reference to the four-course tuning that Bermudo mentions a variant in use in Italy (Capitulo XXXI, f. XXVIII').

Sebastien de Covarrubias Orozco's *Tesoro de la lengua castellana o española* (Madrid) is a dictionary first published in 1611; the 1674 edition is cited here. Covarrubias Orozco describes the guitar as a vihuela, small in size and in number of strings. He indicates that the vihuela has six or more courses. The courses of the *guitarrilla* (four-course guitar) and of the five-course *guitarra* are tuned in octaves rather than in unisons, which was the standard practice for tuning vihuela courses (f. 45). In his definition of vihuela, Covarrubias Orozco indicates that "the guitar is no more than a cowbell [*cencerro*], easier to play, especially in strummed music [*rasgado*] . . ." (f. 209). On the vihuela, however, all forms of plucked music [*punteado*] can be played.

Published in Zaragoza in 1724, after the decline in popularity of the vihuela, Pablo Nassarre's *Escuela musica* also defines the guitar as a type of vihuela. "The vihuela being of seven, six, or five courses (the five-course [instrument]being called *guitarra española*) are not distinguished by material, by form, or by proportions . . ." (p. 461). Later in the text, Nassarre does distinguish the guitar from the vihuela in two respects: in size and in tuning.

Rather than treat the vihuela as a distinctive instrument type in itself, many twentieth-century historians have sought definitions for the

xvii

INTRODUCTION

vihuela by associating it with more familiar instruments. Thus, the vihuela has been called the Spanish lute, quite in contradiction to its origins, history, repertoire, and construction. The fretted, stringed lute with oval belly and curved, ribbed back maintained a quite separate history and enjoyed popularity in European countries outside of Spain. Only once, in regard to tuning, does Bermudo mention the lute [laúd] which he also calls *vihuela de Flandes* (*Declaracion de Instrumentos*, Capitulo LXV, f. XCVI). In this isolated reference, Bermudo uses the term vihuela as a generic—but also a more familiar—term which may have no further bearing on the relationship between the two instruments beyond their similarities in tuning.

Further confusion over the distinctions between the vihuela and lute results from the terminology used by Johannes Tinctoris in his *De inventione et usu musicae* (ca. 1487, Naples).[1] The terms *ghiterra* or *ghiterna* have been incorrectly translated as guitar, and Tinctoris's reference to the stringing and playing of the instrument as that of the lute [*lyra*] has been applied to the discussion of the guitar of four-courses. However, Tinctoris's description of the instrument—tortoise-shaped, though smaller than the lute—indicates that he is describing the gittern.[2] Tinctoris's term for vihuela is *viola*. He designates this term as Spanish and Italian usage, whereas in France it is called *dimitum leutum* [demi-lute]. A clear distinction is made between the lute—larger and tortoise-shaped—and the *viola* which is flat and usually has incurved sides. A second type of *viola* differs from the lute in shape, stringing, and its performance with a bow. In this early source, vihuela is used in a generic sense and is classified as a type of lute.[3]

Luis Milan's 1535 publication for vihuela specifies on the title page the instrument *vihuela de mano* [vihuela played with the hand] which distinguishes it from the *vihuela de peñola* [vihuela played with a plectrum] and the *vihuela de arco* [vihuela played with a bow]. The publications which followed, however, have only the term vihuela in their titles, indicating that the hand-plucked instrument is understood and that there is no concern for confusion between the specific instrument and the generic family of strings. As shown in the previously mentioned sources by Sebastien de Covarrubias Orozco and Pablo Nassarre, in the seventeenth and eighteenth centuries the prepositional phrase *de mano* is no longer in use.

---

[1] Anthony Baines, trans., "Fifteenth-century instruments in Tinctoris's *De inventione et usu musicae*," *Galpin Society Journal* III (March 1950) 19-26 gives the original Latin text concerning the following instruments with an English translation.

[2] See Lawrence Wright, "The medieval gittern and citole: a case of mistaken identity," *Galpin Society Journal* XXX (May 1970) 8-42, especially p. 10 for alternate spellings of the term gittern.

[3] For further discussion of the term *viola*, see John Ward, "The vihuela de mano and its music, 1536-1576," (PhD diss., Music: New York University, 1953) 59-63.

xviii

INTRODUCTION

Guillermo Morphy is responsible for the first transcription of works
of the seven vihuelists from the original tablature into modern notation.
This remarkable, although somewhat inaccurate, work, which exposed
the unfamiliar repertoire of the vihuela, was incorrectly titled. In 1902,
Breitkopf und Härtel published Morphy's *Les luthistes españols du
XVIe siècle* [Spanish lutenists of the sixteenth century]. Also among
those authors who classified the vihuela as a type of lute were Willi
Apel,[4] José Bal,[5] Adolf Koczirz,[6] Walter Starkie,[7] John B. Trend,[8]
and Josef Zuth.[9] Willi Apel's statement in *The notation of polyphonic music, 900-1600*, p. 56, n. 1 serves as an example:

> The Spanish lute, vihuela, actually is a guitar. However, the tuning as well
> as the musical repertoire of this instrument connect it much more closely
> with the sixteenth century lute than with the seventeenth or eighteenth
> century guitar.

This misuse of terminology has resulted in distortions of the history
and the understanding of the repertoire of both instruments.

The perpetuation of misconceptions about the guitar's history have
resulted from a knowledge of misleading source readings in an area in
which sufficient reliable information is lacking. Examples of this occur
in two major transitions in the guitar's stringing: from four courses to
five courses and from five courses to six single strings.

Contradictions exist between sources concerning the origin of the
practice of stringing the guitar with five courses. The conflict results
from the myth which accredits Vicente Espinel (1551-1624) with the
addition of the fifth course to the guitar. His invention is mentioned in
three works by the author Lope de Vega Carpio (1562-1635), including
the play *Dorotea*, which dates the invention ca. 1587. The myth is later
supported in the guitar publications of Nicolas Doizi de Velasco (1640)
and Gaspar Sanz (1674). The publication of music for five-course guitar

---

[4] Willi Apel, "Solo instrumental music," *The new Oxford history of music* IV, ed.
by Gerald Abraham (London: Oxford University Press, 1968) and *The notation of
polyphonic music, 900-1600*, 5th ed. (Cambridge, Mass.: The Mediaeval Academy
of America, 1953).

[5] José Bal, "Fuenllana and the transcription of Spanish lute-music," *Acta Musicologica*
XI (1939) 16-27.

[6] Adolf Koczirz, "Die gitarren Kompositionen in Miguel de Fuenllanas *Orphenica
Lyra* (1554)" [The guitar compositions in Miguel de Fuenllana's *Orphenica Lyra*
(1554)] *Archiv für Musikwissenschaft* IV (1922) 241-61.

[7] Walter Starkie, *Spain. A musician's journey through time and space*, I (Edisli:
Editions Rene Kister Geneva, 1958).

[8] John B. Trend, *The music of Spanish history to 1600* (London: s.n., 1926).

[9] Josef Zuth, *Handbuch der Laute und Gitarre* [Handbook of the lute and the
guitar] (Vienna: Verlag der Zeitschrift für die Gitarre, 1926). Reprint ed. (Hildesheim: Georg Olms Verlag, 1972).

xix

INTRODUCTION

by Miguel de Fuenllana (1554) and references to the five-course guitar in Bermudo's theoretical text confirm previous use of this stringing.[10] Ricardo Aguirre,[11] Bruno Henze,[12] and Diego Vázquez Otero[13] have perpetuated the false claim into the twentieth century. This apparent lack of knowledge of the works of Juan Bermudo and Miguel de Fuenllana is significant in two respects. It is an indication both of the decline in the interest in the vihuela and, likewise, of the limited circulation of the vihuelists's music, a problem which may have contributed to the perpetration of the decline. Juan Carlos Amat's *Guitarra española y vandola*, probably first published in 1586, was the first of numerous five-course guitar books published in Europe. Although Espinel may have been an influential figure in the rise of the popularity of the five-course instrument, evidence is conclusive that the establishment of five-course stringing as common practice in the late sixteenth century results not from its invention but rather from a shift in popularity away from the vihuela and the four-course guitar.

The period of transition from the five-course instrument to that of six single strings in the late eighteenth century presents many questions to the present-day historian. Surviving instruments and publications of guitar music from that period indicate that guitars of five single strings, six courses, and triple courses were in use. Source readings are scant. The addition of the sixth string to the guitar has been attributed to the Weimar instrument maker Jakob August Otto who presumably was the first to add the bass E string at the request of Kapellmeister Johann Gottlieb Naumann. This information is recorded in Otto's treatise (entry 920, pp. 23–24).

> The late Duchess Amelia of Weimar having introduced the guitar into Weimar, in 1788, I was immediately obliged to make copies of this instrument for several of the nobility; . . .
> I must here take the opportunity to observe that, originally, the guitar had only five strings. The late Herr Naumann, chapel master at Dresden, ordered the first guitar with the sixth or low E string, which I at once made for him. Since that time the instrument has always been with six strings; for which improvement its admirers have to thank Herr Naumann.
> During the last ten years, a great number of instrument makers, as well as joiners, have commenced making guitars; . . . The use of covered strings for the D and the G is a small improvement of my own. In the guitar, as brought from Naples, a large violin third-string was used for the D, and only the A was covered.

[10] George Haley, *Vicente Espinel and Marcos de Obregón. A life and its literary representation* (Providence, R.I.: Brown University Press, 1959) 45–46 gives a summary of the publications concerning Espinel.

[11] Ricardo Aguirre, "Noticias para historia de la guitarra," *Revista de Archivios, Bibliotecas y Museo* XLI (1920) 83.

[12] Bruno Henze, *Die Gitarre und ihre Meister des 18. und 19. Jahrhunderts* (Berlin: Verlag ad. Köster, 1920) 8.

[13] Diego Vázquez Otero, *Vida de Vicente Martinez Espinel*, Excma. Diputación Provincial de Málaga. Publicaciones del Instituto de Cultura, Serie B, v. 6 (Málaga, 1948) 220.

INTRODUCTION

Twentieth-century authors who have attributed this addition to Otto are A. P. Sharpe (entry 37), Wilhelm Tappert (entry 42), and Bruno Henze (entry 400). Otto, indeed, may have been important in popularizing the guitar in Germany, and his statement evidences six single string building activities in, or shortly after, 1788; however, extant guitars which pre-date 1788 disprove Otto's claim. The contact with Neapolitan guitars revealed in the text may be significant. Turnbull (entry 43, p. 64) claims that Naumann "had studied the guitar in Italy, and it is more than probable that he met with the six-string instrument there." A six-string guitar made by Antonius Vinaccia in Naples is dated 1785. This guitar is described with illustrative plate in Carl Claudius's *Samlung af Gamle Musikinstrumenter* (Copenhagen: Levin & Munksgaards Forlag, 1931), p. 153, plate 172. In this volume, standard modern six-string guitar tuning is given, and the dimensions of the guitar are listed. Heck (entry 397, pp. 10–12) emphasizes Naples's further significance in the transition from double stringing (courses) to single stringing. An important transitional guitar with five single strings was built by Ferdinando Gagliano in Naples in 1774. In addition to Vinaccia, Turnbull mentions two other six-string guitars which pre-date 1788: by Moutron (France, 1785)[14] and by Michael Ignatius Stadlman (Vienna, 1787).[15] The transition to the six single-string guitar is considered by authors Cox (entry 394), Evans (entry 15), Heck (entry 474) and Turnbull (entry 43).

The history of the guitar and the vihuela is intricate and filled with many unresolved questions. Historians of the early decades of the twentieth century made pioneering efforts to investigate a large body of music and early source material without the benefits of previous research. Among the most recognized authors of the time were Philip J. Bone, Oscar Chilesotti, Adolf Koczirz, Guillermo Morphy, Felipe Pedrell, Erwin Schwarz-Reiflingen, and Josef Zuth. Recent scholarship has contributed notably to the development of a more accurate and well-documented representation of the history of the guitar and the vihuela. Investigations of musical, theoretical, literary, and iconographical sources offer new evidence which has eliminated lacunae and corrected inaccuracies. Yet the problem of insufficient substantiation of theories and of the exclusion of information which defines boundries and properly limits the interpretation of theory and terminology continues to persist even in many recent publications, thus creating the need for a comparative evaluation of available secondary works.

[14] Originally cited in Vladimir Bobri, Martha Nelson, Gregory d'Alessio, "A gallery of great guitars from the XVIth to the XXth century," Part III, *Guitar Review* XXXV (Summer 1971) 21.

[15] Originally cited in Thomas F. Heck, "The birth of the classic guitar and its cultivation in Vienna, reflected in the career and compositions of Mauro Giuliani (d. 1829)," (PhD diss., Music: Yale University, 1970) I, 44.

INTRODUCTION

II. Identifying and Locating Music for Guitar and Vihuela

A number of reference works are available for the identification and location of music for guitar and vihuela. These include bibliographies of specific areas and genres, reference works listing the contents of editions, library catalogs, trade manuals confined to a given year or period, and catalogs based on current publishers' outputs.

For bibliographies of guitar music presently in print, two publications devoted specifically to the guitar are available. Wolf Moser's *Gitarre-Musik. Ein internationaler Katalog*, v. 1, 3rd ed. (Hamburg: Verlag Joachim Trekel, 1979) and v. 2, 1st ed. (Hamburg: Verlag Joachim Trekel, 1977) far exceeds any other reference work of its kind in thoroughness. The first volume contains a list of works available through 105 publishers; the second volume contains a list of works available through 137 publishers. Lists are arranged alphabetically by composer. *Guitar music index. A cross-indexed and graded listing of music in print for classical guitar and lute* (Honolulu, Hawaii: Galliard Press, Ltd., 1976) by George Gilmore and Mark Pereira and volume 2, published under the same title, by George Gilmore and Peter Kun Frary (George Gilmore, 1981) are more selective lists of music for guitar. The first volume contains a list of music available through 92 publishers; the second volume contains a list of music available through 199 publishers.

In preparation is *Classical guitar music in print*, edited by Mijndert Jape, which is expected to be published by Music Data Incorporated at some time in 1985. It is organized by instrumentation and includes anthologies. Chapters on Francisco Tárrega and J. S. Bach contain thematic indexes of their works.

The *National Union Catalogue* is an extensive, multi-volume bibliography of printed books on any subject with their library locations in the United States. This includes a series on *Pre-1956 imprints.* Catalogs of individual music library holdings are also useful for locating music and books in specific collections. The *Directory of music research libraries, including contributors to the International Inventory of Musical Sources (RISM)*, edited by Rita Benton, is an international guide to music research libraries published in four parts:

Part 1: Canada and the United States (Iowa City: The University of Iowa, 1967).
Part 2: Thirteen European Countries (Iowa City: The University of Iowa, 1970).
Part 3: Spain, France, Italy, Portugal (Iowa City: The University of Iowa, 1972).
Part 4: Australia, Israel, Japan, New Zealand (Kassel: Bärenreiter-Verlag, 1979).

These publications give details on library services, publications, and holdings. Vincent Duckles's *Music reference and research materials. An annotated bibliography*, 3rd ed. (New York: Schirmer Books, 1974)

xxii

INTRODUCTION

contains a chapter entitled "Catalogs of music libraries and collections" (pp. 271–386). This section is international in coverage and is organized by city with a final listing of private collections.

Thomas F. Heck's *Guitar music in the archive of the Guitar Foundation of America and at cooperating collections: a computerized catalog* (Columbus, Ohio: Guitar Foundation of America, 1981) includes information on obtaining copies of original editions and other rare music and on borrowing microfilms. The catalog is organized alphabetically by composer and by medium of performance. It contains many nineteenth- and early twentieth-century works and some eighteenth-century works.

Guitar music published in collections and anthologies can be located through available indexes. The most extensive general survey of publications with listings of complete contents is Anna Harriet Heyer's *Historical sets, collected editions, and monuments of music. A guide to their contents*, 3rd ed., v. 1 (text), v. 2 (index), (Chicago, Illinois: American Library Association, 1980). Because the index only lists composers, editors, and titles, locating music of a specific genre or for a specific instrument is difficult. This music can be found only by searching under pertinent composers, editors, and titles. Such a search would reveal a large body of literature for guitar. Sydney Robinson Charles's *A handbook of music and music literature in sets and series* (New York: The Free Press, 1972) indexes some music for guitar and vihuela. This is less extensive than Heyer's publication.

Of particular interest in locating music for guitar in ensemble is Margaret K. Farish's *String music in print*, 2nd ed. (New York and London: R. R. Bowker Company, 1973). The author's sources are publishers' catalogs, and the work provides information on obtaining music through sales and rentals. Although it is primarily a guide to literature for bowed instruments, listings of some unusual, lesser-known guitar music are included. Chapters II–VI, music for two, three, four, five, and six instruments, respectively, contain sections which are specifically on music for guitar in ensemble. The chapters on septets, octets, nonets and decets, and voice and instruments have no sub-categories for specific genres; a search through the composer lists exposes several compositions with guitar:

Septets by Morton Feldman, Wlodzimierz Kotonski, Robert McBride, Arnold Schoenberg, and Elias Tenenbaum.

Octets by Jurriaan Andriessen, Jacob Avshalomov, Roberto Gerhard, Bruno Maderna, and Carlo Prosperi.

Nonets and decets by Günther Becker, John Lewis, and Poul Rovsing Olsen.

Voice and instruments by Pierre Boulez, Karl Heinz Füssl, Hans Werner Henze, Riccardo Malipiero, Dieter Schönbach, Humphrey Searle, Mátyás Seiber, Thorkell Sigurbjörnsson, Elias Tenenbaum, and Andrei Volkonsky.

xxiii

INTRODUCTION

The most complete discography on the guitar, lute, and vihuela is
Ronald C. Purcell's *Classic guitar, lute, and vihuela discography* (Mel-
ville, N. Y.: Belwin-Mills Publishing Corp., 1976). The main text is
organized alphabetically by performer. The complete contents of
records are listed. The discography contains an artist index, a composer
index, and a record number index. *Soundboard*, periodical of the
Guitar Foundation of America (GFA), regularly contains an annotated
discography entitled "Current discography," compiled by John W.
Tanno. David Edwin Cooper's *International Bibliography of Discogra-
phies* (Littleton, Colorado: Libraries, unlimited, Inc., 1975) is a bibliography of classical music, jazz, and blues (1962–72). This is especially
valuable for locating material for a particular composer. Vincent
Duckles's *Music reference and research materials. An annotated bibliography*, 3rd ed. (N. Y.: Schirmer Books, 1974) has a chapter on discog-
raphies which includes encyclopedias and collectors' guides.

A large body of music for guitar and vihuela was printed between
1535 and 1800. Appendix II of this bibliography (pp. 223-304) gives a
bibliography of early music locators. The *International Inventory of
Musical Sources (RISM)* has several series of publications which are the
most comprehensive of the works listed. Howard Mayer Brown's *Instrumental music printed before 1600* is invaluable in the study of the sixteenth-century repertoire for guitar and vihuela; entries include full
titles, complete listing of the contents of the publication, historical
commentary, library locations, and a bibliography of literature. Lost
works are included in this volume. Peter Danner's three articles list
guitar tablatures, specifically. Tablature type is identified. Short titles
are given, and the list of library locations is selective. Paul Cox's "The
evolution of playing techniques of the six-stringed classical guitar as
seen through teaching method books from ca. 1780-1850" contains a
bibliography of method books for guitar composed between the years
designated in the title. Warren Kirkendale's *L'aria di fiorenza id est il
Ballo del Gran Duca* specifically treats the history of the musical form
by that title. A bibliography of printed books and manuscripts for
guitar which contain this musical form is included. The accuracy of
Johannes Wolf's *Handbuch der Notationskunde* and Robert Eitner's
Biographisch-Bibliographisches Quellen-Lexikon is questionable because
of their early dates of publication in this century. Libraries since that
time have changed location or have been lost, and *RISM* listings are
more accurate. An effort has been made to update Eitner's work in
Stephen A. Willier's "The present state of libraries listed in Robert
Eitner's *Biographisch-Bibliographisches Quellen-Lexikon*," published in
Fontes Artis Musicae XXVIII/3 (July-Aug 1981) 220-29. James Tyler's
The early guitar: a history and handbook (London: Oxford University
Press, 1980) contains a chronological list of guitar music printed before
1800. Short titles are cited, and tuning, tablature type, and library
locations are given. Lists of "Undated late eighteenth-century printed
sources" and "Manuscript sources" follow. Other appendixes are
"Appendix 2: Vocal music accompanied by guitar alfabeto," "Ap-

pendix 3: Eighteen-century vocal music accompanied by guitar," and "Appendix 4: Available facsimile editions of guitar tablatures."

A comprehensive bibliography of sources of nineteenth-century guitar music is not available at present. Bibliographies of music, however, are in print which contain listings of guitar music from this period. C. F. Whistling's and Friedrich Hofmeister's *Handbuch der musikalischen Literatur* (titles vary slightly) covers the period 1817 to 1943. It is a publishers' catalog, international in coverage and published yearly, and contains an extensive list of nineteenth-century music. Its uses are limited because of its original purpose as a trade bibliography. To the present-day performer and musicologist, it is primarily useful for confirming the existence of a work, for defining a *terminus ante quem* [latest possible date of first edition], and for pursuing statistical studies of a composer's output or a publisher's activities. The first volume of this work and its ten supplements have been reprinted by two publishers, New York: Vienna House, 1972 *and* New York and London: Garland Publishing, Inc., 1975. The introduction by Neil Ratliff in the edition by Garland Publishing, Inc. gives information on the history and the uses of the work. *Universal Handbuch der Musikliteratur* (Wien: Pazdírek and Co., 1904-10), reprint edition by Frits Knuf (Hilversum, 1967), is a thirty-four volume work containing listings of music which dates mainly from the nineteenth century. Organization is by composer, and, although numerous works for guitar are cited, no genre index for locating guitar music specifically is provided.

Two French-language publications of the decade of the 1820s contain limited listings of music for guitar. These are the 1822 bibliography of Cesar Gardeton (entry 387 of this bibliography) and *Journal général d'announces des oeuvres de musique, graveurs, lithographies, publié en France et à l'étranger (1825-1827)*, ed. by François Lesure, Archive de l'edition, tome III (Genève: Minkoff Reprint, 1976).

Reference works are available which contain listings of American guitar music. The most comprehensive bibliography of American music in the eighteenth century is William Treat Upton's revised and enlarged edition of Oscar George Theodore Sonneck's *A bibliography of early secular American music (18th century)* (Washington, D.C.: Library of Congress, 1945), reprint edition (New York: Da Capo Press, 1964). Guitar music is listed in the general index; the main text contains a description of the contents of each work with library locations of copies cited. Nineteenth-century music is listed in two publications. Richard J. Wolfe's *Secular music in America, 1801-1825* contains an extensive list of works with descriptions, a list of contents, and library locations. A trade manual entitled *Board of music trade of the United States of America. Complete catalogue of sheet music and musical works, 1870* (New York: Board of music trade, [1871]) lists the publications of twenty member firms. Music for solo guitar, guitar songs, guitar duetts [*sic*], guitar and piano, and guitar and violin or flute is included. Entries give only the title, publisher, and composer. Its uses are comparable to those of the Whistling/Hofmeister catalog described above.

xxv

INTRODUCTION

III. The Bibliography: Its Purpose, Contents, and Organization

The following bibliography is intended to fill the need for an annotated reference tool for the study of the guitar and vihuela. It contains literature on composers, performers, theorists, music and analysis, iconography, and design and construction in both an historical context and in a technical one. In addition to literature on the six-string classic guitar, literature on the Renaissance four-course guitar, the Renaissance and Baroque five-course guitar, the chitarra battente, the terz guitar, the seven-string Russian guitar, and the modern eight-string, ten-string, and microtonal guitars is included. Texts in the Catalan, Danish, English, French, German, Italian, Latin, Polish, Portuguese, Russian, Spanish, Swedish, and Ukranian languages are listed. Extant theoretical texts and literary works dating from as early as 1549 are important sources of information in the study of early music. These works and articles contained in nineteenth- and early twentieth-century guitar-related periodicals are listed in the present bibliography. The earliest periodical indexed is *The Giulianiad* III (London, 1833). A survey of available issues of guitar periodicals brought to light many articles which have not been indexed in any major bibliographic listing of literature. Literature published as recently as 1981 is indexed. A list of periodicals devoted to the guitar and other fretted instruments and their library locations in the United States and Canada is given in Appendix I.

Among the most comprehensive encyclopedias of music and musicians are *The New Grove Dictionary of Music and Musicians*, ed. by Stanley Sadie (London: Macmillan, 1980) and the German-language encyclopedia *Die Musik in Geschichte und Gegenwart*, ed. by Friedrich Blume (Kassel und Basel: Bärenreiter-Verlag, 1956). Only those general articles on "Guitar" ("Gitarre" in De) and "Vihuela" are indexed in this bibliography. Biographical articles on composers and performers in guitar history with bibliographies of music and literature are also cited in these works. A detailed review of guitar-related material in *Grove* is written by Peter Danner in *Soundboard* VIII/3 (August 1981) 207-10. Further evaluation of the inadequacies of *Grove* is given by John Duarte in "Back to the *Grove*" *Soundboard* VIII/4 (November 1981) 330-32. Further information on the guitar-related material in *Grove* is given in "The guitarist's guide to the *New Grove*" by Peter Danner, *Soundboard* IX/2 (Summer 1982) 110-18; this is a checklist of articles on musicians and guitar-related subjects. In a chart, the dates of the individual, the author of the article, and the number of works written by the individual are given.

Newspaper articles, program notes, exhibition catalogs of instrument collections, and museum catalogs are excluded from the text. Introductions to editions of music and to method books, also excluded, often give information and background on the music that they preface. Appendix II of this bibliography, "Music for guitar and vihuela printed before 1800 and modern editions," includes method books and their modern editions.

INTRODUCTION

Research was undertaken primarily at the libraries of the New York
Public Library System, the Library of Congress, the Philadelphia Free
Library, the University of Pennsylvania Van Pelt Library, Yale University
Music Library, Vassar College George Sherman Dickenson Music
Library, Queens College of the City University of New York Paul
Klapper Music Library, and private libraries which were made available.
The services of the Guitar Foundation of America (GFA), the services
of the interlibrary loan system of the New York Public Library, and the
resources of University Microfilms International were essential in
achieving thoroughness in research.

The bibliography is organized chronologically by historical period
with a separate chapter on general histories, national histories, iconographies, and design and construction. The order of the chapters and the
appendixes is as follows:

Chapter I: General Histories and Dictionaries
Chapter II: National Histories
Chapter III: Histories of the Renaissance Period
Chapter IV: Histories of the Baroque Era
Chapter V: Histories of the Early Six-String Guitar
Chapter VI: From Tárrega to the Present
Chapter VII: Iconographies
Chapter VIII: Design and Construction
Appendix I: Periodicals Devoted to the Guitar and Other Fretted
                  Instruments
Appendix II: Music for Guitar and Vihuela Printed before 1800
                  and Modern Editions

Appropriate entries list the volume and the entry number assigned to
the item in *RILM Abstracts of music literature (International Inventory
of Music Literature)* (1967–). Book reviews are listed. The order
number of dissertations available through University Microfilms International (UMI) is given. The language of the text is cited; unmarked
texts are in English.

Divisions and sub-divisions of subject matter vary in each chapter.
Chapters II through VIII contain sections which list studies devoted exclusively to individuals. Criterion for selection is based exclusively on
the availability of literature. Although the presence of a name and the
number of works devoted to that individual may be indicative of his
importance in the guitar's history, the absence of an individual is by no
means an inference of his insignificance; rather, this may reveal lacunae
and suggest the areas of the guitar's history most in need of study. In
many cases, individual names have been included as sub-headings with
only cross-references given.

xxvii

INTRODUCTION

Acknowledgments

I am especially indebted to Dr. Barry S. Brook, Executive Officer of
the Ph.D. Program in Music, Graduate School and Center of the City
University of New York for his valuable advice and suggestions. I grate-
fully acknowledge Susan Hellauer of Columbia University for her gen-
erous help and scholarly contribution and Professor Dr. Helmut
Rösing of *RISM* Zentralredaktion in Kassel for loaning me the unpublished proofs of volume IX of series A/I "Einzeldrucke" of *RISM*.
Mention should be made of Cynthia Allison for giving of her time.

How to Use the Bibliography

Entries are numbered throughout the bibliography in bold face type. Different types are used to differentiate the three headings used.

Examples:

E. Individual Authors and Theorists

MAIN HEADINGS: These are indented and are preceded by a letter of the alphabet.

BONANNI [BUONANNI], Filippo (1638-1725)

SUB-HEADINGS: These appear in the left-hand margin, printed in capital letters, and sub-divide the material under the main heading. Alternate spellings of names appear in brackets.

Sources

DIVISIONS BEYOND THE SUB-HEADING: These are placed in the left-hand margin and further sub-divide the material under the sub-heading.

Italicized type is used to designate *book titles*, *abbreviations for periodicals*, and headings for *Library locations* (listed under the bibliographic citation), *Reviews* (listed under the annotation), *See* and *See also* cross-references, and *Comments* (listed under the entries in Appendix II).

Library locations have two elements which are distinguished by two different types. The country abbreviation is in bold face type. The specific library in that country is in elite type and follows the country abbreviation.

Examples: B Bc, Gu. E Bc.

B and E designate the countries Belgium and Spain.
Bc, Gu designate libraries in B (Belgium).
Bc, listed after E, designates a library in E (Spain).

Abbreviations

General Abbreviations

A	AUSTRIA
append.	appendix, appendixes
Apr	April
Aug	August
AUS	AUSTRALIA
b	basso
b.	born
B	BELGIUM
bc	basso continuo
B.C.	BRITISH COLUMBIA
Bibl.	Biblioteca [Library]
bibliog.	bibliography
bibliog. ref. in notes	bibliographic references in [foot]notes
bk.	book
BRD	WEST GERMANY
c.	century
C	CUBA
ca.	circa
Ca	Catalan
Calif.	California
Ch.	Chapter
CH	CHILE
CND	CANADA
Co.	Company
comp.	compiler
d.	died
Da	Danish
D.C.	DISTRICT OF COLUMBIA
De	German
Dec	December
Discog.	discography
diss.	dissertation
DK	DENMARK
E	SPAIN
ed.	editor, edition, edited
En	English
ex.	example
f	folio
f.	following [page]
F	FRANCE
facs.	facsicle
facsim.	facsimile
Feb	February
fig.	figure
fl.	fluent
Fr	French

xxx

ABBREVIATIONS

GB	GREAT BRITAIN
GFA	Guitar Foundation of America. 6538 Reefton Avenue, Cypress, California 90630
H	HUNGARY
I	ITALY
iconog.	iconography
illus.	illustration
Inc.	Incorporated
inc.	incomplete
Int	International
It	Italian
Kpl.	Komplett, complete
Jan	January
Jr.	Junior
La	Latin
lit.	literature
Ltd.	Limited
MA	Master of Arts degree
Mar	March
Mass.	Massachusetts
MEX	MEXICO
MM	Master of Music
MS, MSS	Manuscript, manuscripts
music	music example, music examples
n.	[foot]note, [foot]notes
N.C.	North Carolina
n.d.	*see* s.d.
NL	NETHERLANDS
no.	Number
Nov	November
n.p.	*see* s.l.
n. pag.	no pagination
N.Y.	New York
Oct	October
op.	opus
p.	page, pages
Pa.	Pennsylvania
pf	pianoforte
PhD	Doctor of Philosophy
Pl	Polish
pl.	plate, plates
POL	POLAND
port.	portrait
pseud.	pseudonym
Pt	Portuguese
ref.	references
R.I.	Rhode Island
RILM	*RILM Abstracts (International Inventory of Music Literature)*
RISM	*Répertoire International des Sources Musicales (International Inventory of Musical Sources, Internationales Quellenlexikon der Musik)*

xxxi

ABBREVIATIONS

Ru	Russian
S	SWEDEN
s.d.	sans date, no date
Sept	September
ser.	series
s.l.	sans location, no place
s.n.	sans nomme, no name (of publisher)
Sp	Spanish
Sr.	Senior
SU	SOVIET UNION
Sw	Swedish
SWIT	SWITZERLAND
tabl.	tablature
them. cat.	thematic catalogue
trans.	translate (any form)
transcr.	transcribe (any form)
Uk	Ukranian
UMI	University Microfilms International (Ann Arbor, Michigan)
USA	UNITED STATES OF AMERICA
v.	volume, volumes
va	viola
vl	violin

Abbreviations for Periodicals and Dictionaries Indexed

AChitarristica	L'Arte Chitarristica I
Acoustica	Acoustica
ActaMusicol	Acta Musicologica Int
AfMw	Archive für Musikwissenschaft BRD
AmerMTeacher	American Music Teacher USA
AmerRecorder	American Recorder USA
AmerStrT	American String Teacher USA
AMZ	Allgemeine Musikalische Zeitung
AnM	Anuario Musical E
AnnalesM	Annales Musicologiques F
AustralianJMEducation	The Australian Journal of Music Education AUS
Blues	Blues Unlimited GB
Bluegrass	Bluegrass USA
BMG	Banjo, Mandolin, and Guitar USA
BulAmerMusicolSoc	Bulletin of the American Musicological Society USA
BulSocHistArtFrançais	Bulletin de la Société de l'Histoire de l'Art français F
Cadenza	The Cadenza USA

xxxii

ABBREVIATIONS

CahCanadiensM	Cahiers Canadiens de Musique/Canada Music Book CND
CanadianM	Canadian Musician CND
Canon	The Canon. Australian Journal of Music AUS
CGuitarInt	Creative Guitar International USA
Chesterian	The Chesterian GB
Chelys	Chelys (also titled Electric Chelys) USA
Chitarra	La Chitarra I
CollegeMusSym	College Music Symposium USA
Conservatorio	Conservatorio E
Consort	The Consort GB
CourrierMFrance	Le Courriere Musical de France F
Crescendo	The Crescendo USA
CurrentMusicol	Current Musicology USA
DAfMF	Dansk Aarbog for Musik Forskning DK
DanskMt	Dansk musiktidsskrift DK
DieGit	Die Gitarre
EarlyM	Early Music USA
EDance	English Dance and Song GB
Electric Chelys	*see* Chelys
Etude	Etude USA
FontesArtisMus	Fontes Artis Musicae USA
Frets	Frets USA
Fretts	Fretts USA
FINews	Fretted Instrument News USA
Fronimo	il "Fronimo". Rivista Trimestrale de Chitarra e Liuto I
GalpinSocJ	Galpin Society Journal GB
Gfreund	Der Gitarrefreund BRD
Gitarre (Graz)	Die Gitarre. Zeitschrift des Gitarren Collegiums Graz BRD
GitarreLaute	Gitarre + Laute BRD
Giulianiad	The Giulianiad, or Guitarist's Monthly Magazine GB
GMusique	Guitare et Musique Chansons Poesie F
Grove	The New Grove Dictionary of Music and Musicians. Ed. by Stanley Sadie. (London: Macmillan, 1980).
Guitar	Guitar. The magazine for all guitarists GB
GuitarLute	Guitar and Lute USA
GuitarN	Guitar News GB
GuitarP	Guitar Player USA
GuitarR	Guitar Review USA
Guitarist	Guitarist GB
Guitarra (Chicago)	Guitarra Magazine USA
Guitarra (Havana)	Guitarra C
Guitarra (Madrid)	La Guitarra. Revista Mensual E
Harmonie	Harmonie F

ABBREVIATIONS

Heterofonia	Heterofonia MEX
HiFi/MAmer	HiFi/Musical America USA
HinrichsenMYb	Hinrichsen's Musical Yearbook GB
IB	Instrumentenbau Musik International BRD
Instrument	The Instrumentalist USA
IZ	Instrumentenbau-Zeitschrift BRD
JAmerMusicolSoc	Journal of the American Musicological Society USA
JazzJInt	Jazz Journal International GB
JbÖsterreichischen-Volksliedwerkes	Jahrbuch des Österreichischen Volksliedwerkes A
JLuteSocAmer	Journal of the Lute Society of America USA
JMTheory	Journal of Music Theory
JVdGSocAmer	Journal of the Viola da Gamba Society of America USA
Kontakte	Kontakte BRD
LuteSocJ	Lute Society Journal GB
MakingM	Making Music GB
MBildung	Musik und Bildung BRD
MCourier	Musical Courier USA
MDisciplina	Musica Disciplina Int
MDisques	Musica Disques F
MEducatorsJ	Music Educators Journal USA
MensMelodie	Mens en Melodie NL
Mf	Die Musikforschung BRD
MfMg	Monatshefte für Musikgeschichte
MGG	Die Musik in Geschichte und Gegenwart. Ed. by Friedrich Blume. (Kassel und Basel: Bärenreiter-verlag, 1956).
MHaus	Musik im Haus. Zeitschrift für die Gitarre A
Mhandel	Musikhandel BRD
MinEd	Music in Education GB
Musikinstrument	Das Musikinstrument BRD
MJ	Music Journal USA
MLetters	Music and Letters GB
MMaker	Melody Maker GB
MMusicians	Music and Musicians GB
MOpinion	Musical Opinion GB
MQ	Musical Quarterly USA
MR	Musikrevy S
MReview	Music Review GB
MSD	Musicological Studies and Documents USA
MTeacher	Music Teacher and Piano Student GB
MTimes	Musical Times GB
Musart	Musart USA
Musica	Musica BRD

ABBREVIATIONS

Musikerziehung	Musikerziehung. Zeitschrift zur Erneuerung der Musikpflege A
NeueMz	Neue Musikzeitung. Musikalische Jugend Jeunesses BRD
NeueZfM	Neue Zeitschrift für Musik
Notes	Notes. Music Library Association USA
NuestraM	Nuestra Musica MEX
NuevaRevFilHisp	Nueva Revista de Filología Hispánica E
NuovaRMItaliana	Nuova Rivista Musicale Italiana I
OesterreichGitarreZ	Oesterreichische Gitarre-Zeitschrift A
OesterreichMz	Oesterreichische Musikzeitschrift A
OrganYb	Organ Yearbook GB
PanPipes	Pan Pipes of Sigma Alpha Iota USA
Plettro	Il Plettro I
ProcAmerStrTAssoc	Proceedings of the American String Teacher Association USA
RArt	Revue de l'Art F
RBelgeMusicol	Belgisch Tijdschrift voor Muziek-wetenschap/ Revue Belge de Musicologie B
Recherches	Recherches sur la Musique Française Classique F
RecorderM	Recorder and Music GB
RItalianaMusicol.	Rivista Italiana di Musicologia I
Ritmo	Ritmo E
RM	Revue Musicale F
RMCatalana	Revista Musical Catalana. Butlleti de l'Orfeo Catala E
RMChilena	Revista Musical Chilena CH
RMItaliana	Rivista Musicale Italiana I
RMSuisseRomande	Revue Musicale de Suisse Romande SWIT
RMusicol	Revue de Musicologie F
RuchM	Ruch Muzyczny POL
SaturdayR	Saturday Review USA
SchweizerischeMz	Schweizerische Musikzeitung
SIMg	Sammelbande der Internationalen Musikgesell- schaft
Soundb	Soundboard. The Guitar Foundation of America USA
SouthFolkQ	Southern Folk Quarterly USA
SovetskajaM	Sovetskaja Muzyka SU
Stewart	S. S. Stewart's Banjo, Guitar, and Mandolin Journal USA
Strad	The Strad GB
StudMusicol	Studia Musicologica H
SvenskTMf	Svenskt tidskrift for Musikforskning S
TennFolkSoc	Tennessee Folklore Society Bulletin USA
VViolinists	Violins and Violinists USA
YbIAIMR	Yearbook. Inter-American Institute for Musi- cal Research USA
ZfdG	Zeitschrift für die Gitarre. *See* MHaus
ZfMw	Zeitschrift für Musikwissenschaft
ZIMG	Zeitschrift der Internationalen Musikgesell- schaft

ABBREVIATIONS

Sigla for Library Locations as Designated in RISM

*An asterisk before an abbreviation indicates that this library is not listed in *RISM*.

A - AUSTRIA

Iu	Innsbruck, Universitätsbibliothek
M	Melk an der Donau, Benediktiner-Stift Melk
Sca	Salzburg, Salzburger Museum Carolino Augusteum, Bibliothek
Wgm	Wien, Gesellschaft der Musikfreunde in Wien
Wmi	Wien, Musikwissenschaftliches Institut der Universität
Wn	Wien, Österreichische Nationalbibliothek (K. K. Hofbibliothek), Musiksammlung
Wst	Wien, Stadtbibliothek, Musiksammlung

B - BELGIUM

Aa	Antwerpen (Anvers), Stadsarchief
Bc	Bruxelles (Brussel), Conservatoire Royal de Musique, Bibliothèque
Br	Bruxelles (Brussel), Bibliotheque Royale Albert 1er
Gu	Gent (Gand), Rijksuniversiteit, Centrale Bibliotheek
Lc	Liège (Luik), Conservatoire Royal de Musique, Bibliothèque

C - CANADA

On	Ottawa (Ontario), National Library of Canada
Tb	Toronto (Ontario), Canadian Broadcasting Corporation (Canadian Radio Broadcasting Commission), Music Library
Tc	Toronto (Ontario), Royal Conservatory of Music
Tm	Toronto (Ontario), Royal Ontario Museum Library
Tolnick	Toronto (Ontario), Harvey J. Olnick, private collection
Tp	Toronto (Ontario), Toronto Public Library, Music Branch
Tu	Toronto (Ontario), University of Toronto, Faculty of Music (Royal Conservatory of Music) Library
Vmclean	Vancouver (British Columbia), Hugh J. McLean, private collection
Vu	Vancouver (British Columbia), University of British Columbia Libary, Fine Arts Division

xxxvi

ABBREVIATIONS

CH - SWITZERLAND

Bchristen	Basel, Privatbibliothek Werner Christen
Bu	Basel, Öffenliche Bibliothek der Universität Basel, Musiksammlung
BEk	Bern, Konservatorium (Berner Musikschule), Bibliothek
BEl	Bern, Schweizerische Landesbibliothek (Bibliothèque Nationale Suisse)
E	Einsiedeln, Kloster Einsiedeln, Musikbibliothek
Ff	Fribourg, Franziskaner-Kloster
Gu	Genève, Bibliothèque publique et universitaire
N	Neuchâtel (Neuenburg) Bibliothèque Publique de la Villa de Neuchâtel
SGv	St. Gallen, Stadtbibliothek (Vadiana)

CS - CZECHOSLOVAKIA

Bm	Brno, Moravské múzeum-hud. hist. oddĕleni
Bu	Brno, Státní vĕdecká knihovna Universitní knihovna
J	Jur pri Bratislave, Okresný archív, Bratislava-vidiek
JIa	Česká Lípa, Okresný archív
N	Nítra, Štátní archív
Pk	Praha, Archív Státní konservatore v Praze
Pnm	Praha, Národní múzeum - hud. oddĕlení
Ps	Praha, Památnik národního písemnictví, Strahov
Pu	Praha, Státní knihovna ČSR - Universitní knihovna Různá provenience

D-brd or D - WEST GERMANY

As	Augsburg, Staats- und Stadtbucherei (ehem. Kreis- und Stadtbibliothek)
ASm	Aschaffenburg, Stadtbücherei (Städtische Musikschulbibliothek)
B	Berlin, Staatsbibliothek (Stiftung Preussischer Kulturbesitz)
Bds	Berlin, Deutsche Staatsbibliothek
Bhm	Berlin, Staatliche Hochschule für Musik und Darstellende Kunst (ehem. Kgl. Akademische Hochschule für Musik)
BNba	Bonn, Wissenschaftliches Beethovenarchiv
Cl	Coburg, Landesbibliothek
DÜk	Düsseldorf, Goethe-Museum (Anton und Katharina Kippenberg-Stiftung)
F	Frankfurt/Main, Stadt-, und Universitätsbibliothek, Musik- und Theaterabteilung Manskopfisches Museum

ABBREVIATIONS

Hmb	Hamburg, Musikbücherei der Hamburger öffentlichen Bücherhallen
Hs	Hamburg, Staats- und Universitätsbibliothek, Musikabteilung
HEms	Heidelberg, Musikwissenschaftliches Seminar der Universität
HV1	Hannover, Niedersächsische Landesbibliothek
HVs	Hannover, Stadtbibliothek, Musikabteilung (Sammlung Kestner)
KI1	Kiel, Schleswig-Holsteinische Landesbibliothek
LB	Langenburg (Wurttemburg), Furstlich Hohenlohe-Langenburg'sche Schlossbibliothek
LCH	Lich, Kreis Giessen, Fürstlich Solms-Lich'sche Bibliothek
LÜh	Lübeck, Bibliothek der Hansestadt Lübeck (ehemals Stadtbibliothek der Freien und Hansestadt Lübeck), Musikabteilung
Mbn	München, Bibliothek des Bayerischen Nationalmuseums
Mbs	München, Bayerische Staatsbibliothek (ehemals Konigliche Hof- und Staatsbibliothek (ehemals Konigliche Hof- und Staatsbibliothek), Musik-sammlung
Mmb	München, Städtische Musikbibliothek
MGu	Marburg/Lahn, Universitätsbibliothek der Philipps-Universität
MÜs	Münster, Santini-Bibliothek im Bischöflichen Priesterseminar
MÜu	Münster, Universitätsbibliothek
MZsch	Mainz, Musikverlagsarchiv B. Schott's Söhne
Ngm	Nürnberg, Bibliothek des Germanischen National-Museums
OB	Ottobeuren (Allgäu), Bibliothek der Benediktiner-Abtei
OF	Offenbach am Main, Verlagsarchiv André
Rp	Regensburg (Bayern), Proske - Musikbibliothek
SCH or SCHhv	Schwäbisch-Hall, Bibliothek des Historischen Vereins für Württembergisch-Franken
Tu	Tubingen, Universitätsbibliothek der Eberhard-Karls-Universität
W	Wolfenbuttel (Niedersachsen), Herzog-August-Bibliothek, Musikabteilung
WI or WI1	Wiesbaden, Hessische Landesbibliothek (ehemals Nassauische oder Königliche Landesbibliothek)

D-ddr or D - EAST GERMANY

Bds	Berlin, Deutsche Staatsbibliothek (ehem. Kgl. Bibliothek; Preussische Staatsbibliothek; Offentliche Wissenschaftliche Bibliothek), -Musikabteilung

ABBREVIATIONS

Dl or Dlb	Dresden (Sachsen), Sächsische Landesbibliothek, Musikabteilung (ehem. Kbl. Öffentliche Bibliothek)
HER	Herrnhut (Sachsen), Archiv der Bruder-Unität
LEm	Leipzig (Sachsen), Musikbibliothek der Stadt Leipzig (Musikbibliothek der Stadt Leipzig Peters und verschiedene Sammlungen in der Leipziger Stadtbibliothek)
ROu	Rostock, Universitätsbibliothek
SWl	Schwerin, Wissenschaftliche Allgemeinbibliothek Landesbibliothek
WRtl	Weimar, Thuringische Landesbibliothek (ehem. Grossherzogliche Bibliothek), Musiksammlung

DK - DENMARK

A	Åarhus, Statsbiblioteket i Åarhus
Kk	København, Det kongelige Bibliotek
Sa	Sorø, Sorø Akademis Bibliotek

E - SPAIN

Bc	Barcelona, Biblioteca Central
Bd	Barcelona, Biblioteca Central de Cataluña
Bim	Barcelona, Instituto Español de Musicologia
Bu	Barcelona, Biblioteca de la Universidad
E	Escorial, El, Real Monasterio de El Escorial
Mlg	Madrid, Fundacion Lazaro Galdiano
Mmc	Madrid, Biblioteca de la Casa Ducal de Medinaceli
Mn	Madrid, Biblioteca nacional
VAc	Valencia, Archivo de la Catedral
Zsc	Zaragoza, Seminario de San Carlos

EIRE - IRELAND

Dn	Dublin, National Library and Museum of Ireland

F - FRANCE

AG	Agen, Archives départementales
BO	Bourdeaux, Bibliothèque municipale
CH	Chantilly, Bibliothèque du Musée Condé
G	Grenoble, Bibliothèque municipale
Nm	Nantes, Bibliothèque municipale
Pa	Paris, Bibliothèque de l'Arsenal
Pc	Paris, Bibliothèque du Conservatoire national de musique (übergegangen in Paris, Bibliothèque nationale)

ABBREVIATIONS

Pm	Paris, Bibliothèque Mazarine
Pn	Paris, Bibliothèque nationale
Po	Paris, Bibliothèque- Musée de l'Opéra
Psg	Paris, Bibliothèque Sainte-Geneviève
Pthibault	Paris, Bibliothèque G. Thibault
TLm	Toulouse, Bibliothèque municipale

GB - GREAT BRITAIN

Ckc	Cambridge, Rowe Music Library, King's College
Cpl	Cambridge, Pendlebury Library of Music
Cu	Cambridge, University Library
CDp	Cardiff, Public Libraries, Central Library
DRc	Durham, Cathedral Library
DU	Dundee, Public Libraries
En	Edinburgh, National Library of Scotland
Ep	Edinburgh, Public Library, Central Public Library
Er	Edinburgh, Reid Music Library of the University of Edinburgh
Ge	Glasgow, Euing Music Library
Gm	Glasgow, Mitchell Library
Gu	Glasgow, Glasgow University Library
Lbl	London, The British Library
Lbm	London, British Museum
Lbmh	London, British Museum, Paul Hirsch Collection
Lcm	London, Royal College of Music
LEc	Leeds, Leeds Public Libraries, Music Department, Central Library
LI	Lincoln, Cathedral Library
Ob	Oxford, Bodleian Library
Och	Oxford, Christ Church Library
Ouf	Oxford, Oxford University, Faculty of Music Library
T	Tenbury (Worcestershire), St. Michael's College Library

H - HUNGARY

SFm	Székesfehérvár (Stuhlweissenburg), István Király Múzeum Könyvtára (König-Stephan-Museum)

I - ITALY

BDG	Bassano del Grappa, Biblioteca civica
Bc	Bologna, Civico Museo Bibliografico-Musicale (Liceo Musicale "G.B. Martini")

ABBREVIATIONS

BGc	Bergamo, Biblioteca Civica
CDO	Codogno, Biblioteca civica popolare "L. Ricca"
Fc	Firenze, Biblioteca del Conservatorio di Musica "L. Cherubini"
Fn	Firenze, Biblioteca Nazionale Centrale
FEc	Ferrara, Biblioteca comunale Ariostea
Ma	Milano, Biblioteca Ambrosiana
Mb	Milano, Biblioteca Nazionale di Brera
Mc	Milano, Biblioteca del Conservatorio "Guiseppe Verdi"
MOe	Modena, Biblioteca Estense
Nc	Napoli, Biblioteca del Conservatorio de Musica S. Pietro a Maiella
Nn	Napoli, Biblioteca Nazionale "Vittorio Emanuele III" (with: Bibl. Lucchesi-Palli)
Ppapafava	Padova, Biblioteca privata Novello Papafava dei Carreresi
PAc	Parma, Sezione Musicale della Biblioteca Palatina presso il Conservatorio "Arrigo Boito"
PEsp	Perugia, Archivo Storico di San Pietro
Rc	Roma, Biblioteca Casanatense
Rdp	Roma, Archivio Doria Pamphili
Rsc	Roma, Biblioteca Musicale governativa del Conservatorio di Santa Cecilia
Rv	Roma, Biblioteca Vallicelliana
Rvat	Roma, Biblioteca Apostolica Vaticana
REm	Reggio-Emilia, Biblioteca municipale
Tn	Torino, Biblioteca Nazionale Universitaria
TI	Termini-Imerese, Biblioteca Comunale Liciniana
Vc	Venezia, Biblioteca del Conservatorio "Benedetto Marcello" (fondo primitivo, fondo Correr, fondo Giustiniani, fondo dell' Ospedaletto, fondo Carminati, fondo Torrefranca)
Vnm	Venezia, Biblioteca Nazionale Marciana
VEaf	Verona, Biblioteca dell'Accademia filarmonica
VEas	Verona, Archivio di Stato
VIb	Vicenza, Biblioteca civica Bertoliana

J - JAPAN

Tma	Tokyo, Bibliotheca Masashino Academia Musicae

NL - NETHERLANDS

At	Amsterdam, Toonkunst-Bibliotheek
DHgm	Den Haag, Gemeente Museum
Uim	Utrecht, Instituut voor Muziekwetenschap der Rijksuniversiteit

ABBREVIATIONS

P - PORTUGAL

Pm	Porto, Biblioteca Pública Municipal

PL - POLAND

GD	Gdansk (Danzig), Biblioteka Polskiej Akademii Nauk
Kj	Kraków (Krakau), Biblioteka Jagiellónska
Wu	Warszawa, Biblioteka Uniwersytecka
WRu	Wroclaw (Breslau), Biblioteka Uniwersytecka

S - SWEDEN

L	Lund, Universitetsbiblioteket
Skma	Stockholm, Kungliga Musikaliska Akademiens Bibliotek
Uu	Uppsala, Universitetsbiblioteket

US - UNITED STATES OF AMERICA

A	Albany (New York), New York State Library
AA	Ann Arbor (Michigan), University of Michigan, Music Library
AUS	Austin (Texas), University of Texas
BApi	Baltimore (Maryland), Peabody Institute of the City of Baltimore Library
BE	Berkeley (Calif.), University of California, Music Library
BLu	Bloomington (Indiana), Indiana University
BO	Boulder (Colorado), University of Colorado, Music Library
Bp	Boston (Mass.), Boston Public Library, Music Department
BRp	Brooklyn (New York), Brooklyn Public Library
BU	Buffalo (New York), Buffalo and Erie County Public Library
CA	Cambridge (Mass.), Harvard University, Music Libraries (Eda Kuhn-Loeb, Houghton, Harvard College, Theatre Collection)
CAh	Cambridge (Mass.), Harvard University, Houghton Library
*CARu	Carbondale (Illinois), Southern Illinois University
*Ccr	Chicago (Illinois), Center for Research Libraries
CHH	Chapel Hill (North Carolina), University of North Carolina, Music Library
CIp	Cincinnati (Ohio), Cincinnati Public Library
CLp	Cleveland (Ohio), Cleveland Public Library

ABBREVIATIONS

Cn	Chicago (Illinois), Newberry Library
COu	Columbus (Ohio), Ohio State University, Music Library
*Cp	Chicago (Illinois), Chicago Public Library
Cu	Chicago (Illinois), University of Chicago, Music Library
DE	Denver (Colorado), Denver Public Library, Art and Music Division
DM	Durham (North Carolina), Duke University Libraries
Dp	Detroit (Michigan), Detroit Public Library, Music and Performing Arts Library
*DUu	Durham (New Hampshire), University of New Hampshire
EU	Eugene (Oregon), University of Oregon
I	Ithaca (New York), Cornell University Music Library
IO	Iowa City (Iowa), University of Iowa, Music Library
IObenton	Iowa City (Iowa), Rita Benton Library
LA or LAuc	Los Angeles (Calif.), University of California, William Andrews Clark Memorial Library
LAusc	Los Angeles (Calif.), The University of Southern California, School of Music
LEX	Lexington (Kentucky), University of Kentucky, Margaret I. King Library
M	Milwaukee (Wisconsin), Milwaukee Public Library, Art and Music Department
*MOSu	Moscow (Idaho), University of Idaho
NH	New Haven (Conn.), Yale University, The Library of the School of Music
NO	Normal (Illinois), Illinois State University, Milner Library
NYcu	New York (New York), Columbia University, Music Library
NYhs	New York (New York), New York Historical Society Library
NYhsa	New York (New York), Hispanic Society of America, Library
NYp	New York (New York), New York Public Library at Lincoln Center
OB	Oberlin (Ohio), Oberlin College Conservatory of Music
Pc	Pittsburgh (Pa.), Carnegie Library of Pittsburgh
PHf	Philadelphia (Pa.), Philadelphia Free Library, Music Library
PHu	Philadelphia (Pa.), University of Pennsylvania (Otto E. Albrecht Music Library, Van Pelt Library, Furness Shakespeare Library, Yarnall Library of Theology)
PROhs	Providence (R.I.), Rhode Island Historical Society
PROu	Providence (R.I.), Brown University Libraries
PRV	Provo (Utah), Brigham Young University
Pu	Pittsburgh (Pa.), University of Pittsburgh, Music Library (with: Theodore M. Finney private library)

ABBREVIATIONS

R	Rochester (New York), Sibley Music Library, Eastman School of Music, University of Rochester
*RI	Riverside (Calif.), University of California at Riverside
SFs	San Francisco (Calif.), Sutro Library
SLc	Saint Louis (Missouri), Concordia Seminary Library
SLf	Saint Louis (Missouri), Fontbonne College Library
SLKrohn	Saint Louis (Missouri), Ernst C. Krohn private library collection
SLp	Saint Louis (Missouri), Saint Louis Public Library
SLu	Saint Louis (Missouri), Olin Library, Washington University
SLug	Saint Louis (Missouri), Washington University, Gaylord Music Library
SM	San Marino (Calif.), Henry E. Huntington Library and Art Gallery
Sp	Seattle (Washington), Seattle Public Library
STu	Stanford (Calif.), Stanford University, Music Library
Su	Seattle (Washington), University of Washington, Music Library
TA	Tallahassee (Florida), Florida State University
TE	Tempe (Arizona), Arizona State University Library
Tp	Toledo (Ohio), Toledo Public Library
U	Urbana (Illinois), University of Illinois, Music Library
Wc or Wcm	Washington (D.C.), Library of Congress, Music Division
Wcg	Washington (D.C.), General Collections, Library of Congress
WE	Wellesley (Mass.), Wellesley College Library
Ws	Washington (D.C.), Folger Shakespeare Library
Wsc	Washington (D.C.), Scottish Rite Masons, Supreme Council, Library
Wsi	Washington (D.C.), Smithsonian Institution, Music Library

YU - YUGOSLAVIA

Zha	Zagreb, Hrvatski glazbeni zavod, zbirka Don Nikole Udine Algarotti

Abbreviations for Publishers of Modern Editions

BÄRENREITER, Bärenreiter-Antiquariat (Kassel-Wilhelshöhe, Germany)
EdBerben, Edizioni Berben (Ancona, Italy)
BreitkopfHärtel, Breitkopf und Härtel (Wiesbaden, West Germany)

xliv

ABBREVIATIONS

CEstHist, Centro de Estudio Históricos (Madrid, Spain)

EdChanterelle, Editions Chanterelle, distributed by Brian Jordan (London, England)

EdCultCiv, Editions Culture et Civilisation (Brussels, Belgium)

FORNI, Arnaldo Forni Editore s.p.a. (Sala Bolognese, Italy)

HEUGEL, Heugel et Cie (Paris, France)

HOFMEISTER, Friedrich Hofmeister (Hofheim, West Germany)

InstEspMusic, Consejo superior de investigaciones científicas, Instituto español de musicología (Barcelona, Spain)

InstFernCat, Institución "Fernando el Católico" de la Exema. Consejo Superior de Investigaciones cientificas (Saragossa, Spain)

MINKOFF, Minkoff Reprint (Chene-Bourg/Geneve, Switzerland)

OLMS, Georg Olms Verlag (Hildesheim, West Germany)

OXFORD, Oxford University Press (London, England)

PennaStUniv, Pennsylvania State University Press (University Park, Pa.)

SCHOTT, B. Schott's Söhne, Schott and Co. (Mainz, West Germany)

S.P.E.S., Studio per Edizioni Scelte (Florence, Italy)

TECLA, Tecla Editions (London, England; Boston, Mass.)

UMusicEsp, Unión Musical Española (Madrid, Spain)

ZERBONI, Presso Le Edizioni Suvini Zerboni (Milan, Italy)

CHAPTER ONE

General Histories and Dictionaries

Of the general histories of the guitar listed in this chapter, many are histories of plucked instruments and so include the lute, the mandolin, and others. English-, German-, French-, Italian-, and Spanish-language texts are indexed. The chapter is divided into three sections: Section A. The Early Guitar: The Sixteenth through the Eighteenth Centuries (Including Studies of Tablature Notation in that Period), Section B. General Surveys: The Sixteenth through the Twentieth Centuries, and Section C. Dictionaries of Guitarists.

Section A. gives a short list of items which treat the history of the guitar before 1800. All are extensively researched contributions to the study of early music. Other literature on tablature which is restricted specifically to the Renaissance period or to the Baroque period is cited in Chapter III and Chapter IV.

In Section B., the amount of detail and the degree of accuracy of the entries vary. Among the most thoroughly researched studies recently published are Evans (entries 15, 16), Radole (entry 34), Ragossnig (entry 35), and Turnbull (entry 43). A discussion of the research methods, problems, and final opinions of authors Evans and Turnbull is found in an article by Jas Obrecht entitled "Guitar books and their authors", *GuitarP* XIII/10 (Oct 1979) 78–80, 82, 85, 86, 88, 94–96, 98. Several surveys treat specific aspects of the guitar and its repertoire. These are Clark (entry 13) on elementary harmonic analysis, Pujol (entry 32) on timbre and flesh versus nail right-hand technique, Sicca (entries 38–41) on music for guitar and keyboard instruments, Wade (entry 46) on the guitar duo, Wade (entry 47) on trends in the development of the guitar as a solo instrument, and Zvengrowski's dissertation (entry 50) for a specialized treatment of education and Schenkerian analysis.

1

Etching. *Street Singer* by Edouard Manet.

(1-3)

A. The Sixteenth through the Eighteenth Century (Including Studies of Tablature Notation in that Period)

1   HUFFMAN-BLAIN STEARNS, Roland. "A manual of lute, vihuela, and
     guitar tablatures, with surveys of transcription practice, in-
     strumental technique, and beginning pedagogy". MM diss., Music:
     University of Idaho, 1978.
A valuable study of tablature notation before 1800. Musical style,
instrument types, early technique, pedagogy, tablature interpretation,
and transcription methodology are considered. Source material is consulted; modern scholarship is evaluated and compared. Illus., charts,
music (tabl. and transcr.), append., bibliog. (music and lit.), 118p.

2   TONAZZI, Bruno. *Liuto, vihuela, chitarra e strumenti similari
     nelle loro intavolature, con cenni sulle loro litterature*
     [Lute, vihuela, guitar and similar instruments for which tabla-
     ture is used, with comments on their literature]. (Ancona:
     Edizioni Bèrben, 1971). In It.
A study of tablature notation with emphasis on that for lute, vihuela,
four-course guitar, and five-course guitar. Information on tablature
for the archlute, theorbo, chitarrone, pandora, orpharion, mandola,
and angelica is included. Instruments are discussed individually with
comments on tablature interpretation, transcription methodology, performance practices, and ornamentation. Important composers and their
works are surveyed (16th c.-20th c.); some references to modern editions in footnotes. Sources of music for the individual instruments
are listed in the main text with some library locations cited. 17 pl.
(tabl. in facsim., 1507-1692, includes music for vihuela, four-course
guitar, and five-course guitar), illus., tables, music (tabl. and
transcr.), bibliog. ref. in notes, bibliog. (secondary works).

3   TYLER, James. *The early guitar. A history and handbook*. (Lon-
     don: Oxford University Press, 1980).
A study of the four-course guitar and the five-course guitar in the
period from the sixteenth century to the eighteenth century. In 2
parts. Part 1 "History" offers a detailed history of the guitar including discussions of tuning and stringing, repertoire, theoretical
texts, and extant musical instruments. A preliminary study of origins
includes information on the vihuela and on early terminology. The
study of the five-course guitar includes a consideration of extant
sources of music of the Italian school, the French school, and the
Spanish school with principal composers and publication dates listed.
Part 2 "Handbook" is a practical guide, addressed to the modern
reader, for the understanding of tuning and stringing practices and
for the interpretation of notation systems. Main text divisions are
"Tuning and stringing", "Tablature", "Technique", and "Ornaments". A
brief discussion of continuo performance on guitar includes a quotation of an excerpt from the text of Nicola Matteis's *The false consonances of musick* (ca. 1680). Glossary, 4 append. ("Primary sources",
"Vocal music accompanied by guitar alfabeto", "Eighteenth-century

(3-7)   General Histories

vocal music accompanied by guitar", and "Available facsimile editions of guitar tablatures". 29 pl. (iconog., music, instruments),
music (tabl. and transcr.), bibliog., no index, 176p.
Reviews: MMusician XXVIII (May 1980) 35-36; Ephraim Segerman, *EarlyM*
VIII/3 (July 1980) 387-88; Józéf Powrózniak, *Notes* XXXVII/3 (Mar
1981) 588.

4   WOLF, Johannes. "Über Gitarren-Tabulaturen" [On guitar tabla-
        tures]. Report of the fourth Congress of the International
        Musical Society (London, 29 May-3 June 1911) 354. (London:
        Novello, 1912). English abstract in *ZIMG* XIII/3 (Dec 1911)
        105-06. In De.
Italian and Spanish guitar tablature is discussed. Coverage extends
from the late sixteenth century to the eighteenth century. Some inaccuracies.

5   WOLF, Johannes. *Handbuch der Notationskunde. II. Teil. Ton-
        schroften der Neuzeit. Tabulaturen, Partitur, Generalbass und
        Reformversuche* [Handbook of notation. Part II. Musical writ-
        ings of recent times, tablatures, score, generalbass, and
        reform attempts]. (Leipzig: Breitkopf und Härtel, 1913-1919)
        2v. Reprint ed. (Hildesheim: Georg Olms Verlagsbuchhandlung,
        1963). In De.
Ch. III "Guitarrentabulaturen" [Guitar tablatures]: A survey of
guitar tablatures, published and in manuscript. Includes music for
solo guitar, guitar and voice, and guitar in ensemble with other instruments. Emphasis on transcription methodology. Illustrated extensively with musical examples of tablature and with transcriptions in
two-staff systems (treble and bass clef). Includes some music in
facsim. Extensive bibliog. of tablatures, published material and
manuscripts, p. 209-18. Organization of the bibliography is by
country and by tablature type. Library locations cited.

B. General Surveys: The Sixteenth through the
Twentieth Century

6   AZPIAZU, José de. *The guitar and guitarists from the beginning
        to the present day.* (London: G. Ricordi and Co., Ltd., 1960).
        French ed. (Basle, Switzerland: Editions Symphonia-Verlag A.
        G.).
A short historical survey of the guitar's history to the present day.
Theories on ancestry given. Contains many listings of important individuals with little detail. Some inaccuracies. No notes or bibliog.
41 illus., 39p.
Reviews: GuitarN LV (Sept-Oct 1960) 21; *MakingM* XLIV (Autumn 1960)
17; *MTimes* CII (Jan 1961) 32; *GalpinSocJ* XIV (Mar 1961) 86.

7   BAKUS, Gerald J. *The Spanish guitar. A comprehensive reference
        to the classical and flamenco guitar.* (Los Angeles, Calif.:
        Gothic Press, 1977).

4

General Histories   (7-10)

A general reference work in which several subjects are treated
briefly; history, playing, care, construction, techniques, music,
supplies, literature, recordings, and biographies are the topics
covered. Ch. I "History" gives a short general historical survey in
which the reader is frequently referred to other secondary works for
further information. "This book is best suited for the person who
needs a thorough general reference or who has limited experience
with the guitar" (Preface). Append. (music theory, music symbols,
new developments), illus., port., tables, iconog., glossary, music,
bibliog., 204p.
Review: GuitarP XII (Apr 1978) 22.

8   BELLOW, Alexander. *The illustrated history of the guitar*.
       (New York: Belwin Mills Publishing Corp., 1970).
A study of the history and ancestry of the guitar from 2500 B.C. to
the present day. Includes brief discussions of important makers,
performers, and composers. Many theories on the evolution of the
guitar are not well-documented. Some inaccuracies. 100 pl., music,
bibliog., index, 215p.
See also: RILM IV/2 (1970) 2484bm[44].
Reviews: Carl Miller, *GuitarR* XXXIII (Summer 1970) 33; Peter Danner,
JLuteSocAmer III (1970) 64-68; Joan Rimmer, *Notes* XXVII/2 (1970)
275-76; Thomas Heck, *JAmerMusicolSoc* XXIV/2 (1971) 310-13; *PanPipes*
LXIV/3 (1972) 20-21; *IB* XXX/8 (1976) 556-57; James Tyler, *EarlyM*
VII/1 (1979) 121, 123.

9   BRONDI, Maria Rita. *Il liuto e la chitarra. Richerche
       storiche sulla loro origine e sul loro sviluppo* [The lute and
       the guitar. Historical research on their origin and on their
       development]. (Torino: Fratelli Bocca Editori, 1926). In It.
The origins and history of the lute and of the guitar are treated
individually with attention also given to related instrument types.
In three parts: 1. "Origini orientali del liuto e della chitarra"
[Oriental origins of the lute and of the guitar]. 2. "Il liuto et
la chitarra in Europa" [The lute and the guitar in Europe]. 3. "La
chitarra nella construzione, nei musei, nella musica vocale, sin-
fonia, ecc." [The guitar in construction, in museums, in vocal
music, symphony, etc.]. Some inaccuracies. Illus., music, bibliog.
ref. in notes, list of works consulted not cited in notes. No
index, 170p.

10   BUEK, Fritz. *Die Gitarre und ihre Meister* [The guitar and its
       masters]. (Berlin: Schlesinger'sche buch-U. Musikhandlung Rob.
       Lienau, 1926). In De.
A survey of the life and works of representative guitarists and
composers with emphasis on the period from the late eighteenth
century to the early twentieth century. Organization is by country
(Germany, Spain, Italy, Russia, France, Scandinavian countries, and
America) with an additional chapter on the history of guitar making.
Index, 173p.
Review: OesterreichGitarreZ I/2 (Nov 1926) 28-30, 32.

(11-15)   General Histories

11   CARFAGNA, C.; CAPRANI, A. *Profilo storico della chitarra* [A
         profile history of the guitar]. Preface by Mario Castelnuovo-
         Tedesco. (Ancona: Edizioni Bèrben, 1966). In It.
In 4 parts. 1. "Lo strumento" [The instrument]. A description and
early history of the guitar. 2. "La letteratura chitarristica e i
chitarristi" [The guitar literature and guitarists]. A survey of the
repertoire for vihuela and for guitar from the sixteenth to the
twentieth century. Important composers and performers are considered.
3. "Didattica" [Didactics]. An historical survey of instructional
materials. Specific techniques and studies are considered individually. 4. "Appendice" [Appendixes] (3: List of concertos for guitar
and orchestra, notes on flamenco, notes on jazz). Port., iconog.,
music, bibliog., index, 106p.

12   CHARNASSÉ, Hélène; VERNILLAT, France. *Les instruments a cordes
         pincées, harpe, lute et guitare* [The plucked stringed instru-
         ments, harp, lute, and guitar]. (Paris: Presses Universitaires
         de France, 1970). In Fr.
Individual consideration of the history of the following instruments: harp, lute, guitar, vihuela, and cistre. Ch. III: "La guitare"
[The guitar] presents a survey of the history of the guitar mentioning important composers, repertoire, and makers. Organized chronologically with a section on ancestry and building. Ch. IV: "La
vihuela" [The.vihuela] gives a description of the instrument with a
survey of its published repertoire. Illus., music, bibliog., 128p.
See also: RILM IV/3 (Sept-Dec 1970) 3945bm[44].
Review: Mf XXVI/1 (1973) 145-46.

13   CLARK, Matthew. "Harmonic analysis with examples from the
         classical guitar repertoire". *GuitarP* XIII/12 (Dec 1979) 32-38.
Analysis of examples of music for guitar and for vihuela addressed
to the student of harmony. Includes works by Milan, Ponce, Carcassi,
Sor, Giuliani, and Carulli, among others. Music.

14   CONTRERAS, Segundo N. *La guitarra. Sus antecedentes históricos
         y biografias de ejecutantes célebres* [The guitar. Its histor-
         ical antecedents and biographies of famous performers]. (Buenos
         Aires: Librería "La cotizadora económica" de E. Perrot, 1927).
         In Sp.
A brief history of the guitar from its ancestry to Tárrega. Discussion of the general characteristics of the guitar. Biographies of
important composers and guitarists. Some inaccuracies. Illus., port.,
bibliog., 135p.

15   EVANS, Tom and Mary. *Guitars. Music, history, construction,
         and players, from the Renaissance to rock.* (New York and
         London: Paddington Press Ltd., 1977).
A detailed general history of the guitar. Thoroughly researched,
based largely on a study of source materials. Individual treatment
of guitar types with text divided into the following sections: 1.
The classical guitar. 2. The flamenco guitar. 3. The guitar in Latin
America. 4. The steel-string acoustic guitar. 5. The electric guitar
guitar. The section on the classical guitar gives a detailed study

General Histories   (15-20)

of the history of the vihuela, the four-course guitar, and the five-course guitar. Musical and theoretical sources are examined. Design and construction, repertoire, and social history are considered individually in chronological surveys. Illus. (of historical guitars, performers, and iconography), charts of dimensions of historical instruments, glossary, bibliog., index, 479p.
See also: Evans 16 for a French translation.
Reviews: Carl Miller, *GuitarR* XLIII (Spring 1978) 32; *JazzJInt* XXXI (Apr 1978) 24; *MinEd* XLII/392 (1948) 169; *MMusicians* XXVI (May 1978) 36-37; *GuitarLute* VI (May 1978) 6; *GuitarP* XII (June 1978) 10; *MMaker* LIII (Aug 1978) 36; *GuitarLute* VII (Sept 1978) 40-41; *MTimes* CXIX (Oct 1978) 863; Ivor Mairants, *Guitar* VI/5 (Dec 1977) 32-33.

16   EVANS, Tom and Mary. *Le grand livre de la guitare, de la Renaissance au rock: musique, histoire, facture, artistes* [The great book of the guitar, from the Renaissance to rock: music, history, construction, artists]. Trans. by Jean-Dominique Brière et Claude Lefèvre. (Paris: A. Michel [ca. 1979]). In Fr.
A French edition of Evans 15.

17   GARCIA DE BAIGORRI, Maria Antonia. "Musica de guitarra. Su origen y evolucion" [Music for guitar. Its origin and evolution]. *Guitarra* (Havana) I/1 (Dec 1940) 16-17, 23. In Sp.
A survey of the history of the vihuela and the guitar from the sixteenth to the nineteenth century. Some representative composers are mentioned. Little detail is given.

18   GIERTZ, Martin. *Den Klassika Guitarren - musiken ock maestarna* [The classic guitar - music and masters]. (Sweden: Norstedts, 1979). In Sw.
Reviews: MR XXXIV/3 (1979) 139; *DanskMt* LIV/2 (1979) 97-98; Karen Dusen Dusgaard Nielsen, *Guitar* VIII/7 (Feb 1980) 36-37.

19   "Gitarre" [Guitar]. *MGG* V, 174-202. In De.
This entry consists of three articles. Boetticher's essay (C.) is the most accurate of the three and contains the most detail.
A. "Vorgeschichte und aussereuropaische Formen" [Pre-history and forms outside of Europe] by Hans Hickmann is a survey of a broad range of early plucked instruments.
B. "Die Gitarre in Abendland" [The guitar in the Occident] by Kurt Reinhard is a general survey of the guitar and similar instruments from the thirteenth century.
C. "Gitarremusik" [Guitar music] by Wolfgang Boetticher is an extensive survey of important composers, performers, and publications of guitar music. Vihuela included. Some inaccuracies. Illus., music (facsim.), extensive bibliog. (music and lit.).
See also: Heck 474, p. 26-28 for criticism.

20   Grunfeld, Frederic V. *The art and times of the guitar. An illustrated history of guitars and guitarists.* (New York: Macmillan Co., 1969).

(20-23)   General Histories

A general history of the guitar with questionable commentary on ancient
instrument types. Includes a chapter on the guitar in America. Important composers, guitarists, and publications are considered. Musical and
literary sources are quoted. Contains some inaccurate information. This
work is exceptionally valuable for its extensive iconographical survey.
227 illus. (iconog. and historical guitars), port., bibliog., index,
340p.

Reviews: Peter Danner, *JLuteSocAmer* III (1970) 64-68; *HiFi/MAmer* XX
(May 1970) 30; Carl Miller, *GuitarR* XXXIII (Summer 1970) 33; *Instru-
ment* XXV (Oct 1970) 12; *MEducatorsJ* LVII (Dec 1970) 67-68; *TennFolk-
Soc* XXXVI/1 (1970) 20-21; *Blues* LXXXI (Apr 1971) 21; *MensMelodie*
XXVI (May 1971) 158; Thomas F. Heck, *JAmerMusicolSoc* XXIV/2 (Summer
1971) 310-13; *SouthFolkQ* XXXVI/4 (1972) 404-07; Dale Higbee, *Amer-
Recorder* XIII/2 (1972) 65; *MLetters* LIV/1 (1973) 86-87; *AmerMTeacher*
XXIV/6 (1975) 55-56; *GuitarP* IX (May 1975) 57; *Instrument* XXIX (June
1975) 34; *SouthFolkQ* XL/3-4 (1976) 384-86; *MTimes* CXVII (Dec 1976)
1001; *MinEd* XLI/386 (1977) 183-84; *MReview* XXXVIII/2 (1977) 128-29;
MOpinion CII (Dec 1978) 127.

21   "Guitarristas célebres; fichas biográficas" [Famous guitar-
        ists; biographical notes]. *Ritmo* XXII/246 (Sept 1952) 23. In
        Sp.
Biographical sketches of guitarists from the sixteenth to the twen-
tieth century. Nicolás Alfonso (20th c.), Francisco Alfonson (20th
c.), Felipe Alonso (17th c.), Mariano Alonso y Castillo (19th c.),
José Alsina (19th c.), Juan Carlos Amat (16th c.), Narciso de
Ametller Cabrer (19th c.), and José de Azpiazu (20th c.).

22   HUBER, J. *Origines et techniques de la guitare* [Origins and
        techniques of the guitar]. (Lausanne: Editions Morf S. A.,
        1968). In Fr.
Many aspects of the guitar are covered briefly. Includes an historical survey with notes on ancestry. Some inaccuracies. Also has
sections on construction and makers, jazz, folklore and flamenco
idioms, technique for jazz and classical styles. Illus., 17 pl.,
music, 213p.

23   KASHA, Michael. "A new look at the history of the classic
        guitar". *GuitarR* XXX (1968) 3-12.
An attempt to trace the historical origins of the guitar based on
archaeological findings and written evidence. The author states four
postulates which he applies to questions about the guitar's origins.
These are *accordatura, morphology, complexity,* and *geographical con-
tinuity.* Also included is a section entitled "The guitar and the
vihuela in the Renaissance" in which etymology and theories on
stringing and tuning are discussed. This section gives a somewhat
inaccurate history because of its many unclear generalizations.
Illus., iconog., bibliog.
See also: Heck 474, p. 2-5, for comments.

General Histories   (24-30)

24   KOCZIRZ, Adolf; ZUTH, Adolf. *Beiträge zur Geschichte der
      Gitarre und des Gitarrenspiels* [Contributions to the history
      of the guitar and guitar performance]. (Vienna, 1919). In De.

25   LIBBERT, Jürgen. "400 Jahre Gitarre und Gitarristen: Versuch
      eines historischen Überblicks" [400 years of the guitar and
      guitarists: attempt at an historical survey]. *Musica* XXXIII/1
      (Jan-Feb 1979) 17-22. In De.
A general survey of the history of the guitar with background on
pre-1600 plucked instruments. The significance of representative
composers, performers, and publications of music is considered.
Early history includes notes on the vihuela. Bibliog.

26   MARCUSE, Sibyl. *Musical instruments: a comprehensive
      dictionary.* (Garden City, New York: Doubleday and Co., Inc.,
      1964).
A short historical survey of developments in the guitar's design,
stringing, and tuning, p. 218-20.

27   MUÑOZ, Ricardo. *Historia de la guitarra* [History of the
      guitar]. (Buenos Aires: Talleres gráficos de la Penitenciaría
      Nacional, 1930). In Sp.
A general historical survey of the history of the guitar from
antiquity to the early twentieth century. Includes biographies of
important figures, history of the guitar in Latin America. Many
inaccuracies. Pre-dates some definitive historical findings. Illus.,
port., index, 424p.

28   MURPHY, Sylvia. "The guitar". In 2 parts. *AustralianJM-
      Education* XIII (Oct 1973) 27-33; XIV (Apr 1974) 19-23.
A history of the guitar based on an investigation of available
musical and theoretical sources.
Part 1: "The guitar before 1750". A detailed survey of the history
of the guitar from the sixteenth century to 1750. Notes on vihuela
included. Notation, technique, and repertoire are discussed. Music
(tabl. and staff notation), bibliog. ref. in notes.
Part 2: "The guitar: from 1750 to the present day". A discussion of
the history of the guitar from 1750 based on a study of musical and
theoretical sources. Includes commentary on important composers,
performers, publications.

29   NELSON, Martha. "Notes on the tarantella (including a
      collection of tarantellas for guitar)". *GuitarR* XXXIV
      (Winter 1971) 7-17.
A history of the tarantella with emphasis on the relationship of
its style and form to its etymology. 5 music (tarantellas, 19th c.
and 20th c.).

30   NICHOLS, George. "The guitar". *Guitarra* (Chicago) IV/21
      (July-Aug 1966) 16-17.
Quotations by sixteen famous musicians, poets, and authors about
the guitar. Includes Berlioz, Chopin, Beethoven, Paganini, Debussy,

(30-35)   General Histories

Bream, Madame Sidney Pratten, Robert Louis Stevenson, Edward Lear, Padre J.B. Martini, and others.

31   NICOLA, Isaac. "Notas historicas de la guitarra" [Historical
      notes on the guitar]. *Conservatorio* VI/2 (Apr-June 1948) 5-7.
      In Sp.
A survey of the history of the vihuela and the guitar with notes on ancestry included. Some central figures are mentioned. Little detail is given.

32   PUJOL, Emilio. *El dilema del sonido en la guitarra* [The
      dilemma of timbre on the guitar]. Revised and enlarged ed.
      (Buenos Aires: Ricordi Americana, 1960). In Sp, En, and Fr.
Pujol, an advocate of the no-nail right-hand technique, discusses and compares the two different qualities of tone produced by plucking the strings with the nail and with the flesh of the right-hand fingers. The history of the controversy over the manner of plucking the string includes the theories of Thomas Mace, Dionisio Aguado, Fernando Sor, Julián Arcas, and Francisco Tárrega, among others. Quotations of source material. Bibliog., 84p.
Review: GuitarN LVII (Jan-Feb 1961) 7.

33   PUJOL, Emilio. "La guitare" [The guitar]. *Encyclopédie de la
      musique et dictionnaire du conservatoire* II/3, p. 1997-2035.
      (Paris: Librairie Delagrave, 1927). In Fr.
A general historical survey of the guitar includes theories on its ancestry. Early tunings, notation, vihuelists, guitarists, and important publications of music are considered in an historical context. Includes a discussion of makers and a study of the fundamentals of harmony as they relate to the guitar and guitar techniques. Illus., music, bibliog. ref. in notes.

34   RADOLE, Giuseppe. *Liuto, chitarra e vihuela. Storia e
      letteratura* [Lute, guitar and vihuela. History and litera-
      ture]. (Milan: Edizioni Suvini Zerboni, 1977). In It.
The history and music of the lute, guitar, and vihuela are treated individually. Biographies of composers and performers; description of tuning and notation practices. Some representative compositions are listed. Illus., music (tabl. and staff notation), bibliog., index, 133p.
Review: A.G., Fronimo VII/27 (Apr 1979) 36-37.

35   RAGOSSNIG, Konrad. *Handbuch der Gitarre und Laute* [Handbook
      of the guitar and the lute]. (Mainz: B. Schott's Söhne, 1978).
      In De.
A study of the history, literature, and repertoire of the guitar and lute. The history of the two instruments is considered individually in a study of early tunings, notation systems, performance practices, and ornamentation. The text is well-illustrated with musical examples of the original notation and transcription. Also includes chapters on the history of nail- and flesh-playing technique,

General Histories   (35-39)

musical forms (16th c. - 18th c., listed alphabetically with definitions), guitar instruction and study with an extensive list of
studies and repertoire. Illus. (facsim., iconog., historical
guitars), list of makers, bibliog., index, 256p.
Reviews: MR XXXIV/3 (1979) 139; Carl Miller, *GuitarR* XLV (Spring
1979) 4; Henry Adams, *GuitarLute* X (July 1979) 36; *MBildung* XI
(July-Aug 1979) 485; Thomas F. Heck, *Notes* XXXVI/1 (Sept 1979)
107-08; *OesterreichMz* XXXV (Apr-May 1980) 246.

36   SAINZ DE LA MAZA, Regino. *La guitarra y su historia* [The
          guitar and its history]. (Madrid: Ateneo, 1955). In Sp.
A history of the guitar and its ancestry in which a survey of
representative composers and performers is given. Includes notes
on music for vihuela. Covers the period from the seventeenth-century five-course guitar to Tárrega and the early twentieth century.

37   SHARPE, A.P. *The story of the Spanish guitar. A history of
          the instrument with biographies of its famous composers,
          personalities and players.* First ed., 1954. Second ed.
          (London: Clifford Essex Music Co., 1959).
A short history of the guitar from ancient times to the twentieth
century. Significant composers and "personalities" are listed alphabetically with biographical sketches of each. Chronological list of
some methods (from 1551). Also includes an essay on the guitar as
an accompaniment instrument. Inaccuracies. Port. (contemporary
guitarists), illus. (historical guitars with description). No contents or index, 64p.
Reviews: MMaker XXX (July 1954) 2; *Strad* LXV (Sept 1954) 148; *MTimes*
CI (Mar 1960) 161; Appleby, Wilfrid M. "New books on the guitar",
GuitarN XX (Aug-Sept 1954) 14.

38   SICCA, Mario. "La chitarra e gli strumenti a tastiera" [The
          guitar and keyboard instruments]. *Fronimo* I/1 (Oct 1972) 27-
          32. In It.
A discussion of performance practices and problems of the repertoire
for guitar and fortepiano, guitar and harpsichord, and modern compositions for guitar and piano, harpsichord, or fortepiano. Representative works mentioned. Modern compositions for guitar and keyboard
by Castelnuovo-Tedesco, Hans Haug, Manuel Ponce, Josef Dichler,
Stephen Dodgson, and Guido Santorsola are described. List of works
for guitar and keyboard from the Biedermeier period. Port., bibliog.
ref. in notes.
See also: Sicca 39, 41 for translations.

39   SICCA, Mario. "The guitar and the keyboard instruments".
          Trans. from the Italian by Dr. Livio Manes. *GuitarR* XXXIX
          (Summer 1974) 17-22.
An English translation of Sicca 38. Includes additional information,
"A few suggestions for those who do not have a fortepiano and must
use a modern piano". Iconog., illus., bibliog. ref. in notes.
See also: Sicca 40 for corrections.

(40-45)   General Histories

40   "Erratum". *GuitarR* XL (Winter 1976) 33.
Corrections of two captions under the illustrations of Sicca 39.

41   SICCA, Mario. "Gitarre und Tasteninstrumente" [The guitar and
        keyboard instruments]. *GitarreLaute* II/1 (1980) 16-23. In De.
A German translation of Sicca 38. The list of works for guitar and
keyboard is expanded. Iconog., illus., bibliog. ref. in notes.

42   TAPPERT, W. "Zur Geschichte der Gitarre" [On the history of
        the guitar]. *MfMg* XIV/5 (1882) 77-85. In De.
A survey of the guitar's history from the sixteenth century to the
nineteenth century with emphasis on the guitar in Germany. Includes
a description of Kremberg's *Musikalische Gemüthsergötzung*. Quotation
of luthier Jakob August Otto's treatise (918-921) in which he claims
responsibility for the construction of the first six-string guitar.
Introductory notes on the presently active Leipzig guitar club.
Append. (music).

43   TURNBULL, Harvey. *The guitar from the renaissance to the
        present day*. (London: B.T. Batsford, Ltd., 1974).
A concise, well-documented general history of the guitar from the
sixteenth century. Research is based mainly on a study of source
material. 46 pl. (including historical guitars and iconography), 16
music, bibliog., index, 168p.
Reviews: MinEd XXXVIII/370 (1974) 275; *MMusician* XXIV (Dec 1974) 37-
38; *MTeacher* LIII (Dec 1974) 31; *JLuteSocAmer* XVII (1975) 77-79;
Thomas Heck, *JAmerMusicolSoc* XXVIII/1 (1975) 142-43; *NeueMz* XXIV/3
(1975) 16; *EDance* XXXVII/2, 70; *Notes* XXXI/4 (1975) 786-87; Jerrold
Manns, *Soundb* II/1 (Feb 1975) 13-14; Thomas Heck, *Soundb* II/4 (Oct
1975) 82; *MOpinion* XCIX (Nov 1975) 69; *MTimes* CXVI (Aug 1975) 709.

44   TURNBULL, Harvey (text); HECK, Thomas (bibliog.). *Grove* VII,
        825-43.
A detailed historical survey of the guitar from the sixteenth to the
twentieth centuries. Includes discussions of important composers,
performers, repertoire, notation systems, and developments in design
and construction. Section on guitar variants included. Illus.,
iconog., music (tabl. and staff notation), bibliog.

45   VIGLIETTI, Cedar. *Origen e historia de la guitarra* [Origin
        and history of the guitar]. (Buenos Aires: Editorial Albatros,
        1973). In Sp.
A survey of the history of the guitar with many biographies of
important guitarists and composers. Background on composers and
performers of the lute and the vihuela. Includes an extensive consideration of guitarists and composers of Argentina and of Uruguay
with biographies and historical background. Illus., port., bibliog.
ref. in notes, 289p.
See also: RILM IX/1-2 (Jan-Aug 1975) 449bm[21].
Review: Henry Adams, *GuitarLute* VII (Sept 1978) 41.

General Histories   (46-50)

46   WADE, Graham. "An historical perspective on the guitar duo".
         GuitarR XXXI (May 1969) 7-8.
A survey of the literature for the duo for fretted instruments dating
from the vihuela music of the sixteenth century to twentieth-century
works for guitar. Illus., music.
Reviews: MMusician XXVIII (Aug 1980) 40; *MTeacher* LIX (Nov 1980) 25;
MTimes CXXI (Nov 1980) 706-07.

47   WADE, Graham. *Traditions for the classical guitar*. (London:
         John Calder, 1980).
A study of significant trends in the development of the guitar as a
solo instrument. Solo repertoire for vihuela and for guitar are surveyed in an historical context with remarks on the twentieth-century
performer's and scholar's interest in and treatment of the music.
Emphasis is on Segovia's influence and contributions. Information on
construction and on sources of literature and music. Lacks footnotes
and thorough bibliographic citations for the identification of
sources. Append. (recital programs, 1888-1978), illus., iconog.,
music, discog. (includes music for lute, vihuela, early guitars,
and transcriptions), bibliog., index, 270p.

48   WHALEN, Margaret. "Spanish classical guitar". *Fretts* V (1962)
         17-19.
A short sketch of the history of the guitar with comments on the
present status of the guitar in the United States. Port. (author).

49   WITOSZYNSKYI, Leo. "Vihuela and guitar: some historical
         developments". Trans. from the German by J.D. Roberts.
         Guitar IV/2 (Sept 1975) 19-21.
An historical survey of the guitar and the vihuela, tracing develop-
ments based on a study of sources. Includes etymology and design.
Vihuela, lute, and guitar are distinguished. Illus., ports.

50   ZVENGROWSKI, Steven Theodore. "The treatment of idiomatic
         sonority in selected compositions for the guitar as a cur-
         riculum source for comprehensive musicianship". PhD diss.,
         Music: Northwestern University, 1978. UMI 7907957.
A detailed study of sonority in representative works for solo guitar
and for guitar accompaniments for the development of four "Comprehensive musicianship curriculum strategies". Sonority is studied
from an historical and an analytical point of view. Tables, fig.,
charts, music, 6 append. (including music), bibliog., 480p.

C. Dictionaries of Guitarists

See also 73 and 76 for dictionaries of Italian guitarists and
luthiers

See also 903-05 for dictionaries of luthiers, exclusively

(51-55)   General Histories

51   BONE, Philip J. *The guitar and mandolin. Biographies of
      celebrated players and composers.* First ed., 1914. Second
      enlarged ed., 1954. Reprint of the second ed. with new pre-
      face. (London: Schott and Co., Ltd., 1972).
Concise biographies of composers and performers mentioning their
main works and contributions. Arranged alphabetically with no division between guitarists and mandolinists. Sources of information are
not consistently well identified. Many inaccuracies. Illus., port.,
music, 388p.
Reviews: Richard Capell, *MLetters* XXXV (1954) 254; Wilfrid M.
Appleby, *GuitarN* XX (Aug-Sept 1954) 14; *Strad* LXV (Dec 1954) 284;
Charles Ford, *EarlyM* I/4 (1973) 245; *GuitarP* VIII (May 1974) 55;
MTimes CXV (June 1974) 479-80; J.D. Roberts, *Guitar* III/12 (July
1975); *CGuitarInt* III/1 (Fall 1975) 15-17.

52   POWRÓZNIAK, Józef. *Leksykon gitary* [Dictionary of the guitar].
      (Cracow: Polskie Wydawnictwo Muzyczne, 1979). In Pl.
Reviews: Soundb VI/3 (1979) 133; *GuitarLute* XII (Jan 1980) 38; *RuchM*
XXIV/13 (1980) 19.
See also: Powróźniak 53 for a German translation.

53   POWRÓZNIAK, Józef. *Gitarren Lexikon* [Dictionary of the
      guitar]. Trans. from the Polish by Bernd Haag. Enlarged by
      A. Quadt and W. Pauli. (Berlin: Verlag Neue Musik, 1979).
      In De.
A German translation of Powróźniak 52. 165p.
Reviews: John W. Tanno, *Soundb* VII/3 (Aug 1980) 129; Thomas F. Heck,
Notes XXXVII/3 (Mar 1981) 588-89.

54   PRAT, Domingo. *Diccionario biográfico, bibliográfico,
      histórico, crítico de guitarras, guitarristas, guitarreros*
      [Biographical, bibliographical, historical, and critical
      dictionary of guitars, guitarists, and guitar makers].
      (Buenos Aires: Casa Romero y Fernandez, sucesores: J.B.
      Romero e hijos, 1934). In Sp.
A dictionary of guitars, guitarists, makers, and terminology. Some
inaccuracies. Bibliog., 468p.

55   ZUTH, Josef. *Handbuch der Laute und Gitarre* [Handbook of the
      lute and the guitar]. (Vienna: Verlag der Zeitschrift für die
      Gitarre, 1926). Reprint ed. (Hildesheim: Georg Olms Verlag,
      1972). In De.
Alphabetical listing of composers, performers, and terminology
related to the lute and the guitar. Short biographies and definitions. No division is made between items pertaining to the lute and
those pertaining to the guitar. Many bibliographic references to
early twentieth-century German-language periodicals are cited. Some
inaccuracies. 296p.
Review: R. Lach, *ZfMw* XI (1929/30) 185.

CHAPTER TWO

National Histories

The following chapter contains literature on the history of the guitar in specific countries. Organization is alphabetical by country. The main headings are Argentina, Brazil, Czechoslovakia, Denmark, France, Germany, Great Britain, Italy, Latin America, Mexico, Paraguay, Peru, Poland, Portugal, Russia, Spain, United States, and Uruguay. Many cross-references to chapters on periods in history and to Chapter VIII, Design and Construction, are cited. These contain information on national histories within a more limited subject area.

In the field of Latin American music, Gilbert Chase's *A guide to the music of Latin America*, 2nd ed., revised and enlarged, (Washington, D.C.: Pan American Union and the Libraries of Congress, 1962) gives an extensive, annotated list of literature on the music of Latin American countries.

Section Q. United States contains sub-sections in which literature on guitar societies and on important individuals is listed. Many articles on individual composers include facsimile reprints of music.

(56-61)

A. Argentina

See also 45; 946 (construction)

56   CONTRERAS, Segundo N. "Breve historia de la guitarra en la
         republica Argentina" [Short history of the guitar in the
         republic of Argentina]. *GuitarR* X (1949) 108-10. In Sp.
A history of the guitar in Argentina in which some important guitarists and significant musical events are mentioned. In 2 sections:
1. "Periodo Colonial" [The Colonial period]. 2. "Periodo Indepen-
dente" [The Independent period]. Includes political history as it
affected Argentine culture. Bibliog.

57   CONTRERAS, Segundo N. "The guitar and the gaucho", *GuitarR*
         VI (1948) 150.
Historical notes on the importance of the guitar in the poetry and
music of the *gaucho* of Argentina. The role of the *gaucho* in society
is defined. Bibliog.

58   CONTRERAS, Segundo N. *La guitarra argentina; apuntes para su
         historia y otros articulos* [The Argentine guitar; notes on
         its history and other articles]. (Buenos Aires: imprenta de
         Castro Barrera & Cía., 1950). In Sp.
A history of the guitar in Argentina divided into two main sections:
the colonial period (pre-1810) and the independent period (post-
1810). Includes a discussion of the guitar of the *gaucho*, of the
tarantella, and of music in the Jesuit missions of Paraguay.
Bibliog., 76p.

59   MUÑOZ, Ricardo. "La guitarra en la Argentina" [The guitar in
         Argentina]. *Guitarra* (Havana) I/1 (Dec 1940) 19, 23. In Sp.
A survey of the history of the guitar in Argentina. Important
guitarists are mentioned.

60   ROBERTS, John. "Historical notes. Martín Fierro". *Guitar*
         IX/8 (Mar 1981) 13-14.
The guitar was important in the music of the legendary *gauchos*
(*payadores*) of Argentina. The character and life of the *gauchos*,
including that of Martín Fierro, is central to the discussion.
References are made to nineteenth- and early twentieth-century
texts in which the guitar is mentioned.

61   VEGA, Carlos. "The classical guitar in early Buenos Aires".
         Trans. by Eithne Golden. *GuitarR* X (1949) 103-06.
A history of the guitar in early Buenos Aires from its early form
as an accompaniment instrument of five strings. The new interest in
music in Argentina is attributed to the new contact with the world
following the achievement of national independence in 1810. Interest
in the guitar as it was developed by Miguel Garcia, Federico
Moretti, and other important European influences are discussed.

Etching. *Musicians in a Bistro* by Jacques Villon (pseud. of Gaston Duchamp).

National Histories   (62-67)

62   VEGA, Carlos. "La guitarra artística en el Buenos Aires
      antiguo" [The artistic guitar in old Buenos Aires]. *La
      Prensa* LXVI/23 (Apr 1935) 783. In Sp.

B. Brazil

63   BARBOSA-LIMA, Carlos; BOBRI, Vladimir; NELSON, Martha. "A
      musical journey to many lands: Brazil". *GuitarR* XLVII
      (Spring 1980) 16-17 (text), 18-22 (music).
An introduction to Brazilian music with information on musical in-
fluences from other countries. Discussion of three compositions by
Brazilian composers: "Brazilian Song (canção)" by Francisco
Mignone, "Caterete" by José de Oliveira Queiróz, and "Mestiça" by
an anonymous composer. Illus., music.

64   COELHO, Olga. "The guitar in Brazil...and some reminiscences".
      GuitarR XXI (1957) 16-18.
An autobiography of guitarist-singer Coelho. Emphasis is on the de-
velopment of her career with accounts of her experiences with
Andrés Segovia, Heitor Villa-Lobos, Patricio Teixeira, João "Can-
hoto", Mozart Aranjo, and Oscar Lorenzo Fernández.
See also: *GuitarR* XXI (1957) 30-32 for short biographies of Coelho,
Fernández, and Villa-Lobos.

65   CORRÊA DE AZEVEDO, Luis-Heitor. "La guitare archaique en
      Brésil" [The archaic guitar in Brazil]. *Studia Memoriae Belae
      Bartók Sacra,* 123-24. (Budapest: Aedes Acadeniae Scientiarum
      Hungaricae Budapestini, 1956). In Sp.
Discussion of the two popular forms of Brazilian guitar: *violão* and
viola. Description and comments on history, tunings, and technique.
Music.

66   SIMÕES, Ronoel. "The guitar in Brazil". Trans. and ed. by
      Eithne Golden. *GuitarR* XXII (1958) 6-7 (text), 8-11 (music),
      16-21 (music), 28-29 (music).
A history of the guitar of twentieth-century Brazil. Notes on
Brazilian composers who stimulated interest in the guitar as an
instrument for serious study. Survey of composers and performers
of the classical tradition includes Americo Jacomino "Canhoto"
(d. 1928), Agustín Barrios, Josefina Robledo, Regino Sainz de la
Maza, Isaías Savio, Abel Carlevaro, and Maria Lívia São Marcos.
Outstanding figures in the popular and folk tradition and prominent
makers are also mentioned. List of societies. Music.
See also: *GuitarR* XXII (1958) 27 for biographies of M.C. Guarnieri,
Francisco Mignone, A.T. Nogueira, and Ronoel Simões.

C. Czechoslovakia

67   BOSMAN, Lance. "Lubomír Brabec-on contemporary Czech music
      for guitar". *Guitar* IX/8 (Mar 1981) 15-17.

A survey of twentieth-century Czechoslovakian music. Modern composers of guitar music are considered with short descriptions of their compositions. Important influences on their music are noted. Composers include Jana Obrovská, Jan Truhlar, Kucera, Karel Reimer, and Lubor Barta. Music education and performance opportunities in Czechoslovakia are also topics of discussion. Port., music.

D. Denmark

68   RISCHEL, Thorwald. "Zur Geschichte der Gitarre in Dänemark" [On the history of the guitar in Denmark]. *DieGit* XII/9-10 (1931) 70-74. In De.

A survey of the history of the guitar in Denmark. Includes short biographies of important performers and composers from the eighteenth to the early twentieth century. Comments on present day guitar-related activities in Denmark. The problem of a lack of a guitar tradition and a lack of guitar teachers is noted.
See also: 69

69   RISCHEL, Thorwald; BECKER, Sv. A. "Zur Geschichte der Gitarre in Dänemark. (Nachtrag)" [On the history of the guitar in Denmark. (supplement)]. *DieGit* XII/11-12 (1931) 90-91. In De.

As a supplement to Rischel 68, an additional Danish guitarist of the early nineteenth century is discussed. Guitar clubs in the early twentieth century are described.

E. France

See 10, 161, 162, 252, 255, 286, 407, 411, 556, 558; 884 (iconography); 908, 910, 948, 949 (construction)

F. Germany

See also 10, 42, 409; 950 (construction)

70   SCHWARZ-REIFLINGEN, Erwin. "La chitarra in Germania" [The guitar in Germany]. *Chitarra* I/1 (1934) 3f. In It.

G. Great Britain

See also 556, 558, 635

71   APPLEBY, Wilfrid M. "Song and guitar in Britain". *GuitarR* XII (1951) 193-94.

A consideration of composers and performers of music for voice and guitar in nineteenth-century England. Several publications are mentioned. Recent activities of performers in England are also discussed. Illus.

National Histories   (72-76)

72   BUTTON, Stuart W. "The guitar in England, 1600-1900". PhD
      diss. in progress, Music (40 Lees Road, Willesborough, Ash-
      ford, Kent, England).

H. Italy

See also 10, 472, 476, 636

73   CARFAGNA, Carlo; GANGI, M. *Dizionario chitarristico italiano
      (chitarristi, liutisti, tiorbisti, compositori, liutai ed
      editori)* [Dictionary of Italian guitarists (guitarists,
      lutenists, theorboists, composers, luthiers, and publishers)].
      (Ancona: Edizioni musicali Bèrben, 1968). In It.
Alphabetical listing of individuals. Short biographies and comments
on their main contributions. Compositions, publications listed. In
two parts: guitarists, lutenists, theorboists, and composers.
2. luthiers and publishers. 97p.
See also: RILM II/3 (Sept-Dec 1968) 2912bm[03].

74   GIORDANO, M. "La chitarra in Sardegna" [The guitar of
      Sardinia]. *Plettro* XXIX (1933/34) 7f. In It.

75   HECK, Thomas F. "The role of Italy in the early history of the
      classic guitar-a sidelight on the house of Ricordi". Part 1.
      "The earliest music for the classic guitar". *GuitarR* XXXIV
      (Winter 1971) 1-4 (text), 5-6 (music).
Text in five main divisions in which the following subjects are discussed: 1. The popularity of the guitar ca. 1770-1790, primarily as
an accompaniment instrument. 2. Possible reasons for the exodus of
guitarists from Italy. 3. The establishment of the House of Ricordi
in Milan in 1808 with a study of the first publications for six-
string guitar. 4. The notation of guitar music in the single-staff
notation of violin music. 5. An examination of the first publication
by Ricordi (plate no. 1), Antonio Nava's "The seasons of the year,
in four solo sonatas for chitarra francese". Illus., music
(facsim.), bibliog. ref. in notes.
See also: RILM V/2 (May-Aug 1971) 3345ap[89].

76   TERZI, Benvenuto. *Dizionario dei chitarristi e liutai
      italiani* [Dictionary of Italian guitarists and luthiers].
      (Bologna: Editrice Rivista "La chitarra", 1937). In It.
Alphabetical listings of individuals. Short biographies with notes
on their main contributions. In two parts: 1. guitarists and
lutenists. 2. luthiers and publishers. Some inaccuracies. Illus.,
port., bibliog. 286p.

I. Latin America

See also 15, 16, 27, 45, 176

21

(77-82)   National Histories

77   SLONIMSKY, Nicholas. *Music of Latin America*. (New York: Thomas
      Y. Crowell Co., 1945).
A general history of Latin American music with some notes on the use
of the guitar in native music including Brazil, Colombia, Costa Rica,
Mexico, Panama, and Paraguay. (The reference to the guitar on p. 246
is omitted from the index.) Contains a dictionary of Latin American
musicians, songs, dances, and musical instruments. Music, pl.,
index, 374p.

78   STOVER, Richard D. "Guitar in Latin America". *GuitarP* IX/7
      (July 1975) 18, 30, 32, 35-36, 39.
A short historical survey of the guitar in Latin America from the
sixteenth to the twentieth century. Comments on twentieth-century
composers for the guitar including Agustin Barrios Mangore, Heitor
Villa-Lobos, Antonio Lauro, and Leo Brouwer. Some information on
Creole guitar. Music, discog. (alphabetical listing by country
with performer, title, record company, record number cited).

J. Mexico

See also 176; 951, 952 (construction)

79   GRIAL, Hugo de. *Musicos Mexicanos* [Mexican musicians].
      (Mexico: Editorial Diana, S.A., 1965). In Sp.
Short biographical essays on Mexican musicians from the eighteenth
to the twentieth century. Organization is chronological by date of
birth. Important composers of guitar music are Julián Carrillo, p.
101-06, and Manuel M. Ponce, p. 129-33. Index, 275p.

80   "Guitar in Mexico". In two parts. *CGuitarInt* I/2 (Winter 1974)
      3-6; I/3 (Spring 1974) 26-28.
Part 1: A brief cultural history of Mexico. Notes on present day
guitar-related activities in Mexico with emphasis on a discussion
of the educational system.
Part 2: Remarks on the works of the following twentieth-century
Mexican composers for guitar: Manuel Ponce, Rafael Adame, Julian
Carrillo, Luis Sandi, and Carlos Chavez. Includes a summary of
some basic stylistic characteristics of Mexican folk music.

81   OTERO, Corazon. "The guitar in Mexico". *Guitar* IX/2 (Sept
      1980) 16-17.
A survey of twentieth-century composers and performers in Mexico
from Manuel M. Ponce (1886-1948) to the present. Descriptions of
their activities, works. Port (author).

82   SENSIER, Peter. "A gap in the story of the guitar". *Guitar*
      IV/3 (Oct 1975) 16-17.
An examination of guitar types in Mexico and in Latin America.
Illus. (guitars).

22

National Histories   (83-88)

83   STEVENSON, Robert. *Music in Mexico. A historical survey*.
        (New York: Apollo edition, 1971). First ed. by Thomas Y.
        Crowell Co. (New York, 1952).
A detailed general history of music in Mexico from "early aboriginal
music" to the twentieth century. Includes a description of a manuscript of music for vihuela (ca. 1740) in the Biblioteca Nacional
(p. 162-63). Bibliog., index, 300p.

84   TANNO, John C. "The guitar in Mexico". In 2 parts. *Fretts*
        (Fall 1959) 20-21; (1960) 8-10.
Part 1: Comments on the formation and performance activities of the
Mexican guitar quartet "Cuarteto Dona-Dio". Port.
Part 2: A biographical sketch of Dona-Dio, guitarist, with notes on
his career as a performer. Includes comments on other Mexican
guitarists. Port.

K. Paraguay

See also 58

85   SENSIER, Peter. "Guitar topics". *BMG* LX/690 (Oct 1962) 22-23.
A survey of important classical guitarists in the nineteenth and
twentieth centuries with brief comments on their careers. The effect
of the oppressive political circumstances in nineteenth-century
Paraguay on music is discussed.

L. Peru

86   STEVENSON, Robert. *The music of Peru. Aboriginal and Viceroyal
        Epochs*. (Washington: Pan American Union, 1960).
A history of Peru which includes a brief discussion of literature
and manuscripts of music dating from the seventeenth through the
nineteenth century. Description of two manuscripts of guitar music
(tab. and staff notation). Music, music supplement, bibliog., 331p.

M. Poland

See also 485, 486, 487 (on Felix Horetzsky)

87   POWRÓZNIAK, Józef. "The guitar in Poland". Trans. by Czeslaw
        Boniakowski. *GuitarLute* XIV (July 1980) 18-20.
A discussion of the achievements of outstanding Polish guitarists
from the seventeenth century to the present day including Felix
Horetzsky (1797-[1870]), Jan Nepomucan Bobrowicz (1805-1881),
Stanslaw Prus Szczepanowski (1811-1877), and Marek Konrad Sokolow-
ski (1818-1883). Biographical information on the author.

88   WAGNER, Frank. "Guitar in Poland". *CGuitarInt* III/1 (Fall
        1975) 29-30.

A short survey of the activities of Polish guitarists in the nineteenth and twentieth centuries.

N. Portugal

89 PUJOL, Emilio. "The guitar in Portugal". Trans. by Eithne Golden. *GuitarR* V (1948) 114-15. Sp. trans., 128-29.
A history of the guitar in Portugal with emphasis on its early history. Notes on the establishment of educational courses in the study of the guitar, naming students and their achievements. Illus., music.

O. Russia

See also 10 ; 556, 558 (on Fernando Sor)

90 BARBOSA-LIMA, Carlos; BOBRI, Vladimir. "A musical journey to many lands". *GuitarR* LXV (Spring 1979) 5 (text), 28-31 (music).
An introduction to two Russian folk songs, originally written for seven-string guitar, arranged for classical guitar. Includes a history of the seven-string Russian guitar (late eighteenth century to the twentieth century); tuning and repertoire are described. Music, bibliog.

91 BERAN, Alois. "Ueber den Stand der Sechssaitigen Gitarre in Russland" [On the position of the six-string guitar in Russia]. In 2 parts. *ZfdG* V/5 (July 1926) 100-02; V/7 (1926) 150-53. In De.

92 BERAN, Alois. "Zum Stand der Gitarristik in Russland" [On the position of the guitar in Russia]. In 2 parts. *ZfdG* IV/10 (Oct 1925) 1-3; IV/11 (Dec 1925) 2-5. In De.

93 FAMINTSIN, A.S. *Domra i srodnye yei instrumenty russkago naroda* [The domra and similar instruments of the Russian people]. (St. Petersburg, 1891). In Uk.
On the seven-string Russian guitar.

94 IVANOV. *Russkaia semistrunnaia gitara* [The Russian seven-string guitar]. (Moscow: State musical publishing Co., 1948). In Ru.

95 [MAKAROV, Nicolai Petrovich]. "Aus den Lebenserinnerungen des russischen Gitarrevirtuosen N.P. Makarow" [From the memoirs of the Russian guitar virtuoso N.P. Makarow]. Trans. and ed. by Fritz Buek. In 2 parts. *Gfreund* XI (1910) 43-45; XII (1911) 1-3, 11-13, 23-25, 45-47. In De.

96 MAKAROV, Nicolai Petrovich. "The memoirs of Makaroff". Trans. by Vladimir Bobri and Nura Ulreich. In 3 parts. *GuitarR* I/1

National Histories   (97-100)

        (1946) 10-12; I/2 (1947) 32-34; I/5 (1948) 109-11.
The memoirs of Nicolai Petrovich Makaroff (1810-1890), Russian
guitarist, taken from his *Zadushevnaya Ispoved* [Full hearted con-
fession].
Part 1: A biography of Makaroff with emphasis on his activities
as a guitarist.
Part 2: An account of Makaroff's travels and encounters with other
known guitarists including Zani de Ferranti and Schulz. Illus.
Part 3: Makaroff's experiences with two Viennese guitar makers,
Fischer and Schertzer. The rules and procedures of the guitar composition and guitar making contest organized by Makaroff are explained. Makaroff's further contacts with guitarists and his own
recital experiences are mentioned. Bibliog.

97   MASCHKEWITSCH, W.P. "Die Geschichte der sechssaitigen
       Gitarre in Russland, 1900-1923" [The history of the six-
       string guitar in Russia, 1900-1923]. *DieGit* XI/11-12 (1930)
       93-94. In De.
Notes on the "Internationalen Gitarristenbund", the international
movement in Russia for the promotion of guitar playing. Important
members and publications are cited.

98   MASCHKEWITSCH, W.P. "Russische Gitarristen" [Russian guitar-
       ists]. *DieGit* XI/9-10 (1930) 68-72. In De.
Biographies of important Russian six-string guitarist-composers
of the nineteenth and twentieth centuries: J.I. Djakow, P. Pettoletti, J.M. Stockmann, J.A. Klinger, J.F. Decker-Schenk, W.P.
Lebedeff, M.W. Polupajenko, and A.K. Lolikoff.

99   MASCHKEWITZ, W. [sic]. "Zur Geschichte der Gitarre in Russ-
       land" [On the history of the guitar in Russia]. In 3 parts.
       DieGit X/3-4 (1929) 25-27; X/5-6 (1929) 38-40; X/7-8 (1929)
       54-55. In De.
Part 1: A brief introduction to the Russian seven-string guitar.
Biographical sketches of guitarist-composer A.O. Sichra (1772-
1850) and his students S.N. Aksenow (1773/84-1853) and M.T.
Wyssotzki (1791-1837).
Part 2: Biographies of guitarist-composers who were students of
A.O. Sichra: W.S. Sarenko (1814-1881), W.J. Markow (d. 1863), and
N.I. Alexandrow (d. 1890/1900).
Part 3: A biography of guitarist-composer F.M. Zimmermann (d. ca.
1880), student of A.O. Sichra. Other students of A.O. Sichra of
less importance are listed.

100   MASCHKEWITSCH, W.P. "Zur Geschichte der sechssaitigen
       Gitarre in Russland" [On the history of the six-string
       guitar in Russia]. *DieGit* XI/7-8 (1929) 52-56. In De.
Biographical notes on six-string guitarists M.L. Sokolowski (1818-
1883) and N.P. Makarow (1810-1890). Includes a detailed discussion
of the Brussels guitar composition contest organized by Makarow in
1856. Quotation of Zani de Ferranti's opinion of Makarow's playing;
notes on Makarow's travels and associations. List of his literary

(101-107)   National Histories

works and compositions.

101   PEROTT, Boris A. "Incontri con Makaroff" [Meeting Makaroff].
      Trans. from the English by M. Ablóniz. In 2 parts. *AChitar-*
      ristica no. 54 p. 5-6; no. 55 p. 6-7. In It.
Perott's account of his meeting and conversation with Makaroff in
Kiev preceding Makaroff's death. Includes comments on guitarist
Sychra. Port.

102   POWRÓZNIAK, Józef. "Die Gitarre in Russland" [The guitar in
      Russia]. *GitarreLaute* I/6 (1979) 18-20, 22-24. In De.
A history of the guitar in Russia from the eighteenth century to
the twentieth century. The early five-string, the six-string, and
the seven-string guitar are included. The life, works, and main
contributions of important guitarists and composers for the instrument are discussed. Significant in the history of the seven-string
guitar are Andreas Sichra, Ignatz Held, and students of Sichra,
Siemion Aksjonow, Ladislaus Morkow, Fiordor Zimmerman, and Wasil
Sarenko; noted for re-establishing serious interest in the guitar
in the early twentieth century after its late nineteenth-century
decline is Alexander Solowiow. Historically important guitarist-
composers Nikolaus Makarov, Pietro Pettoletti, Johann Dekker-
Schenk, and Wasil Lebiediew are mentioned. Illus., 9 port.

103   POWRÓZNIAK, Józef. "Die Gitarre in der Sowjetunion" [The
      guitar in the Soviet Union]. *GitarreLaute* II/5 (Sept-Oct
      1980) 28-31. In De.
A study of the guitar and guitarists in the Soviet Union from the
October Revolution (1917) to the present. The popularity of the
guitar, guitarists, and guitar-related activities are discussed;
includes notes on both the six-string guitar and the seven-string
guitar. Biographical information is given on seven-string guitarists Vladimir Maškewič (1888-1971) and Wasil Juriew (1881-1962)
and on six-string guitarists Peter Agafošyn (1847-1950), Aleksandr
Iwanow-Kramskoj (1912-1973), Peter Isakow (1886-1958), and Arsenij
Popow (1892-1977). 4 Port.

104   STAKHOVICH, M.A. *Ocherk istorii semistrunnoy gitary* [Essay
      on the history of the seven-string guitar]. (St. Petersburg,
      1844). In Ru.

105   VOL'MAN, Boris L'vovich. *Gitara* [Guitar]. (Moscow: Muzyka,
      1972). 62p. In Ru.

106   VOL'MAN, Boris L'vovich. *Gitara i gitaristy* [Guitar and
      guitarists]. (Leningrad: Muzyka, 1968). In Ru.
Review: SovetskajaM XXXV (Jan 1971) 100-01.

107   VOL'MAN, Boris L'vovich. *Gitara v Rossii: ocherk istorii*
      gitarnogo iskusstra [The guitar in Russia: an outline history
      of guitar technique]. (Leningrad: Muzyka, 1961). 177p. In Ru.
Review: SovetskajaM XXVI (July 1962) 137-38.

National Histories   (108-111)

108   WAGNER, Frank. "Guitar in Russia". *CGuitarInt* III/2 (Winter
        1976) 31-32.
Remarks on the works of composer-guitarists Vladimir Slavski, Peter
Agafoschin (1874-1950), Peter Isekov (1885-1958), B. Asaflev, and
Peter Panin (b. 1940). Also includes a list of the names of some
contemporary guitarists.

P. Spain

See also 556, 558 (on Fernando Sor); 953-957 (on construction)

109   MARSH, William Sewall. "Some Spanish and Spanish-American
        guitarists". In 2 parts. *Crescendo* XXIV/6 (Feb 1932) 3-4;
        XXIV (Sept 1932) 3-4.
Part 1: Biographical sketches of some important lesser-known Span-
ish and Spanish-American guitarists of the nineteenth and twentieth
centuries: José Broca, José Viñas Dias, Sebastian Caldentey Sancho,
José Ferrer Esteve, Domingo Bonet Espasa, Miguel Más Bargalló, and
Tomás Damas.
Part 2: More biographies of Spanish and Spanish-American guitarists
including makers and mandolinists: Baldomero Cateura, Joaquín Casa-
novas, Antonio Jiménez Manjón, Felix de Santos Sebastian, Benito
Sarabia, Enrique Garcia (maker), Francisco Simplicio (maker), Juan
Nogués Pon, and Miguel Llobet. Also included are descriptions of
recitals by Regino Sainz de la Maza and Daniel Fortea.

110   MOSER, Wolf. "Spanische Gitarristen zwischen Aguado und
        Tárrega" [Spanish guitarists between Aguado and Tárrega].
        GitarreLaute I/4 (1979) 26-30. In De.
The author indicates the importance of significant nineteenth-
century guitarist-composers active between Aguado and Tárrega and
objects to present-day guitarists' ignorance of this period. Biographical notes with comments on important contributions of the
following composers: Dionisio Aguado (1784-1849), Trinidad Huerta
(1804-1875), José Broca (1805-1882), Antonio Cano (1811-1897),
José Viñas (1823-1888), Tomás Damas, Julián Arcas (1832-1882),
and José Ferrer (1835-1916). Some methods and compositions cited.
List of some works published by Unión Musical Española. Music
(facsim.).

111   ROBERTS, John. "The guitar in Granada". *Guitar* V/7 (Feb
        1977) 9-11.
A survey of guitarists and guitar makers in Granada in the nineteenth and the twentieth centuries. Emphasis is on important
makers. Illus. (makers and their guitars).

Q. United States

See also 10, 48

(112-118)   National Histories

General

112   BICKFORD, Vahdah Olcott. "The guitar in America". *GuitarR*
       XXIII (June 1959) 17-19.
An historical survey of the guitar in America with information on
the first American publishers, methods, and periodicals. Short
biographies of some American guitarists: William Bateman, Justin
Holland (1819-1887), W. Buckley (late 19th c.), Charles de Janon
(1834-1911), Luis T. Romero (1853-1893), William Foden (1860-
1947), George Krick, Manuel Y. Ferrer (1828-1904), C.W.F. Jansen,
Charles James Dorn (1839-1910), Clarence L. Partee, Walter Jacobs,
Herbert F. Odell, C.F. Fiset, and Zarh M. Bickford. Notes on early
American periodicals. Port., illus.

113   "Errata". *GuitarR* XXIV (Mar 1960) inside cover.
A correction of Bickford 112.

114   DANNER, Peter. "American guitar music: Some notes on a for-
       gotten repertoire". *CGuitarInt* IV/1 (Fall 1976) 3-5.
A survey of the history of the guitar in America from the eighteenth
century to the twentieth century. Biographical notes on outstanding
American guitarist-composers through William Foden. Port. (author).

115   DANNER, Peter. "Breve storia della musica per chitarra in
       America" [A short history of guitar music in America].
       Fronimo V/20 (July 1977) 18-25. In It.
Composers, performers, and publishers active in America in the
eighteenth to the twentieth century. Biographical information on significant figures. Quotations of texts concerning the guitar and
programs with guitar performance, including a program (1824)
featuring A.F. Huerta (1804-1875). Music, bibliog.

116   DANNER, Peter. "Notes on some early American guitar concerts".
       Soundb IV/1 (Feb 1977) 8-9, 21.
A study of guitar concerts in America from the 1770s to the mid-
nineteenth century. Information on several concerts is based on
concert announcements. Concert programs are quoted. Much of the
information is taken from Sonneck 121. Bibliog. ref. in notes.
See also: Tanno 122 for some conflict about turn of the century
publishing activities.

117   "Increasing popularity of the guitar". *Cadenza* XXVIII/3
       (Mar 1921) 45.
The author attributes the rise in the popularity of the classical
guitar to the upsurge in the interest of the "popular" instrument
and the student's subsequent change to the serious instrument upon
discovering its limitations.

118   "The mandolin and guitar". *Cadenza* V/3 (Jan-Feb 1899) 9.
       Reprinted from *Musical America*.
Comments on the current popularity of the two instruments, listing
teachers active in New York City.

National Histories   (119-124)

119   SHEARER, Aaron. "A review of early methods". *GuitarR* XXIII
         (June 1959) 24-26.
A detailed investigation of method books for guitar published in
America between 1820-1906; research was conducted in the Archives
of the Library of Congress. The quality of the available instruction is evaluated. Text from selected methods is quoted. Illus.
(facsim. of title pages of methods), music (facsim.).

120   SIMPSON, Clinton. "Some early American guitarists". *GuitarR*
         XXIII (1959) 16.
Summaries of the activities of some American guitarists, active
from 1760 to the nineteenth century, indicate some interest in the
guitar during that period. Source material is studied. Guitarists
include Benjamin Franklin, Francis Hopkinson, Robert Carter, Mr.
Vidal, and Henry Capron.

121   SONNECK, Oscar G. *Early concert-life in America, 1731-1800.*
         (Leipzig: Breitkopf und Härtel, 1907).
A study of concert life based on an investigation of sources, 1731-
1800. Provides information on the role of the guitar in concert
life and on the type of repertoire performed. Organization is by
city or area. Programs listed. Guitar recitals between 1773 and
1790 in Charleston, Philadelphia, and New York are mentioned.
Bibliog. ref. in notes, index, 338p.

122   TANNO, John C. "American guitar methods published from the
         turn of the nineteenth century to the present". *GuitarR*
         XXIII (June 1959) 28-31.
The author discusses his own philosophies on choosing a method and
gives a description and evaluation of methods published 1827-1957.
Includes a "Summary of American guitar methods", a chronological
list, 1827-1959. Illus.
See also: Shearer 119 for some conflict about turn of the century
publishing activities.

123   VALDEZ-BLAIN, Albert Sr. "Then...and now". *GuitarN* LVI
         (Nov-Dec 1960) 4-5.
Reflections on the progress of the guitar movement in America
dating from 1928.

The American Guild of Banjoists, Mandolinists, and Guitarists

Many articles about the American Guild can be found in issues of
The Cadenza, The Crescendo, and *S.S. Stewart's Banjo, Guitar and
Mandolin Journal.* A few articles have been selected for annotation.

124   "The American guild of banjoists, mandolinists, and guitar-
         ists. Preamble". *Stewart* XVIII/9-10 (Sept 1901) 31.
Notes on the history and present-day popularity of the banjo, mandolin, and guitar in America preface a statement of the "need and ob-
ject of the Guild".

(125-133)   National Histories

125   "Constitution and by-laws of the American Guild of Banjoists,
       Mandolinists and Guitarists". *Cadenza* X/8 (Apr 1904) 13-17.
"Constitution": nine articles. List of members.

126   "Editorial. A brief history of the American Guild of Banjoists,
       Mandolinists, and Guitarists − What the organization has done in
       the interest of the stringed instruments and what it hopes to
       accomplish in the future". *Cadenza* X/9 (May 1904) 22-24, 40.
Detailed notes on the origin and activities of the Guild. Important
members are mentioned. Comments on the future concerts and meetings,
their location and funding.

127   "A memorable day for Boston. The launching of the Guild and
       the holding of a festival". *Stewart* XIX/2 (Feb 1902) 2-4.
An account of activities of the organizational meeting and the
launching of the Guild 22 January 1902 in Boston. Purposes, goals,
and procedures are discussed. Election results recorded.

128   "The President's corner. The first plan for a Guild". *Cadenza*
       XXVIII/10 (Oct 1921) 6-7.
The history and origin of the Guild. Quotations of early issues of
The Cadenza; list of charter members.

129   "Some officers of the Guild". *Cadenza* VIII/7 (Mar 1902) 28-31.
Biographical sketches of the following officers of the Guild:
Charles Morris (Vice-president), W.J. Kitchener, Geo. L. Lansing,
H.F. Odell, Samuel Siegel. Port. (of each officer).

The American Guitar Society

130   BICKFORD, Zarh Myron. "A brief history of the American Guitar
       Society". *GuitarR* XXIII (June 1959) 20.
A history of the Society since its first meeting in September, 1923.
Comments on the contribution of Vahdah Olcott Bickford. List of
publications by the Society. Port.

The Society of the Classic Guitar (New York)

131   "The chronicle". *GuitarR* I (1946) 13.
The program of the first recital (14 May 1946) and of the second
recital (17 June 1946) of the Society of the Classic Guitar.

132   D'ALESSIO, Gregory. "The Society, 1946-1959". *GuitarR* XXIV
       (Mar 1960) 3-10.
A detailed chronology of the history and activities of the Society
with comments on each year, 1946-1959. Early members are listed.
Port., illus.

133   BROWNE, Rosalind. "The Society...early days". *GuitarR* XXIV
       (Mar 1960) 1-2.

National Histories   (134-137)

Recollections of experiences in the 1920s and 1930s of Vladimir
Bobri, George Brandon, Louis Gill, Luigi Moramarco, Arismendi
Polanco, and Fidel Zabal. The early meetings of the Society,
beginning in the spring of 1936, are recalled. Port.

BLANTCHOR, Francis

134   DANNER, Peter. "Return with us now. *Soundboard*'s featured
        facsimile. Cotillions". *Soundb* VII/3 (Aug 1980) 121 (text),
        122-123 (music in facsim.).
An introduction to Francis Blantchor's set of five Cotillions
including a description of the dance.

BLESSNER, E.

135   HECK, Thomas F. "Return with us now. The *Soundboard*'s
        featured facsimile". *Soundb* III/3 (Aug 1976) 52 (text),
        53 (music in facsim.).
Historical background on E. Blessner's "Annie Laurie" (1850 im-
print) for voice and guitar.

CARR, Benjamin (1769–1831)

136   FRANK, Mortimer. "Music for funeral services for George
        Washington". *GuitarR* XXIII (June 1959) 14-15.
Historical notes on "Dead march and monody" for the funeral of
George Washington, the only composition for guitars by Benjamin
Carr. The adaptation for two guitars was one of four duet arrange-
ments by Carr. Stylistic consideration of the music included. Port.
(Carr), music (facsim.).

FERRER, Manuel Y. (ca. 1828–1904)

See also 112

137   PURCELL, Ronald C. "Return with us now. The *Soundboard*'s
        featured facsimile". *Soundb* III/4 (Nov 1976) 76 (text), 77
        (music in facsim.).
Introductory notes to Manuel Y. Ferrer's "Spanish mazurka no. 2"
include biographical information on the composer and commentary
on the work.

FODEN, William (1860–1947)

See also 112, 114, 715

(138-148)   National Histories

138   "William Foden". *Cadenza* IV/2 (Nov-Dec 1897) 12.
A biographical sketch of William Foden. Port.

139   "William Foden". *Crescendo* III/8 (Feb 1911) 19.
A biographical sketch of William Foden with notes on his present
activities. Port.

140   "William Foden". *Crescendo* XXV/8 (June 1933) 1.
A short biography of William Foden. Port.

141   HOSKINS, Arthur C. "William Foden". *GuitarR* XXIII (June 1959)
       21-22.
A biography of Foden. Includes quotations of reviews of Foden's
performances first published in *The Crescendo* and in *The Cadenza*.
Account of his activities in association with Giuseppe Pettine,
Frederick J. Bacon, and William O. Bateman. Port., music (excerpt
of a composition by Bateman).

142   KRICK, George C. "Reminiscences of William Foden". *GuitarR*
       XXIII (June 1959) 27.
Krick's recollections of Foden as a teacher, a composer, and a
performer. Biographical information on Foden included. Port.
(Krick).

143   KRICK, George C. "William Foden". *FINews* VII/5 (Sept-Oct
       1938) 1, 5.
Biographical notes with emphasis on Foden's contribution to the
guitar as a composer and as a performer. Port. (Foden).

144   KRICK, George C. "William Foden 1860-1947". *FINews* XVI/3
       (May-June 1947).
Biographical notes on Foden.

145   MURR, Emma. "William Foden". *FINews* XIV/5 (Sept-Oct 1945) 12.
Biographical notes on William Foden. Port.

146   PETTINE, Giuseppe. "Foden as I knew him". *GuitarR* XXIII
       (June 1959) 23.
Pettine's account of his association with Foden. Frederick Bacon
is also mentioned as an associate. Illus.

147   TANNO, John C. "The *Soundboard*'s featured facsimile". *Soundb*
       II/4 (Oct 1975) 75 (text), 76-79 (music in facsim.).
Biographical notes on Foden as an introduction to the facsimile of
Foden's "Preludes" for guitar.

HAYDEN, William

148   SPALDING, Walter. "William Hayden and the nineteenth century
       American guitar". *Chelys* I/4 (Oct 1976) 20-29.
Historical notes on nineteenth-century American guitarists and their

National Histories   (149-151)

compositions including comments on the life and works of William
Hayden. Contemporaries of Hayden are listed. Illus. (facsim. of
advertisement), port., music (6 works in facsim.).

KRICK, George C.

See also 112, 142-144

149   "George C. Krick". *Crescendo* I/10 (Apr 1909) 7.
Biographical notes on Krick with comments on his accomplishments,
activities as a guitarist and as a mandolinist. Port.

PICK, Richard (b. 1918)

150   TANNO, John C. "Richard Pick, American guitarist". *GuitarR*
      XXIV (March 1960) 12 (text), 13 (music).
A survey of Pick's methods and compositions. Pick's opinion of what
constitutes a valuable and didactic musical composition is considered. Music.

WEILAND, Francis

151   DANNER, Peter. "Return with us now. *Soundboard*'s featured
      facsimile. A much admired air". *Soundb* VIII/2 (May 1981) 82
      (text), 83 (fascim. of title page), 84-85 (music in facsim.).
Introductory notes to the facsimile reprint of Francis Weiland's
variations on "Home sweet home" (1814) for solo guitar. Historical
background on the original composition with a description of Weiland's version.

R. Uruguay

See 45

CHAPTER THREE

Histories of the Renaissance Period

The sixteenth century has been chosen as a starting point in the study of the history of the guitar and vihuela. The earliest extant music, theoretical texts, and instruments date from this century. Information on Renaissance iconography and on design and construction are found in Chapters VII and VIII, respectively. Appendix II lists known sources of music for guitar and vihuela published before 1800; the chronological list (p. 000-000) may be particularly helpful in locating sources of music in the sixteenth century. Modern editions of these musical sources are also listed in Appendix II and often contain introductory material which gives valuable information on the source and biographical data on its composer.

The vihuela was an instrument endemic to Spain, and no music is known to have been published outside of this country. Its shape was that of the guitar, and its surviving music is for vihuela of six-courses (double strings). In sixteenth-century Spain, seven tablature books of music for vihuela were published. The first of these, published in 1535 (colophon reads 1536), is by vihuelist-courtier Luis Milan and contains the earliest-known music for the instrument. Subsequent works were published by Luis de Narvaez (1538), Alonso Mudarra (1546), Enríquez de Valderrábano (1547), Diego Pisador (1552), Miguel de Fuenllana (1554), and Esteban Daza (1576). Four additional composers of music for vihuela are identified in a manuscript entitled "Ramillete de Flores, O Coleccion de Varias Cosas Curiosas", located in the Biblioteca Nacional in Madrid. These composers—Fabricio, Francisco Paez, Mendoza, and Lopez—are not mentioned in any other musical source. López is named as a vihuelist in Juan Bermudo's *Declaracion de Instrumentos* (Ossuna, 1555) and by the Duque of Arcos. This information is given in Ward's dissertation (entry 191, p. 369–70) and in Cook's articles (entries 170–72).

The guitar of the Renaissance was strung with four-courses and five-courses of strings and was probably smaller than the vihuela. Music for four-course guitar was published in two of the works for vihuela. Mudarra's publication contains the earliest-known music for four-course guitar; Fuenllana included music for both four-course and five-course guitar in his 1554 book. Music for guitar appeared in publications of

35

tablature in France, Italy, and Belgium. French publications include works by composers Gregoire Brayssing, Guillaume Morlaye, Simon Gorlier, and Adrian Le Roy. In Italy, books of tablature by editors Pierre Phalèse and Jean Bellère were published. Later in the century, Juan Carlos Amat's *Guitarra española y vandola* (probably first issued in 1586) initiated the age of the Baroque five-course guitar. Amat and other composers for five-course guitar are treated in Chapter IV, Histories of the Baroque Era.

Also cited in this chapter is literature concerning the keyboard works of Antoine de Cabezón, Thomas de Sancta Maria, and Luys Venegas de Henestrosa. Although these works contain music which is intended primarily for performance on the keyboard, the title page of each indicates that the music is also suitable for performance on the vihuela. Some of this music, however, is not idiomatically feasible for performance on the instrument and must be arranged.

The treatise of Juan Bermudo (entries 211–12) is the most detailed source on the vihuela and the guitar. Literary works by Miguel de Cervantes and Luis Milan contain references to the guitar and the vihuela which provide insights into its role in society.

This chapter is divided into four main sections: Section A. General Surveys, Section B. Musical Forms, Section C. Tablature Studies, and Section D. Individual Composers, Performers, Theorists, Publishers, and Authors.

Section A. is divided into three sub-sections according to the instruments which are specifically treated in the texts. These are GUITAR AND VIHUELA, GUITAR, and VIHUELA. This section includes literature which gives an explanation of the differences between the guitar, the vihuela, and the lute. Entries by Chase (154), Kirsch (156), Zayas (159), Denning (174), Poulton (183), Sensier (186), and Ward (191) treat this issue. An examination of sixteenth-century Spanish texts by John Ward, "The lute in sixteenth-century Spain", *GuitarR* IX (1949) 87–88 gives information on sources in which the Spanish preference for the guitar and the vihuela over the lute is indicated.

Section B. includes literature on the romance, villancico, romanesca, folia, tiento, tarantella, pavan, fantasia, lamentation, frottola, French chanson, Italian song, and diferencia in music for both vihuela and guitar.

Section C. includes studies of *musica ficta* practices in tablature (Fox 204) and discussions of transcription practices (Pujol 206, Zayas 207). Section A. of Chapter I gives a list of works which are of particular value in the study of tablature interpretation and transcription methodology.

In Section D. eighteen individuals are listed alphabetically as subsections. Theoretical sources and their library locations are quoted from *RISM* series B VI (2 v.). The list of abbreviations found on p. xxxvi includes library sigla used in this chapter in addition to those used in Appendixes I and II.

(152-157)

A. General Surveys

See also Ch. I, Section A. The sixteenth through the eighteenth centuries, including studies of tablature notation in that period, 1-5; 49, 285, and Ch. VIII, Design and Construction, Section C. The sixteenth century: vihuela and guitar, 906-915.

GUITAR AND VIHUELA

152   APPLEBY, Wilfrid.M. "Some origins of the guitar. Part II."
       GuitarN XVII (Feb-Mar 1954).
A short survey of the origins and early history of the guitar, vihuela, and gittern which precedes definitive findings on the histories of the instruments.

153   BARBOUR, James Murray. *Tuning and Temperament.* Second ed.
       (East Lansing, Michigan: State College Press, 1953). Reprint
       ed., (1973).
A detailed study of tuning systems and temperament based on a study of source materials. The systems of Thomas de Sancta María and Juan Bermudo are considered. Glossary, 180 tables, bibliog., index, 228p.

154   CHASE, Gilbert. "Guitar and vihuela: a clarification".
       BulAmerMusicolSoc VI (1940) 13-14.
An abstract of a paper read 7 Dec 1940, Washington, D.C. A discussion of the incorrect analogies between the guitar and the lute and between the vihuela and the lute made by many authors. Some essential differences are described.

155   CHASE, Gilbert. *The music of Spain.* (New York: W.W. Norton
       Co., Inc., 1941). Second revised ed. (New York: Dover Publi-
       cations, Inc., 1959).
An historical survey of Spanish music from the early Christian Church to the present day. Ch. III: "Early masters of the guitar" is a survey of sixteenth-century music for vihuela and guitar. Consideration is also given to the role of the guitar in Spanish lyric drama and Iberian folk music. Some later history is included. Some inaccuracies. Illus., music, bibliog., discog., index, 383p.

156   KIRSCH, Dieter. "Laute und Gitarre" [Lute and guitar].
       Kontakte V (Oct 1968) 167-72. In De.
"The two instruments are historically differentiated through features of construction, stringing, voicing, and methods of notation. The lute used in 16th-c. polyphonic music requires methods of playing that differ from those of the chord-oriented concert guitar of the 19th c." Illus.-Quoted from *RILM* II/3 (Sept-Dec 1968) 3991ap[44].

157   MUNROW, David. *Instruments of the Middle Ages and Renaissance.*
       (London: Oxford University Press, 1967).

(158-161)   Renaissance Histories

In 2 parts: "The Middle Ages" and "The Renaissance". Organization
within is by type of instrument. Ch. IX: "Strings. The plucked instruments. Vihuela and guitar" is a survey of the history of the
vihuela and the guitar in the sixteenth and seventeenth centuries.
Illus., music (tunings), bibliog. ref. in notes, 97p.

158   PUJOL, Emilio. "Les ressources instrumentales et leur rôle
         dans la musique pour vihuela et pour guitare au XVIe siècle
         et au XVIIe" [Instrumental resources and their role in the
         music for vihuela and for guitar in the XVIth and XVIIth
         centuries]. *La Musique Instrumentale de la Renaissance*,
         205-15. Ed. by Jean Jacquot. (Paris: Éditions du Centre
         National de la Recherche Scientifique, 1955).
Journées Internationales d'études (Paris, 28 March-2 April 1954).
A description of the contents of Spanish publications of vihuela
music and guitar music (1536-1578) with an explanation of tablature
notation. Includes comments on the etymology of the word "vihuela"
and on the influence of vihuela technique on the early Baroque
guitar. Music (tuning, transcr.).

159   ZAYAS, Rodrigo de. "The vihuela: Swoose, lute, or guitar?"
         GuitarR XXXVIII (Summer 1973) 2-5.
An examination of the differences between the vihuela, the guitar,
and the lute. Argument is given for the theory that the vihuela was
a type of guitar. Quotations of sources. Notes on tuning, fretting,
and design. List of modern instrument makers. Illus. (from the publications of Milan and Bermudo).

GUITAR

160   DOBSON, Charles; SEGERMAN, Ephraim; TYLER, James. "The tunings
         of the four-course French cittern and of the four-course
         guitar in the 16th century". *LuteSocJ* XVI (1974) 17-23.
A consideration of possible tunings for cittern and guitar based on
an interpretation of sixteenth-century texts. The tuning instructions for guitar by Phalèse and Bellère (1570) are compared to those
given for the cittern by Vreedman (1568) and Le Roy and Ballard
(1564, 1565). Tuning interpretation given in Heartz 229 is refuted.
Music, bibliog.
See also: Heartz 229 for a translation of the text of Phalèse and
Bellère and Tyler 165 for additional tunings.

161   HEARTZ, Daniel. "Parisian Music publishing under Henry II:
         a propos of four recently discovered guitar books". *MQ* XLVI/4
         (1960) 448-67.
Four books of guitar tablature, three attributed to Guillaume Morlaye, one attributed to Simon Gorlier are examined for their musical
contents and historical significance. Sixteenth-century European
publishing activities are discussed and the publications of Le Roy,
Mudarra, Barberis, and Fuenllana are compared. Music, pl., bibliog.
ref. in notes, map (Paris ca. 1550).

Renaissance Histories   (162-167)

162   LESURE, François. "La guitare en France au XVIè siècle" [The
       guitar in France in the XVIth century]. *MDisciplina* IV (1950)
       (fasc. 2, 3, 4) 187-95.
A discussion of the popularity of the guitar in sixteenth-century
France, including information on contemporary accounts and on the
first publications of guitar music in Paris. Quotations of title
pages, contents of publications listed. Tunings, builders, and
publications are cited.

163   NICKEL, Heinz. "Gitarrentabulaturen II. Die vierchörige
       Gitarre" [Guitar tablatures II. The four-course guitar].
       GitarreLaute I/3 (1979) 42-44.
A survey of music for the four-course guitar, a description of the
instrument, and a discussion of tuning (according to Le Roy) and
of tablature interpretation. Advice to the performer on the performance of the repertoire on the modern guitar. Illus., music,
bibliog. ref. in notes.

164   SUBIRA, José. "Un fondo desconocido de musica para guitarra".
       [An unknown source of guitar music]. *Congrès de la Societat
       International de Musicologia a Barcelona. Programa de les
       sessions i festes que es celibraran de 18 al 25 d'abril del
       1936.* (Barcelona: impr. Casa Caritat, 1936). In Sp.

165   TYLER, James. "Further remarks on the four-course guitar".
       LuteSocJ XVII (1975) 60-62.
A supplement to Dobson 160 in which three additional tunings are
described. The author consults three theoretical sources: Juan
Bermudo's *Declaracion* (1555), Scipione Cerreto's *Della practica
musica* (1601), and Michael Praetorius's *Syntagma musicum* (1619).
Music, bibliog. ref. in notes.
See also: RILM IX/3 (Sept-Dec 1975) 4393ap[44].

166   TYLER, James. "The Renaissance guitar, 1500-1650". *EarlyM*
       III/4 (Oct 1975) 341-47.
A general history of the early guitar including a description of the
instrument, an explanation of terminology, tablature, tuning, and
the definition of other members of the guitar family existing before
1650 (bandurria, chitarriglia, chitarrino, chitarra battente, mandola, and vandola). Theoretical and musical sources are examined.
Iconog., bibliog. ref. in notes, bibliog. of music for four-course
guitar (printed books and MSS), music.

VIHUELA

167   APEL, Willi. "Early Spanish music for lute and keyboard
       instruments". *MQ* XX (July 1934) 289-301.
Music for vihuela, not for lute, is a topic of discussion in this
article. Historical background, tablature interpretation, and some
musical forms are discussed. Individual consideration of the music
of Antonio de Cabezón (keyboard), Luis Milan (vihuela), and Enríquez

(168-174)   Renaissance Histories

de Valderrábano (vihuela). Facsim. (title page and tabl. from
Cabezón's *Obras de música*, 1578), list of works, music.

168   BERNER, Alfred. "Vihuela". *MGG* XIII, 1621-23.
A history of the vihuela includes early etymology and the identification of pre-sixteenth century instruments. A few sources (Praetorius and Bermudo) are described. Bibliog.

169   COOK, Frederick. "The capotasto of the vihuela". *GuitarLute*
       VIII (Jan 1979) 12-13.
A description of the *peñazuela* used for shortening the strings on
the vihuela based on information in Bermudo 211. Biographical notes
on the author included. Diagrams, port.

170   COOK, Frederick. "An unknown vihuela manuscript". *GuitarLute*
       XII (Jan 1980) 13-14.
Four unknown composers of vihuela music (Fabricio, Francisco Paez,
Mendoza, and López) are represented in a 1593 manuscript (MS 6001,
Biblioteca Nacional, Madrid) entitled *Ramillete de Flores, O Colec-
ción de Varias Cosas Curiosas*. Also contained in the manuscript is
a work by Luis de Narváez. The manuscript is described. A list of
compositions is given. Music.
See also: Cook 171 and 172

171   "Composers of works for vihuela". *GuitarLute* XIII (Apr 1980)
       9-10.
A correction of Cook 170.

172   COOK, Frederick. "Ein wenig bekanntes Vihuelamanuskript"
       [A little-known vihuela manuscript]. *GitarreLaute* II/5
       (Sept-Oct 1980) 18-19. In De.
A German translation of Cook 170.

173   DANNER, Peter. "A plain and simple introduction to lutes and
       lute music: the vihuela". *CGuitarInt* V/3 (Spring 1978) 22-28.
General comments on the history of the vihuela with a discussion of
publications of vihuela music. Some notes on performance techniques.
Illus. (facsim.), music (facsim. of tabl. by Mudarra), bibliog. ref.
in text.

174   DENNING, Darryl. "The vihuela – the royal guitar of sixteenth-
       century Spain". *MJ* XXXV/10 (Dec 1977) 19-22. Reprinted in
       Soundb VI/2 (May 1979) 38-41.
A brief general history of the vihuela with a description of the
instrument, a discussion of notation, and a survey of the seven
vihuelists' publications included. Comments on the present-day
interest in the vihuela repertoire and on modern builders. Includes
an investigation of the history and the ancestry of the guitar, the
vihuela, and the lute with distinctions made between the three instruments. Illus., bibliog. ref. in notes, bibliog.

Renaissance Histories   (175-180)

175   FRAENKEL, Gottfried S. *Decorative music title pages. 201 examples from 1500 to 1800*. (New York: Dover Publications, Inc., 1968).
Annotations of 201 plates give the following information: author, title, place, date, library location, author identification, book description, additional comments. Plate 16: a reproduction of the title page of Fuenllana's *Orphenica Lyra* (1554). Plate 17: a reproduction of the title page of Pisador's *Libro de musica de vihuela* (1552). List of sources of illustrations, list of dimensions, bibliog., indexes, 230p.

176   GREBE, Maria Ester. "Modality in the Spanish vihuela music of the sixteenth century and its incidence in Latin American music". In 2 parts. *AnM* XXVI (1971) 29-59; XXVII (1972) 109-29.
A study of polyphonic modality in representative works for vihuela and as explained in contemporaneous theoretical texts. Five main aspects are examined individually for the identification of mode: ranges, cadences, accidentals, modal preferences, and transpositions. Practice and theory are compared and differentiated. An epilogue offers written evidence that the vihuela was an instrument in use in sixteenth-century Mexico and Latin America. Charts, tables, music, bibliog. ref. in notes, bibliog.
See also: RILM IX/1-2 (Jan-Aug 1975) 568ap[24].

177   GREENE, Thomas E. "The hexachord system as it applies to the Spanish vihuelists". *Chelys* I/3 (1976) 23-28.
The Guidonian hexachord system is explained as it applies to vihuela tuning and to the sizes of vihuelas in use in the sixteenth century. Compositions cited. Illus., chart, bibliog.

178   HALL, Monica J.L. "Performing early music on record 6. The vihuela repertoire". *EarlyM* V/1 (1977) 59, 61, 63, 65.
A brief introduction to vihuela technique, tuning, stringing, and the contents of the seven vihuela books. Reviews of nine records include the following information: record company, serial number, performers, contents of the record, citations of other record reviews, and an evaluation of the authenticity and the quality of the performance. Illus.

179   JACOBS, Charles. *Tempo notation in Renaissance Spain*. Musicological studies, VIII. (Brooklyn, N.Y.: Institute of mediaeval music, 1964).
A detailed study of tempo notation in the instrumental music of Renaissance Spain. The source material consulted includes the works of the vihuelists and of Juan Bermudo. Quotation of sources (Sp and En trans.), music (transcr. only), 121p.

180   MARCOS, Juan José Rey. "*Ramillete de flores* inediti per vihuela" [*Ramillete de flores*, unpublished works for vihuela]. *Fronimo* IV/15 (Apr 1976) 15-23. In It.
A detailed discussion of a 1593 manuscript containing ten works for

vihuela. Description of the manuscript and its musical contents. The historical importance of the work is considered. Some background on sixteenth-century vihuela music is given. Music (transcr. only, ex. of each composition. This includes a work by Narváez), bibliog. ref. in notes.

181   MYERS, Joan. "Vihuela technique". *JLuteSocAmer* I (1968) 15-18. A discussion of vihuela technique, addressed to the modern performer, which includes information on intonation, tempo, left-hand and right-hand technique, and ornamentation. List of books on technique. Music (tabl.), bibliog. ref. in notes.

182   POPE, Isabel. "La vihuela y su musica en el ambiente humanis-
      tico" [The vihuela and its music in the Humanistic environ-
      ment]. *NuevaRevFilHisp* XV (1961) 364-76. In Sp.
The influences of Renaissance Humanism on the Spanish vihuelists are shown in a study of the music and the texts contained in the vihuelists' publications. General historical notes on Humanistic thought as it is reflected in music and literature. Bibliog. ref. in notes.

183   POULTON, Diane. "Notes on some differences between the lute
      and the vihuela and their music". *Consort* XVI (July 1959)
      22-26.
Distinctions are made between the ancestry and history of the lute and the vihuela. Descriptions of tuning, technique, and repertoire.

184   POULTON, Diane. "Vihuela". *Grove* XIX, 757-61.
Theoretical, literary, and musical sources are investigated in a survey of vihuela tuning, performance practices, technique, and repertoire. The article is divided into 3 parts: 1. Structure and history 2. Technique and performing practice 3. Repertory. Illus., table (tempi), bibliog. (early theorists, other studies).

185   ROBERTS, John. "Some notes on the music of the vihuelistas".
      LuteSocJ VII (1965) 24-31.
A survey of the contents of the seven extant collections of six-teenth-century vihuela music. Catalogue entries given for those five located in the British Museum include the following infor-mation: quotation of title page, number of books in each collection, dedication, place and date of publication, British Museum number, pagination, number of leaves or folios, missing or mutilated folios, printers' marks. Contents (number and types of pieces) and composers are listed for each book.

186   SENSIER, Peter. "When a vihuela is not a vihuela". *Guitar* IV/4
      (Nov 1975) 25-26.
Notes on the differences between the vihuela and the lute. Includes comments on the problems of vihuela construction. Illus. (vihuelas).

187   WADE, Graham. "The repertoire of the guitar". *BMG* LXV/750
      (Oct 1967) 3-4.

Renaissance Histories   (188-191)

A brief introduction to the sixteenth-century repertoire for vihuela.
Comments on the seven known vihuelists and the types of compositions
included in their publications.

188   WARD, John M. "Parody technique in sixteenth-century instru-
        mental music". *Commonwealth of Music*, 208-28. Ed. by Gustave
        Reese and Rose Brandel in honor of Curt Sachs. (New York:
        The Free Press of Glencoe, 1965).
Definition and analysis of parody technique. Types of parody are
examined in an analysis of the relationship of the compositions
using parody technique to the original music parodied. Works by
vihuelists Valderrábano and Narváez are considered. Music (transcr.
only, treble- and bass-clef), bibliog. ref. in notes.

189   WARD, John M. "Le problème des hauteurs dans la musique pour
        luth et vihuela au XVIe siècle" [The problem of pitch in the
        music for the lute and for the vihuela in the XVIth century].
        *Le luth et sa musique. Colloques internationaux du Centre
        National de la Recherche Scientifique*, 171-78. Ed. by Jean
        Jaquot. Second revised ed. (Paris: Centre National de la
        Recherche Scientifique, 1976). In Fr.
Lecture and discussion (Neuilly- sur- Seine, 10-14 September 1957).
An examination of source writings and of the publications of the
vihuelists. The author concludes that liberties with tuning were
taken by Renaissance musicians and investigates the problems of
modern transcription. Music.

190   WARD, John M. "The use of borrowed material in sixteenth-
        century instrumental music". *JAmerMusicolSoc* V/2 (1952)
        88-98.
A study of vocal repertoire intabulated for lute, for vihuela, and
for keyboard. Examination of the type of repertoire chosen and of
the actual treatment of the borrowed material is illustrated with
references to representative works. Literal transcription and
'glosa', quotation parody and paraphrase parody are distinguished.
Sixteenth-century opinions on ornamentation are considered; references to theoretical texts included. Music (treble- and bass-clef),
bibliog. ref. in notes.

191   WARD, John M. "The vihuela de mano and its music, 1536-1576".
        PhD diss., Music: New York University, 1953. UMI 71-28, 669.
The most detailed history of the vihuela, extensively researched,
with a well-documented investigation of source materials. In 7
chapters. Ch. I: "The instrument" gives description, etymology,
fretting, and tuning and includes information on the differences
between the vihuela and the lute and a definition of the viola.
Ch. II: "The performance practice". Ch. III: "The music" (organized
by musical forms). Ch. IV: "The vihuelists", a biographical-bibliographical study of the vihuelists which includes research on Portu-
gese musicians active in Spain and Spanish lutenists; this section,
organized alphabetically by musician, is presented in catalogue
form. Ch. V: "Indices". In 10 sections, including "composers of

(192-197)   Renaissance Histories

music intabulated by the vihuelists" and listings of vocal music intabulated by the vihuelists organized by genre. Ch. VI: "Bibliography". Ch. VII: "Music examples". Illus., music, bibliog., 490p.
(text); 50p. (music, separate pagination).

192   ZAYAS, Rodrigo de. "The vihuelistas". *GuitarR* XXXVIII (Summer
       1973) 7-9.
Short biographical sketches of the seven vihuelists: Milan, Narváez,
Mudarra, Valderrábano, Pisador, Fuenllana, and Daza.

B. Musical Forms

See also 274, 275, 277, 278, 281

193   BAL Y GAY, José. "Romances y villancicos españoles del siglo
       XVI" [Spanish romances and villancicos of the sixteenth cen-
       tury]. Primera seria. *Mexico, Casa de España* (1939). In Sp.

194   BOSMAN, Lance. "Variations 2". *Guitar* IV/12 (July 1976) 16-17.
An introduction to types of variation technique. Emphasis of the
discussion is on the treatment of the ostinato basses, romanesca and
folia, in representative works by Narváez, Mudarra, and Sanz. Music.

195   DEVOTO, Daniel. "Poésie et musique dans l'oeuvre des
       vihuelists" [Poetry and music in the work of the vihuelists].
       AnnalesM IV (1956) 85-111. In Fr.
A discussion of the poetry used in the songs of the vihuelists with
particular consideration given to the relationship of the poetry to
the music of the romances and villancicos. Emphasis is on the
analysis of the poetic structure. Ex. of poetry, music.

196   HUDSON, Richard. "Chordal aspects of the Italian dance style
       1500-1650". *JLuteSocAmer* III (1970) 35-52.
An analysis of Italian dance compositions. Basic harmonic structure
based on chord schemes in two modes, *per B molle* and *per B quadro*,
and chordal and melodic variation techniques are considered. Works
for vihuela and for guitar are selected as representative examples.
Music, bibliog. ref. in notes.
See also: RILM IV/2 (May-Aug 1970) 1607ap[24].

197   JAMBOU, Louis. "Les origins du *tiento*" [The origins of the
       tiento]. PhD diss., Music: University of Paris, 1974. In Fr.
The objective of this work is to understand the musical significance
of the term *tiento* at the time when the Spanish composers, vihuelists and later organists, adopted the term and illustrated it in
several compositions (1535-1555). The procedure is defined "on a
double level: theoretically, through the principal works of sixteenth-century Spain, and practically, in the composers' realizations.
     Study of the *tiento* in the writings of D.P. Cerone (*El Melo-
peo*, 1613) and M. de Fuenllana (*Orphénica lyra*, 1554). Presentation

Renaissance Histories (198-202)

of Spanish modal theory in the sixteenth-century environment. Appearing first in the vihuela works of Milán (1536), Mudarra (1546), and Fuenllana (1554), the *tiento* is revived by the organists (Bermudo, 1555). The final chapter establishes the relationships and differences between *tiento* and fantaisie. Append. (transcr. of *tientos* by Fuenllana, Mudarra, Milán, and Bermudo). - Translation of the annotation in Jean Gribenski, *French language dissertations in music: an annotated bibliography*. (New York: Pendragon Press, 1979), entry 24.22.

198   NELSON, Martha. "Notes on the tarantella (including a collec-
          tion of tarantellas for guitar)". *GuitarR* XXXIV (Winter 1971)
          7 (text); 8-17 (music).
A short history of the tarantella dance. Includes comments on the etymology of the word as related to the style of the dance. Music (5 tarantellas for guitar, 19th and 20th centuries).

199   POULTON, Diane. "Notes on the Spanish pavan". *LuteSocJ* III
          (1961) 5-16.
A study of various arrangements and uses of the Spanish pavan in English and continental European musical sources. Extensive list of printed sources and manuscripts with bibliographical information given. Emphasis is on lute music in French tablature; a few sources of guitar music are cited.

200   SIMPSON, Glenda; MASON, Barry. "The sixteenth century Spanish
          romance - a survey of the Spanish ballad as found in the music
          of the vihuelistas". *EarlyM* V/1 (1977) 51, 53, 55, 57.
A stylistic analysis of the Spanish romance with a consideration of performance practices including improvisation. Includes comments on the role of the romance in fifteenth- and sixteenth-century Spanish social history. Illus., music (tabl. and transcr., elaboration of a vihuela accompaniment of a romance by Fuenllana), bibliog. (sources, secondary works).

201   WADE, Graham. "The repertoire of the guitar". *BMG* LXV/753
          (Jan 1968) 123.
A simple analysis with remarks on the musical interpretation of a sixteenth-century fantasia by Milan, by Mudarra, and by Fuenllana.

202   ZAYAS, Rodrigo de. "The music of the vihuelists and its in-
          terpretation". *GuitarR* XXXVIII (Summer 1973) 10-12.
A study of the musical style and structure of representative musical forms found in the publications of the vihuelists. Music for voice and vihuela and for vihuela solo is considered. Musical forms described are the villancico, the romance, the Italian song, the lamentation, the frottola, the French chanson, the pavan, diferencias (or variations on a theme), and the fantasy. Some notes on performance practices.

C. Tablature Studies

203 "Escritura para guitarra. Sistema antiquo" [Writing for the guitar. An early system]. *Guitarra* (Havana) II/3 (Dec 1941) 24-25. An excerpt from Emilio Pujol's *Escuela razonada de la guitarra*. In Sp.

A discussion of sixteenth-century tablature notation for vihuela and sixteenth- through eighteenth-century tablature notation for guitar. Some representative composers are cited. Rhythm, tempo, and meter symbols are shown with explanation.

204 FOX, Charles Warren. "Accidentals in vihuela tablature". *BulAmerMusicolSoc* IV (Sept 1940) 22-24.

An abstract of a lecture (5 Nov 1938, Ithaca, N.Y.). The use of vihuela tablature in determining *musica ficta* practices in vocal music is considered. Research is limited to the study of transcriptions of the tablatures of Pisador and Fuenllana that are based on pre-existent vocal models. Comparisons are made between the transcriptions and the modern editions of the models that have *musica ficta* added.
See also: 244, 245 for further discussion of these problems in the work of Pisador.

205 NELSON, Martha. "Notes on *musica en cifra*". *GuitarR* XXXVIII (Summer 1973) 23-29.

Comments on the differences between the Spanish system of tablature notation, *musica en (de) cifra*, and music in tablature notation found in other European countries. Includes etymology and transcription methodology. Music (tabl. and transcr.), bibliog. (original editions: "Works of the seven vihuelistas" and "Additional primary sources from the period of the vihuelistas" with library locations cited).

206 PUJOL, Emilio. "La transcription de la tablature pour vihuela d'après le technique d'instrument" [The transcription of vihuela tablature according to the technique of the instrument]. *Congres de la Societat international de Musicologia a Barcelona. Programa de les sessions i festes que es celebraran de 18 al 25 d'abril del 1936.* (Barcelona: impr. Casa de Caritat, 1936). In Fr.

207 ZAYAS, Rodrigo de. "The transcription of the vihuela tablatures: how and why". *Chelys* I/2 (Aug 1976) 11-15.

Literal and polyphonic methods of transcription and other problems and considerations in the interpretation of tablature notation are discussed. Music (tabl. and transcr. by Luis Milan).

Renaissance Histories   (208-211)

D. Individual Composers, Performers, Theorists, Publishers, and Authors

BALLARD, Robert

See LE ROY, Adrien

BARBERIS, Melchior de

See also 161

208   KOCZIRZ, Adolf. "Die Fantasien des Melchior de Barberis für
      Siebensaitige Gitarra (1549)" [The fantasias for seven-string
      guitar of Melchior de Barberis]. *ZfMw* IV (Oct 1921) 11-17.
      In De.
A study of the four fantasias for four-course guitar found in the
back of Melchior de Barberis's 1549 publication of lute music entitled *Opera intitolata contina*. Analysis of notation, tuning, indications of playing technique, and musical style. Some biographical
information on Barberis included. Music (4 fantasias, transcr. only,
treble clef).

BERMUDO, Juan (ca. 1510–ca. 1565)

See also 153, 165, 168, 169, 179, 197, 228, 875

Theoretical Sources

209   BERMUDO, Juan. *Comiença el libro primero de la declaracion de
      instrumentos, dirigido al clementissimo y muy poderoso don
      Joan tercero deste nombre, rey de Portugal*...(Ossuna: Juan de
      Leon, 1549). (145f). In Sp.
      Library locations: D B, Mbs. E Mn. NL DHgm. P Pm. US Cn, NYhs.

210   BERMUDO, Juan. *Comiença el arte tripharia dirigida a la
      ylustra y muy reverenda señora Dona Ysabel Pachedo, abadessa
      en el monasterio de sancta Clara de Montilla, compuesta por el
      reverendo padre fray Juan Bermudo, religioso de la orden de
      los frayles menores de Observancia*...(Ossuna: Juan de Leon,
      1550). (40f). In Sp.
      Library location: E Mn (facsim.).

211   BERMUDO, Juan. *Comienca el libro llamado declaracion de in-
      strumentos musicales dirigido al illustrissimo senor el senor
      don Francisco de Cuniga, Conde de Miranda, compuesto por el
      muy reverendo padre fray Juan Bermudo de la orden de los
      menores; en el qual hallaran todo lo que en musica dessearen,
      y contiene seys libros: segun en la pagina siguiente se vera:
      examinado y aprovado por los egregios musicos Bernardino de
      Figueroa y Christoval de Morales.* (Ossuna: Juan de Leon,

(212-214)   Renaissance Histories

1555). (142f). In Sp.
Library locations: A Wn. D B. E Bd, Mn, V, Zsc. F CH, Pc, Pn.
GB Lbm. US Cn, NYhs, Wcm.

Modern Editions

212   BERMUDO, Juan. *Declaración de instrumentos musicales 1555.*
       Documenta musicologia. Erste Reihe: Druckschriften-Faksimiles
       XI. Ed. by Macario Santiago Kastner. (Kassel und Basel:
       Bärenreiter-Verlag, 1957). In Sp.
A detailed theoretical source writing on the vihuela and on the
guitar which includes information on types of vihuelas, stringing
and tuning, and information on contemporary musicians. "Libro
quarto. Comiença el arte de la vihuela" folio xci-cx includes a
discussion of "las guitarras", nine diagrams of fingerboards il-
lustrating various tunings, and musical examples of tablature *de
cifras.*

Secondary Works

213   MOSER, Wolf. "Über die Unterschiede zwischen Gitarre und
       Vihuela bei Bermudo" [On the differences between the guitar
       and the vihuela according to Bermudo]. *GitarreLaute* II/5
       (Sept-Oct 1980) 32-34, 36-40, 42-43. In De.
A history of the confusion between the guitar and the vihuela.
Definitions are clarified by Bermudo in his publication *Declaración
de instrumentos musicales* (1555). Types of vihuelas and guitars are
differentiated by their stringing and by their size. Tuning is discussed. Illus. (iconog., historical instruments), bibliog. ref. in
notes.

214   STEVENSON, Robert M. *Juan Bermudo.* (The Hague: Martinus
       Nijhoff, 1960).
Bermudo's three publications are examined in a detailed study
divided into the following sections:
"Biographical summary".
1. "An annotated bibliography of Bermudo's works". The three works
are compared; errors in previous research are discussed.
2. "Introductory matter in the editions of 1549, 1550, and 1555".
Description of contents includes quotations from the texts.
3. "Bermudo's sources". A study of Bermudo's use of sources.
4. "Synopsis of the 1555 *Declaración*". A detailed summary of the
contents of the five books contained in the 1555 edition. Music
included.
5. "Keyboard arrangements and original compositions". Music.
List of works cited, index, 97p.
Reviews: MLetters LXII/4 (1961) 375-6; *Notes* XVIII/3 (1961) 417-18;
JMTheory VI/1 (1962) 156-58; *MReview* XXIII/1 (1962) 71; *NeueZfM*
CXXIII (Oct 1962) 481; *JAmerMusicolSoc* XVI/1 (1963) 86-88; *Mf* XVI/3
(1963) 297-99.

Renaissance Histories (215-218)

CABEZÓN, Antonio de (ca. 1500-1566)

See also 167, 245

215 HUGHES, John. "The tientos, fugas, and differencias in Antonio
        de Cabezón's *Obras de musica para tecla, harpa y vihuela*". PhD
        diss., Music: The Florida State University, 1961. UMI 61-1284.
A stylistic consideration of the tientos, fugas, and differencias.
Includes biographical information on Cabezón, historical background
on the period, and extensive consideration of organs of sixteenth-
century Spain. The author approaches Cabezón's *Obras* (1551) as a
work for keyboard, although Cabezón does indicate the possibility of
the performance of the music on other instruments including the
vihuela. Analysis of Cabezón's style and compositional techniques
with particular consideration given to his treatment of musical subjects. Comparisons of the three forms are included. Music, append.,
bibliog., 182p.

216 SPALDING, Walter. "A dance for the king of Spain". *Chelys* I/8
        (Mar-Apr 1977) 23-28 (text), 29-34 (music).
Historical background on "Tres 'sobre el cantollano de la alta" by
Cabezón as found in Luys Venegas de Henestrosa's *Libro de cifra
nueva para tecla, harpa y vihuela* (1551). The contents of Venegas
de Henestrosa's publication is described, and the problem of the
attribution of this work to Cabezón is examined. Description of the
basse dance tenor melody "La Spagna" with an explanation of its
function within Cabezón's work. Some biographical information on
Cabezón is included. Music (tabl. and transcr., transcr. of Cabezón's "Tres 'sobre el cantollano de la alta" for recorder, viola,
vihuela), bibliog. ref. in notes.

CERVANTES, Miguel de (1547-1616)

See also 330

217 GAVALDÁ, Miguel Querol. *La música en las obras de Cervantes*
        [Music in the works of Cervantes]. (Barcelona: Ediciones
        Comtalia, 1948). In Sp.
A study of musical references in the literature of Cervantes.
Musical forms (romances, canciones, dances, and bailes) are mentioned in Cervantes's literature. In ch. V "Los instrumentos men-
cionados por Cervantes" [Instruments mentioned in Cervantes], the
use and the significance of the guitar (p. 138-39) and the vihuela
(p. 140-41) are considered. Quotations from Cervantes's text,
music, index, 173p.

218 HAYWOOD, Charles. *Cervantes and music* (n.p., 1948). Reprinted
        from *Hispania* (May 1948) 131-50.
A study of the use and the significance of musical forms, instruments, and dances in the literature of Cervantes. The social function of the vihuela and of the guitar as shown in Cervantes's texts

(219-222)   Renaissance Histories

is examined. Cervantes's musical sources are considered. Quotations
of literature included. Bibliog. ref. in notes.

219   MANIFOLD, J.S. "Cervantes, the guitar, and history". *Canon* VII
      (March 1954) 342-44.
Cervantes's tale from *Novelas Ejemplares* about a guitar master is
told. The author interprets the significance of the texts in regard
to sixteenth-century folk music traditions.

220   SALAZAR, Adolfo. *La música en Cervantes y otros ensayos*
      [Music in Cervantes and other essays]. (Madrid: OGRAMA Oficina
      Gráfica Madrileña, 1961). Reprinted with additions from
      NuevaRevFilHisp II/1, 2 (1948). In Sp.
Ch. VII. "Música, instrumentos y danzas en las obras de Cervantes",
127-275. A study of the use of music and musical instruments in the
literature of Cervantes. The musical environment contemporary with
his period of fluency is discussed. The importance of the vihuela
and the guitar is emphasized; background on the composers, the
repertoire, and theoretical sources is given. Section II. "Anota-
ciones" [Annotations] gives extensive annotations of the text.
Table of instruments mentioned in Cervantes, table of dances mentioned in Cervantes, illus., bibliog. ref. in notes.

DAZA [DACA], Esteban

221   EVERS, Reinbert. "Die Fantasien aus Esteban Dazas *El Parnaso*
      und ihre Stellung in der Entwicklungsgeschichte der Fantasie
      für Vihuela" [The fantasias from Esteban Daza's *El Parnaso*
      and their place in the development of the fantasia for vi-
      huela]. PhD diss., Music: Ruhr-Universität-Bochum. In De.

222   PURCELL, Ronald Charles. "Esteban Daza, *El Parnasso*". MA
      diss., Music: San Fernando Valley State College, 1972. 2v.
V. 1. "Analysis and commentary". A study of the text and music of
Daza's *Libro de musica en cifras para vihuela, intitulado el Parnasso* (1576), the last publication for vihuela in sixteenth-century
Spain. Sources are consulted for information on the composer and on
others mentioned in the preliminary text. Previous publications for
vihuela are compared. Analysis of stylistic aspects of the music
with concordances; comparison of entabulations by Daza to the original vocal models. Notes on transcription practices. Music (two-
staff systems, treble- and bass-clef), 110p.
V. 2. "Transcriptions". Transcription in two-staff notation (treble-
and bass-clef) of the three books of tablature contained in *El Parnasso*. Them. cat. (incipits from Libro primero only).

FUENLLANA, Miguel de (d. 1579)

See also 161, 175, 197, 200, 201, 204, 245

Renaissance Histories (223-228)

223 ANGLÈS, Higini. "Dades desconegudes sobre Miguel de Fuenllana, vihuelista" [Unknown facts about Miguel de Fuenllana, vihuelist]. *RMCatalana* XXXIII/388 (Apr 1936) 140-43. In Ca.
A study of the positions held by Fuenllana at the royal Spanish court in the mid-sixteenth century with quotations of court documents concerning payments for his services.

224 BAL, J. "Fuenllana and the transcription of Spanish lute-music". *ActaMusicol* XI (1939) 16-27.
The subject of the article is Fuenllana's music for vihuela. The tablature notation used by Fuenllana is examined with emphasis on a study of its interpretation in relationship to the vocal part. Music (tabl. and transcr.), bibliog. ref. in notes.

225 KOCZIRZ, Adolf. "Die Gitarren Kompositionen in Miguel de Fuenllanas *Orphénica Lyra* (1554)" [The guitar compositions in Miguel de Fuenllana's *Orphénica Lyra* (1554)]. *AfMw* IV (April 1922) 241-61. In De.
A discussion of the guitar music contained in Fuenllana's 1554 publication for vihuela. Includes discussion of Fuenllana's instructional text, notation, tuning, instrumental technique, and musical forms (with emphasis on the romance). Analysis of music included. The author incorrectly uses the term lute to specify vihuela. Music (transcr. only, 9 works for guitar, treble clef), bibliog. ref. in notes.

226 RIEMANN, Hugo. "Das Lautenwerk des Miguel de Fuenllana (1554)" [The lute works of Miguel de Fuenllana (1554)]. *MfMg* XXVII/6 (1895) 81-91. In De.
The author discusses the vihuela music of Miguel de Fuenllana. The complete contents of Fuenllana's 1554 publication is listed by folio number. Music (transcr. of a four-voice fantasia).

227 VILLALBA MUÑOZ, Luis. "La *Orphénica lyra* de Fuenllana". *Musica Sacro-Hispana* (1910). In Sp.

GORLIER, Simon

See 161

GUZMAN, Luis de (d. 1528)

No music by Luis de Guzman is extant; however, he is mentioned as a performer in sixteenth-century texts.

228 ROBERTS, John. "The death of Guzman". *JLuteSocAmer* X (1968) 36-37.
An examination of sixteenth-century literature in which Guzman is mentioned. Authors cited are Pero Mexia (1551), Bermudez de Pedraza (1608), Juan Bermudo (1555), and Paulus Jovius (1562). The quotation

(229-230)   Renaissance Histories

of Bermudo gives detail on "mistuning" the vihuela.

HENESTROSA, Luys Venegas de

See VENEGAS DE HENESTROSA, Luys

LE ROY, Adrian and BALLARD, Robert

See also 160, 161, 163

229   HEARTZ, Daniel. "An Elizabethan tutor for the guitar".
       GalpinSocJ XVI (May 1963) 3-21.
Introductory notes cite early texts which define 'guiterne', 'guiterre', and 'gitterne' as a guitar. The author offers evidence for
the assumption that Adrian Le Roy was the composer of *A briefe and
plaine instruction*... published by James Rowbotham, now lost, and
evidence of its probable plagiarism, *Selectissima elegantissimaque*
... (1570, Louvain), published by Pierre Phalèse. Phalèse's eight
rules and "the manner of stringing the guitar" are printed in facsimile and in English translation. Tuning instructions are explained;
the popularity of the guitar in the sixteenth century is discussed
with references to sources. Illus. (facsim.), music, pl., bibliog.
ref. in notes.
See also: Dobson 160 for criticism.

230   LESURE, François; THIBAULT, G. *Bibliographie des éditions
       d'Adrien Le Roy et Robert Ballard 1551-1598* [Bibliography of
       the editions of Adrien Le Roy and Robert Ballard 1551-1598].
       Deuxième série. V. IX. (Paris: Société Française de Musico-
       logie, 1955). In Fr.
A biographical-bibliographical study based on available sources.
Chapter headings are as follows: 1. "Les Familles" (The families)
2. "L'Association" (The association between Le Roy and Ballard)
3. "Le materiel typographique" (Printing materials) 4. "Repertoire"
(Repertoire). "Documents et Pièces Luminaire inédits" (Documents and
eminent unedited writings concerning their lives and business).
"Bibliographie Chronologique" (Chronological bibliography: List of
publications, 1551-1598). Entries are numbered throughout. Includes
quotation of title page, size, library holdings, contents, and
folios. Tablature books for 'guiterre' are listed as entries 2, 4,
10, 14, and 22; for 'guiterne' as entry 2bis. Table of incipits (by
genre), list of volumes described, names cited, pl., table of contents, 304p.

MILAN, Luis (ca. 1500-ca. 1561)

See also 15, 167, 197, 201, 207

Renaissance Histories   (231-237)

Literary Sources (modern editions)

231   MILAN, Luis. *Libro intitulado El Cortesano*. (Valencia 1561).
       Reprinted in *Coleccion de libros españoles raros o curiosos*
       VII, 1-472. (Madrid: Imprenta y estereotipia de Aribau y C.a,
       1874). In Sp.
Milan's literary work on the ideal courtier. Prose, dialogue, and
verse. References to the vihuela occur in the text.

232   MILAN, Luis. *Libro de motes de damas y caballeros: Intitulado
       el juego de mandar*. (Valencia 1535). Reprinted in *Coleccion de
       libros españoles raros o curiosos* VII, 473-502. (Madrid: Im-
       prenta y estereotipia de Aribau y C.a, 1874). In Sp.
Milan's commentary on court life. Prologue and verse. References to
the vihuela occur in the text.

Secondary Works

233   "Música en la antiguedad. Luis Milan" [Music in antiquity.
       Luis Milan]. *Guitarra* (Madrid) XXI (May 1965) 3-4, 11 (text),
       5-7 (music, tabl. and transcr.). In Sp.
A discussion of the text and music in Luis Milan's *Libro de musica*
(1536) includes notes on musical contents, notation, and Milan's
instructions for tuning.
See also: Guitarra (Madrid) XXII (June-Aug 1965) 6-8 for music
(fantasia in tabl.).

234   JACOBS, Charles. "An introduction to Luis de Milan's *El
       Maestro* (Valencia 1536)". *CahCanadiensM* (Spring-Summer 1970)
       99-104.
A description of the contents of Milan's *El Maestro* includes information on the problems of modern transcription of music for lute and
vihuela. Biographical information on Milan included. Music (facsim.
of tabl.), bibliog.
See also: RILM IV/2 (May-Aug 1970) 1609ap[24].

235   LINDLEY, Mark. "Luis Milan and meantone temperament".
       JLuteSocAmer XI (1978) 45-62.
An explanation of meantone temperament, Pythagorean temperament, and
equal temperament. Milan's tablature notation is examined for evidence of his use of meantone temperament. Music (tabl. and transcr.).

236   MILAN, Luis. "Vihuela". *GuitarLute* I/1 (Apr-June 1971) 19-22.
       In Sp and En.
A facsimile of the prologue and music (1 page) from Milan's publication, *El Maestro*. Trans. of the Prologue by Carol Beresiwsky.

237   MOSER, Wolf, ed. and trans. "Sammlung historischer Quellen.
       Luys Milan: *El Maestro*" [Collection of historical sources.
       Luis Milan: *El Maestro*]. In 2 parts. *GitarreLaute* II/5 (Sept-
       Oct 1980) 24-27; II/6 (Nov-Dec 1980) 28-30. In De.
A German translation of the preface to Luis Milan's *El Maestro*.

(238-242)   Renaissance Histories

Introductory remarks to the translation give history and description
of Milan's publication. Illus. (facsim.), music (tabl.).

238   SCHRADE, Leo. "Luys Milán, the vihuelista". *GuitarR* IX (1949)
      78-81; Sp trans., 99.
A portrait of Luis Milán as a courtier and as a musician. Includes
discussion of Milán's ideal of the "complete musician". Milán's
publication *El Maestro* is considered for its musical and educational
value and for its social significance. Illus. (title page of *El
Maestro*), music (facsim.).

239   TREND, J.B. *Luis Milan and the vihuelistas*. (England: Oxford
      University Press, Humphrey Milford, 1925).
A survey of the life and works of Luis Milan with some mention of
the other vihuelists. The terms *vihuela* and *lute* are used inter-
changeably to indicate *vihuela*. Music (transcr. only), bibliog.,
128p.

240   WADE, Graham. "The guitarist and his repertoire". *BMG* LXV/752
      (Dec 1967) 84-85.
An analysis of Milan's Pavane no. 3 with some discussion of musical
interpretation. Remarks on Pavanes nos. 2, 4, 5, and 6 included.

MORLAYE, Guillaume

See 161

MUDARRA, Alonso (d. 1580)

See 161, 194, 197, 201, 245

NARVÁEZ, Luis (d. ca. 1560)

See also 170, 180, 188, 194, 245

241   BOSMAN, Lance. "Variations 1". *Guitar* IV/11 (June 1976) 23-24.
A survey of early variation forms. Luis de Narváez's "Conde Claros"
is used as a representative example for analysis in a discussion of
the Spanish *diferencia*.

242   ZAYAS, Rodrigo de. "*Passeavase el Rey Moro*, a brief introduc-
      tion". *Chelys* I/2 (Aug 1976) 17-19.
The significance of the texts of Spanish ballads in relationship to
Spanish history is considered. Notes on the ballad *Passeavase el Rey
Moro* by Narváez. Biographical information on Narváez included. Music
(tabl. and transcr.).

Renaissance Histories   (243-245)

PHALÈSE, Pierre and BELLÈRE, Jean

See 160, 229

PISADOR, Diego

See also 175, 204

243   CORTÉS, Narciso Alonso. "Diego Pisador, algunos datos bio-
      gráphicos" [Diego Pisador, some biographical facts]. *Boletín
      de la Biblioteca Menéndez y Pelayo* III (1921) 331-35. In Sp.

244   HONEGGER, Marc. "Les messe de Josquin des Prés dans la tabla-
      ture de Diego Pisador (Salamanque, 1552). Contribution à
      l'étude des altérations au XVIe siècle" [The masses of Josquin
      des Prés in the tablature of Diego Pisador (Salamanca, 1552).
      Contribution to the study of alterations in the sixteenth cen-
      tury]. 2v. PhD diss., Musicology: University of Paris, 1970.
      In Fr.
"The intabulations - which have no added ornaments - include more
than 1,000 chromatic alterations which do not appear in the vocal
originals. Their use derives not from the more harmonic character
of vihuela performance but from the practice of the singers and from
the progress of each voice. In the present edition, the transcriptions from tablature are placed parallel with the versions in the
Josquin complete works edition. The use of accidentals is summarized
in 7 rules (3 for the sharp, 4 for the flat) to which, however, there
are some exceptions. In most cases, alterations in one voice cannot
be applied - following tonal logic - to other voices, since this
logic did not exist at the time." Music, bibliog. - Quoted from
RILM IV/3 (Sept-Dec 1970) 3064dd[24].

245   HONEGGER, Marc. "La tablature de D. [Diego] Pisador et le
      problème des altérations au XVIe siècle" [The tablature of
      Diego Pisador and the problem of alterations in the XVIth
      century]. In 3 parts. *RMusicol* LIX/1 (1973) 38-59; LIX/2
      (1973) 191-230; LX/1 (1974) 3-32. In Fr.
A detailed analysis of the use and implications of accidentals found
in Diego Pisador's intabulations of masses of Josquin des Prés. The
Albert Smijers edition of the complete works of Josquin des Prés is
used for reference to the original models.
Part 1: Introductory notes include a summary of the contents of the
seven books of tablatures contained in Pisador's *Libro de música de
vihuela*. Notes on preliminary text, biographical information on the
composer, source locations cited. Section 2. "Les messes de Josquin
des Prés dans la tablature de Pisador" [The masses of Josquin des
Prés in the tablature of Pisador]. The contents of books four and
five, devoted to intabulations of Josquin's works, are listed with
concordances of intabulations found in other publications for vihuela. A second list of intabulations found in publications for vihuela is organized chronologically by date of publication: Narváez,

(246-247)   Renaissance Histories

Mudarra, Valderrábano, Fuenllana, Venegas de Henestrosa, Cabezón.
The peculiarities of Pisador's transcription techniques and the
treatment of the original models are examined with extensive comments
on his use of accidentals. Tables, music (transcr., one ex. of
tabl.), illus. (facsim. of Pisador's title page), bibliog. ref. in
notes.
Part 2: "Question du dièse (prenant la forme du bécarre en mode
transposé)[The question of the sharp (taking the form of the natu-
ral in transposed modes)]. An analysis of Pisador's use of raised
tones. Includes a study of alterations in the embellished line and
in cadential formulas in relationship to the concept of mode and
the fundamental harmonic structure. Table, music (transcr.),
bibliog. ref. in notes.
Part 3: "Question du bémol" [The question of the flat]. An analysis
of Pisador's use of the flat sign in comparison to its use in the
original models. The conclusion includes a summary of the rules for
the use of sharps and flats as accidentals in sixteenth-century
modal polyphony. Music (transcr., one ex. of tabl.), bibliog. ref.
in notes.
See also: 244 for Honegger's dissertation.

246   HULTBERG, Warren Earle. "Diego Pisador's *Libro de música de
       vihuela* (1552)". *Festival essays for Pauline Alderman. A
       musicological tribute*, 29-51. Ed. by Burton L. Karson.
       (Provo, Utah: Brigham Young University Press, 1976).
A study of Diego Pisador's 1552 publication of music for vihuela.
Preliminary text includes a description of the contents, biographical information on Pisador, and comments on Pisador's text. Section
on "theoretical considerations" includes a discussion of tuning,
clefs, the use of chromaticism, and "voice leading and rhythmic
aspects"; Pisador's system of notation is interpreted. The section
entitled "Transcription and comparative analysis of a *Pater Noster*
by Willaert" includes a transcription of Pisador's intabulation in
two-staff notation with the original tablature shown below. The intabulation is compared to Hermann Zenck's 1950 edition of the work
by Willaert. Analysis in chart form includes detail on accidentals,
musica ficta, and other commentary. Music, bibliog. ref. in notes.

247   HUTCHINSON, Loving. "The vihuela music of Diego Pisador". MM
       diss., Music: Eastman School of Music, University of Rochester,
       1937.
A study of the contents of the seven books of music for vihuela contained in Pisador's *Libro de música de vihuela* with notes on musical
forms, rhythmic aspects, and *musica ficta* practices. Historical
background on the vihuela includes a consideration of theoretical
sources and sixteenth-century publications of music for vihuela.
Biographical information on the composer is based on a study of extant contemporary documents. Preface includes evaluation of scholarship before 1937. 4 append., bibliog., 81p. (text), 71p. (music supplement).

Renaissance Histories   (248-251)

SANCTA MARÍA, Thomas de (ca. 1515-1570)

See also 153

248   HULTBERG, Warren. "Sancta María's *Libro llamado arte de taner
      fantasia*: A critical evaluation". PhD diss., Music: University
      of Southern California, 1964.

249   POULTON, Diane. "How to play with good style by Thomas de
      Sancta María". *LuteSocJ* XII (1970) 23-30.
A translation of excerpts from Sancta María's *Libro* (1565) that deal
with performance practices. In the introductory material, Poulton
indicates that certain theories can be applied to the performance of
instrumental music other than that of the keyboard. In particular,
Sancta María's interpretation of rhythm and ornamentation (redoubles
and trills) is considered in detail. Music.

VALDERRÁBANO, Enríquez de

See also 167, 188, 245

250   AZPIAZU, Lupe de. "Enríquez de Valderrávano". *Guitarra*
      (Madrid) XX (Apr 1965) 12 (text), 13 (music). In Sp.
Biographical notes with a short description of Valderrábano's 1547
publication of music for vihuela.

VENEGAS DE HENESTROSA, Luys

See also 216, 245

251   WARD, John M. "The editorial methods of Venegas de Henestrosa".
      MDisciplina VI (1952) 105-13.
A discussion of the earliest known collection of sixteenth-century
Spanish keyboard music, *Libro de cifra nueva para tecla, harpa y
vihuela* (1557), Luys de Venegas de Henestrosa, editor. Standards and
methods of printing are discussed in a study of Venegas de Henestrosa's publication. Comparison of music in other contemporary editions includes music for vihuela. A list of concordances of works
for vihuela found in Venegas de Henestrosa's publication includes
references to critical modern editions. Section on additional concordances of vocal pieces with attributions cited.

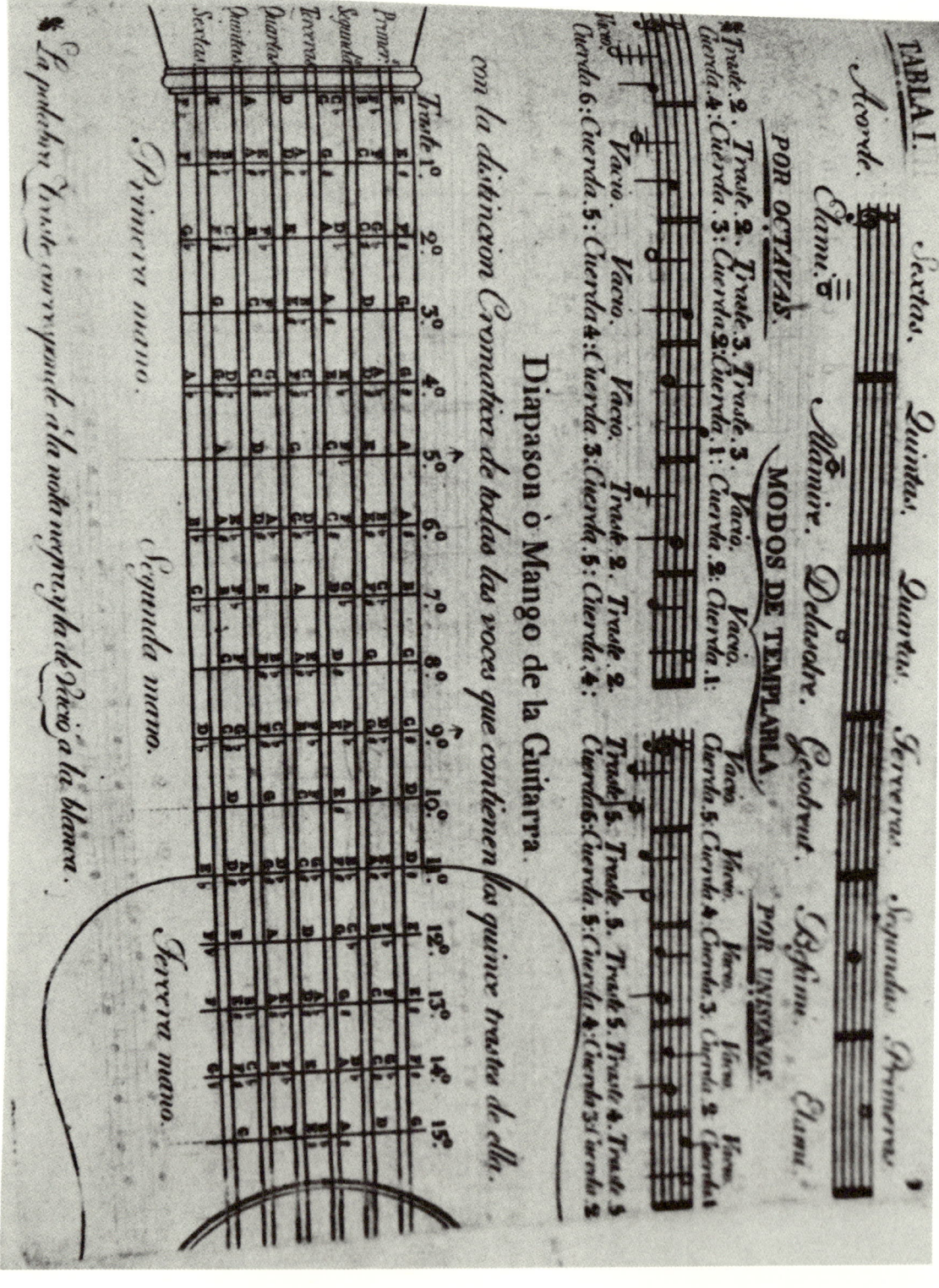

Federico Moretti, *Principios para tocar la guitarra de seis ordenes* (Madrid: por Josef Rico, 1799), Tabla I, p. 9.

CHAPTER FOUR

Histories of the Baroque Era

The guitar of the Baroque Era was most commonly strung with five courses (double strings). It was used in the period from the late sixteenth century to the end of the eighteenth century. A vast body of music, published and in manuscript, was written in this period. Study of this repertoire has been relatively neglected by modern guitarists and scholars. In addition to the studies contained in this chapter, early and modern editions of music make the repertoire more accessible. In many modern editions, the introductory material gives accurate information on performance practices, repertoire, and biography. Appendix II lists sources and modern editions of music from this period.

Publications and instruments of the late eighteenth century indicate that guitars with variant stringings were in use in this period of transition from the five-course instrument to that of six single strings. Music for six-course, for triple-course, and for five single-string guitars survives from this period. Studies which specifically treat the question of the transition to the six single-string guitar are indexed in Chapter V, Histories of the Early Six-String Guitar. Of particular interest in this area are Paul Cox (entries 393, 394) and Thomas Heck (entries 397, 398).

This chapter is divided into six sections: Section A. General Surveys, Section B. The Chitarra Battente, Section C. Musical Forms, Section D. Performance Practice and Tuning, Section E. Individual Authors and Theorists, and Section F. Individual Composers and Performers.

In Section A., French, Italian, Spanish, and German music and its notation are considered. Although some entries are devoted to the treatment of individual national styles, no national divisions have been made in this section. Specifically, these entries are 252 and 255 (France), 256 and 266 (Spain), and 257 (Italy).

The Chitarra battente is the subject of Section B. This was a type of guitar used in the eighteenth century. A problem with the definition of the Chitarra battente has arisen in modern literature because authors have assumed that the instrument was distinguished from the standard Baroque five-course guitar only by its arched back. Bellow (entry 8) defines the instrument in this way. Essential to its definition is the use of

59

HISTORIES OF THE BAROQUE

wire strings which passed over the bridge and were secured at the heal of the instrument. Frets were inlaid and of metal to withstand the pressure of the wire strings. Guitars other than the Chitarra battente were built with arched backs and should not be confused with the true-form variant. Examples of this instrument are extant; no music, however, survives. The instrument is well-defined in Evans (entries 15 and 16), Turnbull (entry 43), Tyler (entry 3), and in the literature listed in Section B. of this chapter.

In Section C., literature on the origins, the sources, and the analysis of musical forms written for solo guitar and for the guitar as an accompaniment instrument is included. Specifically, literature on the following forms is cited: Aria di fiorenza, also called il ballo del Gran Duca (280), canarios (282), canzonette (269), falsobordone (275), fedele (275), folia (270, 273–76), passacaglia and ciaccona (271, 276–78, 284), reprisa (278), ritornello (278), sarabande (276), zarabanda and zarabande francese (279), and zarazuela in Spanish theatre music (283). Discussions of the following Baroque dance forms are found in Chapter III: folia (entry 194), Italian dance forms (entry 196), romanesca (entry 194), and tarantella (entry 198).

In Section D., literature which gives an explanation of *rasguado* [strummed style of playing] and of *punteado* [plucked style of playing], the guitar as a continuo instrument, and ornamentation in guitar music is annotated. The following subject areas are emphasized in the items listed: Tuning (entries 285, 287, 288, 291), *rasguado* and *punteado* (entries 287, 289, 290, 294), ornamentation (entries 287, 293), the guitar in ensemble (entry 286), and the guitar as a continuo instrument (entries 289, 292).

Section E. gives an extensive list of individuals and is subdivided into three categories: *Sources, Modern Editions*, and *Secondary Works.* Sources are listed with short titles; library locations of the works are quoted from *RISM* series B VI (2 v.). The list of abbreviations on p. xxxvi includes library sigla for this chapter in addition to those used in Appendixes I and II. Because all of the sources are large, general works—a dictionary, a study of musical instruments, a theoretical treatise, or a literary essay—in most cases, only a relatively small portion of the text deals with the guitar. For this reason, only studies of the sources in which the guitar is discussed have been selected for annotation.

In Section F., forty-one individuals have been listed as sub-headings. Many of these have been cross-referenced to literature found elsewhere in the chapter. In Chapter I, Section A., literature is listed which is recommended for its detail in a general survey of the period.

(252-256)

A. General Surveys

See also Ch. I, Section A. The sixteenth through the eighteenth centuries, including studies of tablature notation in that period, 1-5.

252   CHILESOTTI, Oscar. "La chitarra francese. Appunti" [The *chitarra francese*. Notes]. *RMItaliana* XIV/4 (1907) 791-802. Reprinted in Oscar Chilesotti. *Studi sulla chitarra e altri scritti*, 191-202 (Bologna: Arnaldo Forni Editore, 1975). In It.
Historical notes on the *chitarra francese* with a description of systems of notation, tuning, and the music of Francesco Corbetta, Robert de Visée, and François Campion. Music (tunings, transcr.).

253   CHILESOTTI, Oscar. "XVIe et XVIIe siècles. Notes sur les tablatures de luth et de guitare" [XVIth and XVIIth centuries. Notes on the tablatures of the lute and the guitar]. *Encyclopédie de la musique et dictionnaire du conservatoire-première partie: Histoire de la musique. Italie-Allemagne*, V. II, 636-84. (Paris: Librairie Delagrave, 1925). In Fr.
An historical survey of the notation, tuning practices, and repertoire for lute and guitar in the sixteenth and seventeenth centuries. Lute and guitar are treated individually (guitar history, p. 676-84). Commentary on the history of the vihuela, incorrectly defined as a Spanish lute, is combined with that of the lute. Guitar history includes commentary on and examples of music by Fasolo, Francesco Asioli, Lodovico Roncalli, François Corbetta, Robert de Visée, and François Campion. Music (facsim. and transcr.), illus.

254   DELL'ARA, Mario. "La chitarra nel 1700" [The guitar in the eighteenth century]. *Fronimo* III/12 (July 1975) 6-14. In It.
A study of the history of the guitar in the eighteenth century: Spain and Portugal, France, Germany and Austria, and Italy. Representative composers and their works are mentioned. General historical background is given in the introductory material. Illus. (iconog.), bibliog. ref. in notes.

255   DENIS, Françoise-Emmanuelle. "La guitare en France au XVIIe siècle: son importance, son répertoire" [The guitar in France in the seventeenth century: its importance, its repertoire]. *RBelgeMusicol* XXXII-XXXIII (1978-79) 143-50. In Fr.
The popularity and the use of the guitar in seventeenth-century France is discussed. References to seventeenth-century texts are given as evidence. Includes a survey of the works for guitar by composers Francesco Corbetta, Henry de Gallot, Antoine Carré Sieur de la Grange, Remy Médard, Henry Grenerin, and Robert de Visée. Bibliog. ref. in notes.

256   HOWELL, Almonte. "Symposium on seventeenth-century music theory: Spain". *JMTheory* XVI/1-2 (1972) 62-71.
The works of Spanish theorists (1592-1724) are considered for their

(257-262)   Baroque Histories

limitations and their usefulness and for indications of Spanish
musical development. The author points out the strong influence of
past traditions and the significant lack of new thought. Works of
the following theorists are considered: Montanos, Cerone, Nassarre,
Torres, and Lorente. Works for guitar which include theoretical
texts are excluded. "A checklist of sources" is divided into two
sections: A. General theory works, 1592-1724 and B. Guitar, harp,
and dance manuals, 1597-1714.

257   HUDSON, Richard. "The music in Italian tablatures for the
       five-course Spanish guitar". *JLuteSocAmer* IV (1971) 21-42.
A survey of seventeenth-century Italian guitar music (1606-1692).
Discussion of the influences of Italian, Spanish, and French dance
styles on the Italian music for five-course guitar with a comparison
of national styles. The evolution of musical forms is explained.
Important publications are described. Fig. (3 charts), bibliog. ref.
in notes.

258   KEITH, Richard. "The guitar cult in the courts of Louis XIV
       and Charles II". *GuitarR* XXVI (June 1962) 2-9. An abstract of
       the paper read in Washington, D.C. (14 Jan 1959) at a meeting
       of the Greater Washington Chapter of the American Musicologi-
       cal Society is printed in *JAmerMusicolSoc* XII/1 (1959) 96.
A survey of seventeenth-century music for five-course guitar includes notes on performance practices, tuning, notation, and social
history. Biographical information on Francesco Corbetta is based on
a study of source material. Illus., music (tabl. and transcr.).

259   KENNARD, Deric. "The guitar tablatures". *GuitarN* XXX (Apr-May
       1956) 11-13.
A brief introduction to the music for four- and five-course guitar.
Description of the repertoire by Francisco Corbetta, Robert de Visée,
and Ludovico Roncalli. Pre-dates some essential bibliographical and
biographical research.

260   KOCZIRZ, Adolf. "Eine Gitarren- und Lautenhandschrift aus der
       zweiten Halfte des 17. Jahrhunderts" [A manuscript for guitar
       and lute of the seventeenth century]. *AfMw* VIII (1927) 433-40.
       In De.
A detailed description of a manuscript containing music in tablature
for angelica and guitar dated ca. 1673. Notation is explained; repertoire, mainly dance movements, is described. Angelica, a type of lute
with seventeen strings, is described. Bibliog. ref. in notes, music.

261   MURPHY, M. "Guitar music in Spain and Italy in the seventeenth
       century". PhD diss., Musicology: London.

262   PINNELL, Richard T. "Baroque guitar. An alternative for clas-
       sical guitarists". *GuitarP* XII/9 (Sept 1978) 32, 115-17.
A general survey of the repertoire for the baroque guitar (ca. 1600-
1750) with major composers and their publications mentioned. Remarks
on the importance of the study of the repertoire for the modern per-

Baroque Histories   (263-266)

former. Biographical information on the author. Illus., music
(tuning, tabl., transcr.).

263   PROVOST, Richard. "The baroque guitar: the forgotten instru-
       ment". *GuitarLute* XI (Oct 1979) 15-16.
Renaissance lute, baroque lute, and baroque guitar techniques are
compared to those of the modern guitar. The problems of the transcription of baroque guitar music for the modern guitar are discussed.
Biographical information is given on the author. Port., music
(tuning, tabl., transcr.), bibliog. ref. in notes.

264   SCHMITZ, Eugen. "Guitarrentabulaturen" [Guitar tablatures].
       MfMg XXXV/9 (1903) 133-47. In De.
Seventeenth-century guitar tablatures and their interpretation are
discussed. Italian tablature is distinguished from Spanish and
French tablature. Music (tuning, tabl., transcr.).

265   STRIZICH, Robert. "The Baroque guitar: then and now". *Soundb*
       VIII/3 (Aug 1981) 128-36.
In 3 main divisions: I. "The Baroque guitar in the seventeenth and
eighteenth centuries": a general survey of the Baroque guitar in
which composers, performers, builders, and repertoire are considered.
Includes a biographical sketch of Francesco Corbetta. The Italian,
French, and Spanish schools of composition are distinguished, as are
the German, Italian, French, and Spanish schools of guitar construction. II. "The Baroque guitar in the twentieth century": a discussion
of the interest in early music which has developed in recent decades:
reasons for the relative neglect of the Baroque guitar are suggested.
Recent contributions to and accomplishments in this area of guitar
performance, history, and construction are mentioned. Two possibilities now present themselves to the classic guitarist: transcription
of the original music to accommodate the modern instrument and performance from the original tablature in facsimile on reproductions
of early instruments. The advantages of the second possibility are
considered. III. "The Baroque guitar and its music in recent articles, books, recordings, and editions": a list of authors' works
with incomplete bibliographical information. List of recording performers, their repertoire, and the record company. List of modern
editions includes transcribers, editors, and publishers of facsimiles. Port. (author), illus.

266   TELLO, Francisco José Leon. *La teoria española de la musica en
       los siglos XVII y XVIII* [Spanish music theory in the seven-
       teenth and eighteenth centuries]. (Madrid: Consejo superior de
       investigaciones cientificas. Instituto español de musicologia,
       1974). In Sp.
The works of theorists which contain information on the guitar and
the works of composers for guitar which contain theoretical texts
are discussed individually. Theorists considered are Tomás Vicente
Tosca (p. 59-62) and Pablo Nassare (p. 148). Composers for guitar
considered are Nicolás Doizi de Velasco, Gaspar Sanz, Lucas Ruiz de
Ribayaz, Santiago de Murcia, Andrés de Sotos, Fernando Ferandière,

(267-271)   Baroque Histories

and Antonio Abreu-Víctor Prieto. 16 pl., music, bibliog., 759p.

B. The Chitarra Battente

See also 3 (glossary), 166, 397, 896, 925, 928

267   HECK, Thomas. "Historical research. Mysteries in the history
       of the guitar". Ch. II. *Guitarra* (Chicago) XXXVIII (May-June
       1980) 8-10.
A definition of the Italian *chitarra battente*, also called *guitare
en bateau* (French terminology). The author suggests possible reasons
for the French terminology, translated "boat-shaped guitar", and for
the use of wire strings, and raises several questions concerning the
practice of double-stringing. The early origins of wire stringing
are considered. References to extant instruments are included. Illus.

268   SORRISO, Marino. "La *chitarra battente* in Calabria" [The
       chitarra battente in Calabria]. *Fronimo* VIII/31 (Apr 1980)
       29-31. In It.
A description of the *chitarra battente* and a discussion of its
history in Calabria. Performance practices are considered. Illus.
(guitars), bibliog. ref. in notes, music (tuning used today).

C. Musical Forms

269   CHILESOTTI, Oscar. "Canzonette del seicento con la chitarra"
       [The *canzonette* with guitar of the seventeenth century].
       RMItaliana XVI (1909) 847-62. Reprinted in Oscar Chilesotti.
       Studi sulla chitarra e altri scritti, 209-24. (Bologna:
       Arnaldo Forni Editore, 1975). In It.
A study of the early seventeenth-century *canzonette* with guitar
accompaniment. Representative works for voice and guitar in *alphabeto* notation are found in the rare publications of Francesco Severi
Perugino (1626) and [Giovanni Battista] Fasolo (1627). Music
(transcr. only: 10 works by Severi; 2 works by Fasolo).

270   GOMBOSI, Otto. "Zur Frühgeschichte der Folia" [On the early
       history of the folia]. *ActaMusicol* VIII/3-4 (July-Dec 1936)
       119-29. In De.
A study of the historical development of the folia in the sixteenth
and seventeenth centuries including a consideration of its possible
origins. Music for vihuela and guitar based on the folia and folia
variants is studied. Folia basses in the music of representative
composers are compared. The author suggests that **certain folia
variants** are the result of technical peculiarities of guitar playing. Music (staff notation), bibliog. ref. in notes.

271   HUDSON, Richard Albert. "The development of the Italian key-
       board variations on the passacaglio and ciaccona from guitar
       music in the seventeenth century". PhD diss., Historical

Baroque Histories   (272-274)

musicology, University of California at Los Angeles, 1967. Now
published as *Passacaglio and ciaccona from guitar music to
Italian keyboard variations in the seventeenth century*. Series
no. 37. (Ann Arbor, Michigan: UMI Research Press). The following annotation is based on the original dissertation.
A study of the origin and development of the passacaglio and ciaccona. The development of the Italian keyboard variation on the passacaglio and ciaccona is shown through a study of the musical forms
found in Spanish and Italian guitar music dating from the early
seventeenth century and through early developments in Italian keyboard music. Works for guitar are studied in detail with comparative
analysis and comments on notation: Representative examples of guitar
music are taken from the works of the following composers: Amat
(1586), Montesardo (1606), Sanseverino (1620), Colonna (1620-1623),
Milanuzzi (1625), Millioni (1627), Pico (1627), Foscarini (1627),
Briceño (1625), and two anonymous composers. Foscarini's variation
techniques are considered in three periods of development. Keyboard
variations discussed are selected from the works of the following
composers: Frescobaldi, Rossi, Storace, Poglietti, Kerll. Analysis
of structure, harmony, form, and style. 10 fig., XIV tables, 43
music (tabl., staff notation), append., bibliog. (music, lit.), xii,
456p.
See also: RILM I/2 (May-Aug 1967) 690dd[25].

272   HUDSON, Richard. "The concept of mode in Italian guitar music
       during the first half of the seventeenth century". *ActaMusicol*
       XLII/3-4 (July-Dec 1970) 163-83.
A study of modal harmony in early seventeenth-century music for
guitar as shown through chordal schemes and their treatment and
variation in musical forms. Indications of the evolution from a
modal system to a tonal system in baroque music is examined. Extensive consideration of source material. Music (staff notation
only), bibliog. ref. in notes.
See also: Kirkendale 280, p. 18 n. 3 for critical comments; *RILM*
IV/2 (May-Aug 1970) 1700ap[25].

273   HUDSON, Richard. "The *folia* dance and the *folia* formula in
       17th-century guitar music". *MDisciplina* XXV (1971) 199-221.
The history and development of the folia dance and the folia formula
are shown through a study of representative examples of seventeenth-
century Spanish and Italian guitar music. Analysis of chordal
schemes and their variants. Comparative analysis of the folia formula in musical forms. Extensive study of source material. Music
(staff notation), fig., bibliog. ref. in notes.
See also: RILM V/1 (Jan-Apr 1971) 447ap[25].

274   HUDSON, Richard. "The folia melodies". *ActaMusicol* XLV/1
       (Jan-June 1973) 98-119.
A detailed study of the historical development of the folia with
analysis and comparisons of its stages of development. Emphasis is
on the analysis of melodic structure. Musical sources from the late
fifteenth century through the mid-eighteenth century are consulted,

including examples from the early guitar repertoire. Music (staff notation), bibliog. ref. in notes.

275   HUDSON, Richard. "The folia, fedele, and falsobordone".
      MQ LVIII/3 (July 1972) 398-411.
A comparative analysis of the folia, fedele, and falsobordone forms with an examination of the relationship between their development in the period from the late fifteenth century to the early seventeenth century. Discussion of the early repertoire includes a consideration of works for vihuela and for guitar. Music (staff notation), bibliog. ref. in notes.

276   HUDSON, Richard. *The folia, the sarabande, the passacaglia, and the chaconne. The historical evolution of four forms that originated in music for the five-course Spanish guitar.* 4 v. Musicological studies and documents, 35. (Texas: American Institute of musicology, 1981).

277   HUDSON, Richard. "Further remarks on the passacaglia and ciaccona". *JAmerMusicolSoc* XXIII/2 (Summer 1970) 302-14.
A valuable companion to Walker 284. Hudson offers additional insights into the early history and musical sources of the passacaglia and ciaccona. Detailed commentary on systems of notation. Stylistic analysis. Music (staff notation), bibliog. ref. in notes.
See also: RILM IV/2 (May-Aug 1970) 1701ap[25].

278   HUDSON, Richard. "The reprisa, the ritornello, and the passacaglia". *JAmerMusicolSoc* XXIV/3 (Fall 1971) 364-94.
The structure and function of the reprisa, the ritornello, and the passacaglia in musical forms of the sixteenth- and seventeenth-century Italian dance style. Terminology is defined. Analysis of the organization of chord-rows, variation techniques, and ostinato forms. A study of musical sources. Tables, music (staff notation), bibliog. ref. in notes.

279   HUDSON, Richard. "The *zarabanda* and the *zarabande francese* in Italian guitar music of the early 17th century". *MDisciplina* XXIV (1970) 125-49.
The development of the *zarabanda* and of the *zarabande francese* in guitar music is traced from Montesardo's publication of the prototype (1606). Analysis and comparison of forms. Charts, diagrams, music (staff notation), bibliog. ref. in notes.
See also: RILM V/3 (Sept-Dec 1971) 3677ap[25].

280   KIRKENDALE, Warren. *L'aria di fiorenza id est il Ballo del Gran Duca.* (Firenze: Leo S. Olschki, 1972). In En.
A detailed history and analysis of the harmonic-bass progression "Aria di fiorenza", also called "Ballo del Gran Duca", which includes a study of early sources of guitar music. The following subject areas are covered: 1. Definition and structural analysis. 2. A study of repertoire for guitar, for keyboard, and for ensemble. Music for guitar is considered in regard to the notation system,

Baroque Histories   (281-284)

stylistic aspects of music (predominantly a *rasgado* or strummed
repertoire), and the use of compositional techniques such as passeg-
giata-practice, transposition, and proportz. 3. Origins. From a
study of the earliest examples, including an investigation of possible alternative titles, the author concludes that Cavalieri's
"Ballo" (1589) is the prototype. 4. Analysis of the treatment of the
text which was troped to the aria. Nine sources and their locations
are cited. One questionable text has no known source. 5. Spanish and
Italian literary sources are considered. 6. Bibliography of musical
sources. 7. 12 compositions (staff notation. Includes one work for
guitar by Montesardo). 12 pl., bibliog. ref. in notes, index, 161p.
Reviews: RItalianaMusicol VII/1 (1972) 145-48; *OesterreichMz* XXVIII
(Jan 1973) 46-47; *MTimes* CXIV (Feb 1973) 173-74; JAmerMusicolSoc
XXVI/2 (1973) 344-50; *Musikf* XXVI/2 (1973) 272-73; *MLetters* LIV/1
98-99; *MQ* LIX/3 (1973) 474; *Notes* XXIX/3 (1973) 467-69; *NuovaRM-
Italiana* VII/2 (1973) 272-77; *EarlyM* II/3 (1974) 183; *NeueZfM*
CXXXIV/12 (1974) 778; *StudMusicol* XVI/1-4 (1974) 284-86; *RMusicol*
LXI/1 (1975) 134; *MBildung* VII (June 1975) 319.

281   MACHABEY, Armand. "Les origines de la chaconne et de la
       passacaille" [The origins of the chaconne and of the passa-
       caille]. *RMusicol* XXVIII (1946) 1-21. In Fr.
A study of the origins of the chaconne and of the passacaille as
indicated in literary and musical sources of the sixteenth and
seventeenth centuries. Sources of guitar music are considered. Includes a discussion of the function of the two forms in variations
and as ostinato basses. Music, bibliog.

282   NELSON, Martha. "Canarios". *GuitarR* XXV (Feb 1961) 12-17
       (music), 18-22 (text).
A discussion of the dance *canarios* which includes notes on Joaquin
Rodrigo's "Fantasia para un gentilhombre" (1954), based on "Canarios" by Gaspar Sanz. Biographical information on Rodrigo with comments on his perception of the work. Biographical information on
Gaspar Sanz includes a discussion of the past research on his life.
History and possible origins of the dance with comments on stylistic
aspects. Illus., music (several examples of *canarios*, ca. 1600-1954,
including transcr. and facsim.), bibliog. ref. in notes.

283   PEDRELL, Felipe. "La musique indigène dans la théâtre espagnol
       du XVIIe siècle" [The music indigenous to the Spanish theater
       of the seventeenth century]. Trans. by Mme. Marthe Chassang.
       SIMg (1903-04) 46-72 (text), 73-90 (music). In Fr.
A definition of the *zarazuela* with a discussion of its stylistic
characteristics, the evolution of its form, and its function in
seventeenth-century Spanish theater. Music (17 works including one
for vihuela solo and two for voice and guitar).

284   WALKER, Thomas. "Ciaccona and passacaglia: remarks on their
       origin and early history". *JAmerMusicolSoc* XXI/3 (Fall 1968)
       300-20.
A study of the earliest literary references to and the earliest

(285-289)   Baroque Histories

musical sources of the ciaccona and the passacaglia. Etymology
studied. Musical sources of Italian guitar music dating from as
early as Montesardo's *Nuova Inventione* (1606) are studied. Analysis
and description of the music with information on systems of notation. Music (*alphabeto* and staff notation), bibliog. ref. in notes.
See also: 277; *RILM* II/3 (Sept-Dec 1968) 3311ap[25].

D. Performance Practice and Tuning

285   CHARNASSÉ, Hélène. "Sur l'accord de la guitare" [On the tuning
        of the guitar]. *Recherches* VII (1967) 25-37. In Fr.
A study of the tunings of the four-course and five-course guitar as
indicated in a survey of publications of guitar music and theoretical treatises dating from the sixteenth through the eighteenth century. Music (staff notation), bibliog. ref. in notes.
See also: RILM I/3 (Sept-Dec 1967) 2255ap[44].

286   COHEN, Albert. "A study of instrumental ensemble practice in
        seventeenth-century France". *GalpinSocJ* XV (Mar 1962) 3-17.
The function of the guitar in instrumental ensembles and as an
accompanying instrument in vocal choruses is examined. Includes
comments on the popularity of the guitar in seventeenth-century
France with references to opinions found in source writings.
Append., music, bibliog.

287   DANNER, Peter. "L'adattamento della musica barocca per chi-
        tarra all' esecuzione moderna" [Adapting baroque guitar music
        for modern performance]. *Fronimo* II/7 (Apr 1974) 11-20. In It.
An examination of three areas of baroque performance practices based
on a study of sources of guitar music: tuning, *rasgueado* [strumming],
embellishments. Music (tabl. and transcr.), bibliog. ref. in notes.

288   GILL, Donald. "The stringing of the five-course baroque
        guitar". *EarlyM* III/4 (Oct 1975) 370-71.
A consideration of various stringings and tunings of the five-course
guitar. References to sources on the subject include the instructions
of Stradivarius. Music (tabl. and transcr.), bibliog. ref. in notes.

289   MARCUS, Robert Samuel. "The use of the five-course guitar as a
        continuo instrument as described in Spanish treatises: 1596-
        1764". MA diss., Music: California State University, Fullerton,
        1978. UMI 13-11, 529.
A detailed study of twelve Spanish sources of guitar music which contain valuable information on continuo performance: Amat (1596),
Arañes (1624), Briceño (1626), Guerrero (n.d.), Minguet y Yrol
(1752), Murcia (1714), Ruiz de Ribayaz (1677), Santa Cruz (n.d.),
Sanz (1674, 1697), Sotos (1764), and Doizi de Velasco (1640). Performance practices, notation systems, and theoretical considerations
contained in the individual works are compared and examined. *Rasgueado* (strumming) and *punteado* (plucked) performance techniques are
considered with greatest attention given to *punteado* continuo prac-

Baroque Histories   (290-293)

tices described by Gaspar Sanz and Santiago de Murcia. Includes an
examination of the role of the guitar in Spanish music theater in
the seventeenth and eighteenth centuries with a study of available
musical and literary sources on the subject. Tables, fig., append.
(an extensive set of appendixes which contain examples of music,
including realizations, and theoretical material selected from
musical sources), bibliog., 203p.

290   MURPHY, Sylvia. "Seventeenth-century guitar music: notes on
       rasgueado performance". *GalpinSocJ* XXI (Mar 1968) 24-32.
Seventeenth-century sources concerning the *rasgueado* (strumming)
style of playing are considered. *Rasgueado* performance is distinguished from *punteado* performance. Survey of musical sources. Music
(tabl. and transcr.), bibliog. ref. in notes.
See also: RILM II/2 (May-Aug 1968) 2637ap[52].

291   MURPHY, Sylvia. "The tuning of the five-course guitar".
       GalpinSocJ XXIII (Aug 1970) 49-63.
Seventeenth-century sources of guitar music are consulted for evi-
dence of tuning practices. Quotations from the sources are included.
Contains an appendix of seventeenth-century tunings by Cellier,
Amat, Montesardo, Sanseverino, Briceño, Mersenne, Velasco, Trichet,
Carré, Corbetta, Sanz, Ribayaz, de Visée, de Rosier, Talbot, and
Diderot. **Extensive study.** Music.
See also: Gill 288 for a summary of some important points made in
the article.

292   STRIZICH, Robert. "L'accompagnamento di basso continuo sulla
       chitarra barocca" [Thorough-bass accompaniment on baroque
       guitar]. *Fronimo* IX/34 (Jan 1981) 15-26. In It.
An examination of musical, literary, and iconographical sources for
evidence of basso continuo practices on the guitar in the late sixteenth century through the eighteenth century. Section A. "Fonti
musicali" [musical sources]: Representative musical sources indicate
significant stylistic traits of music for the guitar in the continuo
body. Includes notes on notation and performance practices. B. "Fonti
letterarie" [literary sources]: Includes quotations of seventeenth-
century source material. C. "Fonti iconografiche" [iconographical
sources]: A description of representative works of art in which the
baroque guitar is depicted as a continuo instrument. Footnotes contain citations of the locations of the original works and bibliographical citations of publications in which they are reproduced.
Bibliog. ref. in notes.

293   STRIZICH, Robert. "Ornamentation in Spanish baroque guitar
       music". *JLuteSocAmer* V (1972) 18-39.
A discussion of six ornaments found in seventeenth- and eighteenth-
century publications of guitar music: trill, mordent, slur, appogia-
tura, vibrato, and arpeggio. Sources of guitar music by Sanz (1674,
1697), Ruiz de Ribayaz (1677), Guerau (1694), and Murcia (1714,
1732). Music (tabl. and transcr.), bibliog. ref. in notes.

294   WEIDLICH, Joseph. "Battuto performance. Practice in early
        Italian guitar music (1606-1637)". *JLuteSocAmer* XI (1978)
        63-86.
A detailed study of early seventeenth-century guitar technique and
performance practices based on an examination of eleven publications
for guitar from the period 1606-1637. The publications of the following composers are studied: Montesardo, Colonna, Sanseverino,
Milanuzzi, Costanzo, Millioni, Millioni and Monte, Pico, Foscarini,
and Abbatessa. Music (tabl. and transcr.), bibliog. of sources
(including library locations), bibliog. ref. in notes.

E. Individual Authors and Theorists

BONANNI [BUONANNI], Filippo (1638-1725)

Sources

295   BONANNI, Filippo. *Gabinetto armonico*... [The showcase of
        musical instruments]. (Rome: Giorgio Placho, 1722). 177p.,
        148pl. In It.
        Library locations: A Wgm. B Br. CH Fc. D Bds (2 ex.), Dl, ERu,
        F, G, HEu, LEm (2 ex.), Rp. DK Kk, Km. F Dm, Mm, Pa, Pc, Pn,
        Psg. GB Cu, Ge, Lbm (3 ex.). I BGc, Fc, Fn, Mc, Nc (2 ex.),
        PAc, PIu, Ria, Rli, Rsc (2 ex.), Vnm, VIb. J Tma. P Ln, Pm.
        US BA, Cn, NH, NYp, PHu, R, SFsc, U, Wcm, WOh. For library
        locations of the 1723 edition, consult *RISM* B VI[1].

Modern Editions

296   BONANNI, Filippo. *Gabinetto armonico* [The showcase of musical
        instruments]. (New York: Dover Publications, Inc., 1964).
        In It.
A reprint of 152 illustrations from the 1723 edition of *Gabinetto
armonico* with an introduction and captions by Frank L. Harrison and
Joan Rimmer. Pl. 51 "Chitarra Spagnola": a five-course Spanish guitar. Description and commentary.

BROSSARD, Sébastien de (1655-1730)

Sources

297   BROSSARD, Sébastien de. *Dictionnaire de musique*... [Dictionary
        of music]. (Paris: Christophe Ballard, 1703). 56f. In Fr.
        Library locations: A Wmi. B Bc. CH Zs. D Bds, HEs. DK Kk.
        E Mra. F Dm, Nm, Pa, Pc, Pi, Pm, Pn (2 ex.), R. GB Lbm. I Bc,
        Mc, PIu. NL DHgm, Uim. P Mp. US AUS, Cn, NYp, Pu, R, Wcm.
        For full title and library locations of the editions of 1705,
        ca. 1708, and ca. 1710, consult *RISM* B VI[1].
A very short definition of *guitarra* with a description of the stringing and of the national use of the five-course guitar.

Baroque Histories   (298-302)

Modern Editions

298   BROSSARD, Sébastien de. *Dictionnaire de musique* [Dictionary of
      music]. Facsimile of the 1703 edition. (The Hague: Antiqua
      Amsterdam, 1964). In Fr.

CERRETO, Scipione (ca. 1551–ca. 1633)

See also Tyler 3, p. 30 and Tyler 165 for a discussion of Cerreto's
text and musical examples of Cerreto's re-entrant tuning for four-
course guitar.

Sources

299   *Scipione Cerreto napolitano. Della prattica musica vocale et
      strumentale, opera necessaria a colore, che di musica si di-
      lettano. Con le postille poste dall'autore à maggior dichia-
      ratione d'alcune cose occorrenti ne' discorsi.* (Napoli: Gio.
      Jacomo Carlino, 1601). 335p. In It.
      Library locations: B Br. D B, HVI, LEm. F B, Pc, Pn. GB Lbm
      (2 ex.). I Bc, Fm, Nc, Rsc. US AAu, Cn, PESo, Wcm.

Modern Editions

300   CERRETO, Scipione. *Della practica musica* [Of musical prac-
      tice]. Ed. by G. Vecchi, *Bibliotheca musica bononiensis*,
      II, 30. (Bologna: Forni, [1969]). In It.

COVARRUVIAS OROZCO [HOROSCO], Sebastien de (fl. 1611)

Sources

301   COVARRUVIAS OROZCO, Sebastien de. *Tesoro de la lengua castel-
      lana o española* [Thesaurus of the Castilian or Spanish lan-
      guage]. (Madrid: Melchor Sanchez, 1674). Originally published
      (Madrid: 1611). Reprint ed. Ed. by Martín de Riquer. (Barce-
      lona: Hortz, 1943). In Sp.
      Library location: US NYp (1674).
Guitarra, fol. 45-46: A description of the guitar with stringing
practices discussed. The guitar is defined as a small vihuela with
four courses (*guitarrilla*) or five courses.
Viguela, fol. 209: A description of the vihuela, its characteristics
and use. The guitar is criticized in favor of the vihuela.

Modern Editions

302   POULTON, Diana. "Notes and information. Notes on the guitarra,
      laud and vihuela". *LuteSocJ* XVIII (1976) 46-48.
Translations of the definitions of the terms *guitarra*, *laud*, and
vihuela found in Covarrubias Orosco's *Tesoro de la lengua castellana*

o *española* (Madrid, 1611). The guitar is defined as a type of vihuela.

GIUSTINIANI, Vincenzo (1564-1637)

Sources

303   GIUSTINIANI, Vincenzo. *Discorso sopra la musica de' suoi tempi* [Discourse on the music of his time]. MS 1628. In It.
Library location: I Lbc.

Modern Editions

304   GIUSTINIANI, Vincenzo. *Discorso sopra la musica de' suoi tempi* [Discourse on the music of his time]. Ed. by Salvatore Bongi. (Lucca: Tipografia Giusti, 1878). In It.

305   GIUSTINIANI, Vincenzo. *Discorso sopra la musica de' suoi tempi* [Discourse on the music of his time]. Trans. and ed. by Carol MacClintock. Musicological studies and documents, IX. (Texas: American Institute of Musicology, [ca. 1962]).

306   SOLERTI, Angelo. *Le origini del melodramma* [The origins of melodrama]. (Turin: Fratelli Bocca, 1903). Reprint ed. (Hildesheim and New York: Georg Olms Verlag, 1969). In It.
A reprint of excerpts from Giustiniani's *Discorso sopra la musica de' suoi tempi* is found on p. 98-128.

Secondary Works

307   FORTUNE, Nigel. "Giustiniani on instruments". *GalpinSocJ* V (Mar 1952) 48-54.
A translation of an excerpt from Giustiniani's *Discorso* includes comments on *chitarra* in which the popularity of the *chitarra alla spagnola* and the *chitarra napolitana* are discussed.

GRASSINEAU, James (d. 1767)

Sources

308   GRASSINEAU, James. *A musical dictionary...* (London: J. Wilcox, 1740). 348p.
Library locations: A Wn, Wu. B Br, Lc. C O. D Bds, Mbs, Tmi. E Mn. F Pc. GB Cc, Ckc, Cpl, Ctc, Cu, Er, Ge, Lam, Lbm (3 ex.), Lcm, Mp, Ob, T. NL DHgm. S SKma, Sm. US A, AAu, Bpm, BA, BE, Cn, Cu, CH, CH-H, Dp, DN, Eu, F, I, IO, LA, LEX, NBu, NH, N-OR, NYcu, NYp, Pu, PH1c, PO, PROc, R, SFs, STm, U, Wcm, Ws, WC. For complete title and library locations of the 1796 edition, consult *RISM* B VI[1].
Guitarra, p. 90: A short description of the stringing of the five-

Baroque Histories   (309-312)

course guitar with a comment on its Spanish origin and its use in
Italy. This definition is an English translation of Brossard's
definition (entry 297).

Modern Editions

309   GRASSINEAU, James. *A musical dictionary* (London: 1740). Re-
      print ed. *Monuments of music and music literature in facsimile.*
      Second series. Music literature XL. (New York: Broude Brothers,
      1966).

MERSENNE, Marin (1588-1648)

See also 291, 326

Sources

310   MERSENNE, Marin. *Harmonie universelle contentant la théorie et*
      la pratique de la musique... [Universal harmony containing the
      theory and practice of music]. (Paris: Sébastien Cramoisy,
      1636). In Fr.
      Library locations: A Wgm (inc.). B Br, Lc. CH Gu. D B (inc.),
      LEm, Ngm. E Mn. F B, BO, G, LG, LM, Pa, Pc, Pm, Pn. GB Cmc,
      Cu, Ge, Lbm (2 ex.), Ob. I Bc, Pu, PAc, Rsc. S H. US Cn, CAh,
      NYm, R, Wcm.
      For library locations of the 1636 Pierre Ballard and the 1636
      Richard Charlemagne editions, consult *RISM* B VI[1].
"Traité des instruments a chordes. Livre second des instruments"
[Treatise of stringed instruments. Second book of instruments].
Proposition XIV: "Expliquer les figures, l'accord, la tablature, et
les bateries de la guiterre" [To explain the shape, tuning, tablature, and the playing of the guitar]. A discussion of the tuning of
the five-course guitar with a comparison of French, Spanish, and
Italian tablatures. Historical background on the four-course guitar
is included.
Proposition XV: "Donner des examples de la tablature françoise de la
guiterre, et expliquer celle des espagnols, et des italiens" [To give
examples of French tablature for the guitar and to explain that of
the Spaniards and of the Italians]. An explanation of tablature types
with references to contemporary publications. Illus., music (tabl.).

Modern Editions

311   MERSENNE, Marin. *Harmonie universelle* [Universal harmony].
      The books on instruments. Trans. by Roger E. Chapman. (The
      Hague: Martinus Nijhoff, 1957). 596p. In Fr.

312   MERSENNE, Marin. *Harmonie universelle* [Universal harmony].
      Édition facsimilé, de l'exemplaire conservé a la Biblio-
      thèque des Arts et Métiers et annoté par l'auteur. Introduc-
      tion par François Lesure. (Paris: Édition de Centre National

(313-316)   Baroque Histories

de la Recherche Scientifique, 1963). In Fr.

313   COOK, Frederick. "Die *Batteries* auf der Spanischen Barock-
       gitarre nach Marin Mersenne" [The *batteries* on the Spanish
       Baroque guitar according to Marin Mersenne]. *GitarreLaute* I/5
       (1979) 34-38. In De.
Mersenne's discussion of *batteries*, the manner of striking the
strings, in his *Harmonie Universelle* (1636) and in his *Harmonicorum
Libri XII* (1648) is reproduced in the original French in facsimile
and is printed in German translation. Rhythmic considerations and
the fingering and direction of the strumming are studied. Illus.
(facsim. picturing guitars and tablature from both volumes), 3
tables, music.

Secondary Works

314   EGAN, John Bernard. "Marin Mersenne. Traité de *l'harmonie
       universelle*: Critical translation of the second book". PhD
       diss., Music: Indiana University, 1962. UMI 6205029. In Fr.

NASSARRE [NASARRE], Pablo (d. 1730)

See also 256, 266

Sources

315   NASSARRE, Pablo. *Escuela música...* [School of music]. 2 v.
       (Zaragoza: Diego de Larumbe, 1724 [v. 1], Manuel Roman, 1723
       [v. 2]). In Sp.
       Library locations: B Bc, Br, Lc. D Bds, HEs, Mbs. E Bd, CA,
       Mba (v. 2). F Pc, Pn, SO. GB Ckc, Ge, Lbm (2 ex.), T. NL DHgm.
       P Ln. US AAu, AUS, BE, Cn, IO, LEX, NH, NYhs, NYp, R, U (inc.),
       Wcm.
V. 1: "Libro quarto. De proporciones. Capitulo XV. De las proporciones que deven observar los artifices en las fabricas de los instrumentos arpa, vihuelas, guitarras, y todo instrumento de arco",
458-65 [Book four. Of proportions. Chapter XV. Of the proportions
that craftsmen observe in the construction of harps, vihuelas, guitars, and all bowed instruments]. Included in the discussion is a
description of the vihuela of five, six, and seven courses. The
five-course instrument is called *guitarra española*. Tuning practices are described. v. 1 (1724) 501p. v. 2 (1723) 560p.

Modern Editions

316   NASSARRE, Fr(ay) Pablo, OSB. *Escuela música*. 2 v. (Zaragoza
       1724/23). Facsimile ed. Preliminary study by Lothar Siemens.
       (Kassel-Wilhelmshöhe: Bärenreiter Antiquariat, 1980). In Sp.

Baroque Histories   (317-320)

Secondary Works

317   HOWELL, Almonte C., Jr. "Pablo Nasarre's *Escuela Música*: A
      reappraisal". *Studies in musicology. Essays in the history,
      style, and bibliography of music in memory of Glen Haydon*,
      80-108. Ed. by James W. Pruett. (Chapel Hill, N.C.: University
      of North Carolina Press, 1969).
A discussion of the life and works of Pablo Nasarre. Nasarre's
Escuela música (1723-24) is evaluated for its historical significance and theoretical content. Past evaluations and criticisms are
considered. Detailed synopsis of the texts.

NORTH, Roger (ca. 1651-1734)

318   WILSON, John, ed. *Roger North on music being a selection from
      his essays written during the years ca. 1695-1728*. (London:
      Novello and Co., Ltd., 1959).
For insights into the use and social position of the guitar. Information on Nicola Matteis and his publications is included. Append.,
pl., music, 372p.

PEPYS, Samuel (1633-1703)

319   BRIDGE, Sir Frederick. *Samuel Pepys, lover of music*. (London:
      Smith, Elder, and Co., 1903).
An account of the musical activities and opinions of Samuel Pepys.
In Ch. V, p. 78-79, Pepys states his opinions on the *gittar* and on
contemporary English players. Port., music, 126p.
See also: Keith 339 for a quotation of the text.

PRAETORIUS, Michael (1571-1621)

See also 165

Sources

320   *Syntagma musicum*... (Wolfenbüttel: Elias Holwein; Wittenberg:
      Johann Richter, 1614/15; Wolfenbüttel: Elias Holwein, 1618/20).
      3 v. In La.
      Library locations: A Sst (v. 1), Wn, Wgm. B Br. F Pc (3 ex.),
      Pm (inc. v. 3), Pn, T. GB Cu, Er, Ge, Lbm (2 ex.), Mp, Ob, T.
      I Bc (v. 1), MOe, Rvat (v. 1). US AAu, Bp, Cn, CAh, NH, NYpm,
      R, Wcm. For a more extensive list of locations, consult *RISM*
      B VI[1].
In Ch. XXVI "Quinterna", Praetorius describes the tuning of the
four-course guitar and gives a short description of the four-course
and five-course guitar. He gives *chiterna* as an alternate term for
the *quinterna*. Pl. XVI contains an illustration of the instrument.
459p. (v. 1), 236p. + 42 pl. (v. 2), 260p. (v. 3).

(321-328)   Baroque Histories

Modern Editions

321 *Syntagmatis musici Michaelis Praetorii. C. Tomus secundus de
     Organographia*... Gedruckt zu Wolfenbüttel bey Elias Holwein
     Fulstl. Braunsch, Buchtrucker und Formschneider, 1618. Facsim.
     reproduction, Publikation aelterer praktischer und theoreti-
     scher Musikwerke, v. XIII. (Leipzig: 1873-1905).

322 *Syntagma musicum*, v. III. (Wolfenbüttel: 1619). Ed. by Eduard
     Bernoulli. (Leipzig: C. F. Kahnt nachfolger, 1916).

323 *Syntagmatis musici Michaelis Praetorii. C. Tomus secundus De
     organographia*... (Wolfenbüttel: 1619). Ed. by Elias Holwein.
     (Kassel: Bärenreiter-verlag, 1929).

324 *Syntagma musicum. V. 2: De organographia, first and second
     parts*. Trans. into En by Harold Blumenfeld [n.p., 1949].

325 *Syntagma musicum*. Facsimile-edition, ed. by Wilibald Gurlitt.
     Documenta musicologia. Reihe 1: Druckschriften-Faksimiles
     14-15, 21. (Kassel and Bärenreiter Verlag, 1958-59).

TALBOT, James (1665-1708)

See also 291

326 GILL, Donald. "James Talbot's manuscript: V. Plucked strings-
     the wire-strung fretted instruments and the guitar". *GalpinSocJ*
     XV (Mar 1962) 60-69.
A discussion of two sections of text from Talbot's MS (Oxford,
Christ Church Library Music MS 1187): a. "The wire-strung fretted
instruments", p. 60-66. b. "The guitar", p. 67-69. Includes critical
notes on Talbot's discussion of the guitar. Quotations of Talbot's
text include a chart of the dimensions of the five-course guitar,
tuning and stringing. Talbot's sources of information are Francesco
La Tour, Shore, Agutter, Mersenne, and Kircher. Talbot's discrepancies in tuning are noted. Music (tuning).

327 GILL, Donald. "Bandora, orpharion, and guitar". *GalpinSocJ*
     XXXI (May 1978) 144.
A correction of Gill 326 concerning the use of bourdons on the four-
course and five-course guitar.

TRICHET, Pierre (1586/7-?1644)

See also 291

328 LESURE, François. "Le traité des instruments de musique de
     Pierre Trichet" [The treatise of the instruments of music by
     Pierre Trichet]. In 2 parts. *AnnalesM* III (1955) 283-387;

Juan Carlos Amat, *Guitarra Espanola, y Vandola*
(Gerona: Joseph Bro, [ca. 1765]), Title page.

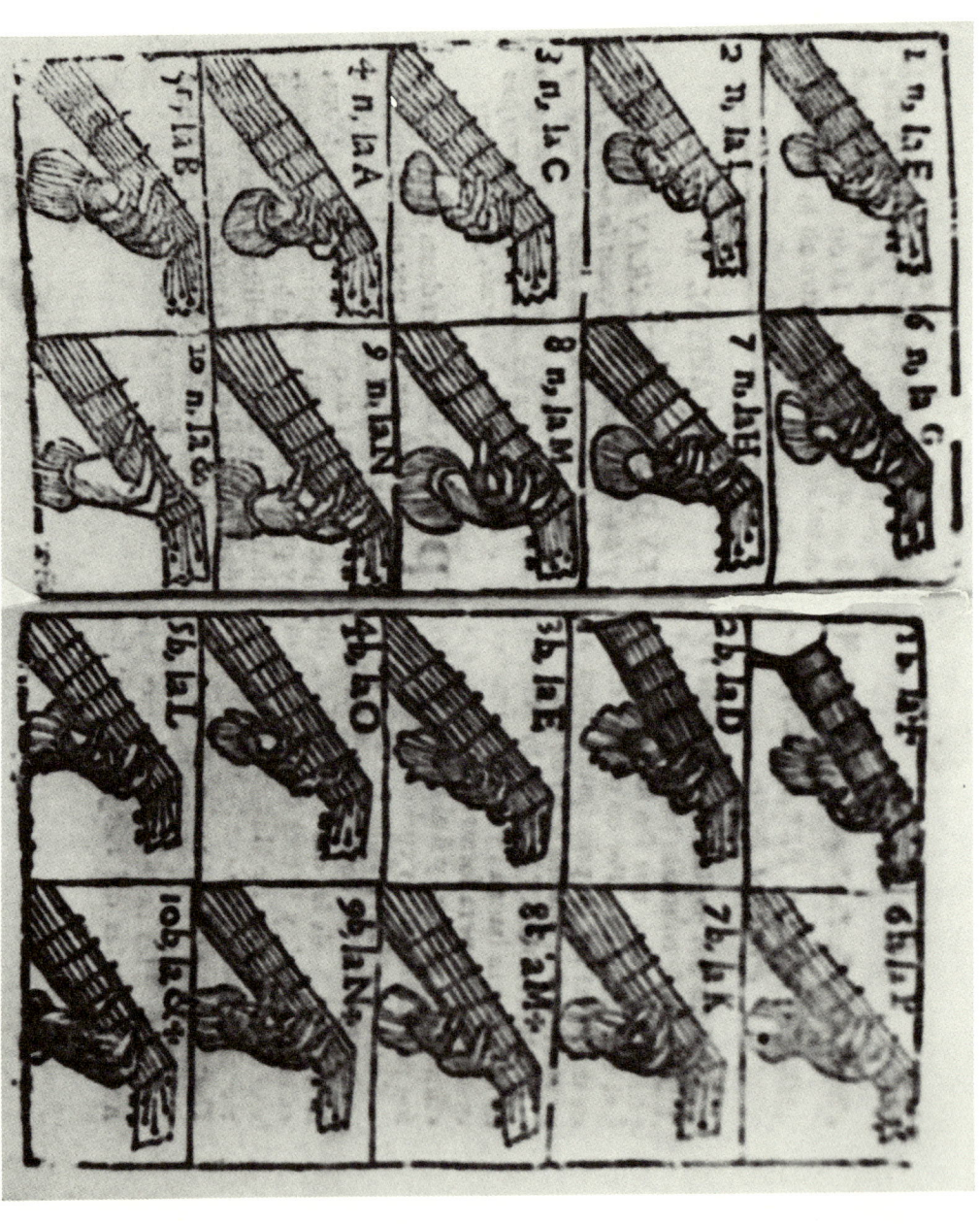

Juan Carlos Amat, *Guitarra Espanola, y Vandola* (Gerona: Joseph Bro, [ca. 1765]), Chord chart.

Baroque Histories   (329-331)

IV (1956) 175-248. In Fr.
Lesure's edition of Trichet's manuscript which dates from ca. 1630.
Part II (in v. IV): "Des instruments de musique a chordes" [The
musical stringed instruments], section 9: "De la guiterre" [Of the
guitar], p. 216-19: Trichet's commentary on the popularity and use
of the guitar indicates his strong dislike for the instrument in
favor of the lute. Description of the instrument, tuning, and publications of music. Music (tuning), bibliog. ref. in notes.
See also: Lesure 162 for a quotation of the text.

TURNER, William

329   TILMOUTH, Michael. "Some improvements in music noted by
       William Turner in 1697". *GalpinSocJ* X (May 1957) 57-59.
A brief discussion of William Turner's 1697 London publication
entitled *A compleat history of the most remarkable providences...*
Quotation of Turner's text on "improvements in musick" includes
comments on the *ghittar*. The popularity of the guitar over "the
nobler lute" is indicated.

F. Individual Composers and Performers

ABREU, Antonio and PRIETO, P. F. Victor

See 266

AMAT, Juan Carlos [Joan Carles](1572-1642)

See also 7, 271, 289, 291

330   HALL, Monica. "The *guitarra española* of Joan Carles Amat".
       EarlyM VI/3 (July 1978) 362, 363, 365, 367, 369, 371, 373.
A description of the contents of Amat's *Guitarra española* (1626).
Music, theoretical considerations, performance practices, and
tunings are discussed. Information on early editions. Notes on the
instrument *vandola*. Synopsis of Cervantes's tale "The jealous
extremaduran" from the *Exemplary Stories*. Iconog., charts, music,
bibliog. ref. in notes.

331   PUJOL, Emilio. "Significación de Joan Carlos Amat (1572-1642)
       en la historia de la guitarra" [The significance of Joan Car-
       los Amat (1572-1642) in the history of the guitar]. *AnM* V
       (1950) 125-46. In Sp.
Biographical information on Amat. Discussion of the editions of
Guitarra española from 1596. Includes historical background on the
vihuela, the four-course guitar, and the five-course guitar. Music,
bibliog. ref. in notes.

(332-334)   Baroque Histories

ARANIES, Juan

See 289

BAILLEUX, Antoine

See 398

BRICEÑO, Luis de

See also 271, 289, 291

332   CHARNASSÉ, Hélène. "A propos d'un récent article sur *la
      méthode pour la guitare de Luis Briceño*" [In regard to a
      recent article on *the guitar method of Luis Briceño*].
      RMusicol LII/2 (1966) 204-07. In Fr.
Commentary on Escudero 333 concerning Briceño's 1626 *Metodo*. The
author introduces theories on tuning and on tablature interpretation
that are contrary to those of Escudero. References to sources included. Music, bibliog. ref. in notes.

333   ESCUDERO, José Castro. "La méthode pour la guitare de Luis
      Briceño" [The guitar method of Luis Briceño] including
      "Appendice. Sur le Séjour de Briceño à Paris" [Appendix. On
      the sojourn of Briceño in Paris] by Daniel Devoto. *RMusicol*
      LI/2 (1965) 131-48. In Fr.
A detailed description of Briceño's *Método* (1626). The importance of
the repertoire is discussed and compared to other Baroque publications of guitar music. Tuning practices and notation are explained.
List of contents. In the Appendix, the author draws conclusions concerning Briceño's sojourn in Paris based on the discovery of a sonnet contributed by Briceño to a 1614 Parisian publication. Quotation
of the sonnet included. Music (facsim., tabl., transcr.).
See also: Charnassé 332 and Murphy 291, p. 62, note 15 for criticism.

334   LESURE, François. "Trois instrumentalistes français au XVIIe
      siècle" [Three French instrumentalists of the seventeenth cen-
      tury]. *RMusicol* XXXVII (Dec 1955) 186-87. In Fr.
Biographical notes on Luis de Briceño (guitarist), Germain Pinel
(lutenist, theorbist), and Henri Grénerin (theorbist, guitarist).
Summary of their works.

CAMPION, François

See 252, 253

Baroque Histories   (335-338)

CARRÉ SIEUR DE LA GRANGE, Anthoine

See 255, 291

CLEMENTI, Orazio (ca. 1637-1708)

335   KOCZIRZ, Adolf. "Eine Gitarrentabulatur des Kaiserlichen
       Theorbisten Orazio Clementi" [A guitar tablature of the im-
       perial theorbist Orazio Clementi]. *Melanges de Musicologie
       offerts a M. Lionel de la Laurencie*, 107-15. (Paris: La
       Société française de Musicologie. Librarie E. Droz, 1933).
       In De.
A tablature for Spanish guitar by Orazio Clementi, MS 10,248 in the
Nationalbibliothek (Vienna) was previously mistaken as a work for
bass lute or theorbe. Description of the manuscript. Discussion of
Clementi's instructional text and musical works (3 ciacones, 4
passagaglios). Notes on tablature notation and performance practices. Some biographical information on Clementi. Also includes
biographical information on Francisco Corbetta. Music (facsim.,
transcr.), bibliog. ref. in notes.

COLONNA, Giovanni Ambrosio

See 271

CORBETTA, Francesco (1615-1681)

See also 252, 253, 258, 259, 265, 291, 335, 359

336   ["The obituary and epitaph of Francisque Corbet"]. *Mercure
       galant* (Apr 1681) 127-33. In Fr.
       Library location: US NH.
This information is cited in Pinnell 344 which includes an English
translation of the obituary.

337   DANNER, Peter. "Prelude in G [by] F. Corbetta. A note on the
       transcription". *Soundb* VIII/3 (Aug 1981) 150-51.
Introductory notes to Danner's transcription of Corbetta's Prelude
in G from *La guitarre royalle* (1671) give an explanation of his
treatment of the original tablature according to Corbetta's tuning
practices and ornamentation. Music (transcr., facsim.).

338   HAMILTON, Anthony. *Memoirs of Count Grammont.* (London: 1905).
Grammont's account of life in the court of Charles II of England
includes references to Corbetta and his position in court.
See also: Grunfeld 21, p. 115-16; Bone 51, p. 81-82; Keith 339,
p. 80-81 (in Fr) for a quotation of the text.

(339-344)   Baroque Histories

339   KEITH, Richard. "La guitare royale – a study of the career and
      compositions of Francesco Corbetta". *Recherches* VI (1966) 73-
      88 (text), 89-92 (music).
A study of the life and works of Corbetta. Contemporary source material is examined for biographical information. Comments on Corbetta's publications of music. General historical background on the
seventeenth-century guitar based on a survey of the works by other
representative composers. Music (tabl., transcr., works by Corbetta).

340   KENNARD, Deric. "A note on Francesco Corbetta and his tabla-
      ture". *GuitarR* XXVI (June 1962) 9 (text), 10-12 (music), 21
      (text).
A brief description of the music in Corbetta's three books of tablature and on the tuning of the guitar. Port., music (transcr.).

341   LACONI. "Corbetta y Corbera. Dos nombres y un solo guitarrista"
      [Corbetta and Corbera. Two names and a single guitarist].
      Guitarra (Havana) III/4 (July 1942) 6. In Sp.
Biographical information on Corbetta. Discussion and quotation of a
reference to the guitarist Corbera in Gaspar Sanz's *Instrucción*
(1674). The author suggests that this is probably an alternate
spelling of the name Corbetta.

342   PINNELL, Richard T. "Alternate sources for the printed guitar
      music of Francesco Corbetta (1615-1681)". *JLuteSocAmer* IX
      (1976) 62-85.
A survey of alternate sources of Corbetta's music found in manuscripts and publications. Discussion of mixed tablature and of
Corbetta's own publications. Includes remarks on Corbetta's influence on contemporary composers. List of concordances is organized
according to dance type with citation of key and date of publication. Music (tabl. and transcr.), bibliog. ref. in notes.

343   PINNELL, Richard T. "Francesco Corbetta the non-guitarist: a
      new look at the racketeer of the Restoration". *Soundb* VIII/3
      (Aug 1981) 146-50.
Some general political history is given as background on Restoration
England under Charles II. Gambling rackets under royal protection
were run by Italian musicians Corbetta and Francesco Finochelli.
Corbetta, although unnamed, is identified as Squire Lottery in the
*Arraignment, trial, and condemnation of Squire Lottery, alias Royal
Oak Lottery* (London, 1699), a fictitious story which reveals certain
truths about a gambling concession in Restoration London and offers
sufficient evidence to incriminate Corbetta.
Port., illus., facsim. of text, bibliog. ref. in notes.

344   PINNELL, Richard T. "The role of Francesco Corbetta (1615-
      1681) in the history of music for the Baroque guitar, in-
      cluding a transcription of his complete works". PhD diss.,
      Musicology, University of California at Los Angeles, 1976.
      Now published as *Francesco Corbetta and the Baroque guitar:
      with a transcription of his works*. 2 v. (Ann Arbor, Michigan:

Baroque Histories   (345-348)

UMI Research Press). The following annotation is based on the
original dissertation.
Corbetta's music in its contemporary environment is examined in
three periods: the early period (1596-1639), the middle period
(1640-1660), and the last period (1660-1681). His importance, his
influence, and past influences on his style are studied in detail.
V. 2: "A transcription of Corbetta's complete works" includes introductory notes on transcription methodology and ornamentation. Transcription only, treble clef.
     "The goal of the present study is to evaluate Corbetta's music
in the context of the other instrumental guitar music of the seventeenth century. In addition, a concentrated effort has been made to
identify the manuscript sources for this guitarist. Whatever influence he had on the music and life of his day demands explanation;
and if he was 'the best of them all' we need to know in what way,
whether composer, virtuoso, or teacher. A study of Corbetta's music
could add much to our knowledge of the baroque guitar. But in order
to compare his music to that of others, the first necessity is to
make his complete works available, and such a transcription constitutes Volume II of the present study." Pinnell, p. 7-8. V. 1: 2
append. V. 2: in text: facsim., tabl., transcr., table of ornaments,
bibliog. ref. in notes.
Reviews: Fronimo VI/23 (Apr 1978) 30-31; C.S. Smith, *Notes* XXXVIII/1
(Sept 1981) 67-68.

345   "Pinnell completes dissertation". *Soundb* III/4 (Nov 1976)
      65, 79.
An abstract from Pinnell 344.

346   PROVOST, Richard. "Francesco Corbetta: a historical perspec-
      tive". *Soundb* VIII/3 (Aug 1981) 137-39.
A discussion of Corbetta's innovations in notation, tuning, and
musical style. Some remarks on the history of the baroque guitar
before Corbetta including its composers, notation, and stylistic
aspects of the music. Port. (author), music (tabl., transcr.),
bibliog. ref. in notes.

347   ROBERTS, John. "Historical notes. Francisco Corbetta".
      Guitar II/1 (Aug 1973) 19.
Biographical information on Corbetta during the time of Charles II
of England, as based on available sources. Quotations of documents
and obituary notice. Port.

348   ZEIDEL, Scott. "The motivic and harmonic language of Corbetta's
      La guitarre royalle (1671) as seen in three selected pieces
      from Suite no. 12 in g minor". *Soundb* VIII/3 (Aug 1981) 140-44
      (text), 145 (music).
A stylistic analysis of the Prelude, Allemande, and Passacaille. In
the Prelude, Corbetta uses a "quasi-improvisational style" as indicated in the formal, melodic, and harmonic structure of the piece.
In the Allemande, harmonic progressions and motivic relationships
are analysed. The Passacaille is a set of five variations based on

(349-353)   Baroque Histories

a single chord progression; the treatment of the progression is
studied. Bibliog. ref. in notes, music (transcr. only).

DIESEL, Nathanael (d. 1744)

349   LYONS, David Bruce. "The guitar music of Nathanael Diesel,
         lutenist to the royal Danish court, 1736-1744. An analysis and
         transcription of the duets". MA diss., Music: California State
         University, Northridge, 1975.
A detailed study of the guitar music of Nathanael Diesel contained
in two manuscripts located in Det Kongelige Bibliothek, Copenhagen.
Emphasis is on the study of the duet music, including an analysis of
the individual instrumental parts. Stylistic analysis of the solo
music. Biographical information on the composer. Historical background on the guitar. Transcription of the duet music with tablature
shown below. Charts, music, bibliog., 133p. (text), 272p. (music).

350   LYONS, David Bruce. "Nathanael Diesel, guitar tutor to a royal
         lady". *JLuteSocAmer* VIII (1975) 80-94.
A discussion of the guitar music of Nathanael Diesel contained in
two manuscripts found in the Royal Library, Copenhagen. List of contents of each manuscript. Remarks on ornamentation, tuning, musical
style, and form. Biographical information on the composer. Music,
append. (music), bibliog. ref. in notes.

351   RASMUSSEN, Knud. "Nathanael Diesels guitarkompositioner" [The
         guitar compositions of Nathanael Diesel]. *DAfMF* (1963) 27-28.
         In Da.

DOIZI DE VELASCO, Nicolao

See 289

ESPINEL, Vicente (1550-1624)

352   HALEY, George. *Vicente Espinel and Marcos de Obregón. A life
         and its literary representation.* (Providence, R.I.: Brown
         University Press, 1959).
A detailed study of the life and works of Vicente Espinel, author of
the novel entitled *La Vida del escudero Marcos de Obregón.* For information on the sources of the myth that credits Espinel with the
addition of the fifth string to the guitar, see p. 44-47. 7 pl.,
append., bibliog., 254p.

353   POPE CONANT, Isabel. "Vicente Espinel as a musician". *Studies
         in the Renaissance* V (1958).

Baroque Histories   (354-358)

FASOLO

See 253, 269

FIORILLO, Tiberio ("Scaramouche")

354   ROBERTS, John. "Historical notes. A fantastic guitarist".
       Guitar V/4 (Nov 1976) 5.
Two accounts of Tiberio Fiorillo ("Scaramouche") which comment on
his activities as a guitarist in seventeenth-century Paris.

FOSCARINI, Giovanni Paolo

See also 271

355   DANNER, Peter. "Giovanni Paolo Foscarini and his 'nuova
       inventione'". *JLuteSocAmer* VII (1974) 4-18.
The significance of Foscarini's *I quatro libri* (ca. 1630) is considered. Foscarini's system of notation and his repertoire are compared to those of other composers for the guitar. Source material is
consulted. Stylistic analysis included. Port., music (tabl.,
transcr.), bibliog. ref. in notes.

356   LIPSCOMB, Pamela. "Baroque style". *CGuitarInt* II/3 (Spring
       1975) 12-13, 15.
A brief survey of baroque guitar music and performance techniques
based in part on Danner's research 287 and 355. Comments on Foscarini's guitar method are included. Bibliog. ref. in notes.

GALLOT, Henry François de

See also 255

357   DANNER, Peter (commentary); JENSEN, Richard d'A. (transcrip-
       tion). "The guitar trios of 'Gallot D'I'". *Soundb* VI/4 (Nov
       1979) 128-31.
A brief discussion of the contents of the anthology of guitar music
collected by Gallot which is located in the Bodleian Library, Oxford.
The manuscript (ca. 1660-1684) contains trios for guitar. Music
(facsim., transcr.).

358   GILL, Donald. "The de Gallot guitar books". *EarlyM* VI/1 (Jan
       1978) 79-81, 83, 85-87.
A detailed description of the contents of the manuscript anthology
of guitar music collected by Gallot which is located in the Bodleian
Library, Oxford (1660-1684). Examination of repertoire, tablature
notation, and tuning. Historical background on the seventeenth-
century guitar included. Illus., music (facsim., tuning).

359   PINNELL, Richard T. "Return with us now. The *Soundboard*'s
       Featured Facsimile". *Soundb* IV/1 (Feb 1977) 14-15.
A short description of the contents of the manuscript "Pièces de
guitarre de differenda autheur a recueillis par Henry François de
Gallot" found in the Bodleian Library, Oxford. Introductory notes
to the facsimile and transcription of "Allemande Francisco" attributed to Francesco Corbetta. Music (facsim., transcr.).

GRAGNANI, Filippo

See 471

GRANATA, Giovanni Battista

360   DELL'ARA, Mario. "Giovanni Battista Granata, chitarrista,
       compositore e barbiere chirurgico" [Giovanni Battista Granata,
       guitarist, composer, and barber surgeon]. *Fronimo* VII/26 (Jan
       1979) 6-15. In It.
A biographical study of Giovanni Battista Granata, a guitarist active in seventeenth-century Bologna. Description of his publications
of guitar music. A survey of works for guitar published in seventeenth-century Bologna includes a chronological list (1607-1684).
Bibliog.

GRÉNERIN, Henri

See 255, 334

GUERAU, Francisco (mid-17th c.–early 18th c.)

See also 293

361   STEVENSON, Janis M. "A transcription of *Poema Harmonico* by
       Francisco Guerau for baroque guitar". MA diss., Music: San
       José State University, 1974.
An edition of Guerau's *Poema Harmonico* (1694). In the preface,
repertoire, notation, ornamentation, and transcription methodology
are discussed. Guerau's text, which is presented in facsimile and
in English translation, gives information on notation, ornamentation, and guitar technique. Illus., append., music (tabl., transcr.),
bibliog., 282p.

KREMBERG, Jakob (ca. 1650–ca. 1718?)

See also 47, 878-80

Baroque Histories   (362-364)

362   KOCZIRZ, Adolf. "Alte Gitarrenmusik. Jakob Kremberg:
       Musicalische Gemüths - Ergökung oder Arien (1689)" [Old
       guitar music. Jakob Kremberg: *Musicalische Gemüths - Ergö-
       kung oder Arien* (1689)]. *DieGit* III/4 (Jan 1922) 35-36. In De.
A very short survey of the contents of Kremberg's 1689 publication
of forty arias for voice and continuo. Notes on notation, tuning,
and instrumentation. Description of vocal text and musical style of
the arias: characteristics of the accompaniment and the idiomatic
use of the guitar is considered. Biographical information on the
composer.

LEMOINE, A.

See 398, 615

MATTEIS, Nicola (?late 1670s–?ca. 1749)

See also 3, 318

363   GARNSEY, Sylvia. "The use of hand-plucked instruments in the
       continuo body: Nicola Matteis". *MLetters* XLVII/2 (Apr 1966)
       135-40.
A discussion of the instructions for realization of figured bass on
guitar as found in Nicola Matteis's *The false consonances of musick*.
Tunings of the five-course guitar are discussed. Comparison of Matteis's publication to the manuscript of lute music, Euing collection,
Glasgow University Library, which contains a plagiarism of Matteis's
work. Bibliog. ref. in notes.

364   TILMOUTH, Michael. "Nicola Matteis". *MQ* XLVI/1 (Jan 1960)
       22-40.
A detailed description of the contents of Matteis's *The false consonances of musick* with quotations of text and information on early
editions. Biographical information on Matteis. Port., music (no guitar music), bibliog. ref. in notes.

MÉDARD, Remy

See 255

MILANUZZI, Carlo

See 271

MILLIONI, Pietro

See 271

(365-367)   Baroque Histories

MINGUET Y YROL, Pablo

See 289, 878-80

MONTESARDO, Girolamo

See 271, 280, 291

MURCIA, Santiago de (fl. 1700-1732)

See also 266, 289, 293

365   LOWENFELD, Elena M. "Santiago de Murcia's thorough-bass
        treatise for the baroque guitar (1714). Introduction, trans-
        lation, and transcription". MA diss., Music: City College of
        the City University of New York, 1975. UMI 1307910.
A study of Santiago de Murcia's *Resumen de acompañar la parte con la
guitarra* (1714), a treatise on thorough-bass accompaniment, includes
a discussion of notation, performance practices, and historical background on musical and theoretical sources. The original edition of
the *Resumen* is described. The text is presented in facsimile and in
English translation. Iconog., illus., tables, music (tabl.,
transcr.), bibliog. (sources, secondary works), music (selected
compositions of Murcia, transcr. with tabl.), 72p. (preliminary
text), 126p. (text translation, music).
See also: RILM IX/1-2 (Jan-Aug 1975) 2571dm[52].

366   LOWENFELD, Elena M. "U.S.A. Abstracts". *Soundb* II/3 (Aug
        1975) 49.
An abstract of Lowenfeld 365.

367   PENNINGTON, Neil Douglas. "The development of Baroque guitar
        music in Spain, including a commentary on and transcription of
        Santiago de Murcia's *Passacalles y Obras* (1732)". PhD diss.,
        Music, University of Maryland, 1979. Now published as *The
        Spanish Baroque guitar with a transcription of de Murcia's
        Passacalles y obras*. 2 v. Series no. 46. (Ann Arbor, Michigan:
        UMI Research Press). The following annotation is based on the
        original dissertation.
V. 1: "Background and commentary". A general survey of Spanish political, social, and economic history. General historical background
on the Spanish baroque guitar includes a study of notation systems,
tunings, technique, and ornamentation based on a study of sources of
Spanish guitar music. Detailed study of the contents of Murcia's
*Passacalles y obras de guitarra por todos los tonos naturales y
accidentales* (1732). Illus., tables, append., music, bibliog.
(sources, secondary works, modern and facsim. editions, discog.),
393p.
V. 2: Transcription with preface.

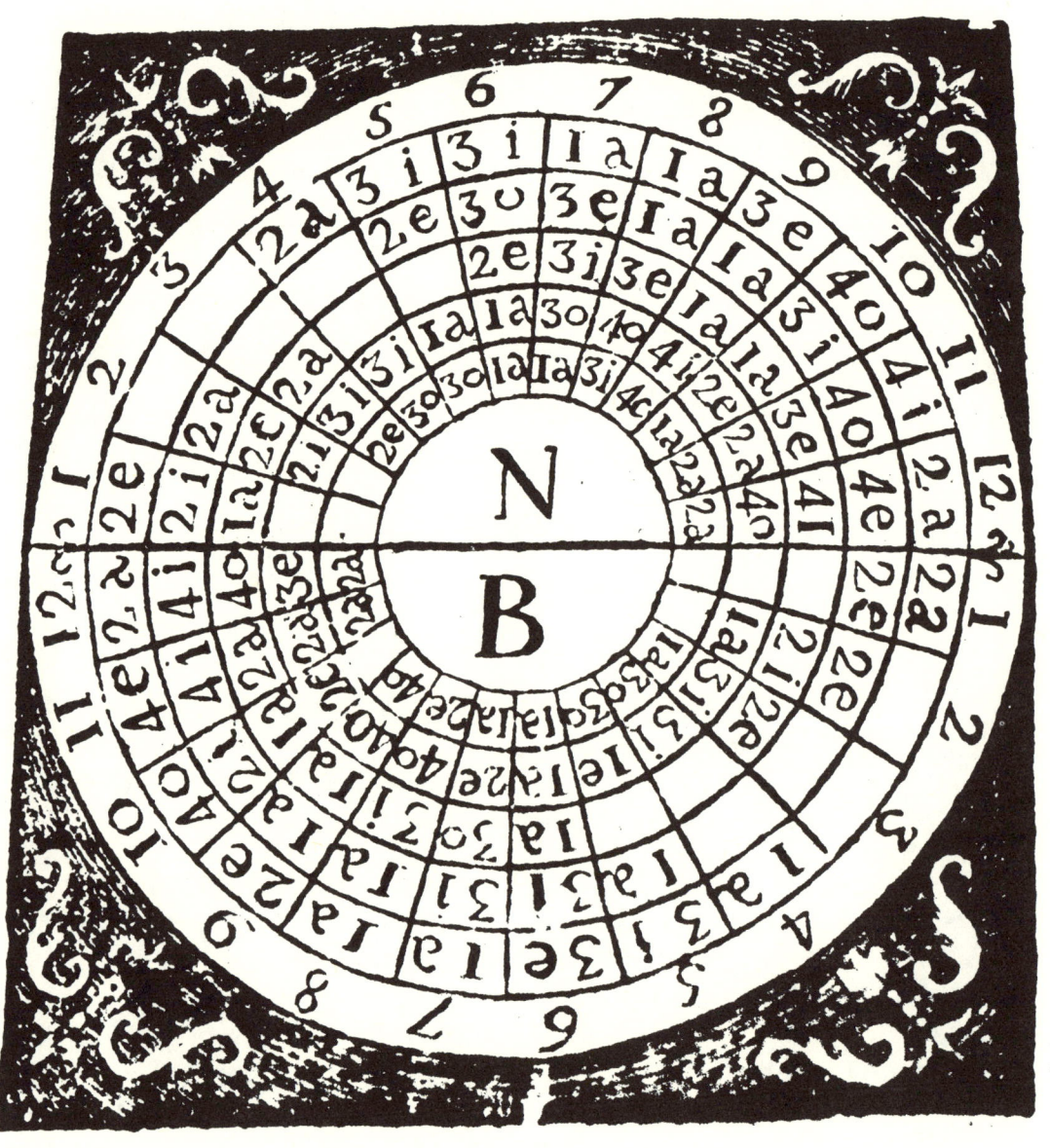

Andres de Sotos, *Arte para aprendre con facilidad* . . . (Madrid:
imprenta de Cruzada, 1764), "La Tabla Laberinto", p. 36.

Lucas Ruiz de Ribayaz, *Luz, y Norte Musical*
(Madrid: Melchor Alvarez, 1677), Title page.

Baroque Histories (368-371)

368 PINNELL, Richard T. "Return with us now. *Soundboard*'s fea-
    tured facsimile". *Soundb* VI/4 (Nov 1979) 134 (text), 135-37
    (facsim., transcr.).
Introductory notes to the facsimile reproduction and transcription
of Santiago de Murcia's *Sarabande* and *Giga* from his 1732 manuscript
in the British Museum. Brief description of the contents of his two
publications for guitar (1714, 1732). Music.

PELLEGRINI, Domenico

369 BELLOW, Alexander. "Domenico Pellegrini". *GuitarR* XXIX (June
    1966) 23 (text), 24 (music).
A description of Pellegrini's *Armoniosi concerti sopra la chitarra
spagnuola* (1650). Music.

PICO, Foriano

See 271

RONCALLI, Ludovico

See 253, 259

RUIZ DE RIBAYAZ, Lucas

See also 266, 289, 291, 293

370 "Lucas Ruiz de Ribayaz". *Guitarra* (Madrid) XXII (June-Aug
    1965) 4 (text), 5 (music). In Sp.
A short biographical introduction to Lucas Ruiz de Ribayaz, composer
of the 1677 publication of guitar music *Luz y norte musicale*. Music
(transcr. by Lupe de Azpiazu), bibliog. ref. in notes.

371 STRIZICH, Robert. "A Spanish guitar tutor: Ruiz de Ribayaz's
    Luz y norte musical (1677)". *JLuteSocAmer* VII (1974) 51-81.
A detailed examination of the contents of Ruiz de Ribayaz's guitar
tutor, including quotations from the text in translation and comparisons to the publications of Gaspar Sanz and others. Biographical information on the composer. Music (tabl., transcr.).

SAN SEVERINO, Benedetto

See 271, 291

(372-376)   Baroque Histories

SANTA CRUZ, Antonio de

See 289

SANZ, Gaspar (1640-1710)

See also 194, 266, 282, 289, 291, 293, 341, 371, 763

372   ARTZT, Alice. "Gaspar Sanz. An overview of various editions".
         GuitarR XL (Winter 1976) 33.
The problems of transcribing Sanz's music for modern guitar are discussed. Various alternatives and solutions are suggested for making
Sanz's music accessible to the modern performer. Tuning practices
are described.

373   KOCZIRZ, Adolf. "Alte Gitarremusik. Gaspar Sanz *Unterweisung
         in der Musik der spanischen Gitarre* (1674) [Old guitar music.
         Gaspar Sanz's *Instruccion de musica sobre la guitarra española*
         (1674)]. *DieGit* I/8 (May 1920) 121-22. In De.
A short summary of the contents of Sanz's *Instruccion* (1674) including notes on tuning, notation, technique, ornamentation, repertoire, and Sanz's instructional text. Biographical information on
Sanz and on Don Juan of Austria, to whom the work is dedicated.
Description of two representative works by Sanz: "Preludio o Capricho arpeado" and "Passacaglia".

374   MANNS, Jerrold Allen. "Gaspar Sanz' *Instruccion de musica
         sobre la guitarra española* (1674). Translation, transcription,
         commentary". MA diss., Music: Case Western Reserve, 1974.
Introductory notes include a general historical survey of Spanish
history and historical background on the seventeenth-century guitar
and its notation. Biographical information on Sanz and a description
of the contents of his publication. Translation of the text with
some reproductions in facsimile. Discussion of transcription methodology and of musical forms contained in the publication. 5 append.
(appendix 2 is a collection of transcriptions and facsimiles of the
original tablature of 30 examples of dance forms), music, bibliog.,
163p.

375   ROBERTS, [John] D. "Historical notes. Approbation of Sanz".
         Guitar V/8 (Mar 1977) 5.
Quotation of the approbations by Licentiates Sebastian Alfonso and
Diego Xarava y Bruna found in Sanz's book of tablature (Saragossa
1697) concerning Sanz's publication of music for guitar. Iconog.

376   ZAYAS, Rodrigo de. "Gaspar Sanz and his music". *GuitarR* XL
         (Winter 1976) 2-11 (text), 12-32 (music); XLII (Fall 1977)
         2-5 (music).
A detailed consideration of the life and compositions of Gaspar
Sanz. Explanation of the tablature and transcription methodology
are included. History and performance, p. 2-9; music, p. 10; tran-

Baroque Histories   (377–380)

scription of 'Libro primero' of Sanz's *Instruccion* (1674), p. 11–32; continuation of the transcription, *GuitarR* XLII (Fall 1977) 2–5. Music (tabl. and transcr.).

SEVERI PERUGINO, Francesco

See 269

SOTOS, Andrés de

See 289

VARGAS Y GUZMAN, Juan Antonio

377   STEVENSON, Robert. "Un olvidado manual mexicano de guitarra de 1776" [A forgotten Mexican guitar manual of 1776]. In 2 parts. *Heterofonía* VIII/44 (Sept–Oct 1975) 14–16; VIII/45 (Nov–Dec 1975) 5–9. In Sp. English summary VIII/45 (Nov–Dec 1975) 28.
A discussion of the contents of Juan Antonio Vargas y Guzman's manuscript "Explicación para tocar la guitarra de punteado" (1776). Information on notation and tuning practices is included. Comments on the significance of the work in an historical context. Bibliog. ref. in notes.

378   "The original classic guitar". *CGuitarInt* III/3 (Sept 1976) 5–8.
A description of the 1776 manuscript "Explicación para tocar la guitar de punteado" by Juan Antonio Vargas y Guzman. The author indicates that the manuscript is the first work for the six-course guitar and the first work in standard music notation. Quotations of the manuscript text in En translation.

VISÉE, Robert de (ca. 1660–ca. 1720)

See also 252, 253, 255, 259, 291

379   CHILESOTTI, Oscar. "Notes sur le guitariste Robert de Visée" [Notes on the guitarist Robert de Visée]. *SIMg* IX/1 (Oct–Dec 1907) 62–74. In Fr.
A discussion of the contents of de Visée's publication entitled *Livre de guitarra*. Information on ornamentation and on tuning practices included. Music (12 ex., 1 tabl., 11 transcr.).

380   PRUD'HOMME, Brian. "A passacaille by Robert de Visée". *GuitarLute* IV (Mar 1977) 10 (text), 11 (music).
Introductory notes to the transcription of the passacaille from de Visée's *Suite in d minor* in his *Livre de Pieces pour la guitarre* (1686).

(381-385)   Baroque Histories

381   WADE, Graham. "The guitarist's repertoire". *BMG* LXVI/762
      (Oct 1968) 4.
A short evaluation of de Visée's *Suite in d minor*.

382   WADE, Graham. "The guitarist's repertoire". *BMG* LXVI/763
      (Nov 1968) 55.
A simple analysis and notes on the interpretation of the Prelude
and the Allemande from de Visée's *Suite in d minor*.

383   WADE, Graham. "The guitarist's repertoire". *BMG* LXVI/764
      (Dec 1968) 71-72.
A simple analysis and notes on the interpretation of the Courante
and the Sarabande from de Visée's *Suite in d minor*.

384   WADE, Graham. "The guitarist's repertoire". *BMG* LXVI/765
      (Jan 1969) 129.
A simple analysis and notes on the interpretation of de Visée's
Suite in d minor.

385   WADE, Graham. "The guitarist's repertoire". *BMG* LXVI/766
      (Feb 1969) 166.
A simple analysis and notes on the interpretation of the Bourree
and the Gigue from de Visée's *Suite in d minor*.

Lucas Ruiz de Ribayaz, *Luz, y Norte Musical* (Madrid: Melchor Alvarez,
1677), Xacaras, Folias, and Pabanas in *Alfabeto* Tablature, p. 66.

CHAPTER FIVE

Histories of the Early Six-String Guitar

This chapter contains literature on the six-string classic guitar of the late eighteenth century and the early nineteenth century. It is divided into four sections: Section A. Early Nineteenth-Century Sources, Section B. General Studies, Section C. Individual Composers and Performers, and Section D. The Terz Guitar. Studies which treat the transition from the Baroque guitar, most commonly strung with five courses, to the six single-string guitar are included in Section B. In particular, entries 393, 394, 397, and 398 are directed toward questions about this period and its lacunae.

A selection of the first products of journalism in guitar history is cited in Section A. Texts exist which confirm contemporary opinion on the guitar and provide information on early concert activities and repertoire. Many reviews and descriptions of recitals are recorded in early periodicals. *The Giulianiad, or Guitarist's Monthly Magazine* (London, 1933/34?) is the first periodical devoted to the guitar. It gives information on English concerts, exposes attitudes toward performers, and contains a supplement of printed music. Entries 388–91, 468, 564, and 926 are articles found in Volume III of *The Giulianiad*; a copy of this volume is located at the New York Public Library at Lincoln Center (New York, N.Y.). A facsimile reprint of articles and music in this volume is listed as entry 386. Heck (entry 486) is based on an investigation of material in *The Giulianiad* which specifically concerns guitarist Felix Horetzky. Information on *The Giulianiad* is also given in entry 520 in an article on Ferdinand Pelzer. French-language concert reviews appear in *Revue et Gazette Musicale de Paris* (entry 411); German-language concert reviews appear in *Allgemeine Musikalische Zeitung* (entry 413). The prejudices of reviewers against the guitar are protested by François Fétis in his 1834 article (entry 467) on guitarist Zani de Ferranti.

In Section B., works which treat a variety of aspects of the early classic guitar are included. General surveys of the period are given in entries 402 and 409. Studies of a biographical nature are given in entries 395, 396, 400, 401, 405, and 410. Repertoire, style, and performance are emphasized in entries 393, 394, 400, 407, 408, and 412.

95

HISTORIES OF THE EARLY SIX-STRING GUITAR

Section C. contains bibliographies of works for both guitarist and non-guitarist composers of guitar music. Among the greatest contributors to the guitar's repertoire are guitarist-composers Fernando Sor, Dionisio Aguado, Mauro Giuliani, Matteo Carcassi, and Ferdinand Carulli. Those composers most commonly associated with genres outside of the guitar are Hector Berlioz, Luigi Boccherini, Anton Diabelli, Niccolò Paganini, Franz Schubert, and Carl Maria von Weber. In addition to these most familiar names, several lesser-known composers, to whom present-day performers and musicologists have given relatively little attention, are cited. The limited amount of available research which acknowledges their contribution is indexed; this exposes an area of the guitar's history where additional repertoire is found. Neglect of this period is primarily the result of the decline in the interest in the guitar at that time and of the consequent struggle of guitarists for recognition of their work. In entry 110, Wolf Moser points out the value of the neglected repertoire of representative Spanish composers between the time of Dionisio Aguado and Francisco Tárrega. The extensive list of articles by Philip J. Bone (entries 590–628) provide biographical information on a number of lesser-known guitarists of the period. As regards his later work (entry 51), the reader is cautioned about Bone's lack of accurate substantiation of his information.

Section D. provides information on the terz guitar, a small guitar in use in the early nineteenth century, which was tuned a minor third higher than the standard classic guitar. Mauro Giuliani and Johann Nepomuk Hummel were among those composers who composed music for the instrument.

A. Early Nineteenth-Century Sources

386   BURTNIEKS, J.A. "The Giulianiad". *GuitarR* XVIII (1955)
       174-86.
Introductory notes to *The Giulianiad*, the first periodical "devoted
solely to the interests of the guitar", give historical background
and a list of twentieth-century European and American periodicals.
Articles and music are reprinted in facsim. from v. I (1833). In
addition to entries 468, 564, and 926, a poem entitled "Stanzas 'to
my guitar' by a lady" and "Musical intelligence, chit-chat, etc."
are also reprinted. Music (facsim., "Introduction and Thema by
Giuliani", "Exercises, or Solfeggi for the voice and guitar").

387   GARDETON, Cesar. *Bibliographie musicale de la France et de
       l'étranger. Archives de l'édition musicale française* [Musical
       bibliography of France and abroad. Archives of French editions
       on music] V, VI. (Genève: Minkoff Reprint, 1978). In Fr.
A reprint of Gardeton's 1822 Paris edition. Extensive lists of
music, methods, and journals include those for guitar. Lists of
music are organized in broad general categories (Aires, Andantes,
Cantates, etc.) and must be searched for guitar-related materials.
A section listing musicians in France and foreign musicians includes
guitarists and builders. 600p.
Review: FontesArtisMus XXVI/4 (1979) 313.

388   "I do not like the guitar! Being an examination of the
       objections raised against that instrument". *Giulianiad* III/1
       (1833) 13-16.
For insights into attitudes towards the guitar in the early nineteenth century. An argument in favor of the guitar in opposition to
those who discredit it. Objections raised against the guitar are
considered and refuted. Giuliani's work with Hummel and Moschelles
is mentioned.

389   "On the capabilities of the guitar". *Giulianiad* III/1 (1833)
       3-5.
For an early nineteenth century opinion of the value of the guitar.
A discussion of the guitar's potential and its advantages over other
instruments. Giuliani's contribution as a composer and as a performer
is mentioned.

390   "On the comparative merits of the piano-forte and guitar,
       as an accompaniment to the voice". *Giulianiad* III/1 (1833)
       9-11. Reprinted in *Soundb* I/4 (1974) 37-39.
A comparison of the guitar and of the pianoforte as accompaniment
instruments. The advantages of the use of each instrument in performance are considered.

391   "Public concerts". *Giulianiad* III/1 (1833) 46-50.
Introductory remarks on the guitar as a concert instrument. Reviews
of seven concerts include an evaluation of the performers and a

(391-397)   Early Six-String Histories

discussion of the repertoire. Mr. Pelzer and his eight year old
daughter are mentioned.
See also: 518-21 for readings on Ferdinand Pelzer and his daughters.

B. General Studies

392   ALVER, Alfred W. "The golden age of the guitar". *Chesterian*
         II (Nov 1929) 37-41.
A brief discussion of the popularity of the guitar in the early
nineteenth century.

393   COX, Paul. "Considerazioni sui primi metodi per chitarra"
         [A consideration of some early methods for guitar]. *Fronimo*
         IX/34 (Jan 1981) 5-15. In It.
Historical background on the evolution of the six-string guitar. The
stylistic development of musical repertoire and opinions on position
and technique are examined in a study of method books for guitar,
1770-1850. Source material is quoted. Bibliog. ref. in notes.

394   COX, Paul. "The evolution of playing techniques of the six-
         stringed classic guitar as seen through teaching method books
         from ca. 1780-1850". PhD diss., Musicology: Indiana Univer-
         sity, 1978. UMI 7909683.
A detailed examination of the development of classic guitar technique
between ca. 1780 and 1850 based on an investigation of European and
American method books. The influences of the literature and the developments in instrumental design before the six-string instrument
are considered. Instructional texts and musical repertoire are
discussed. 2 Append., bibliog., 234p.

395   GRUNFELD, Frederic V. "Introduction to the music in this
         issue". *GuitarR* XLIV (Summer 1978) 21 (text), 22-33 (music).
Includes biographical information on lesser-known early nineteenth-century
composers of guitar music: Antonio Maria Nava (1775-1828), Joseph Meissonnier "Le Jeune" (1790-ca. 1860), Guillaume Pierre Antonio Gatayes
(b. 1774). Music in facsim. for solo guitar and for guitar and voice
by Carulli, Carcassi, Nava, Meissonnier "Le Jeune", and Gatayes.

396   HASKINS, H. Wolcott. "The guitar - facts not generally
         known". *Cadenza* IV/1 (Sept-Oct 1897) 19.
Historical notes on some important European and American guitarists
of the nineteenth century. Includes a quotation of Berlioz's comments on the guitar playing of Zani de Ferranti (1802-1878).

397   HECK, Thomas F. "Historical research. Mysteries in the
         history of the guitar: chapter III". *Guitarra* (Chicago)
         XL (Sept-Oct 1980) 10-12.
Theories on the transition from double stringing to single stringing
are suggested. Includes comments on the single-wire stringing of the
chitarra battente, a description of a five-string guitar by

Early Six-String Histories   (397-402)

Ferdinando Gaglione (1774) as an important transitional instrument, and the influence of the single-string lyre on guitar makers.

398   HECK, Thomas F. "Historical research. More about the transition from double strings (courses) to single strings". *Guitarra* (Chicago) XLI (Nov-Dec 1980) 16-19.
Continued from Heck 397. Additional information on the transition from double stringing to single stringing. An examination of two French methods which provide important information on the transitional period: Antoine Bailleux's *Methôde* (ca. 1773) for guitar of four-courses and single chanterelle and A.M. Lemoine's *Nouvelle Methode* (ca. 1808) for guitar of five single-strings. Tuning, tuning heads, and notation are described. Illus. (facsim.), music (facsim.).

399   HECK, Thomas F. "Ricordi plate numbers in the earlier nineteenth century: A chronological survey". *CurrentMusicol* X (1970) 117-24.
A survey of music published by Ricordi, 1808 to 1857, including historical notes on the Ricordi publishing firm. A list of opera arrangements includes arrangements for the guitar. Plate number, date, composer, title, and instrumentation is given. "Postscript" is a survey of popular arrangements of Rossini's "Zelmira" listing plate numbers and catalogue citations of works including three arrangements for guitar. Bibliog. ref. in notes.
See also: Heck 75.

400   HENZE, Bruno. *Die Gitarre und ihre Meister des 18. und 19. Jahrhunderts* [The guitar and its masters of the 18th and 19th centuries]. (Berlin: Verlag ad. Köster, 1920). In De.
Historical background includes a survey of tablatures from the sixteenth through the eighteenth centuries. The Classical-Romantic repertoire for guitar is described with a chapter devoted to the biographies of Sor and Giuliani and to shorter biographies of other significant composers. Port., music (tabl. and staff notation). No bibliog. or index, 48p.

401   KITCHNER, W.J. "The history and development of the guitar". *Cadenza* V/6 (July-Aug 1899) 5-7.
A survey of the activities and contributions of guitarists of the early nineteenth century. Greatest attention is given to Ferdinand Carulli. The careers of Dionisio Aguado, Fernando Sor, Matteo Carcassi, and Giulio Regondi are also considered.

402   KOCZIRZ, Adolf. "Die Wiener Gitarristik vor Giuliani" [The Viennese guitar school before Giuliani]. In 3 parts. *DieGit* II/7 (Apr 1921) 71-73; II/8 (May 1921) 81-82; II/9 (June 1921) 93-95. In De.
Part 1: A general historical survey of the guitar from the sixteenth century. Emphasis is on the history of the guitar in the eighteenth and early nineteenth centuries. Notes on the lyra guitar and its literature with a description of the instrument by Simon Molitor.

Part 2: A discussion of the use and the popularity of the guitar in Vienna in the late eighteenth and the early nineteenth centuries. Quotations from source material include comments by Simon Molitor from his publication (1804-06) concerning the popularity of the guitar and the problem of dilettantism.
Part 3: A continuation of Molitor's discussion of the popularity of the guitar and his opinion on the decline in musical taste in the early nineteenth century. Comments on Molitor's contribution to the development of the guitar as a serious instrument. Important contemporaries of Molitor are mentioned.

403   MAHLING, Christoph-Hellmut. "Verwendung und Darstellung von Volksmusikinstrumenten in Werken von Haydn bis Schubert" [The utilization and depiction of folk-music instruments in the works from Haydn to Schubert]. *Volks- und Hockunst in Dichtung und Musik*, 110-18. Tagungsbericht eines Colloquiums 19.-22. 10. 1966. Saarbrücken. (Saarbrücken: Mw Inst. der U. des Saarbrücken [1968]). Also in *Jb. Österreichischen Volksliedwerks* XVI (1968) 39-48. In De.
"Surveys those ways in which folk instruments were used, or their sounds approximated by other instruments, in music from Haydn to Schubert. Four instruments were prominent: the hurdy gurdy, bagpipe, mandolin, and guitar. Viennese classical composers used these instruments (or imitations of their sounds) to characterize peasants, farmers, and foreigners, to depict musical genres (serenades, dance music), or to illustrate the usual musical practice of the musicians and their instruments." - Quoted from *RILM* II/3 (Sept-Dec 1968) 3378as[26].

404   OREL, Alfred. "Gitarrenmusik in Wien zur Zeit Beethovens" [Guitar music in Vienna in the time of Beethoven]. *OesterreichGitarreZ* I/3 (Feb 1927) 46-50. In De.

405   PEEL, Douglas. "Guitar composers". *BMG* LXIX/794 (June 1971) 298, 313.
Biographical sketches of Sor, Albeniz, and Granados.

406   PURCELL, Ronald C. "Guitar forum - the evolution of the classic six-string guitar". In 2 parts. *AmerStrT* XXIII (Summer 1973) 12; XXIV (Spring 1974) 58-59.
Part 1: "Introduction". A brief introduction to the history of guitar composition with Fernando Sor mentioned as a composer of central importance.
Part 2: "Fernando Sor". Quotations from Sor's introduction to his method. Some general notes on the history of guitar notation. Port. (author).

407   RIBOUILLAULT, Danielle. "La technique de guitare en France dans la première moitié du siècle" [Guitar technique in France in the first half of the century]. PhD diss., Music: Sorbonne, 1981. Available from the author, 20-C Avenue de la Republique, 94270 Le Kremlin Bicetre, France. In Fr.

Early Six-String Histories   (407-413)

"It traces the evolution of both popular and 'learned' styles of
guitar playing through a study of early nineteenth-century documents
and methods." - Quoted from *Soundb* VIII/3 (Aug 1981) 224.

408   SCHROTH, Andreas. "Dem Gesang verschwistert - Die Gitarre in
      der Romantik" [The sister of song - the guitar in the Romantic
      period]. *Musica* XXXIII/1 (Jan-Feb 1979) 23-26. In De.
The rise in the popularity of the guitar in the early nineteenth
century is attributed to its role as an accompaniment instrument and
to the free-voiced, simple style of the available music. The contemporaneous rise in the virtuoso movement of guitarists is considered
including a summary of Simon Molitor's contributions to the development of the guitar as a serious instrument. Bibliog. ref. in notes.

409   SCHWARZ-REIFLINGEN, Erwin. "Beiträge zur Geschichte der
      Gitarristik nach 1840" [Contributions to the history of the
      guitar after 1840]. In 5 parts. *DieGit* IV/9 (June 1923) 65-
      68; IV/10-11 (July-Aug 1923) 74-78; IV/12 (Sept 1923) 90-93;
      V/1 (Oct-Nov 1923) 103-05; V/5-6 (Feb-Mar 1924) 35-39. In De.
A history of the guitar in the late nineteenth century with emphasis
on the history of the guitar in Germany. Includes a history of the
Leipzig Guitar Club and of the International Guitar Club. A survey
of performers and composers of the period 1788-1845 is given as
background (in part 1).

410   TANNO, John C. "The pentagonal foundation of classic guitar
      culture". *Fretts* II (July-Aug 1959) 24-25.
A short survey of the contributions of the following important
guitarists of the nineteenth and twentieth centuries: Sor, Giuliani,
Aguado, Tárrega, and Segovia.

411   TEMPEL, Hans. "Pariser Gitarrenkonzerte 1829-1839, nach den
      Berichten der *Revue und Gazette musicale de Paris*" [Parisian
      guitar concerts 1829-1839, according to the reports in the
      Revue et Gazette musicale de Paris]. *Gfreund* XXVII (1926)
      92-96, 108-11, 140-43. In De.

412   WADE, Graham. "The guitarist's repertoire". *BMG* LXVIII/792
      (Apr 1971) 223.
A survey of selected compositions by early nineteenth-century
composers Sor, Giuliani, Carcassi, Aguado, Carulli, and Coste.

413   ZUTH, Joseph. "Die Leipziger *Allgemeine musikalische Zeitung*
      (1798-1848) als gitarristische Quelle" [The *Allgemeine
      musikalische Zeitung* (1798-1848) of Leipzig as a source for
      the guitar]. In 12 parts. *DieGit* I/4 (Jan 1920) 64-65; I/5
      (Feb 1920) 83-85; I/6-7 (Mar-Apr 1920) 102-04; I/8 (May 1920)
      123-24; I/9 (June 1920) 140-41; I/10 (July 1920) 156-57; I/11
      (Aug 1920) 168, 170; I/12 (Sept 1920) 183-84; II/1 (Oct 1920)
      2-3; II/2 (Nov 1920) 11-12; II/11 (Aug 1921) 115-17; II/12
      (Sept 1921) 127-30. In De.

(413-415)   Early Six-String Histories

Part 1, I/4: Introductory remarks to a survey of the literature in
the *Allgemeine Musikalische Zeitung* in which references to early
nineteenth-century guitarists are included.
Part 2, I/5: Not available.
Part 3, I/6-7: Reviews of concerts by guitarist Luigi Legnani in
Germany and Switzerland in the years 1823, 1824, 1829, 1833, 1837-
1839. Repertoire performed is listed. Notes on an 1837 concert includes a reference to a performance by Paganini.
Part 4, I/8: Reviews of concerts by the young Giulio Regondi
(1822-1872) in Paris, London, Germany, and Austria. Repertoire
performed is listed. Performance with Joseph Lidel, 'cellist, is
mentioned.
Part 5, I/9: Review of a concert in Germany in which Giulio Regondi
played guitar and melophone (a portable accordion with keyboard).
Joseph Lidel, 'cellist, is also mentioned. Repertoire is listed.
Part 6, I/10: Review of a concert in which Giulio Regondi played
guitar and melophone. Joseph Lidel, 'cellist, is mentioned.
Repertoire is listed.
Part 7, I/11: Review of concerts in which Giulio Regondi played
guitar and melophone. Joseph Lidel, 'cellist, is mentioned.
Repertoire is listed.
Part 8, I/12: Review of concert in which Giulio Regondi played
guitar and concertina. Concertina is described.
Part 9, II/1: A description of the doppelgitarre, a type of melo-
phone. This instrument is not related to the guitar.
Part 10, II/2: Further comments on the doppelgitarre. Parisian
instrument makers, sellers, and players are mentioned.
Part 11, II/11: Biographical information on Luigi Legnani (1790-
1877). Information from Legnani's 1829 passport and from his record
of death and obituary notice are reprinted from the periodical *Il
Plettro* (Milan) XIII/5. Biographical information on Franz de Paula
Stoll, Viennese guitar master and student of Giuliani. Reviews of
German concerts by Stoll in 1825. Repertoire is listed.
Part 12, II/12: Reviews of concerts in Germany in the 1830s and
1840s. Repertoire is listed.

C. Individual Composers and Performers

AGUADO, Dionisio (1784-1849)

See also 32, 110, 401, 410, 412, 568, 810, 814

414   AGUADO, Dionisio. *Hints to guitar players with a description
       of the tripodion* [*sic*]. (London: n.d.).
       Library locations: GB CU (Mus. 25. 8. (4)).
The tripodion, an invention by Aguado, is a machine used for supporting the guitar while playing.

415   BOHR, Heinrich. "Aus der Aguadoschule" [On the Aguado school].
       ZfdG IV/11 (Dec 1925) 12-14. In De.

Early Six-String Histories   (416-423)

416   BONE, Philip J. "Dionisio Aguado". *Cadenza* IX/1 (Sept 1902)
      10-11.
A short biographical sketch of Aguado. List of some works.

417   HUTTIG, H.E. II. "The tripódison of Dionisio Aguado". *GuitarR*
      XXXIX (Summer 1974) 23-25.
A translation of material from Aguado's *Nuevo Metodo de Guitarra*
(n.d.). Aguado's arguments in favor of his invention, the *tripódison*
and his detailed instructions for use are given. The dating of the
Nuevo Metodo is discussed. The name *tripódison* is changed to *tripode*
or *máquina* in the 1843 edition of Aguado's *Metodo*. Illus.

418   JEFFERY, Brian. "I metodi per chitarra di Dionisio Aguado"
      [The guitar methods of Dionisio Aguado]. *Fronimo* VIII/30
      (Jan 1980) 17-25. In It.
A study of the contents of the five editions of Aguado's guitar
method, 1825, 1834, ca. 1837, 1843, and 1849. Music, bibliog. ref.
in notes.

419   JEFFERY, Brian. "La tecnica di unghia e polpastrello secondo
      Dionisio Aguado" [The nail-with-flesh technique according to
      Dionisio Aguado]. *Fronimo* VIII/33 (Oct 1980) 14-20. In It.
A study of Aguado's theories on the nail-with-flesh right-hand technique as discussed in his methods (1825-1850). Comparison to
Segovia's technique. Conflicts in opinion between Sor and Aguado
and Sor's influence on Aguado are discussed. Quotations from the
sources.

420   LEDHUYE, Adolphe. "Aguado". *DieGit* X/9-10 (1929) 79-80. In
      De.
Biographical information on Aguado. Praise of his ability and of
his main contributions to technique and pedagogy. Sor's comments
on Aguado are noted. Includes introductory comments on past traditions in pedagogy.

421   ROBERTS, John. "Historical notes. The tripod". *Guitar* VI/6
      (Jan 1978) 22-23.
Remarks on the tripod, invented by Aguado, which include quotations
by Aguado and by Sor. Illus., port.

422   STEWART, Jimmy. "The guitarist as a complete musician.
      Dionisio Aguado: a tribute". *GuitarP* VII/5 (July-Aug 1973)
      44.
Biographical sketch of Aguado mentioning his compositions and his
activities as a guitarist. Music (by Jimmy Stewart).

423   VELASCO, Venancio García. "Consejos tecnicos de Dionisio
      Aguado" [The technical advice of Dionisio Aguado]. *Guitarra*
      (Madrid) IV/28 (Dec 1966) 2, 7-9. In It.
A list of 100 rules concerning guitar technique by Aguado.

(424-429)   Early Six-String Histories

ARCAS LACAL, Julián Gavino (1832–1882)

See also 32, 110

424   "Julián de Arcas". *Guitarra* (Havana) II/2 (June 1941)
       between pages 16 and 17. In Sp.
A survey of the life and works of Arcas. His date of death is given
here as 1888 in conflict with the date 1882 cited by other authors.

425   ROBERTS, [John] D. "Julián Arcas". *Guitar* IV/12 (July 1976)
       5-7.
Biographical information on Arcas is based on the research of Prat
54. Reviews of Arcas's 1826 concerts in England are included.

426   ROMANILLOS, José. "Julián Arcas, 1832-1882". *La Voz de Almería*
       (21 April 1976).

BASILIO, Padre [né Miguel García]

427   POSELLI, Franco. "L'enigmatica figura di padre Basilio"
       [The enigmatic figure of Padre Basilio]. *Fronimo* I/3 (Apr
       1973) 27-29.
A discussion of the importance of Padre Basilio in the history of
the guitar. Padre Basilio has been accredited with the introduction
of the sixth string to the guitar and with re-establishing the
punteado technique. The research of authors Domingo Prat, Rafael
Mitjana, Emilio Pujol, José Subira, and Mariano Soriano Fuertes is
evaluated. Music, bibliog. ref. in notes.

BERLIOZ, Hector (1830–1869)

See also 30, 396, 515, 642

Modern Editions

428   BERLIOZ, Hector. "Berlioz' *Treatise upon modern instru-
       mentation and orchestration*" *Chelys* I/1 (1976) 20-24.
A reprint of the section on the guitar from Berlioz's *Treatise*.
Illus., music.

429   BERLIOZ, Hector. *Traité d'instrumentation et d'orchestration*
       [Treatise on instrumentation and orchestration]. Nouvelle
       édition suivie de "l'art du Chef d'orchestre". Appendice par
       Ch. M. Widor. (Paris and Brussels: Henry Lemoine et Cie,
       [1856]). Facsim. reprint (Westmead, Farnborough, Hants.,
       England: Gregg International Publishers Limited, 1970).
       In Fr.
Berlioz's treatise was originally published in 1844. The section on
"the guitar", p. 83-86, gives Berlioz's consideration of the guitar's

Early Six-String Histories   (429-435)

tuning, technique, technical difficulties, and harmonics. Berlioz
offers opinions on and recommendations for composing for the guitar.
Music.

430   BERLIOZ, Hector. *A treatise upon modern instrumentation and
       orchestration, opus 10*. Trans. from the French by Mary Cowden
       Clarke. Second ed. (London: Novello, Ewer and Co., 1858).
An English translation of Berlioz's *Treatise*. Section on "the
guitar", p. 66-70.

431   BERLIOZ, Hector. *Instrumentationslehre* [Treatise on instru-
       mentation]. Ergänzt und revidiert von Richard Strauss.
       Revision und ubersetzung eigentum des verlegers. (Leipzig:
       C.F. Peters, 1905). 2 v. In De.
A German edition of Berlioz's *Treatise*, revised and enlarged by
Richard Strauss. Section on "Die Gitarre", p. 156-60. An excerpt
from Verdi's *Otello*, Act II, score with guitar part, p. 160-62.

432   BERLIOZ, Hector. *Treatise on instrumentation*. Enlarged and
       revised by Richard Strauss including Berlioz's essay on con-
       ducting. Trans. by Theodore Front. (New York: Edwin F.
       Kalmus, 1948).
An English translation of Strauss's 1905 German edition. Section on
"the guitar", p. 145-47. Music (an excerpt from Verdi's *Otello* with
guitar part, p. 148-50).

433   BERLIOZ, Hector. "Sammlung historischer Quellen. Hector
       Berlioz" [Collection of historical sources. Hector Berlioz].
       In 2 parts. *GitarreLaute* II/3 (May-June 1980) 22-24; II/4
       (July-Aug 1980) 24-25. In De.
A German translation of the section on the guitar from Berlioz's
Grand traité d'instrumentation et d'orchestration modernes (Paris,
1843). Music.

Secondary Works

434   DELL'ARA, Mario. "Hector Berlioz. 'Il signore che suona la
       chitarra francese'" [Hector Berlioz. 'The man who plays the
       French guitar']. *Fronimo* V/18 (Jan 1977) 6-14. In It.
A biographical survey of the life of Hector Berlioz with emphasis on
Berlioz's involvement with and attitudes toward the guitar. Extensive
quotations from his *Memoirs* and other sources. Includes a discussion
of his *Treatise on instrumentation*. Bibliog. ref. in notes.

435   HENKE, Matthias; STEGEMANN, Michael. "Hector Berlioz - frühe
       Manuskripte mit Gitarrenmusik" [Hector Berlioz - early manu-
       scripts with guitar music]. *GitarreLaute* II/6 (Nov-Dec 1980)
       46-52. In De.
Description and background of the works contained in two early manuscripts by Berlioz. The first, entitled "Recueil de Romances avec
accompagnement de guitarre", contains arrangements of twenty-five

(435-443)   Early Six-String Histories

Romances to which Berlioz added guitar accompaniment. The second
contains a variety of dances and other pieces with added guitar
accompaniment. Includes a history of the guitar in early nineteenth-
century Paris and notes on Berlioz's interest in the guitar. Port.,
illus., iconog., music (facsim.), bibliog. ref. in notes.

436   LEGOUVÉ, Ernest. *Soixante ans de souvenirs* [Sixty years of
         recollections]. 2 v. (Paris: J. Hetzel et Cie, Editeurs,
         1886). In Fr.
V. 2, ch. XVI "Hector Berlioz" contains a reference to the guitar
playing of Hector Berlioz, p. 294-95. V. 1, 398p. V. 2, 384p.

437   LEGOUVÉ, Ernest. *Sixty years of recollections*. 2 v. Trans.
         with notes by Albert D. Vandam. (London and Sydney: Eden,
         Remington and Co., 1893).
An English translation of Legouvé 436 with a reference to Hector
Berlioz's guitar playing in v. 2, ch. XVI, p. 222-23. V. 1, 325p.
V. 2, 330p.

438   MOSER, Wolf. "Die Gitarre im Leben eines romantischen
         Komponisten" [The guitar in the life of a romantic composer].
         GitarreLaute II/4 (July-Aug 1980) 26-34. In De.
Berlioz's interest in and use of the guitar is considered; extensive
quotations of selections from his *Memoirs* contain references to the
guitar. His compositions for guitar include two books of songs with
guitar accompaniment of which only fragments are extant. Includes
discussions of Berlioz's use of the guitar in "Faust", "Les
Troyens", "Benvenuto Cellini", and "Beatrice et Bénédict". Port.,
music (facsim.).

439   ZUTH, Josef. "Die Gitarre des Hector Berlioz" [The guitar of
         Hector Berlioz]. *ZfdG* I/4 (Apr 1922) 8-11. In De.

BOCCHERINI, Luigi (1740-1805)

See also 508

440   BONE, Philip J. "Luigi Boccherini". *Cadenza* XI/10 (June 1905)
         10-12.
A short survey of the life and works of Luigi Boccherini.

441   OPHEE, Matanya. *Luigi Boccherini's guitar quintets - new
         evidence*. (Boston, Mass: Editions Orphée, Inc., 1981). 88p.

442   PENNINGTON, Neil. "The guitar transcriptions of Luigi
         Boccherini". *ProcAmerStrTAssoc. National Guitar Symposium.*
         (1977) 101-09.

443   ROTHSCHILD, Germaine de. *Luigi Boccherini. His life and work.*
         Trans. by Andreas Mayor. (London: Oxford University Press,
         1965).

Early Six-String Histories   (443-448)

A biographical study of the career and compositions of Boccherini.
Of particular interest is Boccherini's reference to his quintets
with a guitar part in letters to Ignace Pleyel, p. 131, 136 (incorrectly indexed). Illus., bibliog. (including MSS and printed
sources), index, 154p.

444   SCARLATTI, Vincenzo. "Clasicos Antiguo". *Guitarra* (Chicago)
       V/25 (March-Apr 1967) 16-18.
A biographical survey of the life and works of Luigi Boccherini.
Port. (Boccherini).

CANO, Antonio (1811-1897)

See 110

CARCASSI, Matteo (1792-1853)

See also 13, 401, 412, 810

445   BONE, Philip J. "Matteo Carcassi". In 2 parts. *Cadenza*
       XIII/5 (Jan 1907) 15-18; XIII/7 (Mar 1907) 10.
Part 1: A biographical survey of the life and works of Carcassi.
A description of his *Method* includes a quotation from the preface
of the first edition.
Part 2: Some important compositions and arrangements are mentioned.

446   NEWCOMB, A.H. "Guitar formerly in the possession of Matteo
       Carcassi". *Cadenza* XIII/11 (July 1907) 11-12.
A detailed description of a guitar purchased from Carcassi in 1849.
Dimensions are given.

447   STEWART, Jimmy. "The guitarist as a complete musician. Matteo
       Carcassi: a tribute". In 2 parts. *GuitarP* VII/6 (Sept 1973)
       45; VII/7 (Oct 1973) 44.
Part 1: A biography of Carcassi. Includes a description of
Carcassi's concert guitar.
Part 2: A description of Carcassi's *Complete method for the guitar*
with a quotation from the preface of the original edition. Music
(by Jimmy Stewart).

CARULLI, Fernando (1770-1841)

See also 13, 401, 412, 467, 567

448   APPLEBY, Wilfrid M. "Carulli". *GuitarN* VII (June-July 1956)
       5-6.
A brief summary of the career of Fernando Carulli addressed to the
student.

(449-456)   Early Six-String Histories

449   "Biography of a composer. Fernando Carulli". *Guitarra*
        (Chicago) II/6 (Jan-Feb 1964) 16.
A brief survey of the life and works of Carulli.

450   BONE, Philip J. "Ferdinando Carulli". In 2 parts. *Cadenza*
        X/4 (Dec 1903) 41; X/5 (Jan 1904) 10-13.
A biography of Carulli with a description of representative works
(publisher, place cited).

451   DANNER, Peter. "Return with us now. *Soundboard*'s featured
        facsimile. Carulli's 'Spanish connection'". *Soundb* V/4
        (Nov 1978) 118-19.
Introductory notes to the facsimile reprint of the bolero from
"Trois morceaux a l'Espagnole" of opus 22 by Carulli. Some bio-
graphical information on Carulli. Description of the bolero.

452   DELL'ARA, Mario. "Ferdinando Carulli (1770-1841). Indagine
        preliminare sulla vita e sull' opera. Elenco delle opere di
        Ferdinando Carulli" [Ferdinando Carulli (1770-1841). A pre-
        liminary study of his life and works. List of works by
        Ferdinando Carulli]. *Fronimo* VII/28 (July 1979) 5-23. In It.
A report of some important observations made by the author in his
research in libraries in Torin. Chronological list of valuable
biographical literature (1826-1971) on Carulli with annotations
and quotations. Chronological list of significant events in
Carulli's life. List of works (with and without opus number. MSS
and printed editions, commentary and library locations).

453   KOLON, V. "Gustav Carulli". *MHaus* I (1927) 1. In De.

CALL, Leonard von (1779-1815)

See also 499

454   BONE, Philip J. "Leonard de Call". *Cadenza* XII/4 (Dec 1905)
        10-11.
Biographical information on Call with a list of some important works
(publisher, place given).

455   MAUERHOFER, Alois. "Leonard von Call - Musik des Mittelstandes
        zur Zeit du Wiener Klassik" [Leonard von Call - Music of the
        middle class in the time of the Viennese Classical Era]. PhD
        diss., Music: University of Graz, 1974. In De.

456   LIBBERT, Jürgen. "Fachliteratur für Gitarristen. Disserta-
        tionen" [Special literature for guitar. Dissertations].
        GitarreLaute I/1 (1979) 47. In De.
An annotation of Mauerhofer 455.

108

Early Six-String Histories   (457-463)

COSTE, Napoleon (1806-1883)

See also 412, 499

457   GELAS, [Lucien]. "Biographische Notiz über Napoleon Coste"
       [Biographical notes on Napoleon Coste]. *DieGit* VIII/11-12
       (Nov-Dec 1927) 82. In De.
A short biography of Coste.

458   GIORDANO, M. "Napoleon Coste e le sue opere" [Napoleon
       Coste and his works]. *Plettro* XXX (1934-35) 68f. In It.

459   RISCHEL, Thorvald. "Bibliographische Notizen zu den
       Gitarrenwerken von Napoleon Coste" [Bibliographical notes
       on the guitar works of Napoleon Coste]. *DieGit* VIII/7-8
       (July-Aug 1927) 47-51. In De.
A survey of the career of Coste from 1840 with a consideration of
the problems of the decline in the guitar's popularity in the mid-
nineteenth century. Catalogue of Coste's works for guitar (published and in MS, organization by opus number). Analytical remarks
on individual works. Bibliog. ref. in notes.

460   SCHWARZ-REIFLINGEN, Erwin. "Costes Bearbeitung der Sor-
       Schule" [Coste's revision of the Sor Method]. *DieGit* VIII/
       7-8 (July-Aug 1927) 51-52. In De.
Commentary on Sor's method and its editions. Description of Coste's
simplified edition of Sor's method.

461   SCHWARZ-REIFLINGEN, Erwin. "Napoleon Coste". *DieGit* VIII/7-8
       (July-Aug 1927) 43-47. In De.
A survey of the life and works of Coste with remarks on the decline
of the popularity of the guitar in the mid-nineteenth century and
its effect on Coste's career.

462   STEWART, Jimmy. "The guitarist as a complete musician.
       Napoleon Coste: a tribute". *GuitarP* VII/4 (May-June 1973)
       48.
A biography of Coste with notes on his activities as a guitarist
and as a composer. Music (by Jimmy Stewart).

DIABELLI, Anton (1781-1858)

See also 499

463   BICKFORD, Vahdah Olcott. "Anton Diabelli and his music".
       GuitarN VIII (Aug-Sept 1952) 7-8.
A general survey of the career of Diabelli. Little information on
his activities as a guitarist and as a composer for the instrument
is given.

464   BONE, Philip J. "Anton Diabelli". *Cadenza* IX/3 (Nov 1902)
         10-11.
A short biographical sketch of Diabelli with a list of some principal works for guitar.

465   HAAS, Robert. "Ein Trauermarsch Anton Diabellis für Gitarre"
         [A funeral march for guitar by Anton Diabelli]. *ZfdG* V/4
         (June 1926) 77-80. In De.

FERANDIERE, Fernando

See also 266

466   KOCZIRZ, Adolf. "Alte Gitarrenmusik. Fernando Ferandiere:
         Die Kunst, die spanische Gitarre musikalisch zu spielen
         (1799)" [Old guitar music. Fernando Ferandiere: *The art of
         playing the Spanish guitar* (1799)]. *DieGit* III/11 (Aug 1922)
         95-98. In De.
A discussion of the contents of Ferandiere's 1799 publication entitled *Arte de tocar la guitarra española*. Ferandiere's theoretical,
pedagogical, and technical considerations are mentioned. Biographical information is given on Ferandiere. Works for solo guitar and
for guitar with other instruments are listed. Music (transcr.,
"Polaca", "Rondo", between p. 100-01).

FERRANTI, Marco Aurelio Zani de (1800-1878)

See also 96, 100, 396, 931

467   FÉTIS, [François]. "La guitare et Zani de Ferranti". *RM*
         VIII/4 (1834) 27-29. In Fr.
Ferranti is praised for his ability as a guitarist. The author
objects to the biases shown by many reviewers against the guitar
and argues in favor of the instrument. Also includes the author's
recollections of Carulli's performance on guitar and Dussek's performance on piano.

GIULIANI, Mauro (1780-1829)

See also 13, 386, 388, 389, 400, 410, 412, 499, 516, 548, 564,
613, 618, 631

468   "Giuliani". *Giulianiad* III/1 (1833) 7-8. Reprinted in *GuitarR*
         XVIII (1955) 177-78.

A portrait of Giuliani as a performer includes a quotation of
remarks by Horetzky in praise of Giuliani.

Early Six-String Histories   (468-474)

469   BONE, Philip J. "Mauro Giuliani. Biographical sketch". *GuitarR*
       XVIII (1955) 171-74. A reprint of Bone 51.
A detailed survey of Giuliani's career and compositions. Contains
inaccuracies. Several works are mentioned. Port. (Giuliani).
See also: Burtniek 472 for corrections.

470   BONE, Philip J. "Mauro Giuliani. Guitar Virtuoso and
       Composer". *Cadenza* X/2 (Oct 1903) 10-15.
A biographical sketch of Giuliani. List of compositions.

471   BOTET, Maria Emma. "Notas sobre algunos compositores
       italianos" [Notes on some Italian composers]. *Guitarra*
       (Havana) II/3 (Dec 1941) 7. In Sp.
A short survey of the life and works of Mauro Giuliani and Felipe
Gragnani (b. 1767).

472   BURTNIEKS, J.A. "Editorial. Mauro Giuliani in England".
       GuitarR XIX (1956) inside cover.
Corrections of Bone's article 469 based on the research of Prof.
Rómulo Ferrari. Dates of birth, death, and activities in London
are verified.

473   ELLIKER, Calvin. "Historical observations on the romance
       La Sentinelle with a comparison of the variations of this
       theme composed by Mauro Giuliani and Fernando Sor". *Soundb*
       IV/4 (Nov 1977) 81-94.
A detailed study of the versions of the romance entitled *La
Sentinelle* by Giuliani, Johann Nepomuk Hummel (1778-1837), and
Fernando Sor. Historical background is based on a study of avail-
able sources which include references to performances. A comparison
of the works by Giuliani and Hummel and by Giuliani and Sor includ-
ing analysis. Music, "Text and translation of *La Sentinelle*".
List of sources (title, instrumentation, composer, locations).
Bibliog. ref. in notes.
See also: Ophee 483 for a refutal of theories concerning authorship.

474   HECK, Thomas Fitzsimons. "The birth of the classic guitar
       and its cultivation in Vienna, reflected in the career and
       compositions of Mauro Giuliani (d. 1829)". PhD diss., Music:
       Yale University, 1970. 2 v. UMI 71-16249.
V. 1: A detailed biography of Giuliani and a study of his compositions. Extensively researched with a thorough examination of important source material. Includes general historical background on the
classic six-string guitar, guitar construction, and systems of
notating guitar music. Musical analysis. Port., illus., music,
append., bibliog., 286p.
V. 2: Thematic Catalogue of the Complete Works of Mauro Giuliani.
Main categories are "Works with opus number", "Works without opus
number", "Posthumous works without opus number". Rubrics used by

(474-478)   Early Six-String Histories

the author are "incipits", "autograph", "first edition", "authen-
tication", "copy" (library location), "date", "later editions",
"comments". Append., 218p.
See also: RILM IV/2 (May-Aug 1970) 1834dd[26]; Heck 475 for a summary.

475   HECK, Thomas Fitzsimons. "A new dissertation on the guitar".
       GuitarN CXII (Apr-June 1971) 3-5.
Heck's summary of his dissertation 474.

476   HECK, Thomas Fitzsimons. "Giuliani in Italia". In 3 parts.
       Fronimo II/8 (July 1974) 16-22; II/9 (Oct 1974) 19-28;
       III/10 (Jan 1975) 13-17.
Part 1: A biographical investigation of the life of Giuliani.
Includes many quotations from sources. Main sections in the text are
"Primi anni (1781-1806)" [The first years (1781-1806)] and "Perché
Giuliani lasciò l'Italia?" [Why did Giuliani leave Italy?]. The
author suggests reasons for Giuliani's departure from Italy based on
a study of musical, social, political, and publishing conditions in
Italy at the end of the eighteenth century. Port. (Giuliani), illus.
(facsim. of baptismal deed; frontispiece of op. 5), music (facsim.,
op. 5, p. 1), bibliog. ref. in notes.
Part 2: A study of the life of Giuliani during the years 1819-1824.
Many quotations of source material. Main sections in the text are "Il
ritorno in patria (1819-1824)" [Return to the country (1819-1824)],
"1819-1820: Giuliani in Italia Settentrionale" [1819-1820: Giuliani
in northern Italy], "1820-1823: 'Giuliani è a Roma', (dai 'Quaderni
di conversazione di Beethoven')" [1820-1823: 'Giuliani is in Rome',
(from the 'Booklet of the conversations of Beethoven')]. Port.
(Giuliani), illus. (facsim. of 1819 letter and frontispiece, op.
108), music (facsim.), bibliog. ref. in notes.
Part 3: A study of the life of Giuliani during the years 1824-1829.
Many quotations of source material. Main sections in the text are
"Perché Giuliani si recò a Napoli?" [Why did Giuliani go to Naples?],
"La situazione musicale a Napoli" [The musical situation in Naples],
"Giuliani a Napoli" [Giuliani in Naples], "L'eredità artistica di
Giuliani" [The artistic heredity of Giuliani]. Port., illus.,
bibliog. ref. in notes.

477   HECK, Thomas Fitzsimons. "Giuliani's works for guitar and
       orchestra (or string quartet): A bibliography". *Soundb* III/2
       (May 1976) 23.
A list of seven works by Giuliani (3 concertos, 4 others in theme
and variation form). Includes information on sources, modern editions, dates of first performance, and first publication.

478   HECK, Thomas Fitzsimons. "Mauro Giuliani, birth and death
       dates confirmed". *GuitarR* XXXVII (Fall 1972) 14-15.
Giuliani's birth and death dates are confirmed from a study of
evidence in contemporary documents. Illus. (facsim. of baptismal
record).

Early Six-String Histories   (479-485)

479   HECK, Thomas Fitzsimons. "Mauro Giuliani, birth and death
        dates established". *GuitarN* CXIV (Oct-Dec 1971) 4-7.
Giuliani's birth and death dates are confirmed in a study of evidence found in contemporary documents. Giuliani's baptismal record
and his death notice in the *Giornale del Regno delle Due Sicilie*
are quoted in translation. 2 pl. (facsim.).

480   HECK, Thomas Fitzsimons. "Return with us now. The *Soundboard*'s
        featured facsimile". *Soundb* I/3 (Aug 1974) 22-23.
Brief introductory notes to Giuliani's guitar duet op. 69, "La lira
notturna". Description of the work, historical background included.
Music (facsim. of "Andante sostenuto no. 3" from op. 69).

481   KOCZIRZ, A. "Wiener hss. von Mauro Giuliani" [Viennese
        manuscripts by Giuliani]. *MHaus* I/2 (1927). In De.

482   MAGULA, George. "The guitar concertos of Mauro Giuliani".
        Soundb III/2 (May 1976) 22-23; reprinted in *Guitar* V/4 (Nov
        1976) 7.
A discussion of the general characteristics of orchestration,
musical style, and the idiomatic writing for the guitar in
Giuliani's concertos op. 30 (1810), 36 (1812), and 70 (1816?).
Bibliog. ref. in notes.

483   OPHEE, Matanya. "Who wrote *La Sentinelle*?". *Soundb* VIII/2
        (May 1981) 75-79.
A response to spurious assumptions concerning the authorship of *La
Sentinelle* in Elliker 473. Available sources indicate that the
French composer Alexander Etienne Choron is the original composer
of "La Sentinelle", not Giuliani, Hummel, or Diabelli. Bibliog. ref.
in notes, music.

484   SHULFER, Glen. "Mauro Giuliani: Grand concerto, op. 30. A
        comparative analysis of various editions. Part I: orchestral
        and string quartet versions". *Soundb* V/3 (Aug 1979) 77-81.
Six editions of the Grand Concerto, op. 30 are listed as available
in the Archives of the Guitar Foundation of America. The editions
are evaluated. The original version for guitar and quartet is compared to the editions for guitar and orchestra. Music, bibliog. ref.
in notes.

GRAGNANI, Felipe (b. 1767)

See 471

HORETZKY, Felix (1796-1870)

See also 87, 468

(485-490)   Early Six-String Histories

485 BONE, Philip J. "Felix Horetzky". *Cadenza* IX/6 (Feb 1903)
     10-11.
Biographical information on Horetzky. List of some compositions for
guitar.

486 HECK, Thomas F. "Horetzky e la Giulianiad" [Horetzky and
     The Giulianiad]. *Fronimo* III/12 (July 1975) 23-26. In It.
Accounts of Horetzky and his publications of music as recorded in
The Giulianiad. Includes reviews of his publications. Historical
background on the periodical *The Giulianiad*, the first periodical
devoted to the guitar. Music, bibliog. ref. in notes.
See also: RILM IX/1-2 (Jan-Aug 1975) 1182ap[27].

487 POWRÓZNIAK, Józef. "Felix Horetzky, un grande maestro della
     chitarra" [Felix Horetzky, a great master of the guitar].
     Fronimo III/12 (July 1975) 19-22. In It.
A detailed biography of Horetzky. List of works for guitar, for two
guitars, and for guitar and voice, with and without opus numbers.
Horetzky's transcriptions are included. Music ("Valzer" by
Horetzky).

HUERTA Y KATURLA [CATURLA], Don Trinidad (1804-1875)

See 110, 115

KREUTZER, Joseph (1780-1849)

488 DANNER, Peter. "Return with us now. *Soundboard*'s featured
     facsimile. Kreutzer's variations on 'God save the king'".
     Soundb VIII/1 (Feb 1981) 24 (text), 25-27 (music).
Introductory remarks to the facsimile of Kreutzer's variations on
"God save the king" from Madame Sidney Pratten's *Guitar School*.
Includes historical background and commentary on the composition.
Biographical information on Kreutzer and on Madame Pratten.

LEGNANI, Rinaldo Luigi (1790-1877)

See also 413, 499, 515

489 FERRARI, Romolo. "A guitarist of yore". *Chesterian* XI/86
     (Apr-May 1930) 169-74.
A biographical sketch of Rinaldo Luigi Legnani.

490 ROSSATO, Daniela. "Luigi Rinaldo Legnani". *Fronimo* VII/27
     (Apr 1979) 5-15. In It.
A study of the life and works of Legnani. List of first editions of
works with their library locations cited. A catalogue of works with
and without opus number (publisher). Illus., music, bibliog. ref.
in notes.

Early Six-String Histories   (491-495)

491   "Dalle antiche cronache" [Of old reports]. *AChitarristica*
      I/4 (Aug 1947) 7. In It.
Quotation of the announcements of and the commentary published after
two concerts (1818) by Legnani. Program cited.

492   "Il terzo concerto Legnani a Modena nel 1819" [The third
      concert of Legnani in Modena in 1819]. *AChitarristica* I/4
      (Aug 1947) 8. In It.
Historical notes on Legnani's 1819 concert in Modena. Program is
listed. Quotation of the correspondence between Legnani and the
Società Filarmonica Modenese preceding the concert.

MATIEGKA, Wenzelslaus Thomas (1773-1830)

See also 499, 535-37, 539

493   LIBBERT, Jürgen. "Ein unbekanntes Werk des böhmischen
      Gitarristen Wenzel Matiegka" [An unknown work of Bohemian
      guitarist Wenzel Matiegka]. *GitarreLaute* I/5 (1979) 14-16,
      18-20, 22-24. In De.
A study of the life and works of Matiegka including a summary of
past research, extensive biography, and an examination of selected
compositions with emphasis on a description of the little-known work
"XII Pièces Faciles", op. 3. Also discussed are the following topics:
"Zwölf Kichte Ländler" op. 1 and "Sonate Nr. I", often confused, are
distinguished; background is given on the theme of "Caprice avec
variations" (Ich bin liederlich - Du bis liederlich)", op. 2; a
history of the trio "Noturno pour flute, viole, et guitarre", op.
21 with a comparison to Schubert's quartet version. Modern editions
are cited. List of works with and without opus numbers includes a
citation of the publisher (place) of the first edition of each work
according to Whistling, Bone (51), and Kramer, "Matiegka" (*MGG* VIII).
Illus. (facsim.), music (facsim., incipits), bibliog. ref. in notes,
append. (bibliog. of lit. and of modern editions of music).

MERTZ, Johann Kaspar (1806-1856)

See also 499

494   BONE, Philip J. "J.K. Mertz". *Cadenza* XIII/12 (Aug 1907)
      15-19, 40-41.
A detailed biographical sketch of Mertz. List of works (publisher,
place).

495   MERTZ, Josephine, née Plantin. "Life of the late J.K. Mertz".
      Trans. by J.M. Miller. *Cadenza* I/3 (Jan-Feb 1895) 4.
A translation by J.M. Miller of the biographical information on
Mertz supplied to Miller by Mertz's wife, Josephine, née Plantin.

(496-501)   Early Six-String Histories

496   OPHEE, Matanya (contributor of music) and *Soundboard*'s
       editorial staff (annotation). "Return with us now. *Sound-*
       board's featured facsimile". *Soundb* VI/2 (May 1979) 50 (text),
       51 (title page), 52-55 (music).

Introductory notes to Mertz's transcription for voice and guitar of
Schubert's "Ständchen". Biographical information on Mertz is given.
Illus. (facsim. of title page), music.

497   TYLER, Thomas C.B. "Some compositions by Mertz". *Crescendo*
       III/8 (Feb 1911) 7.
A survey of the compositions and arrangements of Mertz. Brief
descriptions of selected works included.

MOLITOR, Simon (1766-1848)

See also 402, 408

498   PRUSIK, Karl. "Eine kurze Betrachtung der Gitarrewerke von
       Simon Molitor (1766-1848) und Ferdinand Sor (1780-1839)"
       [A short consideration of the guitar works of Simon Molitor
       (1766-1848) and Fernando Sor (1780-1839)]. *ZfdG* IV/4 (Jan
       1925) 3-8. In De.

499   ZUTH, Josef. *Simon Molitor und die Wiener Gitarristik (um*
       1800) [Simon Molitor and the Viennese guitar school (ca.
       1800)]. (Wien: Anton Goll, 1932). In De.
A detailed biographical-bibliographical study of the life and works
of Simon Molitor. Molitor's compositional style, instrumental tech-
nique, and importance in the history of the guitar are discussed.
Biographies of other guitarists active in Vienna are given in an
appendix: Wenzel Matiegka, Alois Wolf, Anton Diabelli, Leonhard von
Call, Wilhelm Klingenbrunner, Franz Tandler, Bartolomeo Bortolazzi,
Mauro Giuliani, Franziska Bolzmann, Franz Mendl, Karl Töpfer,
Leonhard Schulz, Joseph Böhm, Luigi Legnani, Franz Bathioli, Onorato
da Costa, Karl von Gärtner, Franz Stoll, Johann Kaspar Mertz, Eduard
Pique, Emilia Giuliani-Giulielmi, and Giulio Regondi. Music, 8 pl.
(port., illus., music in facsim.), bibliog. of works by Molitor
with library locations cited, bibliog. of source material, 85p.

MORETTI, Federico

See also 61

500   "Music and musicians". *Chelys* I/6 (Dec 1976) 33 (text),
       34-37 (music).
A brief survey of the life and works of Moretti. Introductory
remarks to the music, "Tema con variationes (Les Folies d'Espagne)".
Port. (Moretti).

501   JEFFERY, Brian. "Return with us now. The *Soundboard's* featured
       facsimile". *Soundb* IV/4 (Nov 1977) 96-97.

Early Six-String Histories   (501-508)

Introductory remarks to the facsimile of Moretti's "El Consejo" from
the song cycle *Doce Canciones* (ca. 1812) for voice and guitar.
English translation of the song text included.

502   POSELLI, Franco. "Federico Moretti e il suo ruolo nella storia
       della chitarra" [Federico Moretti and his role in the history
       of the guitar]. *Fronimo* I/4 (July 1973) 11-19.
A detailed study of the contents of Moretti's works for guitar,
published and in manuscript. Biographical information on Moretti.
Evaluation of other authors' research. List of works by Moretti
with library locations cited. 5 fig. (including music in facsim.),
bibliog. ref. in notes.
See also: RILM VIII/2-3 (May-Dec 1974) 2359ap[26].

PAGANINI, Niccolò (1782-1840)

See also 30, 413

503   "Paganini-guitarist". *BMG* LVI/644 (Dec 1958) 53-54.
A brief discussion of Paganini's interest in the guitar with biographical information included.

504   "Paganini. Violinist and guitarist". *Guitarra* (Chicago)
       II/8 (May-June 1964) 20-21.
A brief survey of the education and early career of Paganini. (The
author credits *Grove's dictionary* as his source.)

505   ALVER, Alfred W. "New light on Paganini". *Strad* XL (1929-1930)
       408-09, 473-74, 535-37, 599-600, 663-65. Reprinted in 4 parts
       in *GuitarR* II (1947) 29-30; III (1947) 51-52; V (1948) 115-17;
       VI (1948) 143-44.
A study of Paganini's activities as a performer on and a composer
for the guitar. Idiomatic aspects of his works for guitar are considered. Music, bibliog. ref. in notes.

506   BONE, Philip J. "Paganini and the guitar". *HinrichsenMYb* VII
       (1952) 475-85. Printed also with some changes in *Strad* LXV
       (Aug 1954) 104, 106, 108; (Sept 1954) 136; (Nov 1954) 138,
       140, 224, 226-28.
A biographical survey of the life and works of Paganini with emphasis
on his experiences with the guitar as a performer and as a composer.
Includes a survey of his compositions for guitar, published and in
manuscript. Illus., music.

507   BONE, Philip J. "Paganini-his associations with the mandolin
       and guitar". *Cadenza* XII/2 (Oct 1905) 15-19.
A survey of the life and works of Paganini with emphasis on his
involvement with and his knowledge of the mandolin and guitar.

508   BURTNIEKS, J.A. "Paganini and Boccherini". *GuitarN* XXXI
       5-6.
A survey of the compositions for guitar by Paganini and Boccherini.
Some important works are cited. No biographical information is
given.

(509-515)   Early Six-String Histories

509   KMOCH, Vladimir. "The guitar quartets of Niccolò Paganini".
       (Typescript, Biblioteca del Conservatorio di Genova, 1971).
See also: Prefumo 513.

510   KRICK, George C. "Niccolò Paganini, guitarist". *Etude*
       LVIII/8 (Aug 1940) 567-71.
A short biography of Paganini with emphasis on his interest in
the guitar. Several compositions for guitar are listed.

511   PEEL, Douglas. "Paganini - Artist Supreme". *BMG* LX/694
       (Feb 1963) 161-62.
A biographical survey of the life and works of Paganini. Illus.

512   PREFUMO, Danilo. "Paganini e la chitarra" [Paganini and the
       guitar]. In 2 parts. *Fronimo* VI/23 (Apr 1978) 6-14; VI/24
       (July 1978) 6-15. In It.
Part 1: "Biografia chitarristica" [Biography as a guitarist]. A
biography of Paganini during the years 1795-1835 with emphasis on
his activities as a composer for the guitar. Bibliog. ref. in notes.
Part 2: "Catalogo delle opere per e con chitarra" [Catalogue of
works for guitar and for guitar with other instruments]. Organization by genre. Title, key, movements, date, information on MSS and
first editions, dedication cited.

513   PREFUMO, Danilo. "I quartetti con chitarra di Paganini" [The
       guitar quartets of Paganini]. *Fronimo* VI/22 (Jan 1978) 7-12.
       In It.
A history of the research on and the publication of Paganini's
fifteen quartets with guitar. Includes comments on the research of
Kmoch 509, Stratton, and de Courcy, among others. List of fifteen
works includes information on key, opus number, editor, date, and
dedication. Bibliog. ref. in notes.

514   RADKE, H. "Paganini und die Gitarre" [Paganini and the
       guitar]. *ZfdG* IV (1926) 4. In De.

515   SCHWARZ-REIFLINGEN, Erwin. "Zur Veröffentlichung der
       gitarristischen Kompositionen Niccolò Paganinis" [On the
       publication of the guitar compositions of Niccolò Paganini].
       In 5 parts. *DieGit* VI/1-2 (Oct-Nov 1924) 7-9; VI/5-6 (n.d.)
       27-30; VI/7-8 (n.d.) 45-46; VI/11-12 (n.d.) 71-72; VII/1-2
       (n.d.) 10-11. In De.
A survey of Paganini's works for guitar and a study of contemporary
accounts of Paganini's activities as a guitarist-composer.
Part 1: A summary of available works for guitar by Paganini, including unpublished manuscripts. Description of stylistic aspects of
the music; discussion of recent discoveries of music (early 20th
century). Some biographical notes included.
Part 2: Accounts of Paganini as a guitarist by his contemporaries.
Part 3: Includes remarks on Schotty's biography of Paganini and
comments about Paganini by Berlioz.
Part 4: Further references to contemporary accounts of Paganini as
a guitarist. Paganini's association with Legnani is mentioned.

Early Six-String Histories   (515-521)

Part 5: A comparison of Paganini's guitar technique to his violin technique based on information from sources.

516   TONAZZI, Bruno. "Gli interessi chitarristici di Paganini" [The guitaristic interests of Paganini]. *Fronimo* III/13 (Oct 1975) 5-10. In It.
A discussion of Paganini's works for solo guitar and for guitar quartet. Mauro Giuliani's influence on Paganini is considered. Includes information on Paganini's original autographs. Music, bibliog. ref. in notes.
See also: RILM IX/3 (Sept-Dec 1975) 3803ap[27].

517   YAMPOL'SKY, Izrail Markovič. "Paganini-guitarist" [Paganini-guitarist]. *SovetskajaM* XXIV (Sept 1960) 133-38. In Ru.

PELZER, Ferdinand (1801-1861) and daughters Catherine Josepha (Madame Sidney PRATTEN) (1821-1895) and Giulia (1839-1938)

See also 30, 391, 488

518   "An eminent guitarist". *Cadenza* VIII/12 (Aug 1902) 10-11.
A biographical sketch of Madame Sidney Pratten.

519   "Madame Giulia Pelzer, mandolin and guitar artiste, of London, England". *Cadenza* VI/3 (Jan-Feb 1900) 19-20. Reprinted from *The Gentlewoman's court review*.
A biographical sketch of Madame Giulia Pelzer.

520   APPLEBY, Wilfrid M. "The story of a guitar". In 3 chapters. *GuitarN* LXIV (March-Apr 1962) 6-11; LXV (May-June 1962) 8-12; LXVI (July-Aug 1962) 20-25.
Ch. 1: "Autobiographical". Appleby's account of his purchase of the concert guitar owned by Catherine Josepha Pratten. Illus. (photograph of the guitar, guitar case, and an engraving of Josepha with the guitar).
Ch. 2: "Ferdinand Pelzer". A biographical study of the life of Ferdinand Pelzer. Commentary on his activities as a guitarist. Compositions cited. Includes information on *The Giulianiad*.
Ch. 3: "Madame Sidney Pratten". A biographical study of Madame Sidney Pratten, née Pelzer, with emphasis on her career as a performer and as a teacher. Biographical sketch of Giulia Pelzer included.

521   HARRISON, Frank M. *Reminiscences of Madame Sidney Pratten, guitarist and composer*. (London, 1899).

PRATTEN, Catherine Josepha (Madame Sidney)

See Pelzer, Ferdinand

(522-528)   Early Six-String Histories

REGONDI, Giulio (1822-1872)

See also 401, 413, 499

522   BONE, Philip J. "Giulio Regondi". *Cadenza* IX/2 (Oct 1902)
       10-12.
A biographical sketch of Regondi. List of works for guitar (title,
opus, publisher).

523   BONE, Philip J. "Regondi's arrival in England, 1831".
       Cadenza X/12 (Aug 1904) 17-18.
An account of Regondi's success as a performer in London. Reports
of contemporary critics are considered.

524   S., A.L. "Regondi e la sua musica" [Regondi and his music].
       AChitarristica V/25-26 (Jan-Apr 1951) 1-2. In It.
An evaluation and a stylistic description of Regondi's "Rèverie
Nocturne" op. 19, "1er Air varié" op. 21, "2eme Air varié" op. 22,
and "Introduction et Caprice" op. 23.

525   ZUTH, Josef. "Eine Handschrift von Giulio Regondi" [A
       manuscript of Giulio Regondi]. *MHaus* VI (1927) 78-80. In
       De.

SCHEIDLER, Christian Gottlieb (ca. 1752-1815)

526   "Christian Gottlieb Scheidler (ca. 1752-1815)". *GuitarN*
       XXXII (Aug-Sept 1956) 29.
The emphasis of the article is on the importance of Scheidler in
the rise of the popularity of the guitar in the early nineteenth
century. Includes an English translation of a quotation of an
account concerning Scheidler in the *AMZ* of 1806.

527   S., K. "Christian Gottlieb Scheidler (ca. 1752-1815).
       Ultimo liutista e primo chitarrista Tedesco" [Christian
       Gottlieb Scheidler (ca. 1752-1815). The last lutenist and
       the first guitarist of Germany]. *AChitarristica* V/28
       (July-Aug 1951) 5. In It.
A survey of the life and works of Scheidler, an important transitional figure in the shift in popularity from the lute to the
guitar. Quotations from the *AMZ* (1806) included.

528   ZUTH, Josef. "Christian Gottlieb Scheidler, der letzte
       Lautenist, der erste Gitarremeister Deutschlands" [Christian
       Gottlieb Scheidler, the last lutenist, the first guitar master
       in Germany]. *DieGit* I/4 (Jan 1920) 65-66. In De.
Scheidler, a virtuoso on both the lute and the guitar, is noted as
an important transitional figure in the shift in popularity from

Early Six-String Histories   (528-533)

the lute to the guitar in Germany. Reference to concerts performed
by Scheidler as reviewed in the *AMZ*. Repertoire discussed.
Scheidler's works in modern editions are cited.

SCHUBERT, Franz (1797-1828)

See also 403, 493, 496

529   DANNER, Peter. "Return with us now. *Soundboard's* featured
       facsimile. An anonymous setting of Goethe's 'Erlkönig'".
       Soundb VIII/3 (Aug 1981) 172 (text), 173 (German song text
       and English trans.), 174 (facsim. of title page), 175-78
       (facsim. of music for voice and guitar).
Background on the song by Schubert and other arrangements of the
song as listed in the Whistling/Hofmeister *Handbuch der Musikalischen Literatur*. Remarks on the anonymous setting reprinted in
facsimile. The musical arrangement in relationship to the meaning
of the text is evaluated.

530   DEUTSCH, Otto Erich. "Schubert ohne Gitarre" [Schubert
       without guitar]. *OesterreichGitarreZ* (Schubert-Gabe, 1928)
       18-26. In De.
Deutsch's refutal of incorrect theories about Schubert's association
with the guitar as a player of and as a composer for the instrument.
Criticism of Schmid 538. Study of the recently discovered quartet
with objections raised to its attribution exclusively to Schubert.
See also: Heck 533, part 3, p. 40, Heck 534 (in It.), and Hoorickx
535 for comments.

531   HECK, Thomas Fitzsimons. "Return with us now. The *Soundboard's*
       featured facsimile. A first edition Schubert Lied with
       guitar". *Soundb* IV/2 (May 1977) 42-43.
Introductory notes to the facsimile reprint of Schubert's Lied
"Nacht und Träume", version with accompaniment for guitar. Infor-
mation on the sources of the work. Translation of the song text.

532   HECK, Thomas Fitzsimons. "Return with us now. The *Soundboard's*
       featured facsimile. A first edition Schubert Lied with
       guitar". *Soundb* VI/1 (Feb 1979) 17-19.
Introductory notes to the facsimile reprint of Schubert's Lied op.
20, no. 3 "Hänflings Liebeswerbung", version with accompaniment for
the guitar. Historical background and description of the work included. Translation of song text.

533   HECK, Thomas Fitzsimons. "Schubert Lieder with guitar ...
       permissible?" In 3 parts. *Soundb* III/4 (Nov 1976) 72; IV/1
       (Feb 1977) 12-13, 16; IV/2 (May 1977) 39-41.
A study of evidence of the publication of Schubert's Lieder arranged
with guitar accompaniment during and immediately after Schubert's
lifetime based primarily on listings in Hofmeister/Whistling *Handbuch
der Musikalischen Litteratur* (1822-1834). Extensive quotations of the

(533-539)   Early Six-String Histories

Handbuch. Opinions on the research of Otto Erich Deutsch. Conclusions
drawn concerning the transcription of Schubert Lieder for voice and
guitar as an historically valid performance practice. "Schubert
Lieder with guitar accompaniment published in Vienna during the composer's lifetime: A preliminary catalog": Organized chronologically
by opus number. Deutsch number, title (poet), and text incipit
listed. Detail on first edition guitar version and first edition
piano version is given. Bibliog. ref. in notes.
See also: Heck 534 for an Italian translation.

534   HECK, Thomas Fitzsimons. "I Lieder di Schubert per chitarra"
       [Schubert Lieder with guitar]. In 2 parts. *Fronimo* VI/24
       (July 1978) 16-21; VI/25 (Oct 1978) 24-29. In It.
An Italian translation of Heck 533.

535   HOORICKX, Fr. Reinhard van. "Schubert's guitar quartet".
       RBelgeMusicol XXXI (1977) 111-35.
Detailed historical background on Schubert's quartet arrangement
of the original trio by Wenzel Matiegka. Discussion of the 1918 discovery of Schubert's manuscript with extensive references to contemporary opinions on authenticity and confusion over the findings.
Examination of the consequences of the subsequent discovery in 1931 of
the trio by Matiegka. Includes a comparison of the two works. Opinions
on the writings of Otto Erich Deutsch and of Georg Kinsky are considered. Discog., music, bibliog. ref. in notes.

536   KINSKY, Georg. "Zu Schuberts Gitarren-Quartett" [On Schubert's
       guitar quartet]. *ZfMw* XIV (1932) 476-78. In De.
Notes on the discovery of the trio for flute, viola, and guitar by
Wenzeslaus Matiegka which Schubert arranged as a quartet. Schubert's
alterations of the original are described. Biographical information
on Matiegka included. Music, bibliog. ref. in notes.

537   KRICK, George C. "The Franz Schubert quartet". *FINews* XXIV/3
       (May-June 1955) 9.
Historical notes on the discovery of Schubert's quartet and on the
subsequent finding of the original trio by Wenzel Matiegka.

538   SCHMID, Heinrich Kaspar. "Franz Schuberts neuendecktes
       Quartett. Ein offener Brief" [Franz Schubert's newly dis-
       covered quartet. An open letter]. *ZfMw* I (Dec 1918) 183-88.
       In De.
The first announcement of the discovery of the Schubert quartet.
See also: Deutsch 530 for criticism.

539   SCHWARZ-REIFLINGEN, Erwin. "Das Rätsel des Schubert-
       Quartetts gelöst!" [The puzzle of the lost Schubert
       quartet]. In 2 parts. *DieGit* XII/11-12 (1931?) 80-82;
       XIII/1-2 (1933) 1-4. In De.

Early Six-String Histories   (539-546)

Historical background on the Schubert quartet and on the subsequent finding of the original trio by Wenzel Matiegka. Discussion
of Schubert's treatment of the original trio with a comparison of
the two versions. Short discussion of each movement.

540   SCHWARZ-REIFLINGEN, Erwin. "Ein unbekanntes Schubert-
       Quartett mit Gitarre" [An unknown quartet with guitar by
       Schubert]. *DieGit* IV/2 (Nov 1922) 11-15. In De.
Speculations about the authenticity of the Schubert quartet and
about Schubert's contact with the guitar and guitarists. Description of the manuscript by Schubert with notes on stylistic aspects
of the music of each movement. Pre-dates the discovery of the
original trio by Wenzel Matiegka.

SOR [SORS], Joseph Fernando Macari (1778-1839)

See also 13, 32, 400, 401, 405, 406, 410, 412, 419-21, 460, 473,
498, 701, 810, 926, 935

541   "Sor". *Encyclopédia pittoresque de la musique*, p. 154-67. In
       Fr.
A biography of Sor published during his lifetime.
See also: Jeffery 558, p. 117-30, for a facsimile reproduction and
Moser 563 for a German translation.

542   [Sor's obituary]. *AMZ* XLI/30 (24 July 1839) 593-94. In De.
The obituary of Fernando Sor. Some biographical information is
included.

543   "Fernando Sor. Zwölf Regeln des Gitarrenspiels" [Twelve
       rules of guitar playing]. *DieGit* V/3-4 (Dec-Jan 1923/24)
       22-23. In De.
Quotation of Sor's twelve rules of guitar playing.

544   ANDERSON, Peter. "The guitarist and the naked lady". *BMG*
       LXVII/764 (Dec 1968) 104-05.
A biography of Sor with information on his patroness, the Duchess
of Alba, and his patron, the Duke of Sussex.

545   APPLEBY, Wilfrid M. "Ferdinand Sor". *GuitarN* XXIII (Feb-Mar
       1955) 2-4.
A short biography of Sor with emphasis on his career as a performer
and on the success of his publications for guitar. Some inaccuracies.

546   APPLEBY, Wilfrid M. "An Italian friend of Fernando Sor. Un
       amico italiano de Ferdinando Sor". In 2 parts. *AChitarristica*
       II/9 (June 1948) 2-3; II/10-11 (Aug-Oct 1948) 4-5. In En
       and in It.
Part 1: A description of four volumes of music in the author's
possession which originally belonged to Philippo Verini (ca. 1782-

123

(546-554)   Early Six-String Histories

ca. 1849), an acquaintance of Sor. The contents of the volumes include early editions of Sor's music, some with Sor's autograph, and
music by Verini dedicated to Sor.
Part 2: Biographical information on Verini. Compositions cited.

547   BOSMAN, Lance. "Variations 5". *Guitar* V/3 (Oct 1976) 32-33.
An analysis of Sor's treatment of the variation form as shown in his
"Variations on a theme from Mozart's *Magic Flute*". Information on
Giuliani's treatment of the variation form is also included. Music
(Sor and Giuliani). Little background in theory is required.

548   BURTNIEKS, J.A. "Fernando Sor". *GuitarR* XVIII (1955) 192.
A short biographical summary of Sor's career. Information is based
on Bone 51. Music.

549   CASANOVA, Maria Julia. "Fernando Sor". *Guitarra* (Havana)
         I/1 (Dec 1940) 13, 15. In Sp.
A biographical sketch of Sor.

550   DELL'ARA, Mario. "La musica di Mozart nelle transcrizioni
         ovvero variazioni per chitarra di Fernando Sor" [The music
         of Mozart in the transcriptions or variations for guitar by
         Fernando Sor]. *Fronimo* IV/17 (Oct 1976) 6-14. In It.
Sor's treatment of the music from Mozart's "The Magic Flute" in
his theme and variation forms is examined. Sor's "Six Airs", op.
19, arranged for guitar are considered individually with comparisons
made to the original models by Mozart. Music (Sor and Mozart).

551   DELL'ARA, Mario. "Le tre sonate per chitarra di Fernando Sor"
         [The three sonatas for guitar by Fernando Sor]. *Fronimo* VI/23
         (Apr 1978) 19-27. In It.
A survey of Sor's career. History and analysis of Sor's three
sonatas for guitar, op. 15b, 22 ("Grand Sonata"), and 25 ("Second
Grand Sonata"). Music.

552   DOUGLAS, Anthony C. "F. Sor and a survey of classical guitar
         music". *Musart* XXVII/1 (1974) 39-41.
A survey of Sor's compositions with some commentary on technical and
structural features of representative works. Includes an annotated
survey of 44 publications of music for classical guitar. Collections,
arrangements, transcriptions, methods, and editions are cited.
Bibliog.

553   EUSEBIO, Font y Moreso. "Una visita a Sors en los últimos
         días de su vida" [A visit with Sor in the last days of his
         life]. *Notas musicales y literarias* XX (12 Nov 1882); XXI
         (19 Nov 1882). In Sp.

554   GUITAR REVIEW EDITORS. "Fernando Sor". *GuitarR* I (1946) 7-8.
"A biographical sketch read at the second recital of the Society of
the Classic Guitar, New York, June 17, 1946". A short biography and
a list of works organized by opus number. Illus.

Early Six-String Histories   (555-560)

555   HARRIS, John. "Fernando Sor in London". *Guitar* III/5 (Dec
       1974) 23-24.
A study of Sor's activities in London based on contemporary records.
Information on the Philharmonic Society included. Illus., port.

556   JEFFERY, Brian. "L'attivita' concertistica di Fernando Sor"
       [Fernando Sor, concert performer]. *Fronimo* II/6 (Jan 1974)
       6-13. In It.
A biographical survey of Sor's performing career. Organization is
chronological with a consideration of his activities in the following countries: Spain, England, France, and Russia. Many contemporary
accounts and reviews of Sor's performances are cited. Bibliog. ref.
in notes.
See also: Jeffery 557 for an English translation.

557   JEFFERY, Brian. "Fernando Sor, concert performer". *GuitarR*
       XXXIX (Summer 1974) 6-10 (text), 11-16 (music).
A translation of Jeffery 556 by the author. Bibliog. ref. in notes.
Illus.

558   JEFFERY, Brian. *Fernando Sor, composer and guitarist.* (London:
       Tecla Editions, 1977).
A detailed account of the life and works of Sor. Extensively re-
searched study of source material. Organized chronologically with
the following chapter divisions: Ch. 1: Spain 1778-1813; Ch. 2:
Paris 1813-1815; Ch. 3: London 1815-1823; Ch. 4: Paris, Berlin,
Warsaw, Moscow, and St. Petersburg 1823-26/7; Ch. 5: Paris 1826/7-
1839. Includes a facsimile reprint of the biography of Sor in
Encyclopédie pittoresque de la musique, published during Sor's
lifetime and possibly written by him. An extensive catalogue of
Sor's works, organized by genre, with information on editions,
library locations, printing format, plate numbers, issues, pages,
date, opus number. Port., illus., music, index, 197p.
Reviews: Richard Pinnell, *Soundb* IV/2 (May 1977) 44; *CGuitarInt*
V/1 (Fall 1977) 12-13; *MMusicians* XXVI (Apr 1978) 38; *GuitarP* XII/4
(Apr 1978) 22; Michael Fink, *GuitarLute* VII (Sept. 1978) 39-40;
Guitar VIII/3 (Oct 1978) 34; *MTimes* CXIX (Jan 1978) 42; *MLetters*
LIX/4 (1978) 490-92.

559   JEFFERY, Brian. "The original version true text of Sor's
       'L'Encouragement'". *Soundb* VII/4 (Nov 1980) 159-60.
An examination of the only copy of the original edition of Sor's
duet for two guitars "L'Encouragement" op. 34 (Paris: Sor and
Pacini, [1828?]). The work is compared to other inauthentic versions; in particular, the arrangement of Napoleon Coste is considered.
See also: Jeffery 560 for an Italian translation.

560   JEFFERY, Brian. "Il vero testo de 'L'Encouragement' di
       Fernando Sor" [The original version true text of Fernando
       Sor's 'L'Encouragement']. *Fronimo* IX/34 (Jan 1981) 34-35.
       In It.
An Italian translation of Jeffery 559.

(561-568)   Early Six-String Histories

561   MACKÉVITCH, M. V.-P. "Fernando Sor en Russie" [Fernando Sor
      in Russia]. *GMusique* XVI (Feb-March 1958) 12-13. In Fr.

562   MOSER, Wolf. "Fernando Sor und seine 'Methode pour la
      guitare'" [Fernando Sor and his 'Method for the guitar'].
      GitarreLaute I/I (1979) 26-32. In De.
The method of Sor is considered in an historical context and for its
instructional text. Biographical information on Sor included. Extensive selections from Sor's text are translated with annotations.
Illus. (facsim.), bibliog. ref. in notes.

563   MOSER, Wolf. "Sammlung historischer Quellen. Sor" [Collec-
      tion of historical sources. Sor]. In 7 parts. *GitarreLaute*
      I/2 (1979) 26-27 (1-2); I/3 (1979) 18-20 (3-5); I/4 (1979)
      14-15 (6-7); I/5 (1979) 26-27; I/6 (1979) 16-17 (10-11);
      II/1 (1980) 24-25 (12-14); II/2 (1980) 23-25 (15-17). (Page
      numbers in parentheses indicate original pagination.) In De.
A German translation of the biography of Sor published in the
Encyclopédia pittoresque de la musique (Paris, 1835) by A. Ledhuy
and H. Bertini. Introductory notes include a discussion of the
possibility that the article may have been written by Sor.
See also: 541 (original source) and Jeffery 558 for a facsimile
reprint.

564   N. "Sor. To the editor of the *Giulianiad*". *Giulianiad*
      III/1 (1833) 27-28. Reprinted in *GuitarR* XVIII (1955)
      179-80.
A letter to the editor in praise of Sor as a composer and as a
performer. The author compares the abilities of Giuliani and Sor.
Editor's response to the letter.

565   PERRY, Francis. "Fernando Sor and the modern guitarist".
      MJ XXXV/6 (July 1977) 55-56.
Notes on Sor's guitar method. Particular attention is given to his
technical considerations as they apply to the concerns of the modern
guitarist. Illus., music.

566   RIERRA, Juan. "Fernando Sor". *GMusique* XXII (June, July,
      Aug 1959) 2-4. In Fr.

567   ROBERTS, John. "Historical notes: A review of Sor's method,
      1831". *Guitar* VII/4 (Nov 1978) 13.
A reprint of a review of Sor's *Method* originally printed in *Revue et
Gazette Musicale* (Paris, 1831). Introductory comments include
information on Carulli and other contemporary guitarists.
Description of the *Method*.

568   ROBERTS, John, trans. "Notes from Sor's tutor". *Guitar* IV/4
      (Nov 1975) 23.
A translation of selections from the text of the 1845 French
edition of Sor's *Method*. Includes comments on guitar technique
and on guitarist Aguado. Port. (Sor).

Early Six-String Histories   (569-576)

569   ROMEA, Alfredo. "Ferdinand Sor". In 3 parts. *DieGit* IX/5-6
      (May-June 1928) 33-36; IX/9-10 (1928) 65-67; IX/11-12 (1928)
      78-81. In De.
A lecture preceding a concert in Barcelona for the "Friends of
music". Portrait of Sor as an artist and as a man. Biographical
notes and anecdotes about his life include references to early
nineteenth-century sources. Summary of some stylistic aspects of
Sor's music.

570   ROSSI, A. "Sor und seine Gitarrenschule" [Sor and his
      guitar method]. In 2 parts. *DieGit* V/3-4 (Dec-Jan 1923/24)
      16-19; V/5-6 (Feb-March 1924) 29-35. In De. A translation of
      an article by Oswald Lorenz in *Il Plettro* (Milan).
A description of the contents of Sor's publication of studies.
Quotations from Sor's text include his remarks on the art of
accompaniment.

571   SASSER, William Gray. "The guitar works of Fernando Sor".
      PhD diss., Music: The University of North Carolina, 1960.
      UMI 6006995.
A biographical-analytical study with historical background on the
guitar. Available sources of Sor's music (published and in MS) and
literature concerning Sor are investigated thoroughly. Detailed
analysis of performance practices and idiomatic writing. 7 pl., 6
tables, append., music, bibliog., list of Sor's works, 177p.

572   SASSER, William Gray. "In search of Sor". *GuitarR* XXVI
      (June 1962) 13-21.
A biography of Sor based on evidence drawn from sources. Catalogue
of Sor's compositions. Illus., ports.

573   SCHÜSSE, Erich. "Wegweiser durch Sors Gitarrewerke" [Guide
      through Sor's guitar works]. *DieGit* V/3-4 (Dec-Feb 1924)
      24-26. In De.
A general survey of Sor's works. Short descriptions of some representative works are given.

574   [SCHWARZ-REIFLINGEN, Erwin]. "Zum Geleit. Ferdinand Sor"
      [Introduction. Ferdinand Sor]. *DieGit* V/3-4 (Dec-Jan
      1923/24) 15. In De.
A short biographical sketch of Sor.

575   SCHWARZ-REIFLINGEN, Erwin, ed. and trans. "Ferd[inand]
      Sor. Über der Anschlag" [Ferdinand Sor. Concerning the
      stroke]. *DieGit* V/3-4 (Dec-Jan 1923/24) 19-22. In De.
A translation of the text from Sor's method concerning right-hand
technique.

576   TEMPEL, H. "Bemerkungen und Gedanken über Sor" [Remarks and
      thoughts about Sor]. *Gfreund* XXIV (1923) 5-7, 21-29; XXV
      (1924) 8-9; XXVI (1925) 3-6, 24. In De.

(577-583)   Early Six-String Histories

577   SCARLATTI, Vincenzo. "Clasicos antiguo". *Guitarra* (Chicago)
       V/27 (July-Aug 1967) 18-19. In En.
Notes on the life and works of Sor. Port.

578   VOLMAN, Boris. "Sor in Russia". Trans. from the Russian by
       A. Chesnakov. *GuitarN* LXIV (Mar-Apr 1962) 17.
An account of the activities of Sor and his wife, Madame Gulièn-
Sor in Russia, 1823-1825. Emphasis is on their contribution to the
theatre.

579   WADE, Graham. "The guitarist's repertoire". *BMG* LXIX/794
       (June 1971) 305.
Some general comments on and an evaluation of Sor's 20 studies.

580   WADE, Graham. "The guitarist's repertoire". *BMG* LXIX/795
       (July 1971) 327.
A brief survey of selected studies by Sor: no. 5 (b minor), no. 6
(D major), no. 9 (a minor), no. 12 (A major). Consideration is given
to technical aspects and to musical interpretation.

581   WADE, Graham. "The guitarist's repertoire". *BMG* LXIX/796
       (Aug 1971) 359.
A discussion of Sor's contribution to the guitar repertoire.
Includes a brief description of stylistic aspects of the "Grand
Solo", op. 14.

582   WAGNER, Frank. "Sor's daughter performed at 8". *CGuitarInt*
       IV/1 (Fall 1976) 28-30.
A report of Sor's concert in Warsaw, Poland. Quotations of reviews
of the concert indicate that a vocal performance by Sor's daughter
was included in the program. Port.

583   ZURFLUH, Jean. "Fernando Sor". *GMusique* I (May 1955) 6.
       In Fr.

STOLL, Franz de Paula

See 413, 499

THOMPSON, General T. Perronet (1783-1869)

See also 926

Note: The enharmonic guitar, invented by Thompson, had a fingerboard
divided into fifty-nine parts. Entry 584 and 585 refer to Thompson's
theoretical text supporting the use of the principles of just intonation in fretting the guitar.

128

Early Six-String Histories   (584-589)

584   *"Instructions to my daughter for playing on the enharmonic
      guitar, by a member of the University of Cambridge. Goulding
      and D'Almaine"*. *Giulianiad* III/1 (1833) 51-53.
A review of Thompson's *Instructions* (1829).

585   JOHNSON, Leonard George. *General T. Perronet Thompson 1783-
      1869. His military, literary and political campaigns*. (London:
      George Allen and Unwin Ltd., 1957).
A biography of General Thompson. Discussion of the purpose and contents of Thompson's *Instructions* (1829) is found on p. 157-58. Pl.,
illus., port., facsim., bibliog. ref. in notes, 294p.

WEBER, Carl Maria von (1786–1826)

586   "Zur Musikbeilage. Carl Maria von Weber. Gitarrelieder"
      [For the music supplement. Carl Maria von Weber. Lieder
      for guitar]. *DieGit* XI/3-4 (1930) 27-29. In De.
A discussion of Weber's use of the guitar as an accompaniment
instrument. Remarks on representative compositions included.

587   HAAS, Robert. "Karl Maria von Webers Theaterlieder zur
      Gitarre" [Karl Maria von Weber's theatre lieder for guitar].
      ZfdG V/5 (July 1926) 97-99. In De.

588   ROEMER, Kammersanger. "Karl Maria von Webers Gitarrewerke"
      [Karl Maria von Weber's works for guitar]. *Gfreund* XXII
      (1921) 49-51. In De.

589   SCHWARZ-REIFLINGEN, Erwin. "Die Gitarre in [Carl Maria von]
      Webers Musik zu 'Donna Diana'" [The guitar in Carl Maria von
      Weber's music for 'Donna Diana']. *DieGit* IX/3-4 (Mar-Apr
      1928) 26-26. In De.
A consideration of Weber's use of the guitar in five of the six
pieces of incidental music for the play "Donna Diana". Background
on the play and the function of music in the play is included.

ZANI DE FERRANTI, Marc Aurelio

See FERRANTI, Marc Aurelio Zani de

MISCELLANEOUS COMPOSERS AND GUITARISTS

Entries 590 through 628, written by Philip J. Bone, are published in *The
Cadenza* (1901-1908). The reader is advised that Bone's information
is often inaccurate. Information in *Grove* and *MGG* on composers'
names and dates which conflict with Bone's information is noted.

129

590   BONE, Philip J. "Aimon". *Cadenza* X/10 (June 1904) 13-14.
A biography of Pamphile Leopold François Aimon (1779-1866), guitarist, violinist, and composer. Some compositions are mentioned.

591   BONE, Philip J. "Johann Andreas Amon". *Cadenza* X/11 (July 1904) 13-14.
A biography of Johann Andreas Amon (1763-1825), guitarist and composer. List of compositions.

592   BONE, Philip J. "Guillaume Pierre Antoine". *Cadenza* IX/4 (Dec 1902) 10-11.
A biography of Guillaume Pierre Antoine ("Gatayes") (1774-1846), guitarist and composer. List of some works for guitar.

593   BONE, Philip J. "Johann Gottfried Arnold". *Cadenza* XI/2 (Oct 1904) 13-14.
A biography of Johann Gottfried Arnold (1773-1806), guitarist, 'cellist, and composer. List of compositions. Also includes biographical notes on Friedrich Wilhelm Arnold (1810-1864), guitarist and composer. List of compositions.

594   BONE, Philip J. "Friedrich August Baumbach". *Cadenza* XI/1 (Sept. 1904) 14.
A biography of Friedrich August Baumbach (1753-1813), guitarist, mandolinist, and orchestra conductor. List of compositions.
Grove: Works for guitar, listed in *MGG,* are now lost.

595   BONE, Philip J. "Henry August Birnbach". *Cadenza* X/11 (July 1904) 10-11.
A biography of Henry August Birnbach (1782-1840), guitarist, 'cellist, and arpeggione player.

596   BONE, Philip J. "Carl Ludwig Blum . *Cadenza* XI/2 (Oct 1904) 27-29.
A biography of Carl Ludwig Blum (1786-1844), guitarist and composer. List of compositions.

597   BONE, Philip J. "Jean Nepomucene de Bobrowicz". *Cadenza* IX/8 (Apr 1903) 10-11.
A biography of Jean Nepomucene de Bobrowicz (1805-1857), guitarist and composer. List of compositions.
Grove: Jan Nepomucen Bobrowicz (1805-1881).

598   BONE, Philip J. "Jan van Boom". *Cadenza* XII/5 (Jan 1906) 10.
A biography of Jan van Boom (b.1773), flutist and composer. List of compositions including some works for guitar.
Grove: Johannes van Boom (1783-1878).

599   BONE, Philip J. "Bartolomeo Bortolazzi". *Cadenza* VII/11 (July 1901) 14-15.
A biography of Bartolomeo Bortolazzi (b. 1773), mandolinist, guitarist, and composer. List of compositions.

Early Six-String Histories   (600-609)

600   BONE, Philip J. "Aubery du Boulley". *Cadenza* XI/9 (May 1905)
        10-11.
A biography of Aubery du Boulley (b.1796), guitarist and composer.
List of compositions.

601   BONE, Philip J. "Luigi Castellacci". *Cadenza* XIII/12 (Aug 1907)
        10-11.
A biography of Luigi Castellacci (b.1797), mandolinist, guitarist,
and composer. List of compositions.

602   BONE, Philip J. "Charles Doisy". *Cadenza* XIII/10 (June 1907)
        10-11.
A biography of Charles Doisy (d.1807), guitarist. List of compositions.

603   BONE, Philip J. "Justus Johann F. Dotzauer". *Cadenza* XII/2
        (Oct 1905) 10-11.
A biography of Justus Johann F. Dotzauer (1783-1860), guitarist,
'cellist, and composer. Description of his work for guitar and 'cello.

604   BONE, Philip J. "Carl Eulenstein, guitarist and composer".
        Cadenza IX/9 (May 1903) 15-17.
A biography of Carl Eulenstein (b.1802). List of compositions.
Grove: Charles Eulenstein (1802-1890).

605   BONE, Philip J. "Josef Fischof". *Cadenza* XII/7 (Mar 1906) 10.
A biography of Josef Fischof (1804-1857), guitarist, pianist, and
composer. List of compositions.
Grove: Josef Fischhof.

606   BONE, Philip J. "Caspar Fürstenau and Anton Bernhard Fürstenau".
        Cadenza XV/2 (Aug 1908) 29.
Biographies of guitarist-composers Caspar Fürstenau (1772-1819) and son
Anton Bernhard Fürstenau (1792-1852). List of compositions.

607   BONE, Philip J. "John Gansbacher". *Cadenza* XV/1 (June 1908) 31.
A biography of John Gansbacher (1778-1844), guitarist, composer, and
capellmeister of the Cathedral at Vienna. List of compositions.

608   BONE, Philip J. "Carl Gollmick". *Cadenza* XIII/5 (Jan 1907) 10.
A biography of Carl Gollmick (1796-1866), guitarist, pianist, and
composer. List of compositions.
MGG: Friedrich Karl (1774-1852), father of Carl, is credited with
works for guitar.

609   BONE, Philip J. "Antoine Graeffer". *Cadenza* XII/7 (Mar 1906)
        11-12.
A biography of Antoine Graeffer (1780-ca. 1830), guitarist and composer. List of compositions.

131

(610-619)   Early Six-String Histories

610   BONE, Philip J. "August Harder – guitarist and composer". *Cadenza*
       XII/5 (Jan 1906) 15-16.
A biography of August Harder (1774-1813), guitarist, pianist, and com-
poser. List of compositions.
Grove: August Harder (1775-1813).

611   BONE, Philip J. "Friedrich Heinrich Himmel". *Cadenza* XIV/4
       (Dec 1907) 12.
A biography of Friedrich Heinrich Himmel (1765-1814), guitarist and
composer. List of compositions.

612   BONE, Philip J. "Don F. Huerta, guitarist, vocalist, and com-
       poser". *Cadenza* VIII/11 (July 1902) 14-15.
A biography of Don F. Huerta (b.1805). List of compositions.

613   BONE, Philip J. "Johann Nepomuk Hummel". *Cadenza* XI/6 (Feb
       1906) 10-12.
A biography of Johann Nepomuk Hummel (1778-1837), guitarist, pianist,
and composer. Includes comments on his association with Giuliani.
List of compositions.

614   BONE, Philip J. "Joseph Kuffner". *Cadenza* XII/12 (Aug 1906)
       11-14.
A biography of Joseph Kuffner (1776-1856), guitarist and composer.
List of compositions.
MGG: Lists Joseph Küffner II (1777-1856) as a guitarist-composer.

615   BONE, Philip J. "Antoine Lemoine". *Cadenza* XII/10 (June 1906)
       10-11.
A biography of Antoine Marcel Lemoine (1763-1817), guitarist and
publisher. List of compositions for guitar.
Grove: Antoine Marcel Lemoine (1753-1817).

616   BONE, Philip J. "C. Lintant". *Cadenza* XIII/11 (July 1907) 10.
A biography of Lintant (1758-1830), guitarist, violinist, and composer. List of compositions.

617   BONE, Philip J. "Victor Magnien". *Cadenza* XII/6 (Feb 1906) 13-14.
A biography of Victor Magnien (1804-1885), guitarist, violinist, and
composer. List of compositions.

618   BONE, Philip J. "Joseph Mayseder". *Cadenza* XIII/1 (Sept 1906)
       10-11.
A biography of Joseph Mayseder (1789-1863), guitarist, violinist, and
composer. Notes on his association with Giuliani. List of compositions
for guitar.

619   BONE, Philip J. "Antoine and Joseph Meissonnier". *Cadenza* XI/11
       (July 1905) 14-16.
A biography of the brothers Antoine and Joseph Meissonnier, guitarists, composers, and publishers. List of compositions.

Early Six-String Histories   (620-628)

620   BONE, Philip J. "Giacomo Merchi". *Cadenza* XII/10 (June 1906) 10.
A biography of the father and son Giacomo Merchi, (son born 1730),
performers and teachers of the guitar, mandoline, and colascione. List
of compositions by both musicians.
Grove: Brothers Giacomo and Joseph Bernard were both guitarists-
composers and are often confused. No mention of the father Giacomo is
made. In *Grove*, Joseph Bernard is credited with the composition of two
methods which are attributed to Giacomo in *RISM* and in Appendix II of
this bibliography.

621   BONE, Philip J. "Don François Molino". *Cadenza* X/9 (May 1904)
       13-14.
A biography of Don François Molino (1775-1847), guitarist, violinist,
and composer. List of compositions.

622   BONE, Philip J. "Ignaz Moscheles". *Cadenza* XI/6 (Feb 1905) 10-12.
A biography of Ignaz Moscheles (1794-1870), guitarist, pianist, and
composer. List of compositions.

623   BONE, Philip J. "Andrew Oberleitner". *Cadenza* XIII/7 (March 1907)
       15-16.
A biography of Andrew Oberleitner (b.1786), guitarist, mandolinist, and
composer. List of compositions.

624   BONE, Philip J. "Hieronimus Payer". *Cadenza* XV/3 (Sept 1908) 29.
A biography of Hieronimus Payer (1787-1845), guitarist, mandolinist,
and composer. List of compositions.

625   BONE, Philip J. "Luigi Picchianti". *Cadenza* XII/11 (July 1906)
       10.
A biography of Luigi Picchianti (1787-1864), guitarist and music
critic. List of compositions.

626   BONE, Philip J. "Pollet". *Cadenza* XI/12 (Aug 1905) 18-19.
A biography of Charles François Alexander Pollet (1748-ca. 1811),
Jean Joseph Benoit Pollet (1753-1818), and L. M. Pollet (1783-1830).
List of compositions by each.

627   BONE, Philip J. "Stanislaus Sczepanowski, guitar virtuoso".
       Cadenza IX/9 (May 1903) 10-11.
A biography of Stanislaus Sczepanowski (b.1814), guitarist, 'cellist,
and composer. List of compositions for guitar.

628   BONE, Philip J. "Gottfried Weber". *Cadenza* XV/6 (Dec 1908) 16,
       33.
A biography of Gottfried Weber (b.1779), guitarist and composer. List
of compositions.
Grove: (Jacob) Gottfried Weber (1779-1839).

(629-631)   Early Six-String Histories

D. The Terz Guitar

See also 803, 896

629   ELLIKER, Calvin. "On gasogenes, penang lawyers, echiquiers and
         terz guitars". *Soundb* V/4 (Nov 1978) 112-13.
An examination of historical evidence for a description of the terz
guitar. Bibliog. ref. in notes.

630   OPHEE, Matanya. "Chamber music for terz-guitar. A look at the
         options". *GuitarR* XLII (Fall 1977) 12-14.
A discussion of the performance of music on the terz guitar or guitar
with capotasto. Explanation of tuning, notation, use of the capotasto,
and string gauges. Illus., ref. to compositions in footnotes.

631   OPHEE, Matanya. "La chitarra terzina" [The terz guitar]. *Fronimo*
         VI/25 (Oct 1978) 8-24.
A detailed study of the history of the terz guitar. Description of the
instrument. Tuning and terminology is explained. Repertoire is discussed; problems of performance in the early nineteenth-century and
for the present-day performer are considered. Several works were
written by Giuliani. Illus., table, music, bibliog. ref. in notes.

Engraving. *Music Party with Guitar and Mandolins* by Vincent M. Langlois.

CHAPTER SIX

From Tárrega to the Present

The renewal of interest in the guitar in the late nineteenth and early twentieth centuries has been attributed to Francisco Tárrega. As a composer, transcriber, and teacher, Tárrega made a great contribution to the instrument. Although he left no written method, Tárrega has been accredited with the formulation of the basic foundations of the modern school of guitar technique. His teachings have been espoused by his students Miguel Llobet (1878–1938) and Emilio Pujol (1886–1980). For this reason, the period of Tárrega's career has been chosen as a starting point in the investigation of the literature on the history of the guitar as a modern instrument. The question of the existence of a "school" of Tárrega is treated in Hofmeester's article (entry 810) and, more extensively, in Ophee's article (entry 814). In these articles, authors' opinions are compared and criticized.

Andrés Segovia (b. 1893) may be considered the greatest contributor and inspiring influence in the promotion of the classic guitar as a legitimate instrument and in the development and organization of a valid repertoire for study and for performance. The most comprehensive bibliographical tool on Andrés Segovia is Ronald C. Purcell's *Andrés Segovia, contribution to the world of guitar* (New York: Belwin Mills Publishing Corp., n.d. [1975]). In addition to extensive bibliographies of works by and about Segovia, listings of modern editions of music and a discography of Segovia's recordings are included.

Gilardino's article (entry 638) is a discussion of the roles of Tárrega, Llobet, and Segovia in the revival of the interest in the guitar in the twentieth century. Leeb's article (entry 786) gives biographical sketches of Segovia, Pujol, and Llobet with a comparison of their careers and of their musical interpretation. Other listings of studies of these artists are found under their headings in Section C.

This chapter is divided into four sections: Section A. General Surveys, Section B. Notation, Section C. Individual Composers, Performers, and Publishers, and Section D. Selected Interviews of Performers and Composers.

FROM TARREGA TO THE PRESENT

In Section A., a number of entries treat specific aspects of the twentieth-century guitar. Entries 640 and 641 are portrait issues of *Guitar News* and *Guitar Review*. Biographical sketches of representative composers are given in entries 639 and 642–45. Style, repertoire, and performance are emphasized in entries 636, 637, 642, and 643. Modern guitar duos are discussed in entries 632 and 633.

Section B. gives a list of a few articles on systems of notation idiomatic to the guitar.

In Section C., sixty individuals are listed. Articles, including interviews, and book-length texts are included.

Section D. is a short list of interviews of thirteen individuals. This includes presently active performers and teachers.

(632-637)

A. General Surveys

632   DUARTE, John W. "The future of the guitar duo". *GuitarR*
        XXXI (May 1969) 12-13.
Comments on the careers of three contemporary guitar duos: Sergio
and Eduardo Abreu, the Athenian guitar duo, and Henri Dorigny and
Ako Ito. Ports. (the duos).

633   DUARTE, John W. "Rationale of the guitar-duo form". *GuitarR*
        XXXI (May 1969) 9-11.
A discussion of the musical advantages and potentials of the guitar
duo. Performers of guitar duos are mentioned, including Sor and
Aguado and many twentieth-century duos. Some detail is given on the
careers of the Pomponio-Martinez duo, the Zarate duo, and the
Presti-Lagoya duo. Illus.

634   GILARDINO, Angelo. "Aspetti della musica per chitarra del
        secolo XX" [Aspects of music for guitar of the twentieth
        century]. *Fronimo* I/2 (Jan 1973) 7-10. In It.
A discussion of the musical style of important twentieth-century
composers, including Frank Martin, Castelnuovo-Tedesco, Tansman,
Villa-Lobos, Britten, Rodrigo, Henze, and Dodgson. Twentieth-century
composers of guitar music who are not guitarists themselves are
distinguished from the guitarist-composers of earlier centuries.
See also: RILM VIII/2-3 (May-Dec 1974) 2764ap[28].

635   GILARDINO, Angelo. "La musica contemporanea per chitarra
        in Gran Bretagna" [Contemporary music for guitar in Great
        Britain]. *Fronimo* I/5 (Oct 1973) 8-14. In It.
A discussion of the revived interest in the guitar in England in the
twentieth century. Remarks on contemporary performers and composers
of guitar music. Several compositions are briefly considered. 31
works (title, publisher, and editor) are listed in the footnotes.
See also: RILM VIII/2-3 (May-Dec 1974) 2765ap[28].

636   GILARDINO, Angelo. "La musica italiana per chitarra nel
        secolo XX" [Italian music for guitar in the twentieth
        century]. *Fronimo* II/7 (Apr 1974) 21-25. In It.
A discussion of twentieth-century music for guitar by Italian composers dating from Luigi Mozzani (1869-1943). Representative works
are briefly considered. 47 works (title, publisher, and editor) are
listed in the footnotes.
See also: RILM VIII/2-3 (May-Dec 1974) 2766ap[28].

637   GILARDINO, Angelo. "La musica per chitarra nel secolo XX"
        [Guitar music in the twentieth century]. In 4 parts. "Italia"
        [Italy], *Fronimo* VIII/31 (Apr 1980) 25-29; "Spagna" [Spain],
        VIII/32 (July 1980) 21-25; "Gran Bretagna" [Great Britain],
        VIII/33 (Oct 1980) 25-29; "Francia" [France], IX/34 (Jan
        1981) 30-33. In It.
The output of solo guitar music by twentieth-century composers is
considered. Organization is by individual country. Music is listed

(637-643)   Modern Histories

alphabetically by composer with title and publisher cited. Discussion following the list of works is divided into four main categories: "La quantità" [The quantity], "Le Tendenze" [Tendencies],
"La qualità" [The quality], and "Gli interpreti" [The performers].

638   GILARDINO, Angelo. "La rinascita della chitarra" [The
       rediscovery of the guitar]. *Fronimo* I/1 (Oct 1972) 10-12.
       In It.
A discussion of the causes of the waning of the interest in the
guitar in the Romantic period and of the subsequent renewal of
interest at the end of the nineteenth century. The importance of
Tárrega, Llobet, and Segovia in the development of this new interest is considered. Ten developments of the modern movement are
listed.

639   *Guitar Player* Magazine, editors. *The guitar player book.*
       (New York: Grove Press, 1978).
Section "Great guitarists" is a series of articles on contemporary
guitarists including interviews and biographies. Guitarists of the
classical tradition include Almeida, Bream, Segovia, and Williams.
Other main headings are "The guitar in contemporary society",
"Acquiring guitars and keeping them in shape", and "Guitars and
accessories". Ports., append., index, ix, 403p.

640   "[Portraits of contemporary guitarists and composers]".
       GuitarN LX (July-Aug 1961) entire issue.
A tenth anniversary issue of *Guitar News* featuring thirty-five
photographs of contemporary guitarists and composers.

641   "Portrait issue". *GuitarR* XI (1950) entire issue.
The complete issue of *Guitar Review* is devoted to portraits of
important guitarists, composers, musicologists, and guitar makers
of the nineteenth and twentieth centuries. Emphasis is on the
twentieth century.

642   SCHNEIDER, John. "Twentieth-century guitar: the second
       golden age". *GuitarLute* X (July 1979) 14-18.
A chronological survey of twentieth-century composers of guitar
music who are not guitarists themselves. Many works and their
general stylistic characteristics are mentioned. Historical background on the six-string classical guitar is given. Biographical
notes on the author. Ports., including Boulez, Stockhausen, Berlioz,
Britten, Schoenberg, Berg, Stravinsky, and Webern. Port., bibliog.
ref. in notes.

643   SCHNEIDER, John. "Twentieth-century guitar: the second
       golden age". *GuitarLute* XII (Jan 1980) 22-26.
Twelve "specialist" composers who are well-known for their contribu-
tion to the guitar repertoire are discussed: Villa-Lobos, Barrios
Mangoré, Moreno-Torroba, Turina, Ponce, Castelnuovo-Tedesco,
Rodrigo, Smith-Brindle, Duarte, Dodgson, Biberian, and Brouwer.

Modern Histories   (643-648)

Biographical information on the composers and a consideration of
stylistic aspects of their music. Compositions cited. Ports.

644   SOPEÑA, Federico. *Historia de la música española contem-
       poranea* [History of contemporary Spanish music]. (Madrid:
       Ediciónes Rialp, S.A., 1958). In Sp.
A general history of twentieth-century Spanish music, organized
chronologically. Many important figures associated with the guitar
are mentioned including Pedrell, Segovia, Rodrigo, and Salazar.
Index of Spanish composers, bibliog., index, 415p.
Review: RMChilena XIII (May-June 1959) 160-61.

645   VIDAL, Robert J. "Quelques grands guitaristes" [Some
       great guitarists]. *MDisques* XXXI (Oct 1956) 27-31. In Fr.
A brief discussion of the contributions of Tárrega, Pujol, Segovia,
Presti, and Lagoya. Several contemporary composers are also men-
tioned. Illus., port.

B. Notation

646   BURLESON, Spencer. "Avant-garde composition for the electric
       guitar". *GuitarP* X/10 (Oct 1976) 14-15, 64, 66, 68.
A consideration of selected contemporary compositions in which the
electric guitar is included in the instrumentation. Includes comments on notation and on the performance of the works. List of
"Selected references for contemporary electric guitar" (scores,
records, books). Music (8 ex. of notation).

647   MARRIOTT, David F. "The contemporary guitar". *Soundb* VIII/1
       (Feb 1981) 39-41.
An examination of the use of and notation of silence in twentieth-
century guitar music as contrasted with rhythmic notation in nineteenth-century music. The notation systems of Alvaro Company and
Maricio Kagel, among others, are considered. Bibliog. ref. in notes.

648   TANNO, John C. "The classic guitar. Harmonic notation". In
       2 parts. *Fretts* II (1967) 8-10; III (1967) 2-4.
Part 1: A discussion of systems of harmonic notation with examples
selected from guitar methods and compositions of the nineteenth and
twentieth centuries. Historical background on notation systems and
some information on the laws of acoustics. Port., music, bibliog.
ref. in notes.
Part 2: Further remarks on methods of notating harmonics. Notes
on the technique of producing harmonics on the guitar. Discussion
of notation includes an explanation of the methods of nineteenth-
and twentieth-century composers. Port., music.

C. Individual Composers, Performers, and Publishers

ABREU, Sergio and Eduardo (Duo)

See 632

ALMEIDA, Laurindo

See also 639

649 BALL, Ernie. "Laurindo Almeida". *Fretts* (Dec 1958-Jan 1959) 4-5.
A biographical sketch of Almeida.

ANIDO, Maria Luisa

650 "Biography of a classical guitarist. Anido Gonzales Isabel Maria Luisa". *Guitarra* (Chicago) I/4 (Sept-Oct 1963) 14.
A portrait of Anido.

651 "Contemporary guitarist (no. 5)". *GuitarN* VI (Apr-May 1952) 1-2.
A biographical sketch of Anido. Port.

652 NICOLA, Isaac. "María Luisa Anido". *Guitarra* (Havana) III/4 (July 1942) 8-9. In Sp.
A biographical sketch of Anido. Port.

653 RÓVERI, Ercole Remo. *Maria Luisa Anido*. (Milan: Edizioni Ercole Remo Róveri, 1957). In It.
The most extensive biography of Anido. Includes Anido's comments on Llobet and remarks on a Torres guitar in Anido's possession which originally belonged to Tárrega. Letters in Italian translation, port., music (autograph copies in facsim.), list of honors awarded to Anido, list of works (published and unpublished, transcriptions), discog., 58p.

ARGENTO, Dominick (b. 1927)

654 "Introducing Dominick Argento". *GuitarR* XLV (Spring 1979) 11.
Biographical notes on Argento. Port.

655 SCLAR, Joyce Rohr. "Guitar: Consort to the voice". MA diss., Music: Ithaca College, Ithaca, N.Y. [1975-?].
This thesis is listed in *Soundb* IV/1 (Feb 1977) 13. It consists of discussions of the following works: Argento's *Letters from composers*, Britten's *Songs from the Chinese*, and Henze's *Kammermusik*.

Modern Histories   (656-661)

656   SCLAR, Joyce Rohr. "Guitar: Consort to the voice. Chapter II.
        Dominick Argento: Letters from composers". *GuitarR* XLV
        (Spring 1979) 6-11.
A discussion of Argento's song cycle "Letters from composers" for
voice and guitar with text based on letters from seven composers.
Sclar considers the songs based on letters of Bach, Debussy, Chopin,
and Schubert. Comments on text. Analysis of musical style and structure in relationship to the text. Quotations of the letters. Music,
illus., bibliog. ref. in notes.

ATHENIAN Guitar Duo (Liza ZOI and Evangelos ASSIMAKOPOULOS)

See 632, 739

BARRIOS MANGORÉ, Agustín Pìo (1885-1944)

See also 78, 643

657   BALADA, Juan Ruano. "Agustín P. Barrios". *Guitarra* (Madrid)
        XVII (Nov 1964) 7 (text), 8-9 (music). In Sp.
Biographical notes on Barrios as an introduction to his music
"Humoresca".
See also: Guitarra (Madrid) XVIII (Dec 1964) 8-9 for Barrios's
"Romanza".

658   SENSIER, Peter. "Guitar topics". *BMG* LX/691 (Nov 1962) 53-54.
A biographical sketch of Barrios.

659   STOVER, Richard. "Agustín Barrios Mangoré. Forgotten master
        of the guitar". In 2 parts. *Soundb* V/2 (May 1978) 44-47; V/3
        (Aug 1978) 65-69.
A detailed biography of Barrios with extensive comments on his com-
positions and on his performing career. Concert programs listed.
Port., bibliog. ref. in notes.

660   STOVER, Richard. "Agustín Barrios Mangoré. Un genio della
        chitarra dimenticato" [Agustín Barrios Mangoré. Forgotten
        master of the guitar]. *Fronimo* V/20 (July 1977) 6-14. In It.
An Italian translation of Stover 659. Port., music, list of published works, bibliog. ref. in notes, discog., bibliog.

661   STOVER, Richard. "Return with us now. The *Soundboard*'s
        featured facsimile". *Soundb* V/3 (Aug 1978) 82-83.
A facsimile of Barrios's *Preludio Saudade* (1938) with a short discussion of the history of the work.

(662-667)   Modern Histories

BELLOW, Alexander (1912-1977)

662   "Contemporary guitarist (no. 4)". *GuitarN* V (Feb-Mar 1952)
      1-2.
A biographical sketch of Alexander Bellow. Port.

BERG, Alban (1885-1935)

See 642

BIBERIAN, Gilbert

See 643

BICKFORD, Vahdah Olcott [née Ethel Lucretia Olcott] (1885-1980)

663   PURCELL, Ronald C. "In memoriam: Vahdah Olcott Bickford
      Revere". *Soundb* VII/3 (Aug 1980) 120. Reprinted from *Overture*
      LX/3 (June 1980).
A biographical sketch of Bickford in memory of her on her death in
May 1980. Port.

664   "Vahdah Olcott Bickford". *GuitarLute* XIV (July 1980) 7.
A portrait of Bickford in memory of her on her death (18 May 1980).

BOULEZ, Pierre (b. 1925)

See also 642

665   WAGER-SCHNEIDER, John. "The contemporary guitar". *Soundb*
      VII/3 (Aug 1980) 126-27.
A discussion of Boulez's works in which the guitar is used: *Le
Marteau sans maitre* (1953-54), *Pli selon pli* (1958-62), *Eclat*
(1965), and *Domaines* (1968).

BREAM, Julian (b. 1933)

See also 30, 639, 686, 775

666   "Biography of a guitarist. Julian Bream". *Guitarra* (Chicago)
      II/6 (Jan-Feb 1964) 20.
A short biographical survey of Bream with notes on his education
and career as a performer.

667   "A conversation. Julian Bream-Malcolm Weller". *GuitarR*
      XXXVII (Fall 1972) 10-13.
Bream and Weller discuss performing, guitars, and technique.

Modern Histories   (668-672)

668   "Incontri. Colloquio con Julian Bream". *Fronimo* II/9 (Oct
       1974) 4-7.
Bream is interviewed by Pier Luigi Cimma. Includes a discussion of
Bream's early education and career, Segovia's influence on him, and
his opinions on repertoire and transcription.

669   "Man with a guitar: Julian Bream. A self-portrait, with
       music". *GuitarN* LXII (Nov-Dec 1961) 13-14.
A short biography of Bream. Includes quotations of comments made by
Bream in an interview broadcasted on B.B.C. London Regional in Sept
1961.

670   McCREADIE, Sue. "Julian Bream. 'Music may use mechanics, but
       it must always be at the service of the human spirit'". *Guitar*
       VIII/7 (Feb 1980) 18-22.
Bream discusses his concert activities, repertoire (including
opinions on the music of Ponce and Henze, concerto performance, and
duo performance), interpretation, performing, and opinions on early
music. Illus., port.

BRINDLE, Reginald Smith (b. 1917)

See 643

BRITTEN, Benjamin (1913-1976)

See also 642, 655

671   FROESE, Reinhard. "Benjamin Brittens *Nocturnal* und John
       Dowlands *Come heavy sleep*" [Benjamin Britten's *Nocturnal*
       and John Dowland's *Come heavy sleep*]. *GitarreLaute* I/2
       (1979) 20-25. In De.
A discussion and analysis of Benjamin Britten's *Nocturnal* for solo
guitar and the song on which it is based, John Dowland's "Come heavy
sleep", song no. 20 in *The first booke of songes or ayres of fowre
partes* (1597). Background on Britten's significance as a composer
and on the 1964 premier performance on Britten's *Nocturnal*. The
compositional techniques of Britten are considered with a detailed
comparison of the thematic material of the *Nocturnal* to that of the
original model. Illus., port. (Britten), music (Dowland and
Britten).

672   MILLER, Carl. "Meditation on Benjamin Britten's *Nocturnal*".
       GuitarR XLII (Fall 1977) 15-16.
A discussion of Britten's *Nocturnal* for solo guitar and its relationship to the original model, John Dowland's song "Come heavy
sleep" song no. 20 in *The first booke of songes or ayres of fowre
partes* (1597). Examination of the musical structure and of the
technical aspects of each of the eight sections of the *Nocturnal*.
Illus.

(673-678)   Modern Histories

673   SCLAR, Joyce Rohr. "Guitar: consort to the voice". *GuitarR*
        XLII (Fall 1977) 17-24.
"Prologue and chapter 1. Benjamin Britten: *Songs from the Chinese*".
Analysis of Britten's *Songs from the Chinese* op. 58 for high voice
and guitar, a cycle of six songs written in 1958. Study of the
relationship of the music to the text. Detail on the idiomatic use
of the guitar as an accompanying instrument. Illus., music, bibliog.
ref. in notes.

CANO, Antonio (1811-1897)

See 110

CARRILLO-TRUJILLO, Julián Antonio (1875-1965)

See also 79, 80

674   BENJAMIN, Gerald R. "Julián Carrillo and 'Sonido Trece'".
        YbIAIMR III (1967) 38-68.
A study of the life and work of Carrillo, inventor of the microtonal system of composition called "Sonido Trece". Detailed
biography. Analysis of Carrillo's systems of notation. Extensive
list of Carrillo's compositions and theoretical writings. Discog.
of Carrillo's music. Charts, music, bibliog. ref. in notes.

675   FORD, John. "Carrillo after 100 years". *CGuitarInt* III/1
        (Fall 1975) 11-14.
A short introduction to Carrillo's microtonal system "Sonido Trece".
Part 1: "Notation". Carrillo's method of notation is described.
Music (facsim. of guitar music), bibliog. (works for guitar com-
posed in the "Sonido trece" system).
See also: Ford 676.

676   FORD, John. "Carrillo: Music pioneer". *CGuitarInt* III/2
        (Winter 1976) 14-17.
A continuation of Ford 675. Biographical notes on Carrillo with
emphasis on his accomplishments in music. Port.

677   FORD, John. "Carrillo's *sonido trece*". *CGuitarInt* III/3
        (Spring 1976) 12-14.
A continuation of Ford 676. Conclusion of Carrillo's biography with
a discussion of his method of composition. Port.

CARLEVARO, Abel

See also 66

678   AZKOUL, Jihad; DÍAZ, Bartolomé. "Abel Carlevaro: Looking
        ahead". *GuitarLute* IX (Apr 1979) 21-24.

Modern Histories (678-685)

Carlevaro's philosophies on guitar technique and on methods of teaching are discussed, including a consideration of the ideas put forth in his method entitled *Escuela de la guitarra: Exposición de la teoría instrumental*. The authors indicate the uniqueness of his approach and the depth of his technical analysis. Biographical information on the authors. Port., illus.

CASTELNUOVO-TEDESCO, Mario (1895-1968)

See also 38, 643

679 DUARTE, John W. "Death of Castelnuovo-Tedesco". *BMG* LXV/ 758 (June 1968) 280-81.
In memory of Castelnuovo-Tedesco, a discussion of his life and works.

680 HIGHAM, Peter. "Mario Castelnuovo-Tedesco". *Guitar* VI/7 (Feb 1978) 24-25.
A biography of Castelnuovo-Tedesco with many compositions mentioned. Biographical information on the author. Port., bibliog. ref. in notes.

681 HIGHAM, Peter. "Castelnuovo-Tedesco's works for guitar". MA diss., Music: University of Alberta, Edmonton, Canada.

682 MÖLLER, Dirk. "Mario Castelnuovo-Tedescos *24 Caprichos de Goya*". *GitarreLaute* III/1 (Jan-Feb 1981) 42-46. In De.
A discussion of Castelnuovo-Tedesco's *24 Caprichos de Goya* based on a selection from Goya's 80 "Caprichos", political characterizations. Historical background on Goya in his contemporary environment. Analysis of Castelnuovo-Tedesco's music with comments on the relationship of the music to Goya's art. Chart, 5 iconog. (reproductions of Goya's "Caprichos"), music, bibliog. ref. in notes.

683 PURCELL, Ronald C. "Mario Castelnuovo-Tedesco and the guitar". *GuitarR* XXXVII (Fall 1972) 2-4.
A short biographical sketch mentioning his important works for the guitar. Castelnuovo-Tedesco's relationship with Segovia is discussed. Port., complete list of guitar works (date, title, opus no., publisher).

684 STEWART, Jimmy. "The guitarist as a complete musician. Castelnuovo-Tedesco". *GuitarP* VIII/2 (Feb 1974) 44.
A short biographical sketch with some important compositions mentioned. Music (by Jimmy Stewart).

CHILESOTTI, Oscar (1848-1916)

685 DIAZ, Alirio. "Oscar Chilesotti". *Fronimo* VI/22 (Jan 1978) 21-22. In It.

(685-689)   Modern Histories

A discussion of Chilesotti's major contributions to the study of
the guitar and his publications. Bibliog. ref. in notes.

COMPANY, Alvaro

See 647

CUARTETO, Dona-Dio

See 84

DODGSON, Stephen (b. 1924)

See also 38, 643

686   FARRELL, Terrence. "Interview: Stephen Dodgson". *GuitarLute*
        IX (Apr 1979) 13-14, 39.
Introductory notes include biographical information on Dodgson.
Dodgson discusses composition for guitar, his future plans, and his
association with Julian Bream, John Williams, and Hector Quine.
Port.

687   PROVOST, Richard. "The guitar music of Stephen Dodgson".
        Soundb VI/1 (Feb 1979) 3-5.
Biographical notes on Dodgson. Description and evaluation of his
works for guitar, published and unpublished.

688   TOLLY, Kevin. "Stephen Dodgson: his works for guitar".
        GuitarLute IX (Apr 1979) 15-17.
A survey of Dodgson's works for guitar through 1978 with remarks on
each. 20 works considered. Biographical notes on the composer. List
of publishers. Port. (Dodgson and the author).

DORIGNY, Henry and ITO, Ako (Duo)

See 632

FALLA. Manuel de (1876-1946)

See also 752

689   CHRICHTON, Ronald. *Manuel de Falla. Descriptive catalogue of
        his works*. (London: J. & W. Chester, Edition Wilhelm Hansen
        Ltd., 1976).
History and description of the works of de Falla. Discussion of de
Falla's "Homenaje 'Le tombeau de Claude Debussy' for solo guitar",
p. 35.

Modern Histories   (689-694)

Reviews: MMusician XXV (Feb 1977) 30; *MTimes* CXVIII (Mar 1977) 211-12; *Strad* LXXXVII (Apr 1977) 1019; *MinEd* XLI/385 (1977) 385.

690   "Falla's 'Homenaje pour le tombeau de Claude Debussy'. A
        master lesson with Rey de la Torre - taped in the form of a
        conversation with Walter Spalding, Sept. '76". *Chelys* I/5
        (1977) 37-41. In Fr.
A dialogue between Walter Spalding and Rey de la Torre. Historical
background on de Falla's "Homenaje", originally published in 1920 in
Revue Musicale. Comments on the musical interpretation of the work
and on the close association between de Falla and Miguel Llobet
during its composition. Port. (Llobet).

691   JENSEN, Richard d'A. "A closer look at Falla's 'Homenaje'".
        Soundb V/4 (Nov 1978) 101-03.
An examination of Manuel de Falla's "Homenaje" (1921) for solo
guitar. Comments on the relationship of the work to the music of
Ravel and Debussy. Analysis of thematic material with a comparison
to the material from Debussy's *Soirée dans Grenade* and *Parfums de
la nuit*. Music, bibliog. ref. in notes.

692   KEIM, Betty. "Manuel de Falla: the guitar and his music".
        GuitarR XLI (Winter 1976) 22-23.
A brief discussion of de Falla's opinions on the guitar and the
influence of the guitar on his musical style. De Falla's use of
guitaristic effects is illustrated in representative examples of
orchestral works and works for piano. Illus., bibliog.

693   MEIJERING, Cord. "Analyse von Manuel de Fallas 'Homenaje'
        auf den Tod von Claude Debussy" [Analysis of Manuel de Falla's
        "Homenaje" on the death of Claude Debussy]. *GitarreLaute* II/2
        (Mar-Apr 1980) 14-16, 19-22. In De.
Historical background and detailed analysis of de Falla's "Homenaje"
with particular emphasis on the analysis of de Falla's motivic development. Comments on the derivation of the work from Debussy's
La soirée dans Grenade included. Illus., music, bibliog. ref. in
notes.

694   TONAZZI, Bruno. "Considerazioni sull' 'Omaggio a Debussy'
        per chitarra di Manuel de Falla" [Considerations of Manuel
        de Falla's 'Hommage to Debussy']. *Fronimo* II/8 (July 1974)
        9-15. In It.
Historical background on de Falla's "Homenaje", originally written
in memory of Claude Debussy for *La Revue Musicale* (1921). Comparison
of the original version for guitar to the versions for piano and for
orchestra. Miguel Llobet's edition for the guitar is described.
Music, bibliog. ref. in notes.

(695-700)   Modern Histories

FALÚ, Eduardo

695   SENSIER, Peter. "Eduardo Falú". *BMG* LXVIII/789 (Jan 1971)
       133.
A discussion of the career of Argentinean guitarist Eduardo Falú.
Port.

FORTEA, Daniel (1878-1953)

See 109

HENZE, Hans Werner (b. 1926)

See also 655, 670

696   "Incontri. Intervista a Hans Werner Henze" [Encounters.
       Interview with Hans Werner Henze]. *Fronimo* I/4 (July 1973)
       3-5. In It.
Henze, interviewed by Ruggero Chiesa, discusses his compositions for
guitar and his opinions on the instrument. Port.

697   KESSNER, Daniel. "Contemporary guitar music". *Soundb* IV/1
       (Feb 1977) 17.
A discussion of Toru Takemitsu's "Folios for guitar" and Hans Werner
Henze's "Drei Tentos für Gitarre". Comparison of the two works.

698   LEISNER, David. "Contemporary guitar music. Three perspectives
       on Henze's 'Drei Tentos'". *Soundb* IV/2 (May 1977) 36-38.
       Italian trans. "Tre vedute prospettiche dei drei tentos di
       Henze". *Fronimo* V/21 (Oct 1977) 19-23.
A study of Henze's "Drei Tentos" from his *Kammermusik 1958*. In 3
sections: 1. Analysis. 2. Relationship of music. 3. "Stage design".
Music.

699   WAGER-SCHNEIDER, John. "The contemporary guitar". *Soundb*
       VII/4 (Nov 1980) 173-75.
A discussion of Henze's compositions for guitar. Short descriptions
of the works.

HINDEMITH, Paul (1895-1963)

700   SCHWARZ-REIFLINGEN, Erwin. "Paul Hindemith. Musik für drei
       Gitarren" [Paul Hindemith. Music for three guitars]. *DieGit*
       XI/5-6 (1930) 39-40. In De.
Background on Hindemith as a composer with general remarks on his
style. Discussion of the history of and first performance of *Music
for three guitars* in Berlin (1930).

Modern Histories   (701-707)

JEFFERY, Brian

701   KOZINN, Allan. "Brian Jeffery. Historian, music editor,
       Fernando Sor's biographer". *GuitarP* XIII/7 (July 1979)
       61-64, 66, 68.
A survey of Jeffery's career and main contributions to the field of
guitar research. Remarks on the activities of his publishing company, Tecla Editions, and on his research on Fernando Sor are included. Music (Sor, "El que quisiera amando" for voice and guitar).
Port.

KAGEL, Mauricio (b. 1931)

See 647

LECKIE, Walter J.

702   ROBERTS, John. "Historical notes". *Guitar* VII/1 (Aug 1978)
       28-29.
Biographical notes on Dr. Walter J. Leckie. Emphasis is on his
association with Tárrega. Quotations by Pujol and Prat. Port.

LLOBET, Miguel Soles (1878-1938)

See also 109, 638, 690, 694, 786, 808, 814, 829

703   "Guitar music. The artistry of Miguel Llobet (1878-1938)".
       GuitarN LXVII (Sept-Oct 1962) 14-15.
A biographical sketch of Llobet with notes on his arrangements and
transcriptions for guitar.

704   "Miguel Soles Llobet". *Guitarra* (Chicago) I/2 (May-June
       1963) 13-15.
Biographical information on Llobet. Port.

705   RIERA, Juan. "Miguel Llobet, composer and guitarist (1878-
       1938)". Trans. from the Spanish by Mrs. A. Korwin-Rodziszewski.
       GuitarN XXVII (Oct-Nov 1955) 7-8.
A biographical sketch of Llobet.

706   ROBERTS, John. "Miguel Llobet". *Guitar* I/5 (Dec 1972).

707   SCHWARZ-REIFLINGEN, Erwin. "Miguel Llobet". *DieGit* IX/1-2
       (Jan-Feb 1928) 9-13. In De.
A biography of Llobet with comments on his significance as a guitarist-composer. Quotation of a review of a 1927 Berlin concert with
repertoire listed. Port.

(708-713)   Modern Histories

708   SCHWARZ-REIFLINGEN, Erwin. "Miguel Llobet (zu seinem 50.
        Geburtstag am 18. Oktober 1928)" [Miguel Llobet (on his
        50th birthday on 18 October 1928)]. *DieGit* IX/9-10 (1928)
        59-63. In De.
A biographical survey of the life and work of Llobet. Includes comments on Tárrega's influence on Llobet. Information on concert tours
and repertoire interests. Port.

709   TONAZZI, Bruno. *Miguel Llobet, chitarrista dell'impression-
        ismo*. (Ancona: Edizioni Bèrben, 1966). In It.
A detailed biographical study of Llobet with a discussion of his
career as a performer and a summary and evaluation of his major
contributions to the guitar as a composer and as a transcriber.
A short history of the guitar from the sixteenth century. Description of Llobet's original compositions. Concert programs cited.
List of works organized in the following categories: compositions
published and unpublished, transcriptions for guitar published and
unpublished, and transitions for voice and guitar. Annotated
bibliog., music, port., 51p.
Review: Terrence Farrell, *GuitarLute* VIII (Jan 1979) 37.

710   VECHTEN, Carl van. "A critic's view of Llobet". *Chelys* I/5
        (1977) 42. Reprinted from [CHASE, Gilbert] *The music of Spain*.
        (New York: Alfred A. Knopf, 1918), p. 39-41.
The author's reflections on the artistry of Llobet in a recital in
April 1916. Port. (p. 43).

LORCA, Federico García (1898-1936)

711   DELL'ARA, Mario. "La chitarra nella poesia di Federico García
        Lorca" [The guitar in the poetry of Federico García Lorca].
        Fronimo IV/16 (July 1976) 15-19. In It.
A biographical sketch of Lorca includes remarks on his involvement
with music. Quotations of poetry on the subject of the guitar with
commentary. Consideration of the influence of Lorca's poetry on
contemporary composers with representative compositions listed.

712   MAXSON, Gloria, trans. "Six strings from a Spanish guitar.
        Poems translated from the Spanish by Gloria Maxson". *GuitarP*
        VI/8 (Nov-Dec 1972) 18.
Quotations in English translation of the poetry of Lorca, Paz, and
Machado.

MARTIN, Frank (1890-1974)

713   BOSMAN, Lance. "Analysis 6". *Guitar* IX/1 (Aug 1980) 7-8.
A short analysis of the "Prelude" from Martin's *Quatre pièces brèves*
(1933). Music.

Modern Histories   (714-717)

MOZZANI, Luigi (1868-1943)

714   FERRARI, Romolo. "La vita e le opere di Mozzani" [The life and
        works of Mozzani]. In 6 parts. *AChitarristica* I/1 (Jan 1947)
        5-6; I/2 (Mar 1947) 5-6; I/3 (June 1947) 5-6; I/4 (Aug 1947)
        5-6; I/8 (Apr 1948) 5-6; I/10-11 (Aug-Oct 1948) 12-13. In It.
A study of the life and works of Mozzani with discussion of his
career as a guitarist and as a luthier. Anecdotes recalled.
Mozzani's main contributions, including innovations in construction, are noted.

715   HUTTIG, H. E. II. "Luigi Mozzani, a vignette". *GuitarR*
        XXXVII (Fall 1972) 19. Originally written in German by F.
        Buek in *La Guitarra* magazine (Buenos Aires, 1926). Trans.
        into Spanish by Federico Canno. Trans. from Spanish to English
        by Huttig.
A brief account of some experiences of Mozzani as a guitarist, including his association with William Foden. Illus.

PEDRELL, Carlos (1878-1941)

See 717

PEDRELL, Felipe (1841-1922)

See also 644, 808, 829. The first nine articles of *Anuario Musical*
XXVII (1972) are in the memory of Felipe Pedrell. Among them are
Pujol 716.

716   PUJOL, Emilio. "El Maestro Pedrell, la vihuela y la guitarra"
        [The Maestro Pedrell, the vihuela and the guitar]. *AnM* XXVII
        (1972) 47-59. In Sp.
A homage to the late Felipe Pedrell in which he is honored for his
musicological research on the guitar and vihuela. Pujol recalls his
own experiences in working with Pedrell's studies and examines the
value of Pedrell's accomplishments. Includes a comparison of the
transcription methodology used by Pedrell, Conte de Morphy, and
Leo Schrade. Music (2 works for voice and vihuela, transcr. only,
vihuela music in 2-staff system, treble and bass clef), bibliog.
ref. in notes.

PETRASSI, Goffredo (b. 1904)

717   "Guitar music. Pedrell and Petrassi". *GuitarN* LXVI (July-
        Aug 1962) 30.
Short biographical surveys of composers Carlos Pedrell, nephew of
Felipe, and Petrassi.

(718-724)   Modern Histories

718   "Incontri. Intervista a Goffredo Petrassi" [Encounters.
      Interview with Goffredo Petrassi]. *Fronimo* I/1 (Oct 1972)
      7-9. In It.
Petrassi is interviewed by Ruggero Chiesa. Port., music.

719   WAGER-SCHNEIDER, John. "The contemporary guitar. Goffredo
      Petrassi". *Soundb* VIII/2 (May 1981) 92-94.
A stylistic analysis of works for guitar solo and for guitar with
other instruments: "Suoni notturni" (1959), "Seconda-serenata trio"
(1962), "Nunc" (1971), "Alias" (1977), "Grand septuor" (1978).
Port., music.

POMPONIO-MARTINEZ DUO

See 633

PONCE, Manuel M. (1882-1948)

See also 13, 38-41, 79-81, 643, 670, 776

720   ANGEL, Miguel. "En memoria a Ponce" [In memory of Ponce].
      FINews XVII/6 (Nov-Dec 1948) 12.
A portrait of Ponce in his memory. Port.

721   BOSMAN, Lance. "Variations 6". *Guitar* V/4 (Nov 1976) 28-29.
A discussion of Ponce's treatment of variation form in "Variations
sur Folia de Espania". Analysis included. Music.

722   CHAVEZ, Carlos. "Historical evaluation of Manuel M. Ponce".
      GuitarR VII (1948) 6.
Commentary on Ponce's influence on the development of Mexican music,
his development of larger forms, and his use of national folk music
in his compositions. Port.

723   COELHO, Olga. "Ponce, lover of Mexican folklore". *GuitarR*
      VII (1948) 8-9.
The author recalls his first meeting with Ponce, expresses his
admiration for Ponce as a man and as a composer, and comments on
Ponce's interest in Mexican folk music. Illus.

724   JEFFERY, Brian. "24 preludes for guitar of Manuel M. Ponce".
      Soundb VIII/3 (Aug 1981) 160-62.
An introduction to Ponce's "24 Preludes" (one for each major and
minor key) which have been recently published in an edition by
Miguel Alcázar. Alcázar bases his research on the original manuscript composed in the late 1920s in Paris. A general stylistic
description includes remarks on representative works. Segovia's
objection to the inappropriateness of certain choices of key in
guitar composition is revealed in a letter from Segovia to Ponce.
Music (incipits of the 24 Preludes).

Modern Histories   (725-734)

725   LUSE, Marvin W. Jr. "Interval, contour, and shape as struc-
        tural elements in Manuel Ponce's 'Sonata III'". MA diss.,
        Music: University of South Florida.
A reference copy is available through the GFA Archive.

726   MENDEZ, Guillermo Flores. "Manuel M. Ponce". *AChitarristica*
        I/10-11 (Aug-Oct 1948) 13. In It.
A portrait of Ponce in which his contributions and accomplishments
as a composer of guitar music are noted.

727   MENDEZ, G. [Guillermo] F. [Flores]. "Manuel M. Ponce".
        Trans. from the Spanish by Mrs. A. Korwin-Rodziszewski.
        GuitarN XXX (Apr-May 1956) 3-4.
A short biographical sketch in which Ponce is praised for his contribution to the guitar repertoire. Includes general comments on his
musical style with some works mentioned.

728   "Obituary notice". *GuitarR* VI (1948) 152.
An announcement of the death of Ponce, 24 April 1948 in Mexico City.

729   OTERO, Corazon. "Book review: *Manuel M. Ponce y la guitarra*"
        [Book review: *Manuel M. Ponce and the guitar*]. *Guitar* IX/10
        (May 1981) 21-23. In En.
A pre-publication review. No publication information is given. Ports.

730   PINCHERLE, Marc. "A letter". *GuitarR* VII (1948) 11.
A portrait of Ponce in his memory.

731   RAYGADA, Carlos. "Manuel Maria Ponce". Trans. by Eithne
        Golden. *GuitarR* VII (1948) 5-6.
A biographical sketch of Ponce including the author's own reflections
on his personal relationship with the composer. Illus.

732   SEGOVIA, Andrés. "Manuel M. Ponce: sketches from heart and
        memory". Trans. by Olga Coelho and Eithne Golden. *GuitarR*
        VII (1948) 3-4 (English text), 15-16 (Spanish translation).
Segovia's praise of Ponce for his outstanding character and contribution. Includes anecdotes of Segovia's own personal experiences
with Ponce.

733   SILVA, Jesus. "Reminiscences of Manuel M. Ponce". *GuitarR*
        VII (1948) 11.
Silva's recollections of his final moments with Ponce. Segovia's
last words to Ponce are recalled.

734   SMITH, Carleton Sprague. "Impressions of Manuel Ponce".
        GuitarR VII (1948) 10.
A portrait of Ponce based on the author's recollections of the
composer on his meeting with him in Mexico City (1941). Notes on
Ponce's areas of interest in composition and his style of composition. Music.

(735-743)   Modern Histories

735   SPALDING, Walter. "Manuel Maria Ponce". *Chelys* II/2 (1978)
          29-30.
A brief description of Ponce's style of composition. Biographical
notes included. Port.

736   STEWART, Jimmy. "The guitarist as a complete musician. Manuel
          Ponce: a tribute". *GuitarP* VII/1 (Jan 1974) 45.
A biographical sketch of Ponce with some compositions mentioned.

737   VILLA-LOBOS, Heitor. "Nostalgic recollections". *GuitarR*
          VII (1948) 11.
Villa-Lobos's recollections of his friendship with Ponce on the
event of Ponce's death.

PRESTI, Ida (1924-1967) and LAGOYA, Alexander (b. 1929) (Guitar Duo)

See also 633, 645

738   ARTZT, Alice. "Presti in New York". *GuitarR* XXXI (May
          1969) 4.
The author's recollections of her experiences with Presti during
Presti's New York visit. Remarks on Presti as a teacher.

739   THE ATHENIAN GUITAR DUO (Liza ZOI and Evangelos
          ASSIMAKOPOULOS). "Ida Presti - in memoriam". *GuitarR*
          XXXI (May 1969) 5.
Recollections by the authors of their experiences with Ida Presti
and with the Presti-Lagoya duo.

740   DORIGNY, Henri. "Ida Presti". *GuitarR* XXXI (May 1969)
          4-5. Trans. from the French by Chantal Dubourg.
Praise of Presti for her contribution to the guitar as a performer
and as a teacher.

741   DUARTE, John W. "Ida Presti". *BMG* LXIV/746 (June 1967)
          303-04.
A portrait of Presti immediately following her death. The author
recalls his association with her. Port.

742   DUARTE, John W. "Presti-Lagoya duo". *GuitarR* XXXI (May
          1969) 6.
Biographical accounts of the childhoods and the careers of Presti
and Lagoya. Illus.

743   LAWRENCE, Catherine. "Viewpoints: Alexandre Lagoya and
          Guitarra". *Guitarra* (Chicago) XXXVIII (May-June 1980)
          2-5.
An interview with Lagoya on 23 Feb 1980. Includes a discussion of
Lagoya's concert activities. Comments on the history of technique
and position in reference to Lagoya's development of the technique

Modern Histories   (743-751)

of playing on the right side of the nail. Port., illus. (including
right hand positions).

744   "Presti + Lagoya + two guitars". *Guitarra* (Chicago) II/8
        (May-June 1964) 14-19.
An interview with Presti and Lagoya. Emphasis of the discussion is
on their concert careers and on the guitar repertoire.

745   SEGOVIA, Andrés. ["Ida Presti"]. *GuitarR* XXXI (May 1969) 3.
Segovia's tribute to Ida Presti in which he expresses his grief for
her death in 1967. Port. (Presti).

746   SHERRY, James. "Ida Presti leaves us". *Guitarra* (Chicago)
        V/26 (May-June 1967) 10-15.
A tribute to Presti with biographical notes on her life as a performer. Port.

PUJOL, Emilio (1886-1980)

See also 38, 427, 645, 702, 716, 786, 808, 810, 814, 815-21, 858

747   ADAMS, Henry. "Interview: Emilio Pujol". *GuitarLute* IX
        (Apr 1979) 8-10.
Introductory notes give biographical information on Pujol. The
interview includes a discussion of Pujol's opinions on recording,
transcriptions, the influences on his career and his influences on
others, Torres guitars, and education. References to Tárrega's
influences throughout. Port.

748   AUGUSTINE, Rose L. "Emilio Pujol (Biographical sketch)".
        GuitarR V (1948) 117.
A sketch of Pujol's career as an artist, composer, teacher, and
author.

749   CHIESA, Ruggero. "I novant'anni di Emilio Pujol" [The nine-
        tieth year of Emilio Pujol]. *Fronimo* IV/15 (Apr 1976) 6-10.
        In It.
A biography of Pujol with emphasis on his contributions to the
guitar. Illus. (facsim. of a 1927 recital program), port.

750   "Emilio Pujol: a complete list of works". *GuitarLute* VI
        (May 1978) 12-14.
A reprint of the list of works in Riera 756.

751   "Incontri. Colloquio con Emilio Pujol" [Encounters. Inter-
        view with Emilio Pujol]. *Fronimo* III/10 (Jan 1975) 3-4.
        In It.
Emilio Pujol, interviewed by Silvio Cerutti, discusses his work as
a musicologist, transcription, and the teachings of Tárrega. Port.

(752-759)   Modern Histories

752   KOZINN, Allan. "Emilio Pujol. 'If you cannot live your art
       in this secret intimate way, there is no reason to continue'".
       Guitar V/12 (July 1977) 9-11.
Pujol discusses his study with Tárrega, his work on his method, *La
escuela razonada de la guitarra*, the work of de Falla, transcription, and recordings. Port.

753   KOZINN, Allan. "Emilio Pujol. Teacher, performer, master of
       classical guitar". *GuitarP* XI/4 (Apr 1977) 20 (text), 21
       (music), 48, 52, 76, 81 (text).
A biography of Pujol with notes on his contributions, activities,
and philosophies. Quotations of Pujol. "Selected works by Emilio
Pujol", port., music ("Becqueriana" by Pujol).

754   PORTA, A. "Emilio Pujol, a world-famous Leridan". *GuitarN*
       XXI (Oct-Nov 1954) 3-5. Trans. from the Spanish by A.
       Rodziszewska from *Labor*, Lérida, Spain (10 Feb 1954).
A defense of Pujol's contribution to the guitar in a reaction
against the Leridan's lack of recognition of the artist. Pujol's
main accomplishments are noted. Includes comments on his continuation of the teachings of Tárrega.

755   PURCELL, Ronald C. "Emilio Pujol. In memoriam. 1886-1980".
       Soundb VIII/2 (May 1981) 65-69.
A portrait of Pujol with notes on his career and accomplishments
in the field of the guitar. Chronological listing of important
events in the life of Pujol based on information taken from Riera
756. Includes a facsimile of a review by Isolde Radclyffe of a
recital by Pujol (London 1912), reprinted from *BMG*. Facsim of a
program (France 1922). Port.

756   RIERA, Juan. *Emilio Pujol*. (Lérida: Instituto de Estudios
       Ilerdenses, 1974). In Sp.
A detailed biography of Pujol in 2 parts: "Biografia" [Biography]
and "El artista y su obra" [The artist and his work]. Emphasis is
on his life in music, his activities, his contributions, and his
associations. Comments on his relationship with Tárrega are included. Programs of recitals, port., 7 append., bibliog., 201p.
Review: John Roberts, *Guitar* IV/8 (Mar 1976) 35.

757   ROBERTS, John. "Emilio Pujol. 1886-1980". *Guitar* IX/8
       (Mar 1981) 27, 29.
A biographical survey of the life of Pujol. Notes on his association
with Tárrega included. Port.

758   SANUY, Ignacio María. *Notas biográficas sobre Emilio Pujol*
       [Biographical notes on Emilio Pujol]. (Lérida: Publicaciones
       del Instituto de Estudios Ilerdenses, 1952). In Sp.

759   SCHWARZ-REIFLINGEN, Erwin. "Emilio Pujol und die spanische
       Gitarristik" [Emilio Pujol and Spanish guitar music]. *DieGit*
       VII/9-10 (Sept-Oct [1926]) 63-65. In De.

Modern Histories   (759-765)

A biographical sketch of Pujol with notes on his technique, his major contributions, and his publications. Includes a summary of the history of the guitar in Spain with some important guitarists mentioned. Port.

QUINE, Hector

See 686

RODRIGO, Joaquin (b. 1902)

See also 282, 643, 644

760   C., M.G. "Il 'Concierto de Aranjuez' per chitarra e orchestra di Joaquin Rodrigo" [The "Concerto de Aranjuez" for guitar and orchestra by Joaquin Rodrigo]. *AChitarristica* II/10-11 (Aug-Oct 1948) 6-7. In It.
A description of the first performance of Rodrigo's "Concerto de Aranjuez" (Madrid, 1940) performed by Regino Sainz de la Maza. Stylistic consideration of the work.

761   GOMEZ-SANTOS, Marino. *[Once] Españoles universales.* [Eleven renown Spaniards]. (Madrid: Ediciones Cultura Hispanica, 1969). In Sp.
Includes five interviews with Joaquin Rodrigo in July 1959, p. 269-303, and five interviews with Andrés Segovia in July 1960, p. 335-68. Port., 417p.

762   "Incontri. [Joaquin Rodrigo]" [Encounters. Joaquin Rodrigo]. *Fronimo* III/11 (Apr 1975) 3-5. In It.
Silva Cerutti interviews Joaquin Rodrigo. Topics of discussion include Rodrigo's compositions for guitar, guitar technique, and, in particular, composing for guitar with orchestra. Port.

763   IRVINE, Kip. "Joaquin Rodrigo: *Fantasia para un gentilhombre.* Analysis and comments". *GuitarLute* IV (Mar 1977) 17-19.
A discussion and analysis of the six movements of Rodrigo's *Fantasia para un gentilhombre.* Relationships between the music of Gaspar Sanz, Rodrigo's model, and Rodrigo's work are considered. Music, bibliog.

764   RODRIGO, Joaquin. "L'analisi tecnica dell'autore sul 'Concierto'" [Technical analysis of the "Concerto" by the composer]. *AChitarristica* II/10-11 (Aug-Oct 1948) 7-8. In It.
Rodrigo's analysis of the three movements of his "Concerto de Aranjuez". Music.

765   RODRIGO, Joaquin. "Concerto de Aranjuez". *GuitarN* LV (Sept-Oct 1960) 16-17.

(765-770)   Modern Histories

Rodrigo's personal reflections on his composition "Concerto de
Aranjuez".

766   STEWART, Jimmy. "The guitarist as a complete musician. Joaquin
       Rodrigo". *GuitarP* VIII/4 (Apr 1974) 45.
A short biography of Rodrigo with some compositions cited. Music (by
Jimmy Stewart).

767   VÁYA PLA, Vicente. *Joaquin Rodrigo: Su vida y su obra* [Joaquin
       Rodrigo: His life and his work]. (Madrid: Real Musical
       Editores, 1977). In Sp.
A detailed study of the life and works of Rodrigo. Analysis of
selected compositions including "Concerto de Aranjuez". Also includes
general discussion of all of Rodrigo's music for guitar. Catalogue
of works organized by genre (title, duration in min., publisher),
24 pl., append., bibliog., discog., 245p.

ROSETTA, Giuseppe

768   BOSMAN, Lance. "Variations 8". *Guitar* V/5 (Dec 1976) 29.
A short analysis of Rosetta's treatment of theme and variation in
the rondo movement of the *Sonatine* (1969). Music.

SCHÖNBERG, Arnold (1874–1951)

See also 642

769   HAAS, Theodor. "Schönbergs Serenade, op. 24 mit obligater
       Mandoline und Gitarre" [Schönberg's Serenade, op. 24 with
       obligato mandolin and guitar]. *ZfdG* IV/4 (1925) 11-15. In
       De.

SAINZ DE LA MAZA, Regino

See 66, 109, 760, 870

SEGOVIA, Andrés (b. 1893)

See also 47, 64, 410, 419, 638, 639, 644, 645, 668, 683, 724, 732,
733, 745, 761, 804, 831, 843, 860, 890, 973, 1032, 1033

770   ANDERSON, Peter. "Segovia at Los Olivos". *BMG* LXV/757
       (May 1968) 247-48.
A description of Christopher Nupen's film documentary "Segovia
at Los Olivos". Procedures and events in the making of the film
are discussed.

Modern Histories   (771-776)

771   "Andrés Segovia. Celebrated guitarist". *Crescendo* XX/8
        (Feb 1928) 5-6.
A portrait of Segovia as a performer. Quotation of a review of
Segovia's New York debut. Recital program listed.

772   "Andrés Segovia - Golden Jubilee. Fifty years of concertizing
        in the United States". *Soundb* V/1 (Feb 1978) 1-15.
A tribute to Segovia in a commemorative issue of *Soundboard* "in
celebration of the Golden Anniversary of his first American concert
in New York". Includes essays on the contributions of Segovia with
biographical information. Description of the Andrés Segovia exhibit
in January and February. Photographs of Segovia with descriptive
captions (p. 4-7). Sketches of Segovia and other sketches by Andrés
Segovia Jr. (p. 8-15).

773   BOBRI, Vladimir. *The Segovia Technique*. (New York: The
        Macmillan Co., 1972).
A detailed consideration of Segovia's technique for both the left
and the right hand. Includes an "Historical outline" in which the
history of the guitar is traced briefly from ancient times to the
present; chapter on "Virtuosi" includes comments on outstanding
guitarists from the early nineteenth century to the present. Biographical information on Segovia, praise of Segovia for his genius
and for his influence on others. Illus., port., iconog., append.,
bibliog. (of instruction books, annotated), index, 94p.
Reviews: GuitarR XXXV (Summer 1971) 32; *GuitarR* XXXVII (Fall 1972)
23; *TennFolkSoc* XXXVIII/3 (1972) 88; *MJ* XXX (Sept 1972) 45; *Instrument* XXXVII (Aug 1972) 16; *Musart* XXVI/2 (1973) 45; Dieter Kreidler,
MBildung VI/7-8 (July-Aug 1974) 462-63; *GuitarP* XIV (Sept 1980) 90.

774   BURTNIEKS, J.A. "Andrés Segovia". *GuitarN* XXIV (Apr-May
        1955) 2-3.
A brief discussion of the career and contributions of Segovia.

775   CLINTON, George, comp. and ed. *Andrés Segovia - An apprecia-
        tion*. (London: Musical News Service Ltd., 1978).
Twenty-eight articles include biography, accounts of important
events, interviews, and essays on opinions on and associations with
Segovia. Authors include Prat, Cooper, Hardie, Moffatt, Clinton,
Walker, Mills, Mairants, Randolph, Biberian, Maccaferri, Roberts,
Artzt, Bream, Bobri, Diaz, Duarte, Matsuda, Williams, and Nupen.
Includes a reproduction of Segovia's baptismal record and the
script to the film "Andrés Segovia - The song of the guitar"
(Christopher Nupen). Autograph letter, many photographs, 100p.
Reviews: H. de C., *Guitar* VI/9 (Apr 1978) 32; *Gitarre* (Graz) I/2
(July 1978) 30; *GuitarP* XII (July 1978) 10; Tom Vollmer, *GuitarLute*
VII (Sept 1978) 40-41; *MTimes* CXIX (Oct 1978) 863; *AmerStrT* XXVIII/
3 (1978) 42.

776   CLINTON, George. "Segovia". *Guitar* III/5 (Dec 1974) 20-21.

Clinton interviews Segovia. Includes a discussion of Segovia's performing experiences, his family, his recordings, and his association with Manuel Ponce. Port.

777   CLINTON, George. "Segovia in the Alhambra". *Guitar* V/3 (Oct 1976) 20-23.
An account of the making of the film of Segovia by filmmaker Christopher Nupen. Photos.

778   CROCKETT, Jim. "Andrés Segovia". *GuitarP* V/4 (June 1971) 22-23, 44.
Biographical information on Segovia including notes on his childhood, career, opinions on the guitar, and his activities. Port.
See also: Oribe 788 for criticism.

779   DOMINGUEZ, F. "'Segovia' and 'Guitar' are inseparable words". *Guitarra* (Chicago) I/1 (Mar-Apr 1963) 13-16.
Biographical with information on Segovia's concert career, influence on others, and his main accomplishments. Port.

780   GAVOTY, Bernard. *Andrés Segovia*. Portraits by Roger Hauert. (Geneva: Éditions René Kister, 1955). In Fr.
Reflections on Segovia as a performer and accounts of his conversations with Segovia. Autograph letter by Segovia with French translation (New York, 1956). Biography. Illus. (17 pages of photographs), discog., 32p.

781   GAVOTY, Bernard. *Andrés Segovia*. Portraits by Roger Hauert. Trans. by F.E. Richardson. (Geneva: Éditions René Kister, 1955).
An English translation of 780.

782   GELATT, Roland. *Music Makers*. (New York: Alfred A. Knopf Inc., 1953). Reprint ed. (New York: Da Capo Press, Inc., 1972).
Ch. IV, p. 195-203. A biography of Segovia with emphasis on his performing career. Some inaccuracies.
Reviews: SaturdayR XXXVI (28 Mar 1953) 19; *MCourier* CXLVII (June 1953) 26; *Instrument* VIII (Sept 1953) 74; *Notes* X (Sept 1953) 638; *HiFi/MAmer* III (Sept-Oct 1953) 116; *MTimes* CXIV (Sept 1973) 901-02; *Strad* LXXXV (Aug 1974) 217.

783   GORNER, Peter. "Golden hands from a quieter age". *Guitarra* (Chicago) XL (Sept-Oct 1980) 2-6.
A biographical sketch of Segovia as a performer. Port.

784   "Incontri. Intervista ad Andrés Segovia" [Encounters. Interview with Andrés Segovia]. *Fronimo* I/2 (Jan 1973) 3-6. In It.
Segovia is interviewed by Silvio Cerutti. Includes a discussion of performance, instruction, interpretation, and repertoire. Port.

785   KOZINN, Allan. "Andrés Segovia". *GuitarP* XII/6 (June 1978) 26-28, 104, 106, 110.

Modern Histories   (785-794)

An interview with Segovia in which the changes in the guitar and the
public view of it over the past fifty years, the repertoire, transcription and methods, recording and performing are among the topics
discussed. Includes a list of "Selected works by Segovia" (transcr.,
exercises, records). Port.

786   LEEB, Hermann. "Von Segovia, Pujol, und Llobet". [On Segovia,
       Pujol, and Llobet]. *GitarreLaute* II/6 (Nov-Dec 1980) 32-33.
       In De.
Short biographies of the three guitarists with comparisons of their
musical interpretation and of their background. Port.

787   NORDAU, Max. "The artistry of Segovia". Trans. from the French
       by George Giusti. *GuitarR* IV (1947) 87.
The author's reflections on his first impressions of Segovia upon
seeing him at the Ateneo in Madrid. The article was originally
written on 20 Mar 1919.

788   ORIBE, José. "An open letter to Andrés Segovia". *GuitarP*
       V/7 (Oct 1971) 16-17.
The response of guitar maker José Oribe to Crockett's article on
Segovia 778 expressing his objection to comments made by Segovia
concerning strings, guitars, and performance.

789   PEEL, Douglas. "Segovia - the legend and the dream". *BMG*
       (May 1974) 24-25.
A portrait of Segovia with quotations by him. Biographical notes
included. Port.

790   PEROTT, Boris A. "A letter". *GuitarR* IV (1947) 94.
A letter by Perott expressing his admiration for Segovia.

791   "Return with us now. The *Soundboard*'s featured facsimile".
       Soundb V/1 (Feb 1978) 16-17.
Segovia's manuscript of "Macarena" with a brief explanation of the
significance of the work.

792   SCHWARZ-REIFLINGEN, Erwin. "Andrés Segovia". *DieGit* VIII/3-4
       (Mar-Apr 1927) 23-24. In De.
A portrait of Segovia with reports of recent concerts. Description
of his concert tour in Europe. Port.

793   SEGOVIA, Andrés. "Adventures in Argentina". Trans. by Eithne
       Golden-Sax. *GuitarR* XLVIII (Spring 1981) 4-6.
Segovia's recollections of his experiences on his 1920 concert tour
of Argentina. Illus.

794   SEGOVIA, Andrés. *Andrés Segovia, an autobiography of the
       years 1893-1920*. Ed. by Tana de Gámez. Trans. by W.F. O'Brien.
       (New York: Macmillan Publishing Co., Inc., 1976).
A personal account of Segovia's childhood, early career, travels,
and acquaintances. Letters included. Illus., pl.

(794-799)   Modern Histories

Reviews: P.K. Thomajan, *GuitarR* XLI (Winter 1976) 28; Dolber B.
Spalding, *Chelys* I/8 (Mar-Apr 1977) 10-11; *MEducatorsJ* LXIII (Apr
1977) 75; Ivor Mairants, *Guitar* VI/6 (Jan 1978) 32-33; *MMusician*
XXVI (Jan 1978) 34; *MTimes* CXIX (Feb 1978) 143; *MTeacher* LVII (Feb
1978) 37; *MinEd* XLII/389 (1978) 37.

795   SEGOVIA, Andrés; BOBRI, Vladimir. "A conversation". *GuitarR*
       XLIII (Spring 1978) 2-5.
A dialogue between Segovia and Bobri which took place in Jan 1977.
Includes a discussion of Segovia's concertizing and recording plans,
repertoire, technique, and guitar makers. Illus.

796   SEGOVIA, Andrés. "The guitar and myself". Trans. by Eithne
       Golden. In 6 parts. *GuitarR* IV (1947) 77-86; VI (1948) 133-
       40; VIII (1949) 31-36; X (1949) 111-18; XIII (1952) 4-13;
       XXV (Feb 1961) 7-11. Pagination for parts 1 through 5
       include supplements of the text in Spanish.
Part 1: "Granada", "Cordoba", "Seville". Segovia's recollections of
his childhood and early career including accounts of experiences
with acquaintances and of incidents significant to the development
of his career. Illus., port.
Part 2: "Towards Madrid". Segovia's experiences as a guitarist-
performer in Seville and in Cordoba leading up to his departure for
Madrid. Illus.
Part 3: "Madrid". Segovia's meeting with José Ramirez. Illus.
Part 4: "Madrid". Segovia's experiences in Madrid including an
encounter with a student of Tárrega and a period of illness. Illus.
Part 5: An account of Segovia's recollections about his preparation
for his first Madrid recital at the Ateneo. His reflections on the
outcome of his recital include recollections of letters regarding
his debut which he was able to obtain from various sources. Illus.
Part 6: Segovia's amusing anecdotes and accounts of experiences with
acquaintances in Madrid. Illus.

797   SEGOVIA, Andrés. "Japan revisited". Trans. by Eithne Golden-
       Sax. *GuitarR* XLVIII (Spring 1981) 7.
An account of the events surrounding Segovia's arrival in Japan on
his 1980 tour.

798   STEWART, Jimmy. "Segovia at 80". *GuitarP* VIII/4 (Apr 1974)
       14.
Comments on Segovia's activities at 80. Quotations of Segovia
included. Port.

799   USILLOS, Carlos. *Artistas españoles contemporaneos - Andrés
       Segovia (No. 65)* [Contemporary Spanish artists: Andrés
       Segovia (no. 65)]. ([Madrid]: el Servicio de Publicaciones
       del Ministerio de Educación y Ciencia, 1973). In Sp.
A detailed biography of Segovia including numerous quotations of
authors and reviewers about Segovia. Photos., bibliog., discog.,
139p.

Modern Histories   (800-804)

800   VEGA, Carlos. "The miracle which is Segovia". *GuitarR* IV
      (1947) 88.
The author's opinion of Segovia as a man and as an artist.

801   WALKER, Donald. "*Guitar*'s first family". *Guitar* V/11 (June
      1977) 20-21.
An account of an interview with Segovia and his family. Port.

STOCKHAUSEN, Karlheinz (b. 1928)

See 642

STRAVINSKY, Igor (1882-1971)

See 642

TAKEMITSU, Toru (b. 1930)

See also 697

802   MARRIOTT, David F. "Interview: Toru Takemitsu". *Soundb*
      VIII/3 (Aug 1981) 167-68.
Takemitsu discusses his use of the guitar in composition, his association with guitarist Kiyoshi Shomura, other contemporary composers,
and the popularity of the guitar in Japan, among other topics. Port.

803   WAGER-SCHNEIDER, John. "The contemporary guitar. Toru
      Takemitsu". *Soundb* VIII/3 (Aug 1981) 169-71.
A study of the chronological development of the compositional style
of Takemitsu with emphasis on his works for guitar. Short descriptions with remarks on the peculiarities of the performance and notation are given for the following works for guitar: The trilogy of
works "Ring" (1961) for flute, terz guitar, and lute; "Sacrifice"
(1962) for flute, lute, vibraphone, antique cymbals; "Valeria"
(1965) for two piccolos, guitar, violoncello, and electric organ;
"Stanza I" (1969) for voice, piano, guitar, harp, and vibraphone;
"Folios" (1974) for solo guitar, dedicated to Kiyoshi Shomura; "12
songs for guitar" (1977). The influences of composers Boulez and
Messaien shown in the works of the trilogy are pointed out. Port.,
music.

TANSMAN, Alexander (b. 1897)

804   "Incontri. Intervista ad Alexander Tansman di Ruggero Chiesa"
      [Encounters. Interview with Alexander Tansman by Ruggero
      Chiesa]. *Fronimo* VI/23 (Apr 1978) 3-5. In It.
Tansman's discussion includes comments on the possibilities and
problems of composing for guitar, his association with Segovia,

(804-812)   Modern Histories

opinions on Villa-Lobos's and other contemporary composers' understanding of the guitar, his compositions, and musical style. Port.

805   STEWART, Jimmy. "The guitarist as a complete musician.
       Alexander Tansman". *GuitarP* VIII/5 (May 1974) 52.
A short biography of Tansman with compositions mentioned. Music (by
Jimmy Stewart).

TÁRREGA, Francisco (1852-1909)

See also 32, 410, 638, 645, 653, 702, 747, 751, 752, 754, 756, 757

806   BUEK, Fritz. "Francisco Tárrega". *Gfreund* XXV (1924) 18-22.
       In De.

807   "Francisco Tárrega: a complete list of works". *GuitarLute* V
       (Nov 1977) 17-18.
In 2 main divisions: Original works and transcriptions.

808   "Francisco Tárrega según...". *Guitarra* (Havana) II/3 (Dec
       1941) between pages 16-17. In Sp.
Quotations of comments on Tárrega by Lopez Chavarri, Felipe Pedrell,
Victor Monagne, Luis Millet, Ricardo Muñoz, Miguel Llobet, Emilio
Pujol, and Luis de Soto.

809   HECK, Thomas F. "Historical notes to a Tárrega recital of
       1888". *GuitarN* CVII (Jan-Mar 1970) 24-27.
The works listed on an 1888 recital program of Tárrega are original
works by Tárrega and transcriptions of late nineteenth-century compositions. The transcriptions on the program are discussed with
conclusions drawn concerning program choice. Program listed.

810   HOFMEESTER, Theodorus M. Jr. "Is there a school of Tárrega".
       GuitarR I (1946) 4-6.
Hofmeester examines Tárrega's contribution to guitar technique and
the resulting formation of a "rational system". Domingo Prat's
theory that there can be no "school of Tárrega" because he left no
written method is refuted. The ideas of Roch, Pujol, Sor, Aguado,
and Carcassi on selected technical points are compared to those of
Tárrega. Port., bibliog. ref. in notes.

811   LLOBET, Miguel. "Francisco Tárrega". *DieGit* IX/9-10 (1928)
       64. In De.
A short sketch of Tárrega as a man and as an artist. Notes on his
compositions and transcriptions.

812   LLOBET, Miguel. "Francisco Tárrega". *RMCatalana* VII/73
       (1910) 9-10. In Ca.
A portrait of Tárrega with notes on his outstanding qualities as an
artist.

Modern Histories   (813-819)

813   LÓPEZ, Antonio. "Francisco Tárrega Eixea (1854-1909)". *DieGit*
        XI/1-2 (1930) 1-5. In De.
A biographical survey of the life of Tárrega. Author's sources are
not indicated. Quotation of a contemporary report on Tárrega's vir-
tuosity. List of some compositions.

814   OPHEE, Matanya. "The promotion of Francisco Tárrega - a case
        history". In 2 parts. *Soundb* VIII/3 (Aug 1981) 152 (port.),
        153-58; VIII/4 (Nov 1981) 256-61.
Part 1: The author investigates and compares the opinions on
Tárrega's historians Pujol, Prat, and Llobet. The subjectivity
which has caused the aggrandizement of Tárrega's name is distin-
guished from historically documented facts. In particular, Pujol
has over-emphasized the influence of Tárrega on his own teachings.
His contribution independent of Tárrega and the influence of Aguado
on Pujol are pointed out. Prat's critical portrayals of Pujol and
Tárrega are evaluated. Port., bibliog. ref. in notes.
Part 2: A discussion of the reputation of Tárrega by his disciples
at the expense of past traditions, especially of the teachings of
Sor and Aguado. Includes the ideas of Prat, Llobet, Roch, Pujol,
Sagreras. Views on what constitutes the school of Tárrega. The
author evaluates Tárrega's contribution to technique in a comparison
of Tárrega's teachings to past traditions. Bibliog. ref. in notes.

815   PUJOL, Emilio. *Tárrega. Ensayo biográfico* [Tárrega.
        Biographical essay]. Prologue by Eduardo L. Chavarri.
        (Valencia: Artes Graficas Soler, 1978). In Sp.
A detailed biographical study of the life and works of Tárrega.
Recital programs are shown. List of works (original compositions and
transcriptions). Ports., index, 266p.
Review: GuitarLute IV (Mar 1977) 25-28.

816   PUJOL, Emilio. "El 32 aniversario de la muerte de Tárrega"
        [The 32nd anniversary of the death of Tárrega]. *Guitarra*
        (Havana) II/3 (Dec 1941) 14. In Sp.
A commentary on Tárrega with a discussion of his contributions to
the guitar. Illus.

817   PUJOL, Emilio. "Tárrega as teacher". *GuitarN* IX (Oct-Nov 1952)
        2-3.
Pujol's praise of Tárrega. No detail on technical approach to or
philosophy of teaching.

818   PUJOL, Emilio. "Pedagogía de Tárrega" [The pedagogy of
        Tárrega]. *Guitarra* (Havana) II/2 (June 1941) 7, 30. In Sp.
A portrait of Tárrega with information on his teaching philosophies.

819   PUJOL, Emilio. "Tárregas Wohnhaus" [Tárrega's home].
        ÖsterreichGitarreZ III/3-4 (Apr-July 1929) 49-52. In De.
Pujol's reflections on Tárrega's home with a description of Tárrega
as a man and as a musician at home in his daily routine.

(820-829)   Modern Histories

820   PUJOL, Emilio. "Tárrega's home". *ÖsterreichGitarreZ* (Aug
         1930) 15-18.
An English translation of 819.

821   PUJOL, Emilio. "Tárrega's home". *Crescendo* XXIII/4 (Dec
         1930) 13, 16.
An English translation of 819.

822   ROBERTS, John D. "Historical notes: Tárrega". *Guitar* I (Oct
         1972).

823   ROBERTS, John D., trans. "Notes on Tárrega". *Guitar* IV/5
         (Dec 1975) 29.
A translation of comments on Tárrega made by Rafael Balaguer.

824   ROBERTS, John D. "Tárrega concert". *BMG* LXIII/729 (Jan 1966)
         133.
Comments on a concert by Tárrega translated from the journal *La
Vanguardia* of Vall de Uxo (1904). Discussion of Tárrega as a per-
forming artist.

825   SAINZ DE LA MAZA, Regino. "Homage". *GuitarN* IX (Oct-Nov
         1952) 2-3.
A tribute to Tárrega and his contribution to the guitar.

826   SAVIO, Isaias. "Clasicos antiguo". *Guitarra* (Chicago)
         V/29 (Nov-Dec 1967) 12-18. In En.
A discussion of the life and major contributions of Tárrega. Port.

827   SCHWARZ-REIFLINGEN, Erwin. "Tárregas Gitarrentechnik" [The
         guitar technique of Tárrega]. *DieGit* XI/1-2 (1930) 9-11.
         In De.
Analysis of Tárrega's teachings with a comparison to methods before
him. Tárrega's influence in Germany is considered with notes on
recent guitar-related activities in Germany.

828   STEWART, Jimmy. "The guitarist as a complete musician.
         Francisco Tárrega: a tribute". *GuitarP* VII/1 (Jan-Feb
         1973) 43.
A short biography of Tárrega.

829   "Tárrega als Mensch und Künstler im Urteil seiner Zeit-
         genossen" [Tárrega as a man and as an artist in the judgment
         of his contemporaries]. *DieGit* XI/1-2 (1930) 5-8. In De.
Quotations of writings by Felipe Pedrell, Miguel Llobet, and Emilio
Pujol. Eulogies, comments on his significance as a composer, ar-
ranger, and performer.

TORROBA, Federico Moreno (b. 1891)

See also 643

Modern Histories   (830-836)

830   "Biography of a composer. Federico Moreno Torroba". *Guitarra*
       (Chicago) I/3 (July–Aug 1963) 17.
A short biography of Torroba with a summary of his compositions.

831   "Incontri. Incontro con Federico Moreno Torroba di Griselda
       Ponce de Léon" [Encounters. Interview with Federico Moreno
       Torroba by Griselda Ponce de Léon]. *Fronimo* VI/24 (July 1978)
       3–6.
Torroba discusses his own compositions, problems in composing for
the guitar, musical style, and the influence of Segovia. Port.,
bibliog. ref. in notes.

832   STEWART, Jimmy. "The guitarist as a complete musician.
       Federico Moreno Torroba". *GuitarP* VIII/3 (Mar 1974) 45.
A short biography of Torroba with a summary of his compositions.
Music (by Jimmy Stewart).

TURINA, Joaquin (1882–1949)

See also 643

833   STEWART, Jimmy. "The guitarist as a complete musician. Joaquin
       Turina". *GuitarP* VII/8 (Dec 1973) 45.
A short biography of Turina with some compositions mentioned.

VILLA-LOBOS, Heitor (1887–1959)

See also 64, 78, 643, 737, 804

834   ABLÓNIZ, Miguel. "More about the Choro". *GuitarN* XLV (Nov–
       Dec 1958) 12.
The dates for Villa-Lobos's works in the *Suite Brasilienne* and
Prelude no. 3 and no. 4 are established.
See also: Appleby 835.

835   APPLEBY, Wilfrid M. "The choro – and Villa-Lobos". *GuitarN*
       XLIV (Sept–Oct 1958) 21.
Comments on the meaning and the use of the term chŏro and on the
works of Villa-Lobos by that title. Notes on his publications as
of 1958.
See also: Ablóniz 834.

836   GLADSTONE, Ralph J. "An interview with Heitor Villa-Lobos".
       GuitarR XXI (1957) 13.
An interview with Villa-Lobos by Vladimir Bobri, John Richter, and
the author in Feb 1957. Includes Villa-Lobos's discussion of his
association with the guitar and guitarists from childhood. Music
("Modinha" by Villa-Lobos, Rio, 1926), p. 11–13.

(837-844)   Modern Histories

837   JAFFEE, Michael. "Harmony in the solo guitar music of Heitor
          Villa-Lobos". *GuitarR* XXIX (June 1966) 18-22.
An analysis of harmony and structure in Villa-Lobos's works for solo
guitar. Influences on his style are noted. Music examples are taken
from "Suite populaire bresilienne", "Chôros", the "Etudes", the
"Preludes", and "Brazilian folk tunes". Text is divided into the
following sections: 1. "General tonal organization" 2. "Modulatory
procedures" 3. "Parallelism" 4. "Polytonality" 5. "Chord vocabu-
lary". Music, bibliog. ref. in notes.

838   KELLY, Christine Kuehn. "The twentieth century's preeminent
          classical guitar composer. Villa-Lobos". *GuitarP* XV/7 (July
          1981) 70-71.
A survey of Villa-Lobos's education, career, and the influences on
his style of composition. Includes some brief comments on his works
for guitar. Port.

839   LORIMER, Michael. "Prelude no. 1. An analysis". *GuitarP* XV/7
          (July 1981) 71-72.
Passages selected from Villa-Lobos's Prelude no. 1 are analyzed for
their technical difficulty. Villa-Lobos's idiomatic writing creates
a musical texture which is quite accessible to guitarists. No background in theory is required. Music examples are notated in the
original staff notation and in tablature.

840   SANTOS, Turibio. *Heitor Villa-Lobos e lo violão* [Heitor Villa-
          Lobos and the guitar]. (Rio de Janeiro: Museu Villa-Lobos,
          1975). In Pt.
"Discusses problems of performance, analyzes the guitar music, and
gives pertinent biographical details. Port., music, bibliog., list
of works." - Quoted from *RILM* IX/1-2 (Jan-Aug 1975) 1614bm[28].

841   SCARLATTI, Vincenzo. "Clasicos Antiguo". *Guitarra* (Chicago)
          V/26 (May-June 1967) 18-19. In En.
Notes on the life and works of Villa-Lobos. Port.

842   SCHAFFER, John W. "The published solo guitar music of Heitor
          Villa-Lobos". MA diss., Music: Southeastern Community College,
          P.O. Box 151, Whiteville, N.C. 28472.
See also: Soundb VI/4 (Nov 1979) 149 for announcement.

843   SCHAFFER, John W. "Voice-leading: Towards a better under-
          standing of select passages in Villa-Lobos' Preludes for
          guitar". *Soundb* VII/4 (Nov 1980) 155-59.
Schenkerian analysis of voice-leading in passages selected from
Villa-Lobos's Preludes no. 1 and no. 4. Background on Schenkerian
theory included. Bibliog. ref. in notes. Music.

844   SEGOVIA, Andrés. "I meet Villa-Lobos". Trans. from the
          Spanish by Eithne Golden. *GuitarR* XXII (1958) 22-23.
Segovia's account of his meeting with Heitor Villa-Lobos at the home
of the Countess Olga de Moraes Sarmento in Paris in 1924. Illus.

Modern Histories   (845-850)

845 STEWART, Jimmy. "The guitarist as a complete musician. Heitor
     Villa-Lobos". *GuitarP* VIII/6 (June 1974) 61.
A short biography of Villa-Lobos with some compositions mentioned.
Music (by Jimmy Stewart).

846 ZVENGROWSKI, Steven. "Structural patterns found in Prelude
     number 4 by Hector Villa-Lobos". *Soundb* VI/3 (Aug 1979)
     86-89.
A detailed analysis of structural patterns in [Heitor] Villa-
Lobos's Prelude no. 4 provides insights into performance possi-
bilities. Music.

WEBERN, Anton (1883-1945)

See 642

WILLIAMS, John (b. 1941)

See 639, 686, 775

YEPES, Narciso (b. 1927)

See also 1035

847 JIMENEZ, Salvador. "With Narciso Yepes". *Guitarra* (Chicago)
     II/9 (July-Aug 1964) 3-12.
Topics of discussion include Yepes's career and education, his
interests, and his opinions on the ten-string guitar. Port.

848 KOZINN, Allan. "Narciso Yepes. Classical master of the ten-
     string guitar". *Frets* II/2 (Feb 1980) 39-42.
A discussion of Yepes's views on the value of the ten-string guitar.
Includes his comments on the guitar repertoire and his experiences
as a guitarist. Illus.

849 SENSIER, Peter. "Narciso Yepes and the ten-string guitar".
     Guitar III/9 (Apr 1975) 27.
Yepes's reason for using four additional bass strings on the guitar
are given.

850 SNITZLER, Larry. "Narciso Yepes. The ten-string guitar:
     overcoming the limitations of six strings". *GuitarP* XII/3
     (Mar 1978) 26, 42, 46, 48, 52.
Yepes discusses the use, the value, and his reasons for developing
the ten-string guitar. Also considered in the conversation are
Yepes's early education, right-hand techniques, and teaching. Biographical information is given in the introductory notes. Port.,
selected discog. of the recordings by Yepes.

(851-856)   Modern Histories

851   WALTER, E. "Narciso Yepes: la guitare classique en pleine
      renaissance" [Narciso Yepes: the classic guitar in full
      renaissance]. *Harmonie* CXXXV (Mar 1978) 44-48.

ZARATE-DUO

See 633

D. Selected Interviews of Performers and Composers

ARTZT, Alice

852   BOSMAN, Lance. "My guitar obeys instructions ... says Alice
      Artzt". *Guitar* II/1 (Aug 1973) 23.
Alice Artzt discusses performance and recalls personal experiences
of her performing career. Her attitudes toward teaching, her
guitars, and the effect of the particular instrument on her interpretation and technique are also topics of discussion. Port.

853   "Incontri. Colloquio con Alice Artzt". [Encounters. Meeting
      with Alice Artzt]. *Fronimo* II/8 (July 1974) 5-8. In It.
Alice Artzt is interviewed by Angelo Gilardino. Artzt discusses her
concert tours, teaching, recording, contemporary performers and
repertoire, and guitar makers. Port.

854   "Interview: Artzt". *GuitarLute* I/1 (Apr-June 1974) 11-12, 33.
A 1973 interview with Alice Artzt includes a discussion of her background and education, her opinions on the role of women in music,
experiences in recording, and her opinions on non-classical styles.
Port.

BARRUECO, Manuel

855   ADAMS, Henry. "Interview: Manuel Barrueco". *GuitarLute* XVI
      (Jan 1981) 7-10, 12, 14, 16.
A biography of Barrueco and a discussion of Latin American music
and concert repertoire, Barrueco's career, teaching philosophy,
and future plans are considered. Port.

BOYD, Liona

856   LAWRENCE, Catherine. "Liona Boyd and *Guitarra*". *Guitarra*
      (Chicago) XXXVII (Mar-Apr 1980) 2-3.
The interview includes a discussion of Liona Boyd's education, technique, career experiences, and reflections on being a woman in
music. Port.

Modern Histories   (857-861)

BROUWER, Leo (b. 1939)

See also 78, 643

857   BREUKERS, El. "Leo Brouwer in Holland". *Guitar* V/9 (Apr
       1977) 7-8.
Brouwer is interviewed during a concert tour in Holland. Brouwer
discusses his feelings for Cuba, opinions on the 'avant-garde', and
his compositions "Metafora del amor" and "Hommage a Lenin".

CHIESA, Ruggero (b. 1933)

858   FARRELL, Terrence. "Interview: Ruggero Chiesa". *GuitarLute*
       XI (Oct 1979) 13-14.
Chiesa discusses his views on repertoire, composition, recordings,
performance and transcription of early music, Pujol's influence, and
chamber music. Biographical information on Chiesa included.

DIAZ, Alirio (b. 1923)

See also 775, 866

859   BREUKERS, El. "Alirio Diaz in Zwolle". *Guitar* IX/4 (Nov
       1980) 20-21.
Commentary on the guitar course in Zwolle, Holland, where Diaz
taught in the summer of 1980. The interview includes a discussion
of Diaz's early study, musical preferences, opinions, activities,
and views on teaching. Port.

860   "Incontri. Intervista ad Alirio Diaz" [Encounters. Interview
       with Alirio Diaz]. *Fronimo* II/6 (Jan 1974) 3-5. In It.
Diaz is interviewed by Ruggero Chiesa and Silvio Cerutti. Includes a
discussion of composers and repertoire of the nineteenth and twentieth centuries, Diaz's interest in South American folk music, Segovia,
repertoire, and transcription. Port.

DUARTE, John (b. 1919)

See 643, 775 (an interview)

FISK, Eliot

861   KOZINN, Allan. "Eliot Fisk. Dynamic classical performer,
       outspoken teacher". *GuitarP* XIV/6 (June 1980) 30-34, 36.
Introductory notes on Fisk's achievements and activities as a
guitarist. Fisk's work with Ralph Kirkpatrick, aspects of performance, his own values and attitudes towards performance,

(861-867)   Modern Histories

technique, rhythm, and transcription are among the topics discussed. Port.

862   WAGER-SCHNEIDER, John. "A feature conversation with Eliot
       Fisk". *Soundb* VIII/1 (Feb 1981) 10-17.
The interview offers a detailed discussion of Fisk's views on
transcribing music for guitar, transcription methodology, and
interpretation. References to specific works. Concluding remarks
on his activities as a performer and as a recording artist. Port.

GHIGLIA, Oscar

863   "Incontri. Intervista a Oscar Ghiglia". [Encounters. Inter-
       view with Oscar Ghiglia]. *Fronimo* I/3 (Apr 1973) 3-5.
Oscar Ghiglia is interviewed by Ruggero Chiesa. Includes commentary
on the study of the guitar, repertoire, and fingering and technique
in relationship to musical interpretation. Port.

ISBIN, Sharon

864   BOSMAN, Lance. "Sharon Isbin. 'As a woman you don't have
       models". *Guitar* VI/2 (Sept 1977) 23-24.
Sharon Isbin discusses fingering and practicing, her concert career,
her feelings on being a woman in music. Port.

865   LAWRENCE, Catherine. "Viewpoints. Sharon Isbin in Chicago".
       Guitarra (Chicago) L (Sept-Oct 1980) 16-19.
Introductory notes give biographical information on Sharon Isbin.
The interview includes a discussion of Isbin's recent activities
as a performer and as a teacher, her education, her research on
Bach (with specific references to the performance of Bach on the
guitar), and her views on technical studies. Port.

LAURO, Antonio (b. 1913)

See also 78

866   ADAMS, Henry. "Interview. Antonio Lauro". *GuitarLute* XII
       (Jan 1980) 8-12.
Introductory notes on Lauro include biographical information and
comments on his compositions. The interview includes a discussion
of Lauro's approach to composition, his association with Alirio
Diaz, his knowledge of Venezuelan music and instruments, and their
influence on his style of composition. Port., map of Venezuela,
list of works (for solo guitar, for guitar with other instruments,
and arrangements and transcriptions).

867   "Antonio Lauro in conversation with Sue McCreadie". *Guitar*
       IX/2 (Oct 1980) 16-17.

Modern Histories   (867-870)

Lauro discusses his early interests and influences, his compositions, and his method of composing. Port.

THE ROMERO FAMILY (Celedonio [father], Celín, Pepe, Angel [sons])

868   ADAMS, Henry. "Interview. The Romeros". *GuitarLute* VII
        (Sept 1978) 15-17.
Biographical information on the Romero family is given in the
introductory notes. The family discusses composers and their choice
of repertoire, recording plans, and transcription, among other
topics. Information on the guitar curriculum at USC is included.

869   *Guitarra* magazine. "An evening with Angel Romero". *Guitarra*
        (Chicago) XXXVIII (May-June 1980) 11-13.
Angel Romero is interviewed by James Sherry, Eve Warren, and Nico
Angel. Includes a discussion of technique, composers of guitar
music, and teaching. Port.

SAINZ DE LA MAZA, Regino (b. 1896)

See also 66, 109, 760

870   ADAMS, Henry. "Interview. Regino Sainz de la Maza". *Guitar-
        Lute* XIII (Apr 1980) 12-15.
Introductory notes give biographical information on Sainz de la
Maza. Sainz de la Maza discusses influences on his early interest
in guitar, guitar composition, transcription, repertoire, perfor-
mance, and education. Illus. (concert program by Sainz de la Maza).
Port.

CHAPTER SEVEN

Iconographies

The study of musical iconography has contributed to the understanding of performance practices, technique, social function, and the question of pre-Renaissance origins of the vihuela and the guitar. Available literature written on vihuela and guitar iconography is limited. Representations of the instruments, however, are found in the works of significant artists. Artists Edgar Degas, Francisco José de Goya, Edouard Manet, Henri Matisse, Pablo Picasso, Marc-Antoine Raimondi, and Antoine Watteau are among those who chose the guitar or vihuela as a subject for their art.

The following chapter is divided into four sections: Section A. General Surveys, Section B. The Seventeenth Century, Section C. Nineteenth-Century Lithography, and Section D. Individual Artists.

In Section A., cross-references are made to those general histories of the guitar which contain a substantial number of reproductions of guitar iconography. In addition to the wealth of iconography in Grunfeld's work (entry 20), a number of reproductions are also contained in Bellow (entry 8), Evans (entries 15, 16), Ragossnig (entry 35), and Turnbull (entry 43).

(871-875)

A. General Surveys

See also 8, 15, 20, 35, 43, 896, 897

871   BECK, Sydney; ROTH, Elizabeth E. *Music in prints*. (New York:
        The New York Public Library, 1965).
52 plates from the New York Public Library collection of prints.
Descriptive notes on each plate cites artist, date, nationality,
title, and type of print. Guitars are represented in the works of
Vincent M. Langlois the younger (pl. 35), Francisco José de Goya y
Lucientes (pl. 38), Edouard Manet (pl. 41), Jacques Villon (pseud.
of Gaston Duchamp) (pl. 45), Henri Laurens (pl. 46), Hans Fischer
(pl. 48).

872   DUFOURCQ, Norbert. *La musique, les hommes, les instruments,
        les oeuvres* [Music, men, instruments, works]. 2 v. (Paris:
        Librarie Larousse, 1965). In Fr.
A chronological survey of the history of musical instruments. Includes a brief historical discussion of the guitar and of the
vihuela mentioning significant composers and their works.
V. 1: 11 illustrations of historical guitars and iconography of
the guitar including art works by Marc-Antoine Raimondi, David
Teniers le Jeune, Antoine le Nain, Jean Garnier, and Goya. "Glos-
saire des instruments" [Glossary of instruments], bibliog., index,
391p.
V. 2: 3 representations of the guitar including works by Gouache
de Gauthier Dagoty and N.A. Taunay. Bibliog., index, 399p.

873   GIANOLI, L.; MASCHERPA, G. *La pittura e la musica* [Painting
        and music]. (Milan: Arti Grafiche Ricordi, 1967). In It.
60 plates of works of art representing musical subjects from ancient
times to the twentieth century. Description and location of the work
is given. The guitar is pictured in works by François Pujet (pl. 32),
Francisco Goya (pl. 38), and George Braque (pl. 54). 29p. (text).

874   "Guitar Gallery". In 4 parts. *Guitarra* (Chicago) V/25 (Mar-
        Apr 1967) 19; V/26 (May-June 1967) 16-17; V/27 (July-Aug
        1967) 12-13; V/29 (Nov-Dec 1967).
Reproductions of works of art in which the guitar is represented.
Part 1: A work by David Ryckaert III (17th c. Vienna).
Part 2: Includes a work by Edouard Manet.
Part 3: Includes a work by Marguerite Gérard (Leningrad, early
19th c.).
Part 4: A work by Henri Matisse.

875   HARRISON, Frank; RIMMER, Joan. *European musical instruments*.
        (London: Studio Vista Limited, 1964).
A chronological survey of the history of musical instruments. Includes illustrations of historical guitars (2) and iconography of
the guitar (6). Little information is given on the guitar in the
text. Artists represented include frescos of the Renaissance,
Velasquez, Theodoor Rombouts, and the instrument maker's shop

(875-882)   Iconographies

from Diderot and D'Alembert's *Encyclopédie* (1751 onwards). Plate 93,
a vihuela from Bermudo's *Declaracion*, is omitted from the index. 248
illus., index, 74p. (text), 210p.

876   HÖHNE, Erich. *Musik in der Kunst* [Music in art]. (Leipzig:
        Veb E.A. Seemann Verlag, 1965).
46 plates with descriptive commentary in German, Russian, English,
and French. Information on artist, title, type of art, and location
is given. Illustration 29: Jean-Baptiste Oudry, "Table in the
artist's studio with musical instruments" (1713) includes a representation of a guitar. 18p. (text).

877   KENDALL, Alan. *The world of musical instruments*. (London:
        Hamlyn Publishing Group Ltd., 1972).
A general historical survey organized by instrument type. Includes a
short, inaccurate survey of the history of the guitar. Representation
of an historical guitar (Tielke, 1693) and iconography including
works by Degas, Ben Shahn, and the instrument maker's shop in Diderot
and D'Alembert's *Encyclopédia* (1751 onwards). 128p.

878   KINSKY, Georg. *A history of music in pictures*. Introduction
        by Eric Blom. (New York: E.P. Dutton & Co., Inc., 1930).
An iconographical survey of the history of musical instruments from
ancient times through the eighteenth century. Includes 29 reproductions of iconography of guitars and of historical guitars. Among the
works of art are those by Bernhard Schmid l'aîné, Giov. Filoteo
Achillini, Caravaggio, Bernard Jobin, François Pujet, Gaspard
Duiffiproncart, Etienne Picart, Gonzales Coques, Theodor Rombouts,
Jan Fijt, Watteau, Jean-Honore Fragonard, M. Barth, and plates from
the publications of music by Jacob Kremberg (1689), Jacques-Champion
de Chambonnières (1670), and Pablo Minguet (1752-54). 1560 reproductions. 364p.

879   KINSKY, Georg. *Storia della musica attraverso l'immagine*
        [A history of music in pictures]. Introduction by Gaetano
        Cesari. (Milan: Sperling & Kupfer S.A., 1930). In It.
An Italian translation of 878.

880   KINSKY, Georg. *Album Musical* [Picture album of music]. Preface
        by Henry Prunière. (Paris: Librairie Delagrave, 1930). In Fr.
A French translation of 878.

881   MORECK, Curt (pseud.) [Haemmerling, Konrad]. *Die Musik in
        der Malerei* [Music in painting]. (Munich: G. Hirth's Verlag,
        n.d.). 2 parts in 1 v. In De.
Representations of the guitar include works by Bernardino Pinturicchio, Diego Velasquez, Antoine Watteau, Nicolas Lancret, Gottlieb
Schick, and Francisco de Goya. Part 1, 113p. (text); Part 2, 147p.
(plates).

882   PINCHERLE, Marc. *An illustrated history of music*. Trans. by
        Rollo Myers. (New York: Reynal & Co., 1959).
                              180

Etching. *Blind Guitarist on the Horns of a Bull*
by Francisco José de Goya Y Lucientes.

Lithograph. *The Clown Andreff with Guitar* by Hans Fischer.

Iconographies (882-887)

A chronological survey of the history of music in art from ancient times to the twentieth century. Commentary on iconography includes information on artist, title, date, description, location of the work. The guitar is represented in the works of the following artists: Larmessin, Marc-Antoine Charpentier, Claude Gillot, Eugène Manet, Pablo Picasso, Georges Braque, and the engraving of an instrument maker's workshop in Diderot and D'Alembert's *Encyclopédie*. Index, 221p.

883 WELLER, M.P.I. "Some steps in the evolution of the Spanish guitar and related instruments, based on a consideration of iconographic evidence". Dissertation in progress, Newcastle (MLH).

B. The Seventeenth Century

884 MIRIMONDE, A.P. de. *L'iconographie musicales sous les rois bourbons. La musique dans les arts plastiques (XVIIe-XVIIIe siècles)* [Musical iconography under the Bourbon kings. Music in plastic arts (XVIIth-XVIIIth centuries)]. (Paris: Éditions A. et J. Picard, 1975). 2 v. In Fr.
V. 1, Ch. V "Musiciens isolés et portraits au XVIIe siècle". "La guitare" [Isolated musicians and portraits in the XVIIth century. The guitar], p. 144-45. A brief explanation of the role of the guitar in XVIIth-century France as shown through iconography. Fig. 105: by Stéphano della Bella; Fig. 106: by A. Quensel. V. 1: LXXII plates containing 142 figs., 202p. (text).
Reviews: CourrierMFrance LII (1975) 156; *MTimes* CXVII (July 1976) 593-94; *RMSuisseRomande* XXIX/5 (1976) 172; *SchweizerischeMz* CXVI/3 (1976) 211-12.

C. Nineteenth-Century Lithography

885 FROMLICH, Yane. *Musique et caricature en France au XIXe siècle* [Music and caricature in nineteenth-century France]. (Genève: Éditions Minkoff, 1973). In Fr.
136 plates organized by subject. Annotations give title, description, artist, original source of publication, date. Plates 19, 20, and 70 are lithographs by Honoré Daumier in which the guitar is pictured. Includes introduction, chronology, table of illustrations, and bibliog.

886 GRUNFELD, Frederic V. "L'Accord parfait en amour. Incidental notes to the graphic music of Balzac's Paris". *GuitarR* XLIV (Summer 1978) 1-2.
A study of lithography in nineteenth-century France. Social attitudes and the concurrent age of *Guitaromanie* are revealed.

887 [GRUNFELD, Frederic V.]. "A portfolio of nineteenth-century lithographs and wood engravings from F.V. Grunfeld's

(887-892)   Iconographies

collection". *GuitarR* XLIV (Summer 1978) 3-20.
20 works are reproduced. Title, description, artist, publisher, and
date are cited.

D. Individual Artists

DE GOYA Y LUCIENTES, Francisco José (1746-1828)

See also 682

888   FENTON, Edward. "Aveugle enlevé sur les cornes d'un taureau
        [Goya]" [Blind man tossed by a bull]. *GuitarR* XIII (1952) 14.
Brief notes on Goya and his use of the guitar in art. Iconog.

889   FENTON, Edward. "Goya and the guitar". *GuitarR* XIV (1952)
        36-38.
A short history and interpretation of Goya's art in which the guitar
is pictured. Five representative works shown are "Scene populaire",
"Blind man singing", "Brabisimo", "Dancers and guitarist", and "Nun
frightened by a ghost". Iconog.

PICASSO, Pablo (1881-1980)

890   D'ALESSIO, Gregory. "Pablo Picasso – monument or mountebank?
        A guitarist's reaction to the guitar in modern art". In 2
        parts. *GuitarR* XLVI (Winter 1979) 2-6; XLVII (Spring 1980)
        1-6.
Part 1: Author's reflections on and opinions of the guitar in modern
art. Emphasis is on the discussion of Picasso's sculpture entitled
"Guitar" (1911). Iconog. (Picasso, Braque, Bobri).
Part 2: Further opinions and analysis of Picasso's representation of
the guitar with emphasis on a study of Picasso's sculpture "Guitar"
(1911). Segovia's reaction to the sculpture is included. Iconog.
(Picasso).

891   HAWARD, Lawrence. *Music in painting*. (London: Faber and
        Faber, 1945). Second impression (1946).
10 plates and discussion. Plate 10: Pablo Picasso, "Les trois
masques" (1921). A discussion of Picasso's treatment of the guitar
in art with a comparison to Watteau's treatment. 22p.

892   SPIES, Warner. "La guitare anthropomorphe" [The anthropo-
        morphic guitar]. *RArt* XII (1971) 89-92. In Fr, summary in
        En (p. 109) and in De (p. 110).
The role of the musical instrument and the function of its form in
cubist art are discussed. Emphasis is on Picasso's representations.
Bibliog. ref. in notes, iconog.
See also: RILM V/2 (May-Aug 1971) 1932ap[10].

Iconographies   (893-894)

WATTEAU, Jean Antoine (1684-1721)

See also 891

893   FENTON, Edward. "Jean Antoine Watteau". *GuitarR* XVI (1954)
       111-12.
Introductory notes on Watteau's style and his representation of the
early guitar. Historical background on the guitar contains inaccuracies. Two engravings: "Leçon d'amour" and "La game d'amour".

894   MIRIMONDE, A.P. de. "Les instruments de musique chez Antoine
       Watteau" [The musical instruments in the works of Antoine
       Watteau]. *BulSocHistArtFrançais*. *Extrait* (May 1927) 47-53.
       In Fr.
A study of the representation of musical instruments in the works of
Watteau. The significance of Watteau's work in the study of guitar
performance practice is considered.

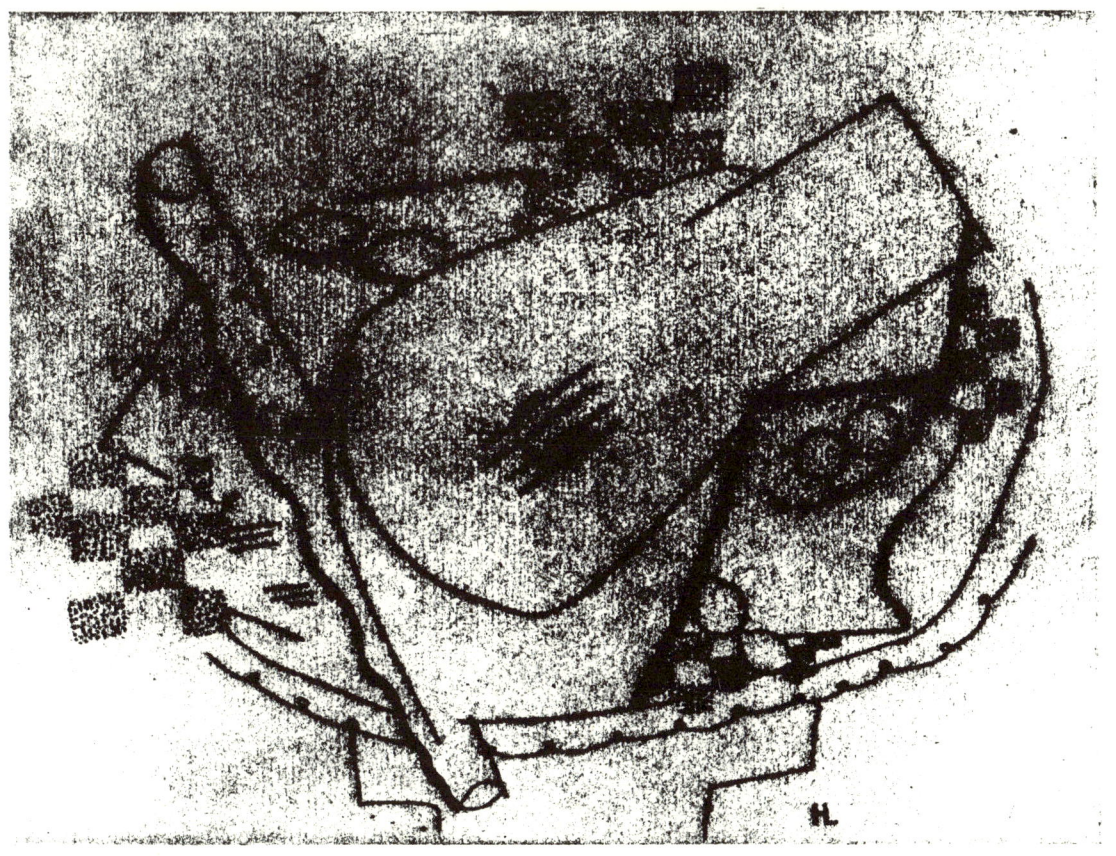

Etching. *Still Life* by Henri Laurens.

CHAPTER EIGHT

Design and Construction

This chapter contains literature on both the historical aspects and the technical and scientific aspects of the design and construction of the guitar and the vihuela. These aspects are documented as early as the sixteenth century in extant instruments, treatises, and other texts in which builders' activities are described. Iconographies, also valuable in determining the physical structure of the guitar, are listed in Chapter VII.

Instrument exhibition catalogs and museum publications are excluded from this chapter. Several reference works are available which give information on musical instrument collections, instrument makers' businesses, and manufacturers. A listing of musical instrument collections in museums, libraries, conservatories, and private collections is available in *International directory of musical instrument collections*, ed. by Jean Jenkins (Buren, Gld., Netherlands: Frits Knuf for the International Council of Museums ICOM, 1977). In this reference work, the contents of collections are summarized, and available services and publications are listed. *A survey of musical instrument collections in the United States and Canada*, compiled by William Lichtenwanger (Ann Arbor, Michigan: Music Library Association, 1974) is organized by county, state, and city and gives detail on 572 collections. James Coover's *Musical instrument collections. Catalogues and cognate literature*, Detroit Studies in Music Bibliography, no. 47, (Detroit, Michigan: Information Coordinators, 1981) gives further information on publications concerning collections. Also useful is Vincent Duckles's chapter on "Catalogs of musical instrument collections" in *Music reference and research materials. An annotated bibliography*, 3rd ed. (New York: Schirmer Books, 1974). This contains an international listing of catalogs, organized by city. Susan Caust Farrell's *Directory of contemporary American musical instrument makers* (Columbia and London: University of Missouri Press, 1981) includes guitar makers in its listing. Appendixes give information on instrument making schools, societies, and a bibliography. In a section on music industries in Christopher Pavlakis's *The American music handbook* (New York: The Free Press, 1974), sixteen manufacturers of fretted instruments are listed with information on their businesses.

This chapter is divided into twelve sections: Section A. General Surveys, Section B. Dictionaries of Luthiers, Section C. The Sixteenth Century: Vihuela and Guitar, Section D. From 1600 to 1900, Section E. National Histories, Section F. Individual Luthiers of the Twentieth

187

DESIGN AND CONSTRUCTION

Century, Section G. Construction Manuals, Section H. Studies of Acoustics and other Scientific Aspects of the Guitar's Construction, Section I. Guitar Strings, Section J. The Eight-String Guitar, Section K. The Ten-String Guitar, and Section L. The Microtonal Guitar.

Section A. includes a selected number of general histories of musical instruments which contain information on historical guitars. Specifically, these are entries 897–900.

Section B. lists French- and German-language texts. Cross-referenced texts are in Italian.

Section C. is divided into three sub-sections: SOURCE READINGS, SECONDARY WORKS, and MODERN LUTISTRY. The only entry cited in SOURCE READINGS is a 1556 French-language treatise which gives a detailed explanation of the Pythagorean system of fretting. SECONDARY WORKS includes studies of extant instruments, luthiers' records, and luthiers' marks. MODERN LUTISTRY contains a list of articles in which present-day makers' techniques for constructing reproductions of early instruments are discussed.

Section D. is divided into three sub-sections: SOURCE READINGS INCLUDING CONSTRUCTION MANUALS, SECONDARY WORKS: LUTHIERS AND HISTORICAL INSTRUMENTS, and INDIVIDUAL LUTHIERS. The third sub-section is further divided by individual luthier.

Section E. contains sub-sections of individual countries. These are Argentina, Austria, France, Germany, Mexico, and Spain.

Section F., organized alphabetically by luthier, includes interviews, biographies, and discussions of makers' construction techniques and materials.

Section G. contains annotations which give general descriptions of the contents and the organization of the literature. No attempt has been made to evaluate the actual quality of the advice and instruction contained in these publications.

Section H. lists works which treat the study of acoustics and physical sound production, including works based specifically on the results of experiments in physics. Many of these are detailed and highly technical.

Section I. contains material on early twentieth-century string manufacturing (entries 1031, 1032) and a debate over the addition of bass strings to the guitar (entry 1033).

Section J. lists one article in which the advantages of the eight-string guitar in the performance of early music are considered.

Section K. contains literature in which the ten-string guitar is described and its advantages over the six-string guitar are discussed. Further readings are found under Narcisco Yepes (entries 847–51) in Chapter VI.

In Section L., works on the construction of the microtonal guitar are listed. Cross-references refer to literature on Julián Antonio Carrillo-Trujillo (entries 674–77), who is noted for his experiments in notation and composition in a microtonal system.

(895-899)

A. General Surveys

See also 10, 12, 872

895   APPLEBY, Wilfrid M. "In a museum". *GuitarN* LV (Sept-Oct
      1960) 8.
Short descriptions of several guitars by makers of the seventeenth
through the twentieth centuries which are exhibited in the Horniman
Museum (London S.E.).

896   BOBRI, Vladimir; NELSON, Martha; D'ALESSIO, Gregory. "A
      gallery of great guitars from the XVIth to the XXth century".
      In 3 parts. *GuitarR* XXX (Aug 1968) 13-27; XXXII (Fall 1969)
      14-31; XXXV (Summer 1971) 9-27.
A pictorial history of the development of the guitar's design with
front, back, and side views shown. Type, maker, date, location,
physical description, and dimensions are cited.
Part 1: [ca. 1500 - XVIIth century]. Twenty-two extant guitars and
a vihuela. Several examples of the *chitarra battente* and of the terz
guitar are included.
Part 2: "The XVIIth Century". Twenty-three extant guitars including
the *chitarra battente* and the double guitar. Illus.
Part 3: "The XVIIIth Century". Twenty-one extant guitars including
the *chitarra battente* and theorbo guitar (ten single strings),
iconog.

897   BUCHNER, Alexander. *Musical instruments: An illustrated
      history*. Trans. by Bořek Vančura. (New York: Crown Publishers,
      Inc., 1973).
A general survey of the history of musical instruments from ancient
times to the twentieth century. Includes illustrations of historical
guitars from the seventeenth through the twentieth centuries and
iconography (one work by J. Massys, 16th c.). 332 pl., illus. in
text, bibliog., index, 275p.
Reviews: MJ XXXI (Dec 1973) 6; *MEducatorsJ* LXI (Nov 1974) 75-76.

898   BUCHNER, Alexander. *Musical instruments through the ages*.
      Trans. by Iris Urwin. (London: Batchworth Press Ltd., 1961).
An historical survey of musical instruments including historical
guitars of the seventeenth and the eighteenth centuries. Includes
the guitars of makers Georgius Sellas (early 17th c.), Matthias
Fux (1692), and Thomas A. Hulinzký (1754). 323 illus., tables,
index, 38p. (text).

899   GÁBRY, György. *Old musical instruments*. Trans. by Eva Rácz.
      (Budapest: Corvina Press, Kossuth Printing House, 1969).
A general history of musical instruments which includes some comments on guitars, p. 19-20. Plate 23 pictures a lady's guitar from
the possessions of Kornélia Lotz built by José Fernandez Silva,
Orense (ca. 1900). Information on stringing, dimensions, location,
and bibliography are given. Pl. (55 instruments), 42p.

(899-903)   Design and Construction

Reviews: MTimes III (Apr 1970) 393; *MOpinion* LXLIII (July 1970) 527;
Musica XXIV/6 (1970) 597; *Mf* XXV/2 (1972) 230-31.

900   HIPKINS, Alfred James. *Musical instruments. Historic, rare
       and unique.* Illustrated with a series of forty-eight plates
       in colours drawn by William Gibb. (London: Adam and Charles
       Black, Ltd., 1921). First published (Edinburgh, 1888).
An illustrated survey of historically significant musical instruments. Annotations of plates give information on owner, location,
description, and the history of the instrument. Pl. X "The Rizzio
guitar"; pl. XXIX "Guitar by Antonio Stradivarius". 48 pl., index,
123p.

901   NICKEL, Heinz. "Beitrag zur Entwicklung der Gitarre in
       Europa" [Contribution concerning the evolution of the guitar
       in Europe]. PhD diss., Musicology: Univ. Frankfurt am Main,
       1971. (Haimhausen: Biblioteca de la Guitarra, 1972). In De.
       169p.
"Traces certain forms and building techniques of the 16th-c.
guitar to the small boards glued together in the Arabian lute (in
Europe, ca. 800) and to Spain's copies of viols made in the late
Middle Ages. The most highly developed instrument of this family,
the *vihuela da mano*, should not be called a Spanish lute, but a
guitar." - Quoted from *RILM* VII/2 (May-Aug 1973) 2521dd[44]. Illus.,
port., facsim., music, bibliog., list of works.
Reviews: NeueMz XXII (Apr-May 1973) 16; Gertrud Marbuch, *MBildung*
VI/11 (1974) 637; *IZ* XXIX/12 (1975) 762; Andrej Mentschukoff, *Soundb*
II/1 (Feb 1975) 14; *Mf* XXIX/3 (1976) 362-64.

902   SCHWARZ-REIFLINGEN, Erwin. "Zur Geschichte des Gitarren-
       baues" [Towards a history of guitar making]. *DieGit* VIII/5-6
       (May-June 1927) 33-36. In De.
An outline history of guitar construction. Building activities of
luthier Otto Schick and other late nineteenth-century luthiers are
considered. The Spanish Torres school of guitar making and the
German, French, and Italian schools are distinguished.

B. Dictionaries of Luthiers

See also 73 and 76 for dictionaries of Italian luthiers

903   FISSORE, Robert [R. Dupuich, pseud.]. *Traité de luthier
       ancienne* [Treatise on ancient luthiers]. (Paris: R. Fissore,
       1894). In Fr.
A dictionary of luthiers of the sixteenth through the eighteenth
centuries. Organization is by country (French, Italian, and English
schools) with alphabetical lists of luthiers within each category.
Each entry gives name, place, dates, description of instrument,
evaluation of work, price category. Some labels are quoted. Guitar
makers listed are Huel, Lacote, Laprevotte, Panormo, Pons, Saunier
(of France), and Bergonzi and Guadagnini (of Italy). 70p.

Design and Construction   (904-906)

904 LÜTGENDORFF, Willibald Lee, Freiherr von. *Die Geigen- und Lautenmacher vom Mittelalter bis zur Gegenwart* [Violin and lute making from the middle ages to the present]. 2 v. 5th and 6th revised ed. (Frankfurt am Main: Frankfurter Verlags-Anstalt A.G., 1922). In De.

V. 1: An historical survey of stringed instrument making. Organization by country. Includes a list of makers organized by city (dates given). 98 pl., 422p. (text).
V. 2: Alphabetical listing of makers with biographies and descriptions of their work. Facsimiles of brand marks (79) and labels (853). 670p.

905 VANNES, René. *Dictionnaire universel des luthiers* [A comprehensive dictionary of luthiers]. Preface by Giovanni Iviglia. Second ed., augmented and revised. (Brussels: Les amis de la musique, 1951). First ed. (Paris: Librairie Fischbacher, 1932). In Fr.

Main text consists of "Notices biographiques" [Biographical notices]: 15,000 entries arranged alphabetically by luthier with biographical information, main contributions, description of their work, and quotations of their label. Facsimiles of 2583 labels (n. pag.). Port., 408p. (text).

V. 2: Preface by Dr. H. Pourtois. (Brussels: Les amis de la musique, 1959).

Additions and corrections of the 2nd edition. Facsimiles of makers' labels and brands. 198p. (text).
Reviews: *VViolinists* XII (Nov 1951) 326; *RBelgeMusicol* VI (Jan-Mar 1952) 57-58; *MensMelodie* VII (Apr 1952) 124; *Strad* LXIII (Dec 1952) 248; *RMItaliana* LVII (Jan-Mar 1955) 77-78; *GalpinSocJ* XIII (July 1960) 104-06; *Notes* XVII/4 (1960) 577; *RBelgeMusicol* XIV/1-4 (1960) 144.

C. The Sixteenth Century: Vihuela and Guitar

SOURCE READINGS

906 WECKERLIN, Jean Baptiste Theodore. *Nouveau musiciana: extraits d'ouvrages rares et bizarres* [New selections of rare and unusual works]. (Paris: Garnier frères, éditeurs, 1890). In Fr.

This volume contains a reprint of an extrait entitled "La manière de bien et justement entoucher les lucs et guiternes" [The manner of tuning lutes and guitars well and precisely] from the anonymous treatise *Discours non plus mélancoliques que divers* (Poitiers: L'imprimerie d'Enguilbert de Marne, 1556). The text offers a detailed explanation of a Pythagorean system of fretting lutes and guitars. Some preliminary comments on the use and the popularity of the guitar are included. Diagrams.
See also: Turnbull 43 and Lesure 162 for comments.

191

(907-912)   Design and Construction

SECONDARY WORKS

See also 162

907   COOK, Frederick. "A vihuela in Quito?" *GuitarLute* IX (Apr
      1979) 11-12.
A description of an instrument in the Iglesia de la Compañía de
Jesús in Quito, Ecuador. Arguments are given for the identification of the instrument as a guitar and as a vihuela. The instrument
belonged to Santa Mariana de Jesús (1619-1645). Illus.

908   COUTAGNE, Henry. *Gaspard Duiffoproucart et les luthiers
      lyonnais du XVIe siècle* [Gaspard Duiffoproucart and the
      sixteenth-century luthiers of Lyon]. (Paris: Librairie
      Fischbacher, 1893). In Fr.
A detailed study of the life and works of Duiffoproucart (1514-1570)
and the Lyonnais school of luthiers based on a study of sixteenth-
century documents. In addition to Duiffoproucart, Philippe Flac is
also mentioned as a maker of guitars. Port. (Duiffoproucart, 1562),
bibliog. ref. in notes, index, 79p.

909   HELLWIG, Friedemann. "Makers' marks on plucked instruments
      of the sixteenth and seventeenth centuries". *GalpinSocJ* XXIV
      (July 1971) 22-32.
A discussion of instrument makers' marks on plucked instruments.
Marks and method of marking are described. List of marks gives information on type of mark, description of detail, identification of
instrument, location, maker, place, date. Marks on four guitars are
described. 4 pl. (30 marks), bibliog. ref. in notes.

910   LESURE, François. "La facture instrumentale à Paris au
      seizième siècle" [Instrument makers in Paris in the six-
      teenth century]. *GalpinSocJ* VII (Apr 1954) 11-52. In Fr.
An examination of sources on instrument makers from the Minutier
Central des notaires de Paris aux Archives nationales. 30 documents.

911   POULTON, Diana. "Notes and information. A vihuela in Ecuador".
      LuteSocJ XVIII (1976) 45-46.
A discussion of the discovery of a vihuela in a seventeenth-century
church in Ecuador, Chile. Description of the instrument.

912   PRYNNE, Michael. "A surviving vihuela de mano". *GalpinSocJ*
      XVI (May 1963) 22-27.
A detailed description of a vihuela. The author conjectures that it is
the only vihuela to have survived from the sixteenth century. The
instrument is located in the Musée Jacquemart-André of the Institut
de France. Chart of dimensions, pl. (vihuela).

MODERN LUTISTRY

See also 159, 174, 186

192

Design and Construction   (913-917)

913   HEITLAND, Winfried. "Zur Rekonstruktion historischer Musik-
       instrumente: Das Beispiel der Vihuela de mano" [Towards a
       reconstruction of an historical musical instrument: the
       example of the vihuela de mano]. *Musica* XXXIII/1 (Jan-Feb
       1979) 27-30. In De.
Alternative methods of vihuela construction - exact copy and recon-
struction with adaptations - are evaluated. The problem of the lack
of surviving instruments and considerations in the determination of
authenticity through the sources are topics of discussion. Illus.

914   ROBBINS, Lance. "The vihuela lives again!". *GuitarP* VII/8
       (Dec 1973) 18, 36-37.
Notes on the revival of interest in the vihuela by Lorenzo Pimentel
and Hector Garcia. Biographical information on luthier Pimentel with
some comments on his construction techniques. Includes a short
history of the vihuela. Illus., port.

915   ZAYAS, Rodrigo de. "The modern concert vihuela: a challenge
       to instrument builders of today". *GuitarR* XXXVIII (Summer
       1973) 13-22.
A discussion of the careers of Fernando (b. 1934) and César
(b. 1939) Vera, instrument makers of Madrid, who specialize in
the construction of vihuelas and early guitars. Biographical
information is given. 11 fig. (guitars and vihuelas).

D. From 1600 to 1900

SOURCE READINGS, INCLUDING CONSTRUCTION MANUALS

916   BACHMANN, Otto. *Theoretisch-Praktisches Handbuch des geigen-
       baues. Oder, Anweisung, italienische und deutsche guitarren
       und geigenbogen* [Theoretical-practical handbook of violin
       making. Or, instruction, Italian and German violin, viola,
       violoncello, viol, as well as guitar and bow making].
       (Quedlinburg und Leipzig: G. Basse, 1835).
Section "Vom Guitarrenbau" [On guitar making]. A description of the
guitar and an explanation of techniques for construction and for
repair. Pl. 3: a detailed set of plans for construction. 97p.

917   MAUGIN, J.C. *Manuel du luthier, contenant: 1. La construction
       intérieure et extérieure des instrumens a archet tels que
       violons, alto basses et contrebasses. 2. La construction de
       la guitare. 3. La confection de l'archet* [Luthier's manual,
       containing: 1. The interior and exterior construction of
       bowed instruments such as the violin, viola, and contrabass.
       2. The construction of the guitar. 3. The construction of
       the bow]. (Paris: librairie encyclopédique de roret, 1834).
       In Fr.
A practical handbook of instructions for instrument building. Instruction for guitar construction, p. 151-88. Diagrams.

(918-922)   Design and Construction

918   OTTO, Jakob August. *Treatise on the construction, preserva-
       tion, repair, and improvement of the violin, and all bowed
       instruments, together with a dissertation on the most eminent
       makers, pointing out the surest marks by which a genuine
       instrument may be distinguished.* Trans. from the German, with
       notes and additions by Thomas Fardely. (London: Longman,
       1833).
Otto's treatise, primarily a treatise for violin, contains commentary on the guitar in Germany which greatly influenced early
historians of the guitar (p. 41-42 of the text). Otto explains the
introduction of the guitar into Weimar and claims responsibility for
building the first guitar with six strings and for using covered
strings for the D and G strings. Subsequent research has questioned
Otto's claims.
See also: Ragossnig 40, Sharpe (1959 ed.) 42, Tappert 47, Turnbull
48, and Heck 474, v. 1, for a quotation of the text concerning the
guitar and for opinions on the credibility of Otto's claim.

919   OTTO, Jakob August. *Treatise...* Reprint in J.F. Hanks, *A
       complete system for the violin,* 93-101. (Boston: John P.
       Jewett and Company, 1846).
Text on the guitar, p. 98.

920   OTTO, Jakob August. *A treatise on the structure and preserva-
       tion of the violin and all other bow-instruments; together
       with an account of the most celebrated makers, and of the
       genuine characteristics of their instruments.* Trans. from
       the original with additions and illustrations by John Bishop.
       (London: R. Cocks and Co., 1848).
An enlarged edition of Otto's *Treatise* with three appendixes. The
text concerning the guitar is found on p. 23-24.

921   OTTO, Jakob August. *A treatise...* Trans. from the original,
       with additions and illustrations, by John Bishop. 4th ed.,
       further enlarged. (London: W. Reeves, [187-?]).
A further enlarged edition of Otto's *Treatise* with five appendixes.
The text concerning the guitar is found on p. 28-29.

922   WETTENGEL, Gustav Adolf. *Lehrbuch der geigen- und bogen-
       macherkunst, oder Theoretisch-praktische anweisung zur
       anfertigung und reparatur der verschiedenen arten geigen
       und bogen, sowie der guitarren, nebst einer darstellung
       der darauf bezuglichen lehren der physik* [Textbook of the
       art of violin and bow making, or theoretical-practical
       instruction on the construction and repair of various types
       of violins and bows, as also of guitars, including a descrip-
       tion of their physical characteristics]. (Weimar: B.F. Voigt,
       1869). In De.
No text. Pl. IX, figs. 160-78 are plans for guitar construction.
10 pl.

Design and Construction   (923-929)

SECONDARY WORKS: LUTHIERS AND HISTORICAL INSTRUMENTS

See also 265

923   "Antique guitars are going for a song". *Guitarist* (Sept 1973)
       10-11.
A discussion of early nineteenth-century guitars including notes on
construction techniques and present-day prices. Illus.

924   BONE, Philip J. "The museum. Shelley and the guitar". *GuitarR*
       II (1947) 36.
A photograph of a guitar by Ferdinando Bottari (1816), once owned
by Percy Bysshe Shelley, now in the Bodleian Museum of Oxford
University. Description and history of the instrument. This guitar
is believed to be the subject of his poem "With a guitar". Illus.

925   "Collection of guitars". *GuitarR* XII (1951) 191.
Photographs of five historical guitars from the collection of
musical instruments in the Metropolitan Museum of Art (New York).
Guitars from the seventeenth century through the eighteenth century, including three *chitarra battente*, are pictured.

926   "Foreign guitar makers and English music sellers". *Giulianiad*
       III/1 (1833) 56-57. Reprinted in *GuitarR* XVIII (1955) 181-82.
A commentary on European guitar makers outside of England. Includes
a quotation of Fernando Sor's recommendation of particular makers.
The quality of Lacote's guitars is discussed. Thompson's invention
of the enharmonic guitar is considered for its value. List of guitar
music published by London music sellers (composer, title,
publisher).

927   GODWIN, Joscelyn. "Eccentric forms of the guitar, 1770-1850".
       JLuteSocAmer VII (1974) 90-102.
Forms are classified in four categories: 1. guitars with added bass
strings. 2. guitars with added treble strings. 3. guitars with added
bass and treble strings. 4. guitars with multiple necks. Includes
information on makers, dating, tuning, and instrument description.
Illus. (11 fig.), bibliog. ref. in notes.

928   *Guitar Review* editors. "The museum: four guitar variants".
       GuitarR III (1947) 60-61.
A description and historical notes on four guitar variants in the
collection at the Metropolitan Museum of Art: harp guitar, guitar-
tirol, *chitarra battente*, and guitar Russian. Illus. (sketches of
each by George Giusti).

929   SENSIER, Peter. "Guitar topics". *BMG* LVIII/673 (May 1961)
       256.
Brief notes on the predecessors of Torres and their construction
techniques. Also includes a description of the cittern and English
guitar.

(930-935)   Design and Construction

930   USHER, Terence. "The Spanish guitar in the nineteenth and
         twentieth centuries". *GalpinSocJ* IX (June 1956) 5-36.
A consideration of significant developments in design. Charts of
dimensions of representative guitars. Explanation of aspects of
construction. Illus., bibliog.

931   USHER, Terence. "Three historic guitars". *BMG* LVI/644 (Dec
         1958) 75-76.
A description of three guitars (two by Lacote, one by Panormo) in
the possession of Sir Vincent de Ferranti, grandson of Zani de
Ferranti and Stanislaus Sczepanowski. Biographical sketches of
Ferranti and Sczepanowski. Illus. (guitars).

INDIVIDUAL LUTHIERS

Banks, Benjamin (1727-1795)

932   "Guitar history". *BMG* LXIII/728 (Dec 1965) 99-100.
An advertisement in the *Salisbury Journal* (1757) mentions the sale
of guitars by Benjamin Banks, a stringed instrument maker whose
guitars are unknown.

Garcia Castillo, Enrique (b. 1868)

933   "Biography of a luthier. Enrique Garcia Castillo". *Guitarra*
         (Chicago) I/2 (May-June 1963) 21-22.
A brief discussion of the career of guitar maker Garcia Castillo,
teacher of Francisco Simplicio.

Lacote, René François

See 926, 931

Martin, Christian Frederick (1796-1873)

934   AUGUSTINE, Rose. "The Museum. A guitar-maker of two con-
         tinents". *GuitarR* II (1947) 37.
A biography of Martin, pupil of Staufer of Vienna, who later
relocated from Germany to New York. Guitars (1836, New York) are
described. Illus.

Otto, Jakob August

See 918-21

Panormo, Louis (b. 1784)

See also 931

935   SENSIER, Peter. "Louis Panormo". *Guitar* III/11 (June 1975)
         24-25.

Design and Construction   (935-939)

A biography of Louis Panormo and his family. Includes a description
of Panormo's guitars and construction methods; comments on his
association with Fernando Sor. Illus. (guitars by Panormo and
Pages).

Staufer, Johann Georg

936   BLÜMML, Emil Karl. "Der Wiener Geigen- und Gitarrenmacher
      Johann Georg Staufer" [The Viennese violin and guitar maker
      Johann Georg Staufer]. In 5 parts. *ZfdG* III/1 (1923) 6-9;
      III/2 (Nov 1923) 3-5; III/3 (Jan 1924) 2-5; III/4 (Mar 1924)
      2-5; III/5 (May 1924) 2-4. In De.

Stradivari, Antonio (1644-1737)

937   FROSOLI, Patrizia. "The *Museo Stradivariano* in Cremona".
      GalpinSocJ XXIV (July 1971) 33-50.
An exhibition of Antonio Stradivari's tools and materials for con-
struction contained in the Stradivari museum, a subsidiary of the
Museo Civico, Cremona, includes Stradivari's designs for guitar.
These are described on p. 40-41. Bibliog. ref. in notes, fig.
See also: Gill 288 for Stradivari's tuning instructions.

Tielke, Joachim (1641-1719)

938   HELLWIG, Günther. "Joachim Tielke". *GalpinSocJ* XVII (Feb
      1964) 28-38.
A discussion of the life and works of Joachim Tielke. Two lists of
instruments are given. List A cites instruments whose location is
known to the author. 15 guitars are mentioned in this list. List B
cites known instruments whose present location is unknown. 2 guitars
are mentioned in this list. Bibliog. ref. in notes.

939   HELLWIG, Günther. *Joachim Tielke: ein Hamburger Lauten- und
      Violenmacher der Barockzeit* [Joachim Tielke: a Baroque luthier
      and violin maker of Hamburg]. (Frankfurt am Main: Verlag das
      Musikinstrument, 1980).
A detailed study of the life and works of Joachim Tielke. In 3 parts.
Part 1 "Die Familie Tielke" [The Tielke family]. Part 2 "Das Werke
Tielkes" [The work of Tielke] offers a discussion of Tielkes guitars,
p. 44-46 including illustrations and a table of eleven of his
guitars giving year, string length, and body length. Part 3
"Beschreibendes Verzeichnis der ermittelten Arbiten Tielkes"
[Descriptive catalogue of the known works of Tielke]. Plates with
date, location, and description cited. 25 guitars are listed. 139
pl., bibliog., index, 352p.
Reviews: Mhandel XXXI/6 (1980) 334; *RecorderM* VI/10 (1980) 298;
Soundb VII/3 (1980) 129; *JVdGSocAmer* XVII (1980) 74-78; *GalpinSocJ*
XXXIV (1981) 158-60.

(940-946)   Design and Construction

Torres Jurado, Antonio de (1817-1892)

See also 653, 747, 962, 1003, 1012

940   BUEK, M. "Die Torres-Gitarre" [The Torres guitar].
        XXIX (1928) 7-8. In De.

941   HOFMEISTER, Theodorus Jr. "Torres, the creator of the modern
        guitar". *GuitarR* XVI (1954) 121-24.
A study of the achievements and contributions of Antonio Torres.
Biographical information on Torres divides his career into two
epochs. 1. 1850-69. 2. 1880-92. Makers' labels are cited. Includes
a description of the guitar (1867) owned by the author. Detailed
chart of dimensions. Port., illus. (Torres guitar).

942   OPHEE, Matanya. "Torres, the creator of the modern guitar,
        an addend[um]". *GuitarR* XVII (1955) inside cover.
Additional information on Torres as a supplement to Hofmeister 941.
Two more makers' labels are quoted.

943   OPHEE, Matanya. "Historical research. A guest essay by
        Matanya Ophee". *Guitarra* (Chicago) XXXIX (July-Aug 1980)
        13-15.
An examination of extant guitars and texts (in particular, that of
Aguado) which prove the existence of developments in size and
strutting that influenced the Torres guitar design. Illus.

944   SCHWARZ-REIFLINGEN, Erwin. "Die Torresgitarre" [The Torres
        guitar]. *DieGit* IX/7-8 (1928) 47-53. In De.
Text in 2 parts. Part 1: A description and praise of the Torres
guitar. A comparison of the Spanish-made guitar to guitars made in
other countries. The problems of German-made guitars are described.
Illus. Part 2: Biographical information on Torres with notes on his
importance as a guitar maker. Disciples of Torres and developments
in construction after Torres are also considered. Port.

945   SENSIER, Peter. "Torres and the first generation". *Guitar*
        I (Oct 1973).

E. National Histories

ARGENTINA

946   SENSIER, Peter. "Guitar topics. Guitar makers of Argentina".
        BMG LXVI/765 (Jan 1969) 136, 141.
A survey of guitar makers of Argentina, including notes on the maker
José Yacopi.

Design and Construction   (947-950)

AUSTRIA

947   HAUPT, Helga. *Wiener Instrumentenbauer von 1791 bis 1815*
      [Viennese instrument making from 1791 to 1815] in *Studien
      zur Musikwissenschaft, Beihefte der Denkmäler der Tonkunst
      in Österreich* XXIV (1960). In De.

FRANCE

See also 908, 910

948   MILLIOT, S. "Documents inédits sur les luthiers parisien
      du XVIIIème siècle" [Unpublished documents concerning Paris-
      ian string instrument makers of the eighteenth century].
      PhD diss., Music: University of Paris, 1970. Publications de
      la société française de musicologie II/3. (Paris: Heugel et
      Cie, 1970). In Fr.
Text is divided into 2 parts. Part 1 is a study of the lives and
businesses of important Parisian luthiers of the eighteenth century.
Makers are considered individually. Part 2 contains inventories and
personal letters of luthiers. Charts, including a comparative table
of different makers listing their dates, instruments (including
guitars), and instrument cost. Illus. bibliog., 240p.
See also: RILM IV/1 (Jan-Apr 1970) 1087dd[44].
Review: OrganYb III (1972) 110.

949   PIERRE, Constant. *Les facteurs d'instrumentale musique.
      Les luthiers et la facture instrumentale* [Musical instrument
      makers. Luthiers and instrument making]. (Paris: Ed. Sagot
      Librairie musicale, 1893). Facsim. reprint (Genève: Minkoff
      reprints, 1971). In Fr.
A detailed study of the history of instrument making in France.
Source material concerning guitar makers (seventeenth to nineteenth
century). Index, 439p.

GERMANY

See also 944

950   SCHUSTER, Friedrich. "Zur Geschichte des Gitarrenbau in
      Deutschland" [On the history of guitar making in Germany].
      DieGit X/11-12 (1929) 83-87. In De.
A history of guitar making in Germany from the time of Jakob August
Otto (1760-1829). Includes a quotation of a 1797 correspondence
between Korner and Schiller concerning an Otto guitar. Also discussed is the account of an argument over the privilege for a
license for guitar construction (Markneukirchen, early nineteenth
century).

(951-957)   Design and Construction

MEXICO

951   MENDEZ, Guillermo Flores. *Constructores de guitarras finas en Mexico* [Builders of fine guitars in Mexico]. Carnet Musical (Jan 1954). In Sp.

952   MURRAY, D. "The guitars of Paracho: village industry thrives in Mexico". *GuitarP* XII/8 (Aug 1978) 34-35, 106, 108-09.
An account of guitar construction activities in Paracho, Mexico. Includes description of shops, guitars, construction methods, and makers. Illus.

SPAIN

953   ADAMS, Henry. "A partial directory of Spanish guitar builders". *GuitarLute* VIII (Jan 1979) 26-27.
Guitar makers are listed by city: Barcelona, Cordoba, Granada, Jaen, Madrid, Malaga, Sevilla, and Valencia. Makers' addresses are cited.

954   CANO TAMAYO, Manuel. *Un siglo de la guitarra granadina* [A century of the Granadan guitar]. Monograph series no. 38 of "Temas de nuestra andalucia". (Granada: Obra cultural de la Caja de Ahorros de Granada, 1975). In Sp.
A history of guitar making in Granada, Spain. Chronological survey of important makers with descriptions of their instruments. Includes a general history of the guitar. Color facsim. of labels, illus. (color, of historical guitars), [16p.].

955   GILBERT, Alice. "Spain's luthiers. A tour of the shops". *GuitarP* VII/3 (Apr 1973) 22, 35.
A discussion of the makers of Madrid and Barcelona. Shops described; information on pricing. 10 makers listed (name, address). Illus.

956   MAIRANTS, Ivor. "Where have all the Spanish guitars gone?". *BMG* LXVI/772 (Aug 1969) 345-51.
A survey of established Madrid guitar makers with some information on their career and technique. Makers considered include Hermanos Conde, Hernandez and Aguado, Fernandez, Ramirez, Juan and Lorenzo Alvarez, and Contreras. Port.

957   RIOJA, Eusebio. *An inventory of Granadan guitar makers.* (Granada: Gráficas Monachil, S.A., 1976).
Reviews: Guitar V/7 (1977); *GuitarLute* VII (Sept 1978) 2.

F. Individual Luthiers of the Twentieth Century

BARBERO, Marcello (1904-1955)

See also 1012

Design and Construction   (958-963)

958   "Guitarras y guitarrerros" [Guitars and guitar makers].
       Guitarra (Chicago) V/29 (Nov-Dec 1967) 20-23. In En.
Biographical notes on Barbero. Illus. (5 views of a 1946 Flamenco
guitar with description).

BERNABÉ, Paulino

959   MAIRANTS, Ivor. "Paulino Bernabé". *BMG* (Nov 1973) 2-3. In En.
Biographical information on Bernabé. Notes on his career and his
construction techniques. Port., illus.

BOUCHET, Robert

960   CLINTON, George. "Robert Bouchet: luthier". *Guitar* I/7
       (Feb 1973).

CALDERSMITH, Graham

961   CALDERSMITH, Graham. "A letter excerpt from Graham
       Caldersmith". *JGuitarAcous* III (June 1981) 19-22.
"... he discusses low frequency resonance coupling and compares
this phenomena in the frequency response curves of one of his own
instruments along side a Ramirez and a Kohno.", p. 19. Illus.

CONE, Michael

962   "A conversation with Michael Cone". In 3 parts. *Chelys* I/9
       (1977) 12-20; II/1 (1978) 34-41; II/2 (1978) 54-56.
In an interview with Walter Spalding, Cone discusses his own
experiences in building, judging the quality of sound, Ramirez,
Torres, Kasha, and other builders, and his opinions on his own
guitars from the point of view of a performer.

DICKENS, Fred T.

963   "An interview with Fred T. Dickens". *JGuitarAcous* II (Mar
       1981) 5-27.
"He [Dickens] holds the distinction of discovering the bracing
pattern for a guitar back which produces a ring mode in the free
state, all the more remarkable because this was not by accident,
but the result of more than a year's directed research.", p. 5.
Dickens discusses his experimentation. Diagram.

ESTESO LOPEZ, Domingo (1882-1937)

See also 1012

(964-969)   Design and Construction

964   "Biography of a luthier. Domingo Esteso Lopez". *Guitarra*
       (Chicago) I/4 (Sept-Oct 1963) 15-17.
A short biography of Esteso. Includes a chart describing "woods",
"dimensions", "finish and complements". Illus. (guitar).

965   "Guitarras y guitarrerros" [Guitars and guitar makers].
       Guitarra (Chicago) V/25 (Mar-Apr 1967) 20-23. In En.
Information on the Esteso family. Illus. (1959 concert guitar with
description).

966   SHERRY, James. "Guitarras y guitarrerros" [Guitars and
       guitar makers]. *Guitarra* (Chicago) IV/9 (Mar-Apr 1966)
       20-23. In En.
Biographical notes on Esteso. Illus. (1928 concert guitar with
description).

FERNANDEZ, Francisco

See also 956

967   SCARLATTI, V. "Guitarras y guitarrerros" [Guitars and guitar
       makers]. *Guitarra* (Chicago) V/27 (July-Aug 1967) 20-23. In
       En.
Biographical notes on Fernandez. Illus. (1964 concert guitar with
description).

FLETA, Ignacio (b. 1897)

968   MAIRANTS, Ivor. "Ignacio Fleta e Hijos" [Ignacio Fleta and
       sons]. *BMG* LXIII/735 (July 1966) 310. In En.
Biographical information on Fleta with a discussion of his construction techniques. Measurements of the Fleta guitar are given.

FLETA, Francisco Manuel (b. 1902)

969   SHERRY, James. "Guitarras y guitarrerros" [Guitars and guitar
       makers]. *Guitarra* (Chicago) IV/23 (Nov-Dec 1966) 20-23. In
       En.
Biographical notes on Fleta. Illus. (1962 concert guitar with
description).

GARCIA, Enrique

See 109

Design and Construction   (970-976)

HAINES, Daniel

970   "An interview with Daniel Haines". *JGuitarAcous* III (June
       1981) 5-13.
Biographical information on Haines. Acoustics, wood-sound production,
and substitute wood experiments are discussed. Highly technical. Fig.

HAUSER, Hermann (1882-1952)

See also 1012, 1032

971   FARRELL, Terrence. "Interview: Herman Hauser". *GuitarLute*
       VIII (Jan 1979) 28-29.
An interview with Hermann Hauser Jr. and Hermann Hauser III
including a discussion of their training, construction methods,
woods, and tone quality. Port. (Hauser Sr., Jr., and III).

972   SCHEIT, Karl. "Fifty years of Hauser guitars". *GuitarN* XXX
       (Apr-May 1956) 8-9.
Biographical notes on Hermann Hauser Sr.

973   SEGOVIA, Andrés. "In memoriam Hermann Hauser". *GuitarR* XVI
       (1954) inside cover.
Segovia's account of his first encounters with Hermann Hauser Sr.
Includes Segovia's compliments of Hauser guitars. Port.

HERNANDEZ, Sobrinos de Santos (1873-ca. 1940)

See also 1012

974   "Guitarras y guitarrerros". [Guitars and guitar makers].
       Guitarra (Chicago) V/28 (Sept-Oct 1967) 20-23. In En.
Biographical notes on Hernandez. Illus. (guitar with description).

975   SHERRY, James. "Guitarras y guitarrerros" [Guitars and guitar
       makers]. *Guitarra* (Chicago) IV/2 (July-Aug 1966) 20-23. In En.
Biographical notes on Hernandez. Illus. (1940 concert guitar with
description).

IBANEZ, Salvador

976   SCARLATTI, V. "Guitarras y guitarrerros" [Guitars and guitar
       makers]. *Guitarra* (Chicago) IV/22 (Sept-Oct 1966) 22-23. In
       En.
Biographical notes on Ibanez. Illus. (guitar with description).

(977-981)   Design and Construction

KASHA, Michael

See also 962, 993, 994

977   "History and design of stringed instruments. A new look".
        GuitarN CXIII (July-Sept 1971) 8-10.
Kasha's developments in design and construction are discussed. Notes
on Kasha's lectures with recital. Port.

LORCA, Antonio

978   "Guitarras y guitarrerros" [Guitars and guitar makers].
        Guitarra (Chicago) V/26 (May-June 1967) 20-23. In En.
Biographical notes on Lorca and his family. Illus. (1965 concert
guitar with description).

ORIBE, José

See also 788

979   "Making a classical guitar - José Oribe". *GuitarP* II/2
        (1967) 15-17.
A short discussion of Oribe's construction techniques. Illus.,
diagrams.

OROZCO, Juan

980   CLINTON, George. "Juan Orozco. Luthier, string maker,
        impresario". *Guitar* VII/11 (June 1979) 17-18.
An account of the career of Orozco. Port.

PIMENTEL, Lorenzo (b. 1928)

See also 914

981   TANNO, John C. and John W. "The classical guitar. Luthier
        Lorenzo Pimentel of Albuquerque, New Mexico". *Fretts* IV
        (1965) 6-8.
An account of the author's visit to the shop of Pimentel. Methods of
construction and experimentation are discussed. Includes biographical
information on Pimentel. Port., illus.

RAMIREZ, José and family

See also 796, 953, 955, 956, 962, 1036

Design and Construction   (982-990)

982   ADAMS, Henry. "Interview: José Ramirez". *GuitarLute* VIII
       (Jan 1979) 14-16.
An interview with José Ramirez. Includes an historical survey of
the Ramirez family from José Ramirez I. Emphasis is on the Ramirez
family's influence on the Madrid school of guitar making. Port.

983   ALVARADO, A. "José Ramirez III". *Guitarra* (Chicago) I/1
       (Mar-Apr 1963) 17-19.
Remarks on the career of José Ramirez III. Guitar description
("woods", "dimensions", "finish and compliments"). Illus.

984   "Guitarras y guitarrerros" [Guitars and guitar makers].
       Guitarra (Chicago) IV/24 (Jan-Feb 1967) 20-23. In En.
Biographical notes on José Ramirez III (b. 1922). Illus. (1965
concert guitar with description).

985   "Madrid school of guitar makers". *GuitarLute* VIII (Jan 1979)
       22-23.
A chart of the guitar makers of Madrid indicating the Ramirez family
members and those trained by them. Name, place, and dates given.
Also listed are other Madrid builders, beginning with Vannes (1951),
who are not included on the chart.

986   MAIRANTS, Ivor. "Madrid makers". *BMG* LVI/652 (Aug 1959)
       275-76.
Author's account of a visit to the Ramirez shop. Information on the
Madrid school of guitar making.

RODRIGUEZ, Manuel (b. 1927)

987   "Interview: Manuel Rodriguez". *GuitarLute* VIII (Jan 1979)
       24-25.
Biographical information on Rodriguez. Brief discussion of construction techniques with a comparison of traditional and modern methods
and remarks on judging the quality of an instrument. Port.

ROMANILLOS, José

988   CLINTON, George. "José Romanillos, luthier". *Guitar* I/7
       (Feb 1973).

989   FORD, Charles, editor. *Making music instruments. Strings and
       keyboard. 4. José Romanillos: The classical guitar.* Foreword
       by Anthony Baines. (London: Faber and Faber, 1979).

RUBIO, David (b. 1934)

990   "Interview: David Rubio". *GuitarLute* VIII (Jan 1979) 6-8.

(990-996)   Design and Construction

Biographical information on Rubio. Discussion of the quality of
instruments, construction materials and methods, Rubio's views on
building as an art form and as a profession, present-day lute construction.

991   CLINTON, George. "David Rubio". *Guitar* V/9 (Apr 1977) 15,
        17, 19-21.
Rubio, interviewed by George Clinton, discusses wood quality and
its effect on sound, his business. Port., illus.

992   WELLER, Malcolm. "David Rubio. Our cover subject". *BMG*
        LXVIII/786 (Oct 1970) 13.
A discussion of Rubio's career and building techniques.

SCHNEIDER, Richard

993   "An interview with Richard Schneider - the origins of the
        Kasha design are discussed". *JGuitarAcous* I (Dec 1980) 19-25.
Schneider discusses work on sound production and construction technique done in conjunction with Michael Kasha. Innovations in guitar
design are considered.

994   PATERSON, John. "Richard Schneider". *GuitarP* V/4 (June 1971)
        21, 28.
A discussion of Schneider's career and his construction techniques.
Includes comments on his association with Michael Kasha. Illus.

SIMPLICIO, Francisco

See 109, 933

TATAY, Vicente

995   ADAMS, Henry. "Hijos de Vicente Tatay. A visit to Valencia's
        largest guitar factory". *GuitarLute* VIII (Jan 1979) 9-11.
Notes on Tatay's guitar industry and construction procedures.
Illus., port.

996   TANNO, John C. "The classic guitar. A tribute to Vincente
        Tatay, Jr., master luthier and a pioneer of modern classical
        guitar construction in this country". *Fretts* IV (1967) 5-8.
Biographical information on Vincente Tatay, Jr., and his sons. Notes
on construction theories. Includes quotations of the Tatays. Port.,
illus.

Design and Construction   (997-1003)

VELAQUEZ, Manuel (b. 1917)

997   BELLOW, Alexander. "Manuel Velazquez". *GuitarN* XXVIII (Dec
      1955-Jan 1956) 9-10.
A biography of Velazquez with praise of his craftsmanship. Port.

VOGL, Hans

998   "Collectors' pieces". *BMG* (July 1973) 23.
A description of a guitar by Hans Vogl (Munich, 1913). Illus.

G. Construction Manuals

999   BEHLEN, H. AND BROS., INC. *The art of wood finishing*. (New
      York: H. Behlen and Bros., Inc., 1957).

1000 BERNER, A.; VAN DER MEER, J.H.; THIBAULT, G. [Geneviève] with
      the collaboration of Norman Brommelle. *Preservation and
      restoration of musical instruments. Provisional recommenda-
      tions*. (London: Evelyn, Adams and Mackay, 1967).
In 3 parts: "Preservation", "Restoration", Plates. A detailed
investigation of the problems of preserving and of restoring musical
instruments with solutions and methods discussed. Specific problems
related to the guitar and to other plucked instruments are treated
individually. Plate V, p. 45, is an illustration of the four-course
and five-course guitars shown in Mersenne 310. Commentary on p. 44.
21 pl., bibliog., 77p.
Reviews: MTimes CIX (Nov 1968) 1029; *MMusician* XVII (Dec 1968)
42-43.

1001 BROSNAC, D. *An introduction to scientific guitar design*. (New
      York: The Bold Strummer, Ltd., n.d.).
Review: CanadianM I/4 (1979) 16.

1002 CIURLO, E. Fausto. "La chitarra nella liuteria moderna" [The
      guitar of modern lutistry]. *Fronimo* II/6 (Jan 1974) 20-31.
      In It.
An examination of the principles of modern guitar construction based
on a detailed description of the parts of the guitar. In outline
form (parts a-t). Terminology is defined in a glossary. 25 fig.
(diagrams of individual parts). Iconog., illus.
See also: RILM VIII/2-3 (May-Dec 1974) 3696ap[44].

1003 HUTTIG, H.E. II. "The guitar maker and his techniques".
      GuitarR XXVIII (May 1965) 1-27.
A discussion of guitar construction based on the principles of
Antonio Torres Jurado (1817-1892). History and methods examined. In
2 main sections: "General discussion of principles and materials"
and "Assembly of the guitar". Illus., diagrams, tables.

(1004-1011)   Design and Construction

1004   JAHNEL, F. *Die Gitarre und ihr Bau; Technologie von Gitarre,*
       Laute, Sister Tanbur und Saite [The guitar and its construc-
       tion; Technology of the guitar, lute, sister tanbur, and
       strings]. (Frankfurt/Main: Verlag das Musikinstrument,
       [1964]). In De.
Review: CollegeMusSym VIII (1968) 157; *Musikerziehung* XVII/5 (1964)
238-39.

1005   KAMIMOTO, Hideo. *Complete guitar repair.* (New York: Oak
       Publications). 174p.
Reviews: GuitarP IX (July 1975) 57; *Bluegrass* X (Aug 1975) 24-25.

1006   LEWIS LUTHIER SUPPLIES. *Catalogue for musical instrument*
       builders. (Vancouver, B.C., Canada: Lewis Luthier Supplies,
       1976).
Advice, recommendations, and procedures. Detailed descriptions and
evaluation of materials and tools available for the construction of
guitars and other instruments. Supplement contains information on
new woods, tools, plans, books, and other supplies.

1007   McLEOD, Donald; WELFORD, Robert. *The classical guitar. Design*
       and construction. (Northgates, Leicester: The Dryad Press,
       1971).
Construction manual with step-by-step instructions. List of sup-
pliers. Illus., diagrams, 107p.

1008   OVERHOLTZER, Arthur E. *Guitar making.* (Chico, Calif.: Lawrence
       A. Brock, 1974).
A detailed manual on construction with instructions for building.
Append. (includes "Sources for materials and supplies"), photos.
(264), drawings (108), bibliog., index, 323p.
Review: GuitarP VIII (July 1974) 55.

1009   SCHNEIDER, John. "The well-tempered guitar. A discussion of
       temperaments and interchangeable fingerboards". *Soundb* V/4
       (Nov 1978) 108-11.
A discussion of the interchangeable fingerboards developed by Tom
Stone which provide different tuning systems for the guitar. Comparison of equal temperament and just intonation included. Illus.,
music, charts, bibliog. ref. in notes.

1010   SCHNEIDER-KLEMENT, Albrecht; WILLEE, Gerd. "Neue Möglichkeiten
       im Gitarrenbau" [Innovations in guitar construction]. *MInstru-*
       ment XXI/10 (Oct 1972) 1180-81. In De. Summary in En, Fr, and
       It.
"Discusses guitar tuning and construction with reference to two
models. Considers problems of intonation, technique, and scale
systems."–Quoted from *RILM* VI/3 (Sept-Dec 1972) 3899ap[44].

1011   SHARPE, A.P. *Make your own Spanish guitar.* First ed. (1957).
       Revised ed. (London: Clifford Essex Music Co. Ltd., 1963).

Design and Construction   (1011-1017)

A step-by-step construction manual. Illus., 36 fig. (diagrams), 32p.
Review: MTimes CI (Mar 1960) 161.

1012 SLOANE, Irving. *Classic guitar construction.* (New York: E.P.
      Dutton and Co., Inc., 1966).
A detailed construction manual. Introduction includes a history of
guitar building. Fig. 2 "Torres's development of modern guitar" with
six guitars pictured (1843-1888). P. 90-92: Six guitars pictured,
dimensions cited (Hauser, Barbero, Arias, Esteso, and Hernandez).
List of supply sources. 125 fig. (diagrams, photographs), bibliog.,
95p.
Review: MJ XXV (Feb 1967) 72.

1013 SLOANE, Irving. *Guitar repair. A manual of repair for guitars
      and fretted instruments.* (New York: E.P. Dutton and Co.,
      Inc., 1973).
A detailed manual of instructions explaining the techniques for
repairing individual problems. Includes a chapter on "Restoration
techniques for antique instruments". List of supply sources. 95p.
Reviews: GuitarP VII/8 (1973) 48; *GuitarR* XXXVIII (Summer 1973) 33;
Instrument XXIX (Sept 1974) 18; *EarlyM* III/3 (1975) 271.

1014 TANNO, John C. "A brief discussion of the construction and
      assembly of guitars by non-Spanish luthiers". *GuitarR*
      XXVIII (May 1965) 28-31.
Twenty-four steps of guitar construction are listed. Comments on the
differences between Spanish and non-Spanish construction methods.
Illus., bibliog. ref. in notes.

1015 WALLO, Joseph F. *How to make a classic guitar.* (1319 F Street,
      Washington, D.C. 20004).

H. Studies of Acoustics and other Scientific
Aspects of the Guitar's Construction

1016 "Acoustical properties of complex cavities. Prediction and
      measurements of resonance properties of violin-shaped and
      guitar-shaped cavities". *Acoustica* XXXVII/4 (May 1977)
      211-21.

1017 CALDERSMITH, Graham. "Physics at the workbench of the luthier".
      JGuitarAcous II (Mar 1981) 28-34.
"In this article we are exposed to some good data regarding the
guitar bridge's role in high frequency tone production. Comparing
bridge motion to sound-production results in a measure of an instrument's 'radiation efficiency', which is said to vary greatly from
one instrument to another. In Australia the face is called the
'table' and the range of an instrument its 'compass'.", p. 28. In 3
parts. "Frequency responses", "Lower range response and table

(1017-1022)   Design and Construction

tuning", and "Higher range response and bridge tuning". Highly technical. 2 charts.

1018 "Le changement du Spectre et du timbre de la guitare du a la
      qualité differente du bois de la table de resonance" [The
      change of spectrum and of timbre of the guitar caused by the
      different qualities of the wood of the resonance table].
      Acoustica XXXIII/1 (June 1975) 25-31. In Fr.

1019 CHRISTENSEN, Ove; VISTISEN, Bo B. "Simple model for low-
      frequency guitar function". *JGuitarAcous* III (June 1981)
      42-62. Reprinted from *Journal of the Acoustical Society of
      America* LXVIII/3 (Sept 1980) 758-66.
"The frequency response of the sound pressure and top plate mobility
is studied around the two first resonances of the guitar. These
resonances are shown to result from a coupling between the fundamental top plate mode and the Helmholtz resonance of the cavity. A
simple model is proposed for low-frequency guitar function ... ", p.
42. Experimentation and results are discussed. In 4 main sections.
I. "Methods and results", II. "Simplified mode for low frequency
guitar function", III. "Comparison between experiment and theory",
and IV. "Discussion". Highly technical. 1 table, 5 fig., bibliog.
ref. in notes.

1020 CUMPIANO, William. "The origins and derivation of guitar
      scales - and overview". *JGuitarAcous* I (Dec 1980) 32-36.
Discussion includes an explanation of scale types (Pythagorian
theory, scale of nature, just-toned scale, equal temperament),
problems in tuning the guitar due to discrepancies in the fret
board, the experiments of General T. Perronet (enharmonic guitar)
and Tom Stone (interchangeable fingerboards). Highly technical.

1021 CUMPIANO, William. "Popular attitudes in guitar acoustics.
      survey of the popular media". *JGuitarAcous* II (Mar 1981)
      53-57.
"A survey of the popular media.", p. 53. A discussion of problems
and misconceptions of guitar making. Includes a consideration of the
propagandizement of new techniques in guitar production.

1022 HAINES, Daniel. "On musical instrument wood". In 2 parts.
      JGuitarAcous II (Mar 1981) 35-52; III (June 1981) 32-41.
      Reprinted from *The Catgut Acoustical Society Newsletter* XXXI
      (May 1979); XXXIII (May 1980).
"The following work is a classic and will go down in luthiery
history as a central reference for makers of all stringed instruments. . . . the many physical properties relevant to sound production of all commonly used instrument woods are accurately measured
under controlled conditions and tabulated for the first time.", p.
35. Individual consideration of wood types. Results of experimentation are recorded. Highly technical. Tables, fig., bibliog. ref. in
notes.

Design and Construction   (1023-1026)

1023 MEYER, Jürgen. "Das Resonanzverhalten von Gitarren bei
      mittleren Frequenzen" [The resonance of guitars in the middle
      frequencies]. *MInstrument* XXIII/9 (1974) 1095-1102. In De.
"The frequency zone around 1,000 Hz plays a significant role in determining the sound quality of guitars. Therefore, the study investigates the vibration shapes of the soundboard in the individual
resonances, as well as the formation of stationary waves in the
interior of the body in the zone between 700 and 1,400 Hz. The influences of the soundboard-support groupings in various quantities
and positions are scientifically measured in the 800 Hz, 1,000 Hz,
and 1,250 Hz zones. The construction of the guitar back has little
effect on the projection of sound in the middle frequencies." -
Quoted from *RILM* IX/3 (Sept-Dec 1975) 4664ap[86].

1024 MEYER, Jürgen. "Die Abstimmung der Grundresonanzen von Gitar-
      ren" [The synchronization of the fundamental resonances of the
      guitar]. *MInstrument* XXIII/2 (1974) 179-86. In De.
"The two lowest resonance frequencies of the guitar body are viewed
as coupled frequencies of a single system consisting of one soundboard resonance and one cavity resonance; thus the coupling factor
is closely dependent upon the type of soundboard reinforcement by
struts or crossbars. The cavity resonance is similar to a Helmholtz
resonance, but deviates considerably in its frequency from the standard calculated according to the Helmholtz formula because of flat
construction and the eccentric position of the sound holes. The
lowest resonance of the soundboard is particularly influenced by
the type of support. Methods of calculation are given for all of
the usual modes of construction." - Quoted from *RILM* IX/3 (Sept-
Dec 1975) 4665ap[86].

1025 RIMSKI-KORSAKOV, A.V. "Les recherches sur le timbre des
      violons et guitares et sur l'excitation des vibrations d'une
      anche d'harmonium" [Research on the timbre of violins and
      guitars and on the excitation of the vibrations of the tongues
      of the harmonium]. *Acoustique musicale. Colloques internation-
      aux du Centre National de la Recherche Scientifique* LXXXIV.
      (Paris: Éditions du Centre National de la Recherche Scien-
      tifique, 1959) 203-13. In Fr.
A detailed synopsis of experiments in the evaluation of the quality
of sound in the violin, guitar, and harmonium conducted by Jankovski,
Jakovlev, and Rimski-Korsakov. Results recorded. 12 fig. (graphs,
charts), bibliog.

1026 STETSON, Karl A. "On modal coupling in string instrument
      bodies". *JGuitarAcous* III (June 1981) 23-31.
"It is a complicating fact of life that guitar resonances are coupled
to one another in varying degrees. In this paper the mechanical basis
of this coupling is explored. Also demonstrated are some very clear
hologram reconstructions of various low-order resonances in an ideal-
ized soundbox without an air resonance, as well as in a steel string
guitar.", p. 23. Highly technical. Fig., bibliog. ref. in notes.

211

(1027-1033)   Design and Construction

1027   TANNO, John W. "The acoustics of strings as related to the
          guitar". *Soundb* IV/3 (Aug 1977) 63-64.
A study of acoustical properties of strings with emphasis on the
construction of the guitar in relationship to tone production.
Illus., bibliog. ref. in notes.

1028   WHITE, Timothy P. "The guitar's air resonance - a model for
          air-wood interactions is proposed". *JGuitarAcous* I (Dec 1980)
          25-31.
"A model for air-wood interactions is proposed.", p. 25. Individual
instrument resonance is discussed. Highly technical. Illus.

1029   WHITE, Timothy P. "Harmonics of a dead guitar string".
          JGuitarAcous I (Dec 1980) 39-42.
"A Real Time analyzer is used to look at the tone produced by a new
string which sounds like an old string.", p. 39. Experiment procedure
and results are discussed. Fig.

1030   WHITE, Timothy P. "Identification of guitar resonances".
          JGuitarAcous III (June 1981) 14-18.
An examination of individual resonances of a guitar detected by
the use of a "Shaker table". Description of electronic components
used in the assembly of a "Shaker table". Results of experiment are
recorded. Fig.

I. Guitar Strings

1031   BOBZIN, Charles. "The making of strings for musical instru-
          ments from a commercial and sentimental standpoint". *Crescendo*
          II/5 (Nov 1909) 5-6, 9.
A discussion of the string manufacturing industry in Germany, Italy,
England, France, and America. Notes on methods of production and on
the quality of the products.

1032   SEGOVIA, Andrés. "Guitar strings before and after Albert
          Augustine". Trans. by Eithne Golden. *GuitarR* XVII (1955)
          145-48.
Segovia's account of his experiences with guitar strings and of the
early improvements made by Pirastro and Hauser. The circumstances
which led to the manufacturing of nylon strings by Albert Augustine
are described.

1033   SEGOVIA, Andrés. "More strings?". *GuitarR* XXXIX (Summer
          1974) 2-4.
Opinions on the question of the addition of more bass strings to the
guitar. "Editor's note" by Vladimir Bobri gives examples of guitars
with added bass strings built in the late eighteenth century and the
nineteenth century. Quotation of a letter from Segovia (29 Jan 1974)
in which he expressed his objections to the addition of bass strings
to the modern guitar. Some historically important builders and

Design and Construction (1033-1039)

players of the six-string guitar are mentioned. In Sp and in En trans. Illus. (drawing of a 1924 "Schrammel" guitar).

J. The Eight-String Guitar

1034 HARRIS, David. "The eight-string guitar". *GuitarLute* XIII (Apr 1980) 21-23.
A biography of the author is given in the introductory notes. Harris discusses his opinions on the advantages of an eight-string guitar for the performance of early lute music. Representative works for lute by J.S. Bach and by Sylvius Leopold Weiss are used to illustrate the problems of transcription to the modern guitar. Port.

K. The Ten-String Guitar

1035 MARLOW, Janet. "Notes on the ten-string guitar". *Soundb* VII/4 (Nov 1980) 151-54.
The author discusses her early experiences with the ten-string guitar, its advantages and possibilities, and Narciso Yepes's reasons for playing it. Port., append. ("Sources of ten-string guitars, strings, and music"), music, bibliog. ref. in notes.

1036 SHERRY, James. "Commentary on the ten-string guitar". *Guitarra* (Chicago) II/11 (Nov-Dec 1964) 31-35.
A description of the Ramirez ten-string guitar: "Woods", "Finish and Complements". The author gives his opinions and the opinions of other guitarists on the instrument. Illus. (guitar), music (tuning).

L. The Microtonal Guitar

1037 "Una chitarra quartitonale" [A quarter-tone guitar]. *NuovaRM-Italiana* VIII/2 (Apr-June 1974) 337-38. In It.
Description of the design of a quarter-tone guitar constructed by Giuseppe Teti (Rome).

1038 CIURLO, E. Fausto. "Chitarra quartitonale" [The quarter-tone guitar]. *Fronimo* III/10 (Jan 1975) 25-26. In It.
A discussion on the quarter-tone guitar with an explanation of the system of calculating the mathematical division of the fingerboard. The developments of Luthier Giuseppe Teti in collaboration with guitarist Carlo Carfagna represent the first efforts in this area of construction. Illus.
See also: RILM IX/1-2 (Jan-Aug 1975) 2454ap[44].

1039 SCHNEIDER, James. *An introduction to the quarter-tone guitar.* (356 E. Walnut Lane, Philadelphia, PA 19144, the author). 92p.
Review: GuitarP XIV (Feb 1980) 117.

Appendix I.

Periodicals Devoted to the Guitar and Other Fretted Instruments

Appendix I lists periodicals devoted to the guitar and other fretted instruments. This includes current and out-of-print periodicals and newsletters. Library locations are given for the United States and Canada only. All locations cited refer to United States libraries unless they are marked C for Canadian holdings. Brackets placed around a number or numbers indicate that the holdings of these volumes are incomplete. The list of abbreviations for Appendix I is on p. xxxvi.

Periodicals   Appendix I

ACCORDIAN AND GUITAR WORLD. Directory of manufacturers,
     publishers, wholesalers. Accordians, guitars, music
     electronics. Running title: ACCORDIAN AND GUITAR WORLD
     YEARBOOK. (Bedford Hills, N.Y.). I (1956?)-

          BRp   3-
          DM   8-
          NYp   2-3

L'ARTE CHITARRISTICA. Rivista di cultura musicale. (Modena,
     Italy).

          Holdings in the GFA Archive.

B M G; BANJO, MANDOLIN, GUITAR. (D.K. Keogh, 20 Earlham Street,
     WC2H 9LR London, England). Continues *Guitarist*. I (1973)-

          NYp   1973-
          Wc   1973-

BANJO NEWSLETTER. (Banjo Newsletter, 1310 Hawkins Lane,
     Annapolis, Maryland 21401). I (Nov 1973)-

          Bp   1-
          Wc   1-

THE CADENZA. American guild of banjoists, mandolinists, and
     guitarists. (Boston, Mass.). Merged into *Jacob's Orchestra*.
     I/1 (1894) -

          NYp   [27]-[30], 31
          OB   [7-8, 11]
          Wc   I/1-XXXI/2

CHELYS [ELECTRIC CHELYS]. Other title: CHELYS, "Journal of the
     New England Society of the plucked string" (1976-77).
     (Exeter, New Hampshire). [Not to be confused with *Chelys;
     the Journal of the Viola da Gamba Society*]. I/0 (undated),
     I/1 (1976)-

          DUu   1-
          IO   1-

LA CHITARRA. Rivista mensile letteraria e musicale. (Bologna,
     Italy). I (1934)-

                                    216

Appendix I   Periodicals

CREATIVE GUITAR INTERNATIONAL. (Mockingbird Press, Box 1275,
    Edinburgh, Texas 78539).

        NYp   1-
        Wc   1-

CRESCENDO. American guild of banjoists, mandolinists, and
    guitarists. (Hartford, Conn.). I (1908)-

        NYp   1 [2-4, 6, 13, 22, 23]
        OB   [11, 16, 19]
        Wc   1-25

ELECTRIC CHELYS   *See* CHELYS

FRETTED INSTRUMENT NEWS. Official organ of the American
    guild of banjoists, mandolinists, and guitarists.
    (Providence, R.I.). I (1932)-

        NYp   18-   PROu   20-
        PHf   [6-20]-   Wc   [6]-[16, 18]

FRETTS. News from the fretted instrument world. Formed by the
    merger of the *Fretted Instrument News* and *Music Studio
    News*. (Randall Publishing Co., Inc., P.O. Box 928, Santa
    Ana, Calif.). (1958-1968).

        NYp   1958-1968
        PHf   1958-1968
        Wc   1962-1968

IL "FRONIMO". Rivista trimestrale di chitarra e liuto. (Presso
    le Edizioni Suvini Zerboni, Via Quintiliano 40, Milan,
    Italy 20138). I/1 (1972)-

        AA   1-   LEX   1-
        BE   1-   NH   1-
        BLu   1-   NYp   1-
        Bp   1-   PHu   1-
        CARu   1-   PRu   [1]
        Ccr   1-   STU   1-
        CIu   1-   U   1-
        EU   1-   C On   1-
        IO   1-   C Tu   1-
        LAuc   1-

217

Periodicals   Appendix I

THE GENDAI GUITAR. (2-12-4 Ikebukuro, Toshima-Ku, Tokyo, Japan).
    I (1967)-

DIE GITARRE. Monatsschrift zur pflege des Gitarre- und Lauten-
    spiels und der Hausmusik. (Berlin, Germany). I (1919)-

        NYp   [1]-13

DIE GITARRE. Zeitschrift des Gitarren Collegiums Graz. Gitarren
    Collegium Graz. (A-8010 Graz Bruckner Strasse 76, Austria).
    I/1 (1978)-

        Wc   I/2 (July 1978)   1 issue only

GITARRE + LAUTE. (Verlag Gitarre + Laute Verlagsgesellschaft
    mbH, Postfach 41 04 08, 5000 Koln 41). I (1979)-

        NH   1-
        NYp   I/3 (1979)-

DER GITARREFREUND. First titled MITTEILUNG DES INTERNATIONALEN
    GUITARRISTEN-VERBANDS. (Munich, Germany) I (1900)-

THE GIULIANIAD, OR GUITARIST'S MONTHLY MAGAZINE. (Sherwood
    and Co., 23 Paternoster Row, London, England).

        NYp   III/1 (1833)

GUITAR. The magazine for all guitarists. (Musical News Services
    Ltd., 8 Horse and Dolfin Yard, Macclesfield Street, W1
    London, England). I (1972)-

        Bp   4-   NH   1-
        IO   [3]-   Wc   2-

GUITAR AND LUTE. (Galliard Press Ltd., 1229 Waimanu Street,
    Honolulu, Hawaii 96814). I (1977)-

        NH   1-
        NYp   8-

GUITAR AND MANDOLIN. (M.I. Holmes: Silver Springs, Maryland).
    Continues *Mandolin Notebook*. II/2 (Mar 1980)-

218

Appendix I   Periodicals

        Wc   II/2-

GUITAR ET MUSIQUE CHANSONS POESIE. (92 Rue de Richelieu, Paris
        (2e), France).

GUITAR NEWS. International Classic Guitar Association. (Chelten-
        ham, England). I (1951)-

        BApi   33-
        NH   107-119

GUITAR PLAYER. (Eastman Publications, 843 The Alameda, San Jose,
        Calif.). I (1967)-

        AA   [3]-   IO   1-
        BLu   1-   NYp   1-
        BO   1-   U   1-
        Bp   1-   Wc   [1]-

GUITAR REVIEW. Society of the Classic Guitar. (409 East 50th
        Street, New York, N.Y. 10011). I (1946)-

        AA   8-   LAuc   8-
        BE   1, 4, 8-   NYp   1-
        BU   4, 8-   PHf   [1]-
        CHH   8-   SLug   18-
        Cp   [2]-   U   9-
        EU   [1-2]-   Wc   1-10

GUITARIST. (Music Sales Ltd., 78 Newman Street, W1P 3LA London,
        England). Continues *B M G; Banjo, Mandolin, Guitar*. I (1973)-

        Wc   1-

LE GUITARISTE MAGAZINE. (Editions Folk International, 43, rue
        Léon Frot, 75011 Paris, France). I (Nov 1980)-

        NYp   I-X

GUITARRA. Sociedad guitarristica de Cuba. (Havana, Cuba). I
        (1940)-

        NYp   1-
        Wc   [1-3]

Periodicals   Appendix I

GUITARRA MAGAZINE. Flamencos International Association. (A.
    Sherry-Brener Enterprises, 3145 W. 63rd Street, Chicago,
    Illinois 60629).

        PHf   12-29
        Wc   [1]

LA GUITARRA. REVISTA MENSUAL. (Madrid, Spain).

        NYp   9-28

HAWAIIAN GUITARIST   *See* MUSIC TODAY FOR GUITARISTS

JOURNAL OF GUITAR ACOUSTICS. (11,000 Seymour Road, Grass Lake,
    Michigan 49240). I (Dec 1980)-

        NYp   I (Dec 1980)-

JOURNAL OF THE INTERNATIONAL VIOLIN, GUITAR MAKERS, AND MUSI-
    CIANS ASSOCIATION. (William K. Reid, 403 W. Maple Street,
    Jeffersonville, Indiana 47130).

THE LUTE SOCIETY OF AMERICA. JOURNAL. (128 Norwood Avenue, Upper
    Montclair, New Jersey 07043). I (1968)-

AA	1-		NH	1-
AUS	1-		NYp	1-
CA	1-		RI	1-
CARu	1-		Pc	
CIp	1-		PHu	1-
CIu	1-		PRu	2-
I	1-		SLug	1-
IO	1-		Su	1-
LAusc	1-		U	1-
LEX	1-		WE	1-
M	1-		C Tu	1-

THE LUTE SOCIETY OF AMERICA. NEWSLETTER. (Los Angeles, Calif.).

BLu	1977-		NO	1966-
CARu	[1968]-		PROu	1979-
LA	current issues		TE	1979-
MOSu	1979-		WE	1975-

Appendix I   Periodicals

LUTE SOCIETY JOURNAL. Lute Society. (London, England). I (1959)-

BE	2-	LEX	2-
BLu		NH	1-
BO	2-	PRu	4-
CA	1-	Pu	2-
CARu	2-9	RI	1-
COu	2-	STu	2-
Cn	2-	U	2-
Cu	2-	Wc	2-
Dp	2-	Wsi	2-
IO	2-	C Vu	10-

LUTE SOCIETY NEWSLETTER. (Dublin, Ireland).

CA	2-
Wc	1962-

MANDOLIN NOTEBOOK. (M.I. Holmes, 12704 Barbara Road, Silver
    Springs, Maryland 20906). Continued by *Guitar and Mando-*
    lin. I (May-June 1977) -

Wc	[1]-

MUSIC TODAY FOR GUITARISTS. Titles vary: HAWAIIAN GUITARIST
    (1933-Jan 1935), GUITARIST (1935-Sept/Oct 1942), MUSIC
    TODAY. (Cleveland, Ohio). I (1933)- Holdings for 1944-
    are not recorded in the US.

CLp	19-	Tp	[20]-
MOSu	[20]-	Wc	1-
NYp	20-	C Hp	1942-45,
PHf	18-		[1946], 1949
		C Tp	3-8, 10-27

MUSIK IM HAUS. ZEITSCHRIFT FUR DIE GITARRE. (Vienna, Austria)
    I (1921)-

NYp	[[5-6] These issues are now lost.

OESTERREICHISCHE GITARRE-ZEITSCHRIFT. (Musikverlag Haslinger,
    Vienna, Austria). I (1926)-

Wc	I/1 (1926)-

Periodicals   Appendix I

Il Plettro. (Milan, Italy). I (1904)-

SOUNDBOARD. (Guitar Foundation of America, 6538 Reefton Avenue,
    Cypress, Calif. 90630). I (1974)-

        NH   I/1-
        Wc   V/1-VI/2

S.S. STEWART'S BANJO, GUITAR AND MANDOLIN JOURNAL. (Philadelphia,
    Pa.). I (1884)-

        NYp   XVI (1899)-XIX (1902)

DIE ZUPFMUSIK. (Quartalsschrift des Bundes Deutscher des Bundes
    Deutscher Zupfmusiker e. V., Memmingerstrasse 26, 7411 Reut-
    ingen 1, West Germany).

        NYp   XVII/1 (Mar 1964), XVII/4 (Dec 1964) only

Appendix II.

Music for Guitar and Vihuela Printed Before 1800 and Modern Editions

The sources in the appendix are organized first in alphabetical order by composer and then in chronological order. The appendix consists primarily of works for solo guitar and vihuela printed between 1535 and 1800. Method books and ensemble music are also included. Songs with guitar accompaniment have been listed only if they contain tablature. These were included because of their importance in the study of tablature types. No arrangements of music originally composed for another instrument are listed. Numerous listings of songs with guitar accompaniment and arrangements for guitar are found in *RISM A/I*. The majority of works are for five-course (double-stringed) guitar. Music known to be composed for guitar other than of five courses is specified in the comments.

Some publications which are not specifically for guitar or vihuela have been included. On the title pages of the publications of Antonio de Cabeçon, Thomas de Sancta Maria, and Luys Venegas de Henestrosa, the vihuela is cited. These works, however, were written primarily for keyboard, and much of the music is not suitable for performance on vihuela. Also included in the appendix is some music for English guitar, a type of cittern in use in eighteenth-century England. On many of the title pages of publications, the instrument was identified as a guitar with no distinction made between it and the true-form guitar. Because of the resulting confusion,

223

Appendix II

several works for English guitar have been listed in this appendix;
the instrumentation is clarified in the comments. Three publications
for lute by Pierre Phalèse (Phal/1546[1], Phal/1546[2], Phal/1568) contain music by Luis de Narváez which was originally written for
vihuela. These works are listed in the appendix with cross-
references to Narváez.

Below is a list of reference works used in locating the material
for the appendix:

Brown:	Brown, Howard Mayer. *Instrumental music printed before 1600: a bibliography.* (Cambridge, Mass.: Harvard University Press, 1965).
Cox:	Cox, Paul. "The evolution of playing techniques of the six-stringed classic guitar as seen through teaching method books from ca. 1780-1850". PhD diss. Musicology: Indiana University, 1978. UMI 7909683.
Danner:	Danner, Peter. "Bibliografia delle principali intavolature per chitarra" [Bibliography of the principal tablatures for guitar]. *Fronimo* VII/29 (Oct 1979) 7-18.
Danner "Update ...":	Danner, Peter. "An update to the bibliography of guitar tablatures, 1546-1764". *JLuteSocAmer* VI (1973) 33-36. This is an update of the original bibliography published in *JLuteSocAmer* V (1972) 40-51.
Eitner:	Eitner, Robert. *Biographisch-Bibliographisches Quellen-Lexikon der Musiker und Musikgelehrten christlicher Zeitrechnung bis Mitte des neunzehnten Jahrhunderts.* (Graz, Austria: Akademische Druck-U. Verlagsanstalt, 1959).
Fétis:	Fétis, François J. *Biographie universelle des musiciens et bibliographie generale de la musique.* 2nd ed. (Bruxelles: Culture et Civilisation, 1963).

Appendix II

Kirkendale: Kirkendale, Warren. *L'aria di fiorenza id est il Ballo del Gran Duca.* (Firenze: Leo S. Olschki, 1972).

RISM A/I: *Répertoire international des sources musicals. (International inventory of musical sources). Einzeldrucke vor 1800.* 9 v. Ed. by Karlheinz Schlager. (Kassel: Bärenreiter-Verlag, 1971-81).

RISM B I: *Répertoire international des sources musicals. (International inventory of music sources). Recueils imprimés XVIe-XVIIe siècles.* Ouvrage publié sous la direction de François Lesure. (München-Duisburg: G. Henle Verlag, 1960).

RISM B II: *Répertoire international des sources musicals. (International inventory of musical sources). Recueils imprimés XVIIIe siècles.* Ouvrage publié sous la direction de François Lesure. (München-Duisburg: G. Henle Verlag, 1964).

RISM B VI: *Répertoire international des sources musicals. (International inventory of musical sources). Écrits imprimés concernant la musique.* Ouvrage publié sous la direction de François Lesure. 2 v. (München: G. Henle Verlag, 1971).

Wolf: Wolf, Johannes. *Handbuch der Notationskunde. II. Teil. Tonschroften der Neuzeit. Tabulaturen, Partitur, Generalbass und Reformversuche.* (Leipzig: Breitkopf und Härtel, 1913-1919). Reprint ed. (Hildesheim: Georg Olms Verlagsbuchhandlung, 1963).

Titles and library locations were gathered mainly from *RISM*. All sources printed before 1600 are listed as well in *Brown* in which additional information and a complete list of the contents of extant sources is given. Articles by Peter Danner deal specifically with guitar tablature. Paul Cox lists only methods, and Warren Kirkendale presents a study of the Aria di fiorenza. Because *Wolf* and *Eitner* were published in the early part of the century, their accuracy

Appendix II

is questionable. *RISM* has partially superseded them, and many
libraries have since changed location or have been lost. Revisions
of locations have been made according to Stephen A. Willier's "The
present state of libraries listed in Robert Eitner's *Biographisch-
bibliographisches Quellen-Lexikon*", *Fontes Artis Musicae* XXVIII/3
(July-Aug 1981) 220-29.

Manuscripts of guitar music are not included in this appendix.
Lists of manuscripts are found in *Danner*, *Danner* "Update . . .",
Kirkendale, Tyler (entry 3 of the bibliography), *Eitner* and *Wolf*.
An additional text, devoted entirely to manuscripts of music for
guitar, vihuela, and lute, is entitled *RISM B VII; handscriflich
überlieferte Lauten- und Gitarren-tabulaturen des 15. bis 18.
Jahrhunderts* (München: G. Henle Verlag, 1978).

For information about the libraries designated in the appendix, Rita Benton's *Directory of music research libraries, including
contributors to the International Inventory of Musical Sources
(RISM)* is most useful. It gives detail on library collections,
including address, telephone number, services, publications,
catalogue system, hours, and type and size of holdings. This work is
published in four volumes: Part I: Canada and the United States (Iowa
City: The University of Iowa, 1967), Part II: Thirteen European
Countries (Iowa City: The University of Iowa, 1970), Part III:
Spain, France, Italy, Portugal (Iowa City: The University of Iowa,
1972), Part IV: Australia, Israel, Japan, New Zealand (Kassel:
Bärenreiter-Verlag, 1979).

Appendix II

USING THE APPENDIX

Three types of editions are listed in the appendix: original editions, subsequent early editions, modern editions. The entry identifier, placed in the left-hand margin, consists of a four-letter author abbreviation and the date of the work. Brackets around a date indicate that the date was ascertained from a source other than the work itself. Superscript numbers are assigned when two or more works appear in the same year. ND (no date) is given in place of a date for undated works. The letters ca before a date indicate *circa* (approximate dating).

Original Edition

The complete title of the work is quoted in this entry; this is particularly useful for identifying the contents of a work and for distinguishing between editions. Library locations are listed below the title and are preceded by the italicized title abbreviation of the locator where they were found. Bold type indicates the country location and is followed by the libraries in that country.

Example:

Colo/1627 *Intavolatura di chitara spagnuola del primo, secondo, terzo et quarto libro* . . . (Milano: erede di Giovanni Battista Colonna). *RISM A/I:* **I** Nn.

Appendix II

Subsequent Early Editions

      Subsequent early editions are listed after the original
edition. When both modern editions and subsequent early editions
follow the original edition, the modern editions are listed first.
The complete title of the work can be found only in the entry for
the original edition. The entry identifier for the original edition
is given after the equal sign. Any differences between the original
edition and the subsequent early edition are then noted.

Example:

Colo/1637   = Colo/1627 . . . *Nuovamente ristampata.*
                 (Milano: Dionisio Gariboldi).
                 RISM A/I: GB Lbm. I Bc.

Modern Editions

      All known modern editions are cited immediately after
the source. Only complete works editions or almost complete works
editions are included. Sheet music of single pieces, anthologies containing selections, and small booklets of tablature or of transcriptions are not listed. In the entry identifier, an ME appears
before the publication date to indicate <u>M</u>odern <u>E</u>dition. The entry
identifier of the source is given after the equal sign. The modern
publisher's abbreviation is then given. The list of abbreviations
for modern publishers is on p. xliv.

Example:

Colo/ME1637   = Colo/1637 FORNI (1971).

(Abba/1627-Abre/1799)

ABBATESSA [BADESSA], Giovanni Battista

Abba/1627
Corona di vaghi fiori overo nuova intavolatura di chitarra alla spagnola...coretta & di nova agiunta accrescuita. (Venezia: stampa del Gardano, appresso Bartholomeo Magni).
RISM A/I: GB Lbm.

Abba/1635
Cespuglio di varii fiori. Overo intavolatura di chitarra spagnola...et il modo d'accordare, con alcune canzonette da cantarsi à una, due, e tre voci sopra il cimbalo hò altri istromenti, con l'alfabeto del[l]a chitarra spagnola. (Orvieto: Giovanni Battista Robletti).
RISM A/I: GB Lbm.

Abba/1637
= Abba/1635 (Firenze: Zanobi Pignoni).
RISM A/I: F Pthibault. I Bc.

Abba/1652
Intessitura di varii fiori, overo intavolatura di chitara alla spagnola. (Roma-Lucca: Bernardino Pieri & Giacinto Paci).
RISM A/I: I Bc.
Comments: According to *Kirkendale*, the name "Badessa" is written on the title page.

Abba/ND
Ghirlanda di varii fiori, overo intavolatura di ghitarra spagnola, dove che da se stesso ciascuno potrà imparare con grandissima facilità, e brevità. (Milano: Lodovico Monza).
RISM A/I: B Br. GB Lbm. US R.

ABREU, Antonio; PRIETO, P. F. Victor

Abre/1799
Escuela para tocar con perfección la guitarra de cinco y seis ordenes, con reglas generales de mano izquierda y derecha. Trata de las cantorias y pasos dificiles que se pueden ofrecer, con método fácil de executarles con prontitud y limpieza por una y otra mano. Compuesta por D. Antonio Abreu, bien conocido por el Portuguès, ilustrada y aumentada con varios divertimientos honestos y utiles para los aficionados a este instrumento por el P.F. Victor Prieto... (Salamanca: Imprenta de la Calle del Prior).
RISM B VI: E Bd. US Wcm.
RISM A/I: E Mn.
Comments: Music composed for five- and six-course guitar.

(Alba/ND[1]-Amat/[ca1750])   Appendix II

ALBANÈSE, Egidio Giuseppe Ignazio Antonio

Alba/ND[1]   *Les amusements de Melpomène ou IVe recueil d'airs*
                   mêlés d'accompagnement de violon, de guitarre et
                   des pièces de guitarre...par Mrs. Albanèse et
                   Cardon. (Paris: de La Chevardière).
                   RISM A/I: F Pa, Pc (4 ex.). US Cn, Wc.

Alba/ND[2]   = Alba/ND[1]...*les accompagnements par M. Cardon.*
                   (Paris: de La Chevardière).
                   RISM A/I: F Pc.

ALBERTI, Francesco

Albe/1786   *Nouvelle méthode de guitarre dans laquelle on y*
                   trouve différentes variations, une sonate, 12
                   menuets et 6 ariettes. (Paris: Camand).
                   RISM A/I: F Pn.

AMAT, Juan Carlos [Joan Carles y][Ivan Carlos]

Amat/[1586]   *Guitarra Española, Y Vandola en dos maneras de*
                   Guitarra, Castellana, y Cathalana de cinco Or-
                   denes, la qual ensena de templar, y taner ras-
                   gado, todos los puntos naturales, y b, mollados,
                   con estilo maravilloso. Y para poner en ella
                   qualquier tono, se pone una tabla, con la qual
                   podrà qualquier sin dificultad cifrar el tono,
                   y despues taner, y cantarle por doze modos. Y se
                   haze mencion tambien de la Guitarra de quatro
                   ordenes. (Barcelona).
                   Brown: Now lost.
                   Comments: Wolf erroneously attributes this work
                   to Fr. Leonardo de San Martino. As *Brown* ex-
                   plains, Fray Leonardo de San Martin is the
                   author of a letter to Amat in which this edi-
                   tion is mentioned. The letter was published in
                   Amat's 1639 edition. Music composed for five-
                   course guitar and vandola.

Amat/1639   = Amat/[1586] (Gerona).
                   Danner: E Mn. GB Lbl. US R.

Amat/1745   = Amat/[1586] (Gerona: Gabriel Bro).
                   RISM B VI: NL DHgm.

Amat/[ca1750]   = Amat/[1586] (Gerona: Antonio Oliva).
                   RISM B VI: E Bd. GB Lbm.

230

Appendix II   (Amat/1758-Amon/ND[2])

Amat/1758   = Amat/[1586] (Valencia: Agustin Laborda).
                       RISM B VI: E Mn.

Amat/ND   = Amat/[1586] (Valencia: la viuda de Agustin
                       Laborda).
                       RISM B VI: E Bd, Mn. US R.

Amat/ME[ca1761]   = ?Amat/ND BÄRENREITER (1980).

Amat/[ca1765]   = Amat/[1586] (Gerona: Joseph Bro).
                       RISM B VI: D B. E Bim, Mn (2 ex.). F Pc. I Mc.
                       US Cn, NH, NYcu, NYp.

Amat/1596   *Guitarra espanola de cinco órdenes, la qual
                     enseña de templar y tañer rasgado, todos los
                     puntos naturales y b mollados, con estilo mara-
                     villoso, y para poner en ella qualquier tono,
                     se pone una tabla, con la qual podrà qualquier
                     sin dificultad cifrar el tono, y después tañer
                     y cantarle por doze modos. Y agora añadida por
                     el mismo autor. Y a la fin se haze mención tam-
                     bien de la guitarra de quatro órdenes...Autor
                     del estilo, Ivan Carlos, doctor en medicina...*
                     (Lerida: viuda Anglada y Andrés Lorenço).
                       Comments: The privileges and dedication of the
                       1626 edition are dated 1596. No extant source
                       is known.

Amat/1626   = Amat/1596
                       Danner: US Cn.
                       Comments: Eitner cites a 1626 edition as
                       listed in *Fétis.*

Amat/1627   = Amat/1596
                       RISM B VI: E Mn.

Amat/ME1627   = Amat/1627 TECLA

AMON, Johann Andreas

Amon/ND[1]   *Divertissement [C] pour la guitarre, violon,
                     alto ou second violon et violoncelle...oeuvre 16.*
                     (Offenbach: Johann André, No. 2466).
                       RISM A/I: D-brd F, OB.

Amon/ND[2]   *IV Walzes, deux eccossaises et une marche pour le
                     pianoforté et guitarre.* (Bonn: Nikolaus Simrock,
                     No. 946).
                       RISM A/I: A Wgm.

(Amon/ND³-Asun/[ca1765])   Appendix II

Amon/ND³   *Six walzes [C, C, C, C, F, C] à quatre mains*
                    pour le pianoforté avec guitarre obligée...
                    oeuvre 52. (Offenbach: Johann André, No. 2671).
                        RISM A/I: A Wgm. D-brd HEms, LCH.

Amon/ND⁴   *Trois sonates [G, C, D] pour piano-forté, avec*
                    guitarre ad libitum...oeuvre 69. (Offenbach:
                    Johann André, No. 3638).
                        RISM A/I: A Wgm. D-brd BNba (pf).

ARAGONA, Paolo d'

Arag/1616   *Amorose querele, canzonette a tre voci, segnate*
                    con le lettere dell'alfabeto per la chitarra
                    alla spagnolo, sopra la parte del basso, e canto
                    ...parte seconda. (Napoli: Lucretio Nucci).
                        RISM A/I: I Bc.

ARANIES, Juan

Aran/1624   *Libro segundo de tonos y villancicos a una dos*
                    tres y quatro voces, con la zifra de la guitarra
                    espanola a la usanza romana. (Roma: Giovanni
                    Battista Robletti).
                        RISM A/I: I Bc.

ASIOLI, Francesco

Asio/1674   *Primi scherzi de chitarra.* (Bologna: Giacomo
                    Monti).
                        RISM A/I: I MOe.

Asio/ME1674   = Asio/1674 S.P.E.S.

Asio/1676   *Concerti armonici per la chitarra spagnuola...*
                    opera terza. (Bologna: Giacomo Monti).
                        RISM A/I: F Pc.

ASUNI, Ghillini di

Asun/[ca1765]   *The Lady's amusement, being an entire new collec-*
                    tion of favourite French and Italian songs, airs,
                    minuets & marches, none ever before publish'd,
                    compos'd and adapted for the guitar by sr. Ghil-
                    lini di Asuni. (London: P. Welcker).
                        RISM B II: GB Lbm.
                        Comments: Contains works by Ghillini di Asuni,
                        Traetta, Anon.

                                    232

Appendix II   (Asun/[ca1785]-Ball/1780)

Asun/[ca1785]   *A select collection for one, two and three gui-*
                    tars of six favorite English...French...Italian
                    songs and six easy lessons or solos...compiled
                    and composed by Sig. Ghillini di Asuni. Op. 19.
                    (London: Longman and Broderip).
                      RISM B II: GB Gu, Lbm, Ob.
                      Comments: Contains works by Ghillini di Asuni,
                      Paisiello.

AUBERT, Pierre François Olivier

Aube/ND   *Trois duetti pour deux guitares, op. 34.* (Paris:
                    auteur).
                      RISM A/I: D-brd Mbs.

BAILLEUX, Antoine

BaiA/[1773]   *Méthode de guittarre par musique et tablature,*
                    avec différens exercices sur le pincer de cet
                    instrument dans lesquels se trouvent les Folies
                    d'Espagne. Suivis d'une suitte d'airs et menuets
                    ajustés pour un violon et une guittarre et d'une
                    autre suitte d'airs à chanter avec accompagnement
                    de guittarre...Par Mr. B.D.C....Mis au jour par
                    Mr. Bailleux. (Paris:l'éditeur).
                      RISM B VI: F Pc.

BaiA/ME[1773]   = BaiA/[1773] MINKOFF (1972).

BAILLON, Pierre-Joseph

BaiP/1781   *Nouvelle méthode de guitarre selon le sistême des*
                   meilleurs auteurs, contenant les moyens les plus
                   clairs et les plus aisés pour aprendre à accom-
                   pagner une voix et parvenir à jouer tout ce qui
                   est propre à cet instrument...par P.J. Baillon.
                   (Paris: l'auteur).
                     RISM B VI: F Pc.

BaiP/ME1781   = BaiP/1781 MINKOFF (1977).

BALLESTEROS, Antonio

Ball/1780   *Obra para guitarra de seis órdenes.*
                     Comments: No sources are known. Contains music
                     for six-course guitar.

233

BANFI, Giulio

Banf/1653
Il maestro della chitara di Giulio Banfi nobile Milanese academico perseverante all'altezza Ser ma di Ferdinando il granduca di Toscana. (Milano).
Danner: I Ma (inc.).

BARBERIS, Melchioro de

Barb/1549
Opera intitolata contina Intabolatura di lauto di fantasie, motetti, canzoni, discordate e varii modi, fantasie per sonar uno solo con uno lauto, et farsi tenore et soprano: madrigali per sonar a dui lauti: fantasie per sonar a dui lauti: fantasie per sonar sopra la chitara da sette corde. Composta per il reverendo M. Pre Melchioro de Barberis padoano, musico, et sonator di lauto eccellentissimo. Libro decimo. (Venezia: G. Scotto).
RISM B I: A Wn. D W.
Comments: Contains works by J. Mouton, Passereau, and eight anonymous compositions. Music composed for four-course guitar and for lute.

BARTOLOMEO, de Selma e Salaverde

BarS/1638
Primo libro, canzoni fantasie et correnti da suonar ad una 2. 3. 4. con basso continuo. (Venezia: Bartholomeo Magni).
RISM A/I: PL WRu (lacks bc, 2. Stb. def.).

BARTOLOTTI, Angiolo Michele

BarA/1640
Libro p°. di chitarra spagnola. (Firenze: S.N.).
RISM A/I: F Pthibault. GB Lbm. I Bc.

BarA/ND
Secondo libro di chitarra. (Roma: S.N.).
RISM A/I: GB Lbm. I Nc.

BERTI, Giovanni Pietro

Bert/1624
Cantade et arie ad una voce sola con alcune a doi commode da cantarsi nel clavicembalo, chitarrone & altro simile stromento, con le lettere dell'alfabeto per la chitarra spagnola (libro primo). (Venezia: Alessandro Vincenti).
RISM A/I: D-brd Hs. I Bc.

Appendix II   (Bert/1627-Bran/ND)

Bert/1627   *Cantade et arie ad una voce sola commode da can-*
                 tarsi nel clavicembalo, chitarrone, & altro
                 simile stromento, con le lettere dell'alfabetto
                 per la chitarra spagnola, libro secondo...racolte
                 da Alessandro Vincenti. (Venezia: Alessandro
                 Vincenti).
                      RISM A/I: GB Lbm. I Bc.

Bert/1634   = Vinc/1634
                      Comments: Contains two works by Berti.

BOECKLIN, Franz Friedrich Siegmund August von

Boec/ND   *Amusement pour le beau monde, sur le violon avec*
                 deux guitarres et violoncell de la composition de
                 Ms. le conseiller intime, op. 35. (Braunschweig:
                 magasin de musique).
                      RISM A/I: H SFm.

BOTTAZZARI, Giovanni

Bott/1663   *Sonate nuove per la chitarra spagnola.* (Venezia:
                 s.n.).
                      RISM A/I: I Bc.

Bott/ME1663   = Bott/1663 S.P.E.S.

BOULERON

Boul/[ca1770]   *Trios pour la guitarre ou recueil de morceaux*
                 choisis mis en trio pour une guitarre, un violon
                 et un alto. Par Mr. Bouleron...mis au jour par
                 Mr. Parison... (Paris: aux adresses ordinaires
                 de musique; Versailles: Parison).
                      RISM B II: F Pa, Pc.
                      Comments: Contains works by Grétry, Monsigny,
                 Philidor.

BRAND, Aloys Carl

Bran/ND   *VI Walses pour la guitarre seule.* (Mainz: Bern-
                 hard Schott, No. 517).
                      RISM A/I: D-brd Mmb.

(Bray/1553-Busa/1644)   Appendix II

BRAYSSING, Gregor

Bray/1553   *Quart livre de tabulature de guitarre contenant*
                     plusieurs fantasies, pseaulmes, et chansons:
                     avec L'Alouette, & la Guerre. (Paris: Adrian
                     Le Roy & Robert Ballard).
                        RISM A/I: F Pm. GB Lbm.
                        Comments: Music composed for four-course
                        guitar.

BREMNER, Robert

Brem/1758   *Instructions for the guitar; with a collection*
                     of airs, songs and duets, fitted for that in-
                     strument. (Edinburgh: [Robert Bremner]).
                        RISM A/I: EIRE Dn. GB CDp, Ep (inc.), Gu.
                        Comments: Tyler (entry 3, p. 109) indicates
                        that this work contains music for English
                        guitar, a type of cittern.

Brem/ND   = Brem/1758 (London: author)
                        RISM A/I: GB Du, En, Gm.

BRICEÑO, Luis de

Bric/1626   *Metodo mui facilissimo para aprender a tañer la*
                     guitarra a lo español, compuesto por Luis de
                     Briçeño...en el qual se hallaran cosas curiosas
                     de romançes y seguidillas. Juntamente sesenta
                     liçiones diferentes, un metodo para templar,
                     otro para conocer los aquerdos, todo por una
                     horden agradable y façilissima. (Paris: Pierre
                     Ballard).
                        RISM B VI: F Pn.

Bric/ME1626   = Bric/1626 MINKOFF (1972).

BUSATTI, Cherubino

Busa/1640   *Compago ecclesiasticorum motectorum unius vocis*
                     modulatione confecta...opus tertium. (Venezia:
                     Bartolomeo Magni).
                        RISM A/I: B Bc. PL WRu.

Busa/1644   *Settimo libro d'ariette a voce sola [accompagna-*
                     mento per la chitarra alla spagnola]. (Venezia:
                     Alessandro Vincenti).
                        RISM A/I: PL WRu.

236

Appendix II   (Busa/1688-Calv/1644)

Busa/1688   *Arie a voce sola commode da cantarsi nel clavi-*
                   cembalo, chitarone & altro simile stromento, con
                   le lettere dell'alfabetto per la chitarra spag-
                   nola. (Venezia: Alessandro Vincenti).
                   RISM A/I: I Rsc.

CABEÇON, Antonio de

Cabe/1578   *Obras de mú[si]ca para tecla, arpa [y] vihuela,*
                   de Antonio de Cabeçon...recopiladas y puestas en
                   cifra por Hernando de Cabeçon su hijo. (Madrid:
                   Francisco Sanchez).
                     RISM A/I: B Br. D-brd W. D-ddr Bds. E E, Mn.
                     F Pthibault. GB Lbm (inc.). I Nc. US Wc.

Cabe/ME1578   = Cabe/1578 InstEspMusic

CALEGARI, Francesco

Cale/ND[1]   *Dodici walzer progressivi per chitarra sola.*
                   (Leipzig: Friedrich Hofmeister, No. 283).
                     RISM A/I: D-brd Tu.

Cale/ND[2]   *Rondo per chitarra sola...op. 3.* (Leipzig:
                   Friedrich Hofmeister, No. 287).
                     RISM A/I: D-brd Tu.

Cale/ND[3]   *Tre tema con variazioni per chitarra sola...*
                   opera 7ª. (Leipzig: Friedrich Hofmeister, No.
                   350).
                     RISM A/I: D-brd Mmb.

Cale/ND[4]   *Sechs Lectionen für die Guitarre in den gewöhn-*
                   lichsten Positionen um die leichteste Applicatur
                   zu erlernen...op: 11. (Leipzig: Friedrich Hof-
                   meister, No. 380).
                     RISM A/I: D-brd Mmb.

Cale/ND[5]   *Six thêmes avec variations pour la guitarre...*
                   oeuv. 12. (Leipzig: Friedrich Hofmeister, No.
                   425).
                     RISM A/I: D-brd Mmb.

CALVI, Carlo

Calv/1644   *Intavolatura di chitarra e chitarriglia.*
                   (Bologna).
                     Danner: I Bc.

237

(Calv/1646-Camp/1730)   Appendix II

Calv/1646   = Calv/1644 *Intavolatura di Chitarra, e Chitarrig-*
                       lia, con le più necessarie, e facile suonate à
                       chi si diletta di tal Professione. Havute da duo
                       eccellenti Professori... (Bologna: Giac. Monti).
                       Part 2.
                          Eitner: GB Lbm.
                          Wolf and *Danner:* I Bc.

Calv/ME1646   = Calv/1646 S.P.E.S.

CAMARELLA, Giovanni Battista

Cama/[1633]   *Madrigali et Arie di...Academico Fileleutero*
                       detto l'Affretato, & perfetto di detta Academia.
                       Op. 1. (Ven: Appresso Al. Vincenti).
                          Wolf: D-brd Bds.
                          Comments: Contains a section of music for
                          guitar. Date MDXXXIII [1553], cited on title
                          page, is probably incorrect. 1633 is substituted.

CAMPION, François

Camp/1705   *Nouvelles découvertes sur la guitarre contenantes*
                       plusieurs suittes de pièces sur huit manières
                       différentes d'accorder. (Paris: Michel Brunet).
                          RISM A/I: F Pc, Pn (lacks title page).

Camp/ME1705   = Camp/1705 MINKOFF (1977).

Camp/1716   *Traité d'accompagnement et de composition, selon*
                       la règle des octaves de musique. Ouvrage générale-
                       ment utile pour la transposition, à ceux qui se
                       meslent du chant et des instrumens d'accord, ou
                       d'une partie seule, et pour apprendre à chiffrer
                       la basse continue, par le sieur Campion...Oeuvre
                       second. (Paris: veuve G. Adam).
                          RISM B VI: F Pn. NL DHgm (inc.). S Skma.

Camp/ME1716   = Camp/1716 MINKOFF (1977).

Camp/ca1717   = Camp/1716 (Amsterdam: Estienne Roger).
                          RISM B VI: CH BEk. GB Lbm. I Bc.

Camp/1730   *Addition au traité d'accompagnement et de compo-*
                       sition par le règle de l'octave; où est compris
                       particulièrement le secret de l'accompagnement du
                       théorbe, de la guitare et du luth avec la manière
                       de transposer instrumentalement, et de solfier
                       facilement la musique vocale sans l'usage de la
                       gâme. Par le sieur Campion...Oeuvre IV. (Paris:

Appendix II   (Camp/ME1730-Cart/ND)

                    veuve Ribou).
                        RISM B VI: B Br. F Pn. GB Ge. NL DHgm. S Skma.

Camp/ME1730   = Camp/1730 MINKOFF (1977).

Camp/1734   *Second recueil d'airs...oeuvre V.* (Paris: auteur,
                    Vve Boivin, Le Clerc, gravé par Mlle Noel).
                        RISM A/I: F AG, Pc, Pn.

CANOBBIO, Carlo

Cano/ND   *Six sonates [C, D, C, G, a, d-D] pour la guitarre
                    accompagnées d'un violon (avec sourdine)...oeuv II.*
                    (St. Petersburg: auteur, Gerstenberg & Dittmar,
                    No. 121).
                        RISM A/I: D-ddr SWI, WRtl.

CARBONCHI, Antonio

Carb/1640   *Sonate di chitarra spagnola con intavolatura
                    franzese.* (Firenze: Amadore Massi & Lorenzo Landi).
                        RISM A/I: E Mn. I Fn (2 ex.).

Carb/ME1640   = Carb/1640 S.P.E.S.

Carb/1643   *Le dodici chitarre spostate inventate...libro
                    secondo di chitarra spagnola, con due alfabeti,
                    uno alla franzese et uno alla spagnola.* (Firenze:
                    Francesco Sabatini).
                        RISM A/I: D-brd W. I Fc, Fn, Rsc.

Carb/ME1643   = Carb/1643 S.P.E.S.

CARRÉ, Antoine

Carr/1671   *Livre de guitarre contenant plusieurs pièces...
                    avec la manière de toucher sur la partie ou basse-
                    continue.* (Paris: s.n.).
                        RISM A/I: F Pn.

Carr/ME1671   = Carr/1671 MINKOFF (1977).

CARTER, Charles Thomas

Cart/ND   *La lumière [la plus pure]. A favourite French
                    song with variations for the harpsichord or piano
                    forte, also for the violin, german flute or gui-
                    tarr.* (London: Charles & Samuel Thompson).

RISM A/I: GB Ckc, Lbm.

CASTRO

Cast/ND[1]   *Journal de musique étrangère, pour la guitare ou*
lyre, rédigé par Castro, chaque numéro de ce
journal sera composé de trois morceaux, dont un
de chant espagnol, un de chant italien et un
pour l'instrument (Heft 1-12). (Paris: auteur
gravé par Michot).
    RISM A/I: D-brd Mbs.
    Comments: Music composed for five-course guitar
and lyre.

Cast/ND[2]   *Deux airs variées pour la guitarre...oeuvre 7.*
(Paris: auteur, gravé par Michot).
    RISM A/I: D-brd LCH.

Cast/ND[3]   *Boléros pour la guitare ou lyre...oeuvre XIII.*
(Paris: auteur, gravé par Michot).
    RISM A/I: D-brd HVs.
    Comments: Music composed for five-course guitar
and lyre.

CHABRAN, Francesco

Chab/[ca1795]   *Compleat instructions for the Spanish guitar...*
to which is added a collection of favorite
songs... (London: Culliford, Rolfe & Barron).
    RISM B VI: GB Lbm, Ob.

CHERBOURG, Mlle

Cher/ND   *Premier recueil de chansons avec accompagnement*
de guitarre et six menuets en duo pour deux
guitarres. (Paris: Bailleux).
    RISM A/I: F Pn.

CIMAROSA, Domenico

Cima/ND   *IV Duetts [G, D, G, D] für zwei Guitarren [und*
Singst.]. (Braunschweig: Musikalienverlag in der
Neuenstrasse, No. 85).
    RISM A/I: CS Pnm. D-brd ASm, Mbs.

Appendix II   (Colo/1620[1]-Corb/1643)

COLONNA, Giovanni Ambrosio

Colo/1620[1]   *Intavolatura di chitarra alla spagnuola, dove si*
                   contengono passacalli, follie, & altre arie alla
                   spagnuola, pass'emezi, gagliarde, corrente, &
                   arie diverse all'italiana, con facilita passeg-
                   giate, & concertate per sonare a due, & tre chi-
                   tarre, con una sonata in fine in ecco detta la
                   Beolca. (Milano: erede di Giovanni Battista
                   Colonna).
                       RISM A/I: GB Lbm. I Bc (lacks title page).

Colo/1620[2]   *Il secondo libro d'intavolatura di chitarra alla*
                   spagnuola. (Milano: erede di Giovanni Battista
                   Colonna).
                       RISM A/I: I Ma.

Colo/1623   *Il terzo libro de intavolature di chitarra alla*
                   spagnuola, dove si contiene in particolare, di-
                   versi passacalli straordinarij, chiacone, zara-
                   bande, e correnti alla francese. (Milano: erede
                   di Giovanni Battista Colonna).
                       RISM A/I: I Bc.

Colo/1627   *Intavolatura di chitara spagnuola del primo,*
                   secondo, terzo et quarto libro...con una scielta
                   di canzonette a voce sola de più illustri musici
                   di Roma. (Milano: erede di Giovanni Battista
                   Colonna).
                       RISM A/I: I Nn.

Colo/1637   = Colo/1627...*nuovamente ristampata.* (Milano:
                   Dionisio Gariboldi).
                       RISM A/I: GB Lbm. I Bc.

Colo/ME1637   = Colo/1637 FORNI (1971).

CORBETTA, Francesco

See Pinnell 342 and 344 for lists of concordances of alternate
sources of Corbetta's music. A transcription of his complete works
is found in Pinnell 344.

Corb/1639   *De gli scherzi armonici trovati, e facilitati in*
                   alcune curiosissime suonate sopra la chitarra
                   spagnuola. (Bologna: Giacomo Monti & Carlo
                   Zenero).
                       RISM A/I: I Bc, Nc.

Corb/1643   *Varii capricci per la ghitarra spagnuola.*
                   (s.l., s.n.).

(Corb/ME1643-Corb/1729)   Appendix II

                         RISM A/I: GB Lbm.

Corb/ME1643   = Corb/1643 S.P.E.S.

Corb/ND[1]   = Corb/1643 (Milano: Bianchi).
                         RISM A/I: I Bc.

Corb/1648   *Varii scherzi di sonate per la chitarra spagnuola
                     ...libro quarto.* (s.l., s.n.).
                         RISM A/I: F Pn. GB Lbm.

Corb/1671   *La guitarre royalle.* (Paris: H. Bonneuil).
                         RISM A/I: E Mn. F Pc, Pn. GB Lbm, Ob. NL DHgm.

Corb/ME1671   = Corb/1671 MINKOFF (1975).

Corb/1673   = Corb/1671
                         Wolf and *Eitner:* F Pn.
                         Comments: Wolf and *Eitner* list a 1673 edition
                         in F Pn. This may be an incorrect dating of the
                         1674 edition which is listed in *RISM A/I* as
                         located in both F Pn and I Bc.

Corb/1674   *La guitarre royale.* (Paris: H. Bonneuil).
                         RISM A/I: F Pn. I Bc (the second guitar part of
                         the duets is missing).

Corb/ME1674   = Corb/1674 FORNI (1971).

Corb/1677   *Easie lessons on the Guittar for young Practi-
                     tioners; single, and some of two parts. By
                     Seignor Francisco. Printed for Jo. Carr in
                     Middle Temple lane.*
                         Comments: No extant source is known. Pinnell
                         (entry 344, p. 254-55) lists this work as it
                         is cited in *The Term Catalogues* (26 Nov 1677)
                         and suggests that Corbetta is the author of
                         the work.

Corb/ND[2]   *Guitarra española y sus diferencias de sones.*
                         Danner: No locations cited.
                         Comments: Danner suggests 1621-1665 as a pos-
                         sible date range and suggests that this is
                         Corbetta's third book. The composer's name
                         given on this volume is Corbera, Franciscus.

                                   242

Appendix II   (Cori/1670-Criv/1628)

CORIANDOLI, Francesco

Cori/1670   *Diverse sonate ricercate sopra la chitarra spag-*
                       nuola...opera prima. (Bologna: Giacomo Monti).
                       RISM A/I: I FEc.

CORRADI, Flamminio

CorF/1616   *Le Stravaganze d'amore...a una, due et tre voci*
                       con la intavolatura del chitarrone & della chi-
                       tarra alla spagnola & con il basso continuo da
                       sonare nel clavicembalo et altri istromenti
                       simili. (Venezia: Giacomo Vincenti).
                       RISM A/I: F Pc.

CorF/1618   = Corr/1616...*novamente ristampate et con diligenza*
                       corette. (Venezia: Giacomo Vincenti).
                       RISM A/I: A Wgm. I Mc.

CORRETTE, Michel

CorM/ND   *Les Dons d'Apollon. Méthode pour apprendre*
                      facilement à jouer de la guitarre...avec...
                      des jolis airs connus notés en partition...
                      livre 1^r. (Paris: Bayard de La Chevardiere,
                      Mlle Castagnery).
                      RISM A/I: GB Lbm.

COSTANZO, Fabrizio

Cost/1627   *Fior novello. Libro primo di concerti di diverse*
                      sonate, sinfonie, e correnti da sonare con una,
                      con due, con tre, e con quattro chitarre alla
                      spagnuola, con l'alfabetto, et dichiarationi da
                      poterle accordare, e sonare. (Bologna: Nicolo
                      Tebaldini).
                      RISM A/I: I Bc.

CRIVELLATI, Domenico

Criv/1628   *Cantate diverse a una, due, e tre voci, con*
                      l'intavolature per la chitarra spagnola in quelle
                      più approposito. (Roma: Giovanni Battista Rob-
                      letti).
                      RISM A/I: GB Lbm.

243

(Dala/ND[1]-Delv/ND)   Appendix II

DALAYRAC, Nicolas-Marie

Dala/ND[1]   *Air...pour la guittare.* (Hamburg: J.A. Böhme).
                            RISM A/I: CH Bu. D-brd LÜh.

Dala/ND[2]   *Arie...für Forte Piano & Guitarre.* (Hamburg-
                            Altona: Rud. Cranz).
                            RISM A/I: DK Kk.

Dala/ND[3]   *Cavatina...für die Guitarre oder Piano-Forte.*
                            (Wien: J. Cappi, No. 1317).
                            RISM A/I: D-brd Cl.

DAZA [DAÇA], Estevan

Daza/1576   *Libro de musica en cifras para vihuela, intitu-*
                            lado el Parnasso, enel qual se hallara toda di-
                            versidad de musica, assi motetes, sonetos, vil-
                            lanescas, en lengua castellana, y otras cosas,
                            como fantasias del autor, hecho por Estevan
                            Daca, vezino de la muy insigne villa de Valla-
                            dolid... (Valladolid: D. Fernandez di Cordova).
                            RISM B I: D Mbs.
                            Comments: Contains music by Basurto, S.
                            Boileau (6), Ceballos (3), T. Crecquillon (3),
                            F. Guerrero (3), P. Guerrero, J. Maillard,
                            Navarro (3), P. Ordonez (2), J. Richafort,
                            Villalar, Anon. (15).

Daza/ME1576[1]   = Daza/1576 BreitkopfHärtel   (1902, ed. by Conde
                            de Morphy).

Daza/ME1576[2]   = Daza/1576 CEstHist (1923, ed. by E. Martínez
                            Torner).

Daza/ME1576[3]   = Daza/1576 Entry 222 (1972, ed. by Ronald C.
                            Purcell).

Daza/ME1576[4]   = Daza/1576 MINKOFF (1978).

DELVER, Friedrich

Delv/ND   *Drey Lieder für Guitarre & Flöte.* (Altona:
                            L. Rudolphus).
                            RISM A/I: D-brd B.

Appendix II   (Dero/1688-Dois/ND³)

DEROSIER, Nicolas

Dero/1688   *Douze ouvertures pour la guitare, op. 5.*
                       (La Haye).
                           Wolf: No locations cited.

Dero/[ca1690]   *Les principes de la guitare composez par Nicolas*
                       Derosier ... (Amsterdam: Antoine Pointel).
                           RISM B VI: B Br. I Bc. NL DHgm.

Dero/ME1690   = Dero/[ca1690] FORNI (1975).

Dero/1696   = Dero/[ca1690]
                          Wolf: B Br. I Bc.

Dero/1699¹   = Dero/[ca1690]
                          Wolf: B Br. I Bc.

Dero/1699²   *Nouveaux principes pour la guittare, avec une*
                       table universelle de tous les accords qui se
                       trouvent dans la basse-continüe sur cet instru-
                       ment. Ce qui peut servir aussi aux personnes
                       qui joüent du luth, du théorbe et de la basse
                       de viole. Par monsieur Nicolas Derozier [sic], ...
                       (Paris: Christophe Ballard).
                           RISM B VI: F Pn.

DIBDIN, Charles

Dibd/ND   *... a favorite rondo for the harpsichord,*
                       violin, german flute and guitar. (London:
                       Longman & Broderip).
                           RISM A/I: GB Gu, Lbm (inc.), Ob.

DOISY-LINTANT, Charles

Dois/ND¹   *Etudes ou caprices pour la guitare, faisant*
                       suite aux principes généraux. 2e partie.
                       (Paris: auteur).
                           RISM A/I: A Wn. D-brd Mmb.

Dois/ND²   *Fandango pour une guitarre seule.* (Wien: bureau
                       d'arts et d'industrie, No. 134).
                           RISM A/I: A Sca.

Dois/ND³   *Grand concerto composé pour la guitare, avec*
                       accompagnement de deux violons obligés, alto et

245

(Dois/ND[4]-Dois/ND[13])   Appendix II

violoncelle. (Paris: auteur, No. 15).
   RISM A/I: CS Pk (guitarre).

Dois/ND[4]   *Principes généraux de la guitare à cinq et à*
                  six cordes et de la lyre ... première partie.
                  (Paris: Doisy).
                     RISM A/I: A Wn.
                     Comments: Music composed for five-string,
                     five- and six-course guitar, and lyre. *Cox*
                     dates this work 1802. See Dois/ND[6] for a
                     German edition.

Dois/ND[5]   = Dois/ND[4] (Doisy, No. 2).
                     RISM A/I: D-brd Bhm.

Dois/ND[6]   *Vollständige Anweisung für die Gitarre, sowohl*
                  für Anfänger als solche welche schon einige
                  Fortschritte auf siesem Instrumente gemacht
                  haben. von Doisy. (Leipzig: Breitkopf und Härtel).
                     Cox: GB Lbm. US NYp.
                     Comments: A German edition of Dois/ND[4].

Dois/ND[7]   *Quatre sonates faciles pour guitare seule.*
                  (Paris: auteur).
                     RISM A/I: CS Pnm. D-brd B.

Dois/ND[8]   *Sonatine [Nr. 1: C] pour guitare et violon.*
                  (Wien: bureau d'arts et d'industrie, No. 130).
                     RISM A/I: CS N. I Mc.

Dois/ND[9]   *Trois duos pour guitarre & violon, composés par*
                  Doisy & Donneaud. (Amsterdam: A. Kuntze, au
                  magazin de musique, No. 20).
                     RISM A/I: D-brd B.

Dois/ND[10]   *Trois duos, extrèmement faciles pour guitarre et*
                  violon ... liv: I. (Amsterdam: A. Kuntze, au
                  magazin de musique, No. 21).
                     RISM A/I: CS Jla (guitarre).

Dois/ND[11]   *Trois duos extrèmement faciles pour guitarre &*
                  violons ... liv: II. (Amsterdam: A. Kuntze, au
                  magazin de musique, No. 22).
                     RISM A/I: D-brd Mbs.

Dois/ND[12]   *Trois duos concertans et faciles, composés pour*
                  guitare et violon. (Paris: Doisy, No. 23).
                     RISM A/I: S Skma (guitarre).

Dois/ND[13]   *Trois duos concertans composés pour guitare et*
                  alto. (Paris: Doisy, gravé par Doisy, No. 35).
                     RISM A/I: D-brd Bhm.

Appendix II   (Dois/ND[14]-Falc/1619[2])

Dois/ND[14]   *Trois duos faciles pour deux guitarres ...*
                     oeuvre 15. (Amsterdam: A. Kuntze, au magazin de
                     musique, No. 31).
                          RISM A/I: D-ddr Dlb.

Dois/ND[15]   *Walses, rondeaux, allemandes, airs variés et*
                     faciles, &c, &c, composés et arrangés pour une
                     guitare seule, et pour les commençans. (Paris:
                     Doisy, No. 34).
                          RISM A/I: S Skma.

DOIZI DE VELASCO, Nicolao

Doiz/1640   *Nuevo modo de cifra para tañer la guitarra con*
                     variedad, perfección, y se muestra ser instru-
                     mento perfecto, y abundantissimo. (Napoli:
                     Egidio Longo).
                          RISM A/I: E Mn.

Doiz/1645   = Doiz/1640
                          Danner: No locations cited.

EPPINGER, Heinrich

Eppi/ND[1]   *Trio [A] per violino, ghitara, e viola ...*
                     (Wien: Artaria & Co., No. 1564 [durch-scheinend
                     eine alte Pl.]-No. 203).
                          RISM A/I: A Wst.

Eppi/ND[2]   *VI Variations sur le menuet de l'opéra Don Juan*
                     pour un violon et une guitare. (Wien: Traeg,
                     No. 104).
                          RISM A/I: YU Zha.

FALCONIERI, Andrea

Falc/1616   *Libro primo di villanelle a 1. 2. & 3. voci, con*
                     l'alfabeto per la chitarra spagnola. (Roma:
                     Giovanni Battista Robletti).
                          RISM A/I: F Pc. I Bc, Rsc (2 ex.).

Falc/1619[1]   *Musiche ... a una, due & tre voci, libro sexto,*
                     con l'alfabbeto [!] della chitarra spagnola.
                     (Venezia: stampa del Gardano, appresso, Barto-
                     lomeo Magni).
                          RISM A/I: I Rsc.

Falc/1619[2]   *Libro quinto delle musiche a una, due e tre voci*
                     con l'alfabeto per la chitarra spagnuola.

247

(Faso/1627-Ferr/1623)   Appendix II

> (Firenze: Zanobio Pignoni).
>> *Danner:* I Fn, Rsc.
>> *Comments: RISM* and *Eitner* cite a shorter title,
>> but give the publisher's name not identified in
>> *Danner.*

FASOLO, Il (? pseud. MANELLI [MANNELLI], Francesco)

Faso/1627   *Misticanza di Vigna alla Bergamasca; il Canto*
                       della barchetta, et altre cantate et ariette
                       per voce et chitarra. (Rome: Robletti).
                          Wolf: I BDG, formerly Oscar Chilesotti's
                          library.
                          Comments: According to *Grove,* "Manelli" arti-
                          cle, il Fasolo is possibly a pseudonym for
                          Francesco Manelli and should not be confused
                          with Giovanni Battista Fasolo. Both Chile-
                          sotti (entry 269) and *Danner* attribute these
                          works to Giovanni Battista. Chilesotti dis-
                          cusses this work and includes a transcription
                          of two compositions in entry 269.

Faso/1628   *Il carro di Madama Lucia, e una serenata in lin-*
                       gua lombarda, che fa la gola, a carnevale; doppo;
                       un ballo di tre zoppi; con una sguazzata di cola-
                       sone, una morescha de schiavi a 3, et altre arie,
                       e correnti francese, con le littere per la chi-
                       tarra spagnola. (Roma: Giovanni Battista Rob-
                       letti).
                          RISM A/I: GB Lbm.
                          Comments: See *Comments* for Faso/1627.

FERANDIERE [FERRANDIERE], Fernando

Fera/1799   *Arte de tocar la guitarra española.* (Madrid:
                      en la imprenta de Pantaleon Aznar).
                         RISM A/I: A Wgm. CH E. E Mn.
                         Comments: Music composed for six-course guitar.

Fera/ME1799   = Fera/1799 TECLA (1977).

FERRARI, G.

Ferr/1623   = Ghiz/1623
                         Comments: Contains two works by G. Ferrari.

248

Appendix II   (Fosc/ND[1]-Fuen/ME1554[4])

FOSCARINI, Giovanni Paolo (Caliginoso detto il furioso)

Fosc/ND[1]

Il primo, second, e terzo della chitarra spagnola. (s.l.).
  RISM A/I: D-ddr Bds.
  Comments: According to Hudson (entry 271, p. 152), the title pages of Fosc/ND[1] and Fosc/ND[2] may have been exchanged; the index of Fosc/ND[1] cites works found only in Fosc/ND[2].

Fosc/ND[2]

I quatro libri della chitarra spagnola. (s.l.).
  RISM A/I: [various editions]: E Mn. F Pn. GB Cn, Lbm (with the title page of the first edition). I Bc.
  Comments: See *Comments* for Fosc/ND[1].

Fosc/1629

Intavolatura di chitarra spagnola, libro secondo. (Macerata: Giovanni Battista Bonono).
  RISM A/I: F Pc.
  Kirkendale: Photo in D-ddr Bds.

Fosc/1640[1]

Li 5 libri della chitarra alla spagnuola. (Roma: s.n.).
  RISM A/I: I Vnm.

Fosc/ME1640[1]

= Fosc/1640[1] S.P.E.S. (1979).

Fosc/1640[2]

Inventione di toccate sopra la chitarra spagnuola. (Roma: s.n.).
  RISM A/I: I TI.

FUENLLANA, Miguel de

Fuen/1554

Libro de musica para vihuela, intitulado Orphenica lyra. En el qual se contienen muchas y diversas obras. (Sevilla: Martin de Montesdoca).
  RISM A/I: A Wn, Iu. B Br. D-brd WI1. E E, Mn. F Pc, **Pn.** GB Lbm. US Cn, NYp.
  Comments: Music composed for vihuela, four- and five-course guitar.

Fuen/ME1554[1]

= Fuen/1554 BreitkopfHärtel (1902, ed. by Conde de Morphy).

Fuen/ME1554[2]

= Fuen/1554 CEstHist (1923, ed. by E. Martínez Torner).

Fuen/ME1554[3]

= Fuen/1554 OXFORD (1978).

Fuen/ME1554[4]

= Fuen/1554 MINKOFF

(Fuen/[1564]-Ghiz/1623)   Appendix II

Fuen/[1564]   *Libro de música para Vihuela intitulado Orphenica*
                    Lira: en el qual se contienen muchas y diversas
                    obras, comp. ^{to} *por Miguel de Fuenllana, dirigido*
                    al mui alto y mui poderoso Sr. D. Phelipe Prín-
                    cipe de Espana Rei de Inglaterra de Nápoles, &c.
                    Con Privilegio Real. En Madrid por Francisco
                    Sánchez. Ano de 1564.
                        Brown: E Mn.
                        Comments: According to *Brown*, the authenticity
                        of this possible second edition is not proven.
                        The title above is a quotation of a manuscript
                        title page which had been added. The original
                        title page is missing.

GATAYES, Guillaume-Pierre-Antoine

Gata/[ca1800]   *Nouvelle méthode raisonnée de la guittare ou*
                    lyre contenant des principes concisément expli-
                    qués, des airs avec accompagnement pour les com-
                    mençans et terminée par des valces et autre mor-
                    ceaux par P. Gatayes ... (Paris: Cochet
                    [ca1800]).
                        RISM B VI: F Bo, Pc.

GAUDE, F.

Gaud/ND   *Sechs Walzer und Sechs Eccosaisen* [*!*] *für die*
                    Guitarre ... op. 10. (Hamburg: Johann August
                    Böhme).
                        RISM A/I: D-brd Tu.

GHILLINI DI ASUNI

See ASUNI, Ghillini di

GHIZZOLO, Giovanni

Ghiz/1623   *Frutti d'amore in vaghe et variate arie, da can-*
                    tarsi co'l chitarrone clavicimbalo, o altro stro-
                    mento, accomodatovi l'alfabetto con le lettere
                    per la chitarra spagnola. Di Giovanni Ghizzolo
                    maestro di Capella della Veneranda Arca di S.
                    Antonio di Padova. Libro quinto. Et opera vige-
                    sima prima. Novamente composta, et data in luce.
                    (Venezia: A. Vincenti).
                        RISM B I: I Bc.
                        Comments: Contains works by G. Ferrari (2),
                        G. Ghizzolo (35).

250

Appendix II   (Giac/1618-GiuF/ND)

GIACCIO, Orazio

Giac/1618   *Laberinto [!] amoroso, canzonette a tre voci ...*
                     libro terzo. (Napoli: Pietro Paolo Riccio;
                     Giovanni Battista Gargano & Matteo Nucci).
                     RISM A/I: I Bc. S Skma.

GIAMBERTI, Gioseppe

Giam/1623   *Poesie diverse poste in musica de Gioseppe Giam-*
                     berti romano a una e tre voci per cantar nel
                     cimbalo et alcune con l'alfabeto per la chitarra
                     spagnola con due aggiunte una di Gio. Bernardino
                     Nanini, l'altra di Paolo Agostini ambidoi miei
                     maestri. Libro primo. (Roma: L.A. Soldi).
                     RISM B I: F Pc.
                     Comments: Contains works by P. Agostino (1),
                     G.B. Nanino (1), G. Giamberti (15).

GIORDANI

Gior/[ca1790]   = Anon/[ca1790]
                          Comments: Contains works by Giordani.

Gior/[ca1800]^1 = Anon/[ca1800]^1
                          Comments: Contains works by Giordani.

GISTAU, S. Castro de

Gist/ND   *Journal de guitare. Publié par S. Castro de*
                     Gistau. Livraison [3-4]. (Bruxelles: A. La-
                     crosse; Paris: chez l'auteur et l'éditeur, s.d.).
                     RISM B II: S Skma.
                     Comments: Contains works by S. Castro, F.
                     Moretti, F. Sors. S. Castro de Gistau may be
                     the publisher-composer identified as CASTRO
                     (listed above: Cast/ND$^{1-3}$). Both Castro and
                     S. Castro de Gistau were active in Paris.

GIULIANI, Giovanni Francesco

GiuF/ND   *Sei duetti notturni a due soprani con l'accom-*
                     pagnamento d'arpa, o cimbalo, o chitarra fran-
                     cese. (Firenze: Niccolo Pagani & Giuseppe Bardi).
                     RISM A/I: I Bc.

(GiuG/[158?]-Gorl/[156?])   Appendix II

GIULIANI, [Girolamo]

GiuG/[158?]   *Intavolatura de Chitara del Giuliani.* (Venezia:
                        Giacomo Vincenti).
                            Brown: Now lost.

GÖPFERT, Carl Andreas

Göpf/ND[1]   *Sonate pour deux guitarres & flûtes ... oeuvre
                        11.* (Offenbach: Johann André, No. 2570).
                            RISM A/I: CS Bu. D-brd OF.

Göpf/ND[2]   *Sonate pour guitarre & basson ou alto ... oeuvre
                        13.* (Offenbach: Johann André, No. 2504).
                            RISM A/I: CS Bu. D-brd As, OF.

Göpf/ND[3]   *Sonate für Guitarre und Flöte ... 15tes Werk.*
                        (Offenbach: Johann André, No. 2565).
                            RISM A/I: A Wgm.

Göpf/ND[4]   = Göpf/ND[3] (Offenbach: Johann André, No. 3943).
                            RISM A/I: CS Bu. D-brd OF.

Göpf/ND[5]   *Air varié pour guitarre & flûte ... oeuvre 18.*
                        (Offenbach: Johann André, No. 2564).
                            RISM A/I: D-brd OF.

Göpf/ND[6]   *Sonate pour deux guitarres, avec accompagement
                        de flûte.* (Offenbach: Johann André, No. 2353).
                            RISM A/I: D-brd OF (lacks fl).

GORLIER, Simon

Gorl/1551   *Le troysieme livre contenant plusieurs duos, et
                        trios, avec la bataille de Janequin a trois,
                        nouvellement mis en tablature de guiterne, par
                        Simon Gorlier, excellent joueur.* (Paris: R.
                        Granjon et M. Fezandat).
                            RISM B I: CH SGv.
                            Comments: Contains works by Jacotin, C. Jane-
                            quin, and eleven anonymous works. Music composed
                            for four-course guitar.

Gorl/ME1551   = Gorl/1551 BÄRENREITER (1980, published under the
                        title *Four guitar books (1551-1553).*

Gorl/[156?]   *Livre de Tabulature de Guiterne.* (Lyon: Simon
                        Gorlier, n.d.).
                            Brown: Now lost.

Appendix II   (Grag/ND^1-GraG/1680)

GRAGNANI, Filippo

Grag/ND^1 *Trois duos [A, D, F] pour deux guitares ... op. 4.*
                      (Paris: Richault, Momigny, No. 533).
                      RISM A/I: I Nc.

Grag/ND^2 *Sestetto per flauto, clarinetto, violino, due*
                      chitarre, e violoncello ... op. 9. (Paris:
                      Richault, Momigny, No. 726).
                      RISM A/I: D-ddr HER.

Grag/ND^3 *Le déluge. Sonate sentimentale pour guitare*
                      seule ... op. 15. (Paris: Richault, Momigny).
                      RISM A/I: I Nc.

Grag/ND^4 *Sinfonìa [d] per chitarra sola.* (Milano:
                      Giovanni Ricordi, No. 49).
                      RISM A/I: CH Bu.

GRANATA, Giovanni Battista

GraG/1646   *Capricci armonici sopra la chittarriglia spag-*
                      nola. (Bologna: Giacomo Monti).
                      Wolf: I Bc, Fn. GB Lbm.

GraG/ME1646^1 = GraG/1646 BERBEN (1962).

GraG/ME1646^2 = GraG/1646 S.P.E.S. (1978).

GraG/1651   *Nuova scielta di capricci armonici e suonate*
                      musicali in vari tuoni. (Bologna).
                      Wolf: I Bc.

GraG/1659   *Soavi concenti di sonate musicali per la chitarra*
                      spagnuola ... opera quarta. (Bologna: Giacomo
                      Monti).
                      RISM A/I: E Mn. I Bc, Vlb.

GraG/ME1659   = GraG/1659 BÄRENREITER (1979).

GraG/1674   *Novi capricci armonici musicali in varj toni per*
                      la chitarra spagnola, violino, e viola concer-
                      tati, et altre sonate per la chitarra sola,
                      opera quinta. (Bologna: Giacomo Monti).
                      RISM A/I: D-ddr Bds. I Bc.

GraG/ME1674   = GraG/1674 FORNI (1971).

GraG/1680   *Nuovi sovavi [!] concenti di sonate musicali in*
                      varij toni per la chittara spagnola, et altre
                      sonate concertate a due violoni, e basso, opera

(GraG/1684-Guer/ME1694[1])   Appendix II

                  sesta. (Bologna: Giacomo Monti).
                     RISM A/I: I Bc.

GraG/1684   *Armoniosi toni di varie suonate musicali con-*
                  certate, a due violini, e basso, con la chitarra
                  spagnola, opera settima. (Bologna: Giacomo
                  Monti).
                     RISM A/I: GB Lbm. I Bc.
                     Comments: Wolf gives the date 1664.

GraG/ND   *Nuove suonate di chitarriglia spagnuola picci-*
                  cate e battute. (s.d., s.l.).
                     Wolf: I Bc.

GRANDI, Alessandro

GraA/1626   *Cantade et arie a voce sola, commode da cantarsi*
                  nel clavicembalo, chitarrone, & altro simile
                  stromento, con le lettere dell'alfabetto per la
                  chitarra spagnola ... raccolte, & date in luce
                  da ... Andrea Ziotti, libro terzo. (Venezia:
                  Alessandro Vincenti).
                     RISM A/I: GB Lbm.

GraA/1629   = GraA/1626 *Libro quarto.*
                     Wolf: PL WRu.

GRENERIN, Henry

Gren/1680   *Livre de guitarre et autres pièces de musique*
                  meslées de symphonies avec une instruction pour
                  jouer la basse continue. (Paris: Bonneuil, gravé
                  par Hierosme Bonneuil).
                     RISM A/I: F Pc.

Gren/ME1680   = Gren/1680 MINKOFF (1977).

GUERAU, Francisco

Guer/1694   *Poema harmonico compuesto de varias cifras por el*
                  temple de la guitarra española. (Madrid: Manuel
                  Ruiz de Murga).
                     RISM A/I: GB Lbm.

Guer/ME1694[1]   = Guer/1694 Entry 361 (1974, ed. by Janis M.
                  Stevenson).

254

Appendix II   (Guer/ME1694²-Kaps/1610)

Guer/ME1694²   = Guer/1694 TECLA (1977).

GUICHARD, L.

Guic/[ca1795]   *La guitharre rendu facile sans le secours de*
                    l'art, où l'on trouve la manière de préluder et
                    jouer dans tous les tons possibles tant majeur
                    que mineur. Par M.L.G. (Paris: Frère).
                         RISM B VI: F Pn.

HENESTROSA, Luys Venegas de

See VENEGAS DE HENESTROSA, Luys

HUBER, J.N.

Hube/ND   *Trois fantaisies pour la guitarre seule.* (Wien:
                    Jean Traeg, No. 325).
                         RISM A/I: CS Pnm.

INDIA, Sigismondo [D']

Indi/1621   *Le musiche ... a una et due voci da cantarsi nel*
                    chitarrone, clavicembalo, arpa doppia et altri
                    stromenti da corpo, con alcune arie, con l'alfa-
                    betto per la chitarra alla spagnola ... libro
                    quarto. (Venezia: Alessandro Vincenti).
                         RISM A/I: GB Och.

Indi/1623   *Le musiche [a 1 v] ... da cantarsi nel chitarrone,*
                    clavicembalo, arpa doppia & altri stromenti da
                    corpo, con alcune arie, con l'alfabetto per la
                    chitarra alla spagnola ... libro quinto. (Venezia:
                    Alessandro Vincenti).
                         RISM A/I: GB Och.

KAPSBERGER, Johannes Hieronymus

Kaps/1610   *Libro primo di villanelle a I. 2 et 3 voci accom-*
                    modate per qualsivoglia strumento con l'intavola-
                    tura del chitarone et alfabeto per la chitarra
                    spagnola ... raccolta dal Sig^r Cavalier Flamminio
                    Flamminij. (Roma: s.n.).
                         RISM A/I: B Bc, Br. D-brd B. F Pc (lacks title
                         page). GB Lbm, Lcm. I Bc, Rvat-barberini, Rvat-
                         capp. giulia. US Wc.

(Kaps/1612-Krem/1689)   Appendix II

Kaps/1612   *Libro primo di arie passaggiate a una voce, con*
                    l'intavolatura del chitarone ... raccolto dal
                    Sig^r Cav. Fra Jacomo Christoforo ab Andlaw.
                    (Roma: s.n.).
                        RISM A/I: A Wn. B Br. GB Ge, Lbm (2 ex.). I Bc,
                        Rvat-barberini (inc.), Rvat-capp. giulia.
                        US Wc.

Kaps/1619[1]   *Libro secondo di villanelle a 1. 2. & 3 voci;*
                    con l'alfabeto per la chitarra spagnola ...
                    raccolte dal Sig. Ascanio Ferrari. (Roma: Gio-
                    vanni Battista Robletti).
                        RISM A/I: B Br. GB Lbm. I Bc, Rvat-barberini,
                        Rvat-capp. giulia.

Kaps/1619[2]   *Libro terzo di villanelle a 1. 2. et 3. voci*
                    accommodate per qual si voglia stromento con
                    l'intavolatura del chitarone et alfabeto per la
                    chitarra spagnola ... raccolto dal Sig^r Fran-
                    cesco Porta. (Roma: s.n.).
                        RISM A/I: B Br. GB Lbm. I Bc, Rvat-barberini,
                        Rvat-capp. giulia.

Kaps/1623   *Libro quarto di villanelle a una e piu voci con*
                    l'alfabeto per la chitarra spagnola ... raccolte
                    dal Signor Marcello Panocchieschi de Conti
                    d'Elci. (Roma: Luca Antonio Soldi).
                        RISM A/I: B Br. D-brd B. F Pc. GB Lbm (2 ex.).
                        I Bc, Rsc, Rvat-barberini, Rvat-capp. giulia.

KECK, P. L.

Keck/ND   *Six pièces* [C, G, A, A, C, G] *pour flûte et*
                    guitarre. (København: C.C. Lose).
                        RISM A/I: S Skma.

KRAUS, J.

Krau/ND   *Sonate* [C] *pour la guitarre ... dédiée à M^le*
                    Caroline de Reiche ... oe. II. (Leipzig: A.
                    Kühnel, bureau de musique, Ferdinand Schwarz,
                    No. 938).
                        RISM A/I: D-brd F.

KREMBERG, Jakob

Krem/1689   *Musicalische Gemüths-Ergötzung, oder, Arien, samt*
                    deren unterlegten hochdeutschen Gedichten ...
                    Welche also eingerichtet, dass sie entweder mit

                                    256

Appendix II (Laba/[1788]-Laga/1764[4])

einer Stimme allein zu singen, benebenst dem
General Bass, oder aber ... auf der Lauthe,
Angelique, Viola di Gamba, und Chitarra können
gespielet werden. (Dresden: Autor, Christoph
Mathesius).
    RISM A/I: A Wgm. B Bc. DK Kk. GB Lbm. NL DHgm.
US NYp.

LABARRE, Trille

Laba/[1788]
    Etrennes de guitarre ou recueil des plus jolies
romances et couplets qui aient paru dans l'année
1787, suivis d'une sonate avec accompagnement de
violon obligé et de plusieurs autres pièces ...
par Mr. Trille Labarre. Oeuvre IIè ... (Paris:
Baillon).
    RISM B II: F Pn.
    Comments: Contains works by Léonard, Sarti,
Trille Labarre, Anon.

LAGARDE, Pierre (de)

Laga/1764[1]
    I. recueil de brunettes avec accompagnement de
guittare, de clavecin ou de harpe ... les bru-
nettes sont tirées du Journal de musique.
(Paris: auteur).
    RISM A/I: F Pc (3 ex.), Pn (2 ex.). GB Lbm.

Laga/1764[2]
    IIe Recueil de brunettes avec accompagnement de
violon, guitare, clavecin ou harpe ... les bru-
nettes sont tirées du Journal de musique.
(Paris: auteur).
    RISM A/I: F Pc (3 ex.), Pn, Po. GB Lbm.

Laga/1764[3]
    IIIe Recueil de brunettes avec accompagnement de
violon, guitare, clavecin ou harpe ... ces bru-
nettes sont tirés du Journal de musique.
(Paris: auteur).
    RISM A/I: F Pc (3 ex., 2 different editions
    with slightly different contents), Pn (2 ex.),
    Po. GB Lbm.

Laga/1764[4]
    Ve Recueil de duo ... ces duos sont tirés du
Journal de musique. (Paris: auteur, aux addresses
ordinaires).
    RISM A/I: B Br. F Pc (5 ex.), Pn. GB Lbm.

Laga/1764[5]   *VIe Recueil de duo ... ces duos sont tirés du*
                      Journal de musique. (Paris: auteur, aux addresses
                      ordinaires).
                      RISM A/I: B Br. F Pc (5 ex.), Pn. GB Lbm.

LA GRANGE, de

Lagr/1671   *Livre de guitarre, contenant plusieurs pièces ...*
                      avec la manière de toucher sur la partie ou basse
                      continue. (Paris: s.n.).
                      RISM A/I: F Pn.

LANDI, Stefano

Land/1620   *Arie a una voce.* (Venezia: Bartolomeo Magni,
                      stampa del Gardano).
                      RISM A/I: F Pc. GB Lbm. PL WRu.

Land/1621[1]   = Anon/1621[1]
                      Comments: Contains works by Landi.

Land/1621[2]   = Anon/1621[2]
                      Comments: Contains works by Landi.

Land/1637   *Il quinto libro d'arie da cantarsi ad una voce,*
                      con la spinetta & con le littere per la chitara.
                      (Venezia: Bartolomeo Magni, stampa del Gardano).
                      RISM A/I: PL WRu.

LEMOINE, Antoine Marcel

Lemo/ME1773   *Methode de Guittarre par musique et tablature,*
                      avec differens Exercices sur le Pincer de cet
                      Instrument dans les quels se trouvent les Folies
                      d'Espagne, suivis d'une suitte d'Airs et menuets
                      ajustés pour un violon et une Guittarre et d'une
                      autre suitte d'Airs à chanter avec accompagnement
                      de Guitarre ... Dédié a Mlle. Sa Soeur. (Paris:
                      L'Editeur M. de musique ordinaire de la Chamber

Appendix II   (Lemo/ND[1]-LeRo/[1551])

et menus plaisirs du Roi). MINKOFF
    Comments: No library locations of the original
edition were found.

Lemo/ND[1]   *Nouvelle méthode de lyre ou guitarre à six*
cordes. (Paris: auteur, écrit et gravé par
Johannes, No. 2).
    RISM A/I: D-brd Mmb. F Pn.
    Comments: Contains music for six-course guitar.

Lemo/ND[2]   *Nouvelle méthode de guitarre à l'usage des com-*
mençans, divisée en trois parties ... par A.M.
Lemoine,... (Paris: l'auteur).
    RISM B VI: F Pn.

Lemo/ND[3]   *Nouvelle Méthode courte et facile Pour la Gui-*
tarre à l'usage de Commençan composée par Mr.
le Moine Professeur de Guitarre et de lyre.
Deuxième Édition. Augmentée de Principes pour la
Lyre, de Romances et d'Airs variés, et de deux
Estampes représentant la Guitarre et la Lyre
avec leur Doigtés. Prix 9 A Paris, chez Imbault,
Professeur et Editeur de Musique, au Mont d'Or,
Rue St. Honoré No. 125 près celle des Poulties.
Et Peristyle du Theatre de l'Opera Comique Impe-
rial, Rue Favart No. 461.
    Cox: No library locations are cited.
    Comments: Music composed for five-string gui-
tar, six-string guitar, and lyre.

Lemo/ME/ND[3]   = Lemo/ND[3] MINKOFF (1972).

LE ROY, Adrian

LeRo/[1551][1]   *Briefve et facile instruction pour apprendre la*
tabulature a bien accorder, conduire et disposer
la main sur la guiterne.
    Brown: Now lost.
    Comments: See LeRo/[1578] for a later edition.
Because of slight differences between the two
titles, the editions have been listed separate-
ly. Heartz (entry 229) explains that
Rowb/[1568] may be an English translation of
this work; Heartz also discusses the relationship between this work and Phal/1570, a plagiarism with Latin text.

(LeRo/1551² -LeRo/1554)   Appendix II

LeRo/1551²   *Premier livre de tabulature de guiterre, conten-*
                      ant plusieurs chansons, fantasies, pavanes,
                      gaillardes, almandes, branles, tant simples qu'
                      autres: le tout composé par Adrian Le Roy.
                      (Paris: A. Le Roy et R. Ballard, 1551).
                          RISM B I: F Pm. GB Lbm.
                          Comments: Music composed for four-course gui-
                          tar. Contains works by Boyvin (2), J. Maill-
                          ard.

LeRo/ME1551²   = LeRo/1551² EdChanterelle (1979).

LeRo/1552   *TIERS LIVRE DE TABULATURE DE GUITERRE, CONTEn-*
                      ant plusieurs Préludes, Chansons, Basse-dances,
                      Tourdions, Pavanes, Gaillardes, Almandes, Bran-
                      sles, tant doubles que simples. Le tout composé
                      par ADRIAN LE ROY. [Printer's mark] *A PARIS. De*
                      l'imprimerie, d'Adrian le Roy, & Robert Ballard,
                      Imprimeurs du Roy, rue saint Jean de Beauvais, à
                      l'enseigne sainte Genevieve. 1552. Avec privi-
                      lege du Roy, pour neuf ans.
                          Brown: F Pm. GB Lbm.
                          Comments: Music composed for four-course gui-
                          tar.

LeRo/ME1552   = LeRo/1552 EdChanterelle (1979).

LeRo/1553   *Quart livre de tabulature de guiterre contenant*
                      plusieurs fantasies, pseaulmes, et chansons:
                      avec l'Alouette, & la Guerre, composées par M.
                      Gregoire Brayssing de Augusta. (Paris: A. Le
                      Roy & R. Ballard, 1553).
                          RISM B I: F Pm. GB Lbm.
                          Comments: Music composed for four-course gui-
                          tar. Contains works by J. Arcadelt, J. Boy-
                          vin, S. Festa, C. Janequin (3), P. Sandrin,
                          M. Sohier, Anon.

LeRo/ME1553   = LeRo/1553 EdChanterelle (1979).

LeRo/1554   *CINQIESME LIVRE DE GUITERRE, CONTENANT PLUSIEURS*
                      CHANSONS A TROIS & quatre parties, par bons &
                      excelens Musiciens: Reduites en Tabulature par
                      Adrian le Roy. [Table of contents] *A PARIS. De*
                      l'imprimerie, d'Adrian le Roy, & Robert Balard,
                      Imprimeurs du Roy, rue saint Jean de Beauvais,
                      à l'enseigne sainte Genevieve. 6. Decembre.
                      1554. Avec privilege du Roy, pour neuf ans.
                          Brown: F Pm. GB Lbm.
                          Comments: Music composed for solo voice and
                          four-course guitar. (*RISM B I:* Contains works

                                  260

Appendix II   (LeRo/1554-LHoy/ND[5])

                          by J. Arcadelt (13), Bonard, P. Certon (2),
                          De Bussi, A. Le Roy (2).)

LeRo/ME1554   = LeRo/1554 EdChanterelle (1979).

LeRo/1555   *SECOND LIVRE DE GUITERRE, CONTENANT PLUSIEURS*
                   CHANSONS EN forme de voix de ville: nouvelle-
                   ment remises en tabulature, par Adrian le Roy.
                   [Table of contents] *A PARIS. De l'imprimerie,*
                   d'Adrian le Roy, & Robert Balard, Imprimeurs
                   du Roy, rue saint Jean de Beauvais, à l'enseigne
                   sainte Genevieve. 5. Janvier. 1555. Avec privi-
                   lege du Roy, pour neuf ans.
                        Brown: F Pm. GB Lbm.
                        Comments: Music composed for four-course gui-
                        tar.

LeRo/ME1555   = LeRo/1555 EdChanterelle (1979).

LeRo/[1578]   *Briefve & facile instruction pour apprendre la*
                   tabulature à bien accorder, conduire & disposer
                   la main sur la Guiterne. (Paris: Adrian le Roy
                   et Robert Ballard).
                        Brown: Now lost.
                        Comments: A later edition of LeRo/[1551][1].
                        Because of slight differences between the two
                        titles, the editions have been listed separate-
                        ly.

L'HOYER, Antoine de

LHoy/ND[1]   *Air varié pour guitarre.* (Offenbach: Johann
                   André, No. 3732).
                        RISM A/I: D-brd OF.

LHoy/ND[2]   *Air varié pour guitare.* (Paris: Pleyel père &
                   fils ainé, No. 1223).
                        RISM A/I: D-brd Mbs.

LHoy/ND[3]   *Grand sonate [G] pour la guitarre ... oeuvre 12.*
                   (Hamburg: Johann August Böhme).
                        RISM A/I: S Skma.

LHoy/ND[4]   *Six romances pour la guitare ... oeuv. XIV.*
                   (Hamburg: Johann August Böhme).
                        RISM A/I: A Wn.

LHoy/ND[5]   *Six romances composées & arrangées pour la*
                   guittarre ... oeuv. 15. (Hamburg: Mees & Co.).
                        RISM A/I: S Skma.

LHoy/ME/ND[6]

Trois duos concertants pour deux guitarres,
Op. 24. S.P.E.S.
   Comments: No library locations of the original
   edition were found.

LHoy/ME/ND[7]

Trio concertant pour trois guitarres, Op. 29.
S.P.E.S.
   Comments: No library locations of the original
   edition were found.

LHoy/ME/ND[8]

Grand duo concertant pour guitarre et violon,
Op. 28. S.P.E.S.
   Comments: No library locations of the original
   edition were found.

LIGHT, Edward

Ligh/[1795]

The art of playing the guittar, by Edward Light;
to which is added a variety of the most familiar
lessons, airs, divertimentos, songs, &c. properly
adapted for that instrument. (London: J. Preston).
   RISM B VI: GB Lbm. US Wcm.
   Comments: Cox indicates that this work contains
   music for English guitar, a type of cittern,
   and dates it 178-.

LOSY, Jan Antonín

Losy/ND

Pièces de guitarre.
   Grove (article on Losy): CS Pnm.

Losy/ME/ND

= Losy/ND ARTIA (*Musica antiqua bohemica* I/XXVIII,
   1958).

MAJER, Joseph Friedrich Bernhard Caspar

Maje/1732

Museum musicum theoretico practicum, das ist:
Neu-eröffneter theoretisch- und practischer Music-
Saal, darinnen gelehret wird, wie man sowohl die
Vocal- als Instrumental-Music gründlich erlernen,
auch die heut zu Tag üblich- und gewöhnlichste,
blasend- schlagend und streichende Instrumenten in
kurzer Zeit und compendieuser Application in be-
sondern Tabellen mit leichter Mühe begreifen
könne. Nebst einem Appendice derer anjetzo ge-
bräuchlichst-griechisch-lateinisch-italiänisch-
und französisch-musicalischen Kuntswörter nach
alphabetischer Ordnung eingerichtet und erkläret
zum nutzlichen Gebrauch aller und jeder Music-

Appendix II   (Maje/1741-Marc/post1660)

Liebhaber zusammen getragen und mitgetheilet von
Joseph Friederich Bernhard Caspar Majer ...
(Schwäb. Hall: Georg Michael Majer).
   RISM B VI: D Mbn, Mbs, Ngm, Rp (2 ex.), SCH.
F Pc. GB Lbm, T.
   Comments: A theoretical text which contains
music for guitar.

Maje/1741
                Joseph Friederich Bernhard Caspar Majers ... Neu-
eröffneter theoretisch- und pracktischer Music-
Saal, das ist: Kurze doch vollständige Methode,
so wohl die Vocal- als Instrumental-Music gründ-
lich zu erlernen, auch die ... blasend- schlagend-
und streichende Instrumenten ... durch die deut-
lichste Exempla, in besondern Tabellen, mit
leichter Mühe zu begreiffen. Nebst einem ...
Appendice und Erklärung derer anjezo gebräuch-
lichsten griechische-lateinisch- italiänisch-
und französisch- musicalischen Kunst-Wörter.
Zweyte und viel-vermehrte Auflage. (Nürnberg:
Iohann Iacob Cremer).
   RISM B VI: A Wgm. B Bc, Br. D Bds, Dl, LEm,
Mbs, MGu, Ngm (2 ex.), ROu. DK Kk. F Pn. GB Er,
Lbm. NL DHgm. S L, Skma, Uu. US A, I, NYp, PHf,
Wcm.
   Comments: A theoretical text which contains
music for guitar.

MARCHETTI, Tommaso

Marc/1648
                Il primo libro d'intavolatura della chitarra
spagnola. Composto, e dato in luce da Tomasso
Marchetti romano. Con una regola facilissima per
poter'imparar' à sonare, accordare, e far lettere
della detta chitarra da se stesso. Et si conten-
gono anco nel detto libro molte sonate passe-
giate, non più da altri date in luce. (Roma:
Catalani).
   RISM B VI: I Rsc.

Marc/1660
       = Marc/1648 (Roma: Francesco Moneta).
   RISM B VI: F Pn. I Rsc.

Marc/ME1660
       = Marc/1660 MINKOFF

Marc/post1660
       Title unknown.
   Danner: I Rsc.
   Comments: Danner "Update ..." lists this item
as "tablature with mutilated title page".

(MarB/1655-Mart/[ca1790])   Appendix II

MARINI, Biagio

MarB/1655   *Per ogni sorte d'istromento musicale, diversi*
                     generi di sonate, da chiesa, e da camera, a due,
                     tre, & a quattro, con l'alfabeto alle più pro-
                     prie, per la chitarra alla spagnola ... libro
                     terzo, opera XXII. (Venezia: Francesco Magni).
                          RISM A/I: GB Ob. I Bc. PL WRu.

MARINONI, Girolamo

MarG/1614   *Il primo libro de motetti a una voce et in fine*
                     una Salve Regina a doi, posti in musica per
                     alfabeto. (Venezia: stampa del Cardano, aere
                     Bartolomei Magni).
                          RISM A/I: CS Pu.

MARTIN, François

MarF/1663   *Pièces de guitairre [!], à battre et à pinser*
                     ... premier livre. (Paris: „proche l'autheur").
                          RISM A/I: F Psg.

MARTÍN Y SOLER, Vicente

MarV/ND   *Drei Duetts (Il Giuramente, Notturno L'Allegrìa)*
                     für zwei Guitarren ... mit doppeltem Texte.
                     (Braunschweig: Musikalienverlag in der Neuen-
                     strasse, No. 42).
                          RISM A/I: D-brd Mbs.

MARTINI

Mart/[ca1775]   = Anon/[ca1775]
                          Comments: Contains works by Martini.

Mart/[1785]   = Porr/[1785]
                          Comments: Contains works by Martini.

Mart/1788   = Porr/1788
                          Comments: Contains works by Martini.

Mart/[ca1790]   = Anon/[ca1790]
                          Comments: Contains works by Martini.

Appendix II   (Matt/[ca1680]-Merc/ME/ND^2)

MATTEIS, Nicola

Matt/[ca1680]   *Le False consonanse della musica per poter' ap-*
                       prendere a toccar da se medesimo la chitarra
                       sopra la parte. Esempii curioso con havertimenti
                       chiarissimi e dichiarationi dove ciasche d'uno
                       potrà in breve accompagnar le arie in musica, e
                       sonar qual si voglia basso ... Il tutto è diviso
                       in quattro parti. Opera di Nicola Matteis.
                       ([London]).
                          RISM B VI: F Pthibault.

Matt/[1682]   *The False consonances of musick or instructions*
                       for the playing a true base upon the guitarre,
                       with choice examples and cleare directions to
                       enable any man in a short time to play all
                       musicall ayres ... ([London: J. Carr]).
                          RISM B VI: GB Ge, Ob (lacks p. 1-32). I Bc.
                       US NYp.
                          Comments: An English translation of
                       Matt/[ca1680].

Matt/ME1682   = Matt/[1682] BÄRENREITER (1980).

MÉDARD, Rémy

Méda/1676   *Pièces de guitarre.* (Paris).
                          Danner: S Uu.

MERCHI [Giacomo MERCHI DI BRESCIA, Giacomo MERCHI, Mr. MERCHI]

See RISM A/I under MERCHI for a list of works with guitar accompaniment.

Merc/ND^1 *Quatro duetti a due chitarre e sei minuetti a*
                       solo con variationi ... li duetti possono essere
                       anche acompagnati dal violino, opera tersa [!].
                       (Paris: auteur, Bayard, Le Clerc, Mlle Castag-
                       nery).
                          RISM A/I: F Pn. GB Lbm.

Merc/ME/ND^1 = Merc/ND^1 S.P.E.S.

Merc/ND^2 *Raccolta d'ariette francesi ed italiane per la*
                       chitarra, li acompagnamenti sono in musica e
                       tavolatura ... opera quarta. (Paris: auteur).
                          RISM A/I: F Pc.

Merc/ME/ND^2 = Merc/ND^2 S.P.E.S.

(Merc/ND³-Merc/[ca1770])   Appendix II

Merc/ND³   *Le guide des écoliers de guitarre ou préludes*
                    aussi agréables qu'utiles, sur tous les modes,
                    les positions et les arpégemens avec des airs
                    et des variations ... Ve livre de guitarre,
                    oeuvre VIIe. (Paris: auteur).
                      RISM A/I: GB Pc (2 ex.).

Merc/ME/ND³   = Merc/ND³ MINKOFF

Merc/ND⁴   *Dodici suonate per la chitarra, sei a due chi-*
                    tarre o con accompagnamento di violino e sei a
                    solo ... opera XVI. (London: author).
                      RISM A/I: GB Lbm. S Skma.

Merc/[1768]   *XVIè Livre de guitarre contenant des airs, ro-*
                    mances et vaudevilles. Avec des accompagnements
                    préludes et ritournelles par Mr. Merchi. Oeuvre
                    XXè. (Paris: l'auteur).
                      RISM B II: F Pc.
                      Comments: Contains works by Collet and anony-
                      mous works.

Merc/ND⁵   *Twelve divertimentos for two guittars or a*
                    guittar and violin ... opera 21ˢᵗ. (London:
                    Welcker).
                      RISM A/I: GB Lbm.

Merc/ND⁶   = Merc/ND⁵ (London: Robert Bremner).
                      RISM A/I: DK Sa.

Merc/[ca 1766]   *Les Soirées de Paris. XVIIIè livre de guitarre*
                    contenant des airs d'opéra comique avec des
                    accompagnemens d'un nouveau goût, des préludes
                    et des ritournelles par Mr Merchi. Oeuvre XXIIè.
                    (Paris: l'auteur, et aux adresses ordinaires;
                    Lyon, Castaud).
                      RISM B II: F Pc.
                      Comments: Contains works by Duni, Gluck,
                      Monsigny, Philidor, Rinaldo da Capua. Both
                      this work and Merc/ND⁷ are cited as opus 22.

Merc/ND⁷   *A collection of the most favorite Italian, French*
                    & English songs & duets for the guittar, with an
                    accompanyment for an other guittar ... op. XXII.
                    (London: Welcker).
                      RISM A/I: GB Ckc, Lbm.
                      Comments: Both this work and Merc/[ca1766] are
                      cited as opus 22.

Merc/[ca1770]   *XXè. Livre de guitarre contenant des airs d'opera*
                    comique avec des accompagnements d'un nouveau
                    gout, des préludes et des ritournelles par Mr.

                                  266

Appendix II   (Merc/ME/ND^8-Merc/ND^{11})

Merchi. Oeuvre XXIVe ... (Paris: l'auteur).
   RISM B II: F Pc.
   Comments: Contains works by Duni, Grétry,
   Monsigny, Anon.

Merc/ME/ND^8 *XXI Livre de guitarre contenant des Airs connus,*
                      des préludes et des ritornelles, Op. 25. S.P.E.S.
                         Comments: No library locations of the original
                         edition were found.

Merc/ND^9 *Sei duetti a chitarra e violino con sordina o a*
                      due chitarre. XXIXe Livre de guitarre, oeuvre
                      XXXIIIe. (Paris: auteur).
                         RISM A/I: GB Ckc.

Merc/ME/ND^9 = Merc/ND^9 S.P.E.S.
                         Comments: The modern edition is marked as
                         Op. 12.

Merc/ND^{10} *Traité des agrémens de la musique exécutés sur*
                      la guitarre ... oeuvre XXXVe. (Paris: auteur).
                         RISM A/I: F G.
                         Comments: MINKOFF dates Merc/ND^{10} as 1761 and
                         1777. *Cox* dates this work ca. 1777 and indi-
                         cates that it was written for five-string
                         guitar.

Merc/ME1761   = Merc/ND^{10} MINKOFF

Merc/ME1777   = Merc/ND^{10} MINKOFF

Merc/1780   *XXXIVè Livre de guitarre contenant des airs*
                      d'opéra et opéra comique et autres de societez
                      avec des accompagnements, des préludes et des
                      ritournelles par Mr. Merchi. Oeuvre XXXVIè.
                      (Paris: l'auteur et aux adresses ordinaires;
                      Lyon, Castaud).
                         RISM B II: F Pc.
                         Comments: Contains works by Albanèse, Dezède,
                         Gluck, Grétry, Merchi, Mereaux, Piccini,
                         Rousseau.

Merc/ND^{11} *Six lessons and six duets for one and two gui-*
                      tars ... book first. N.B. These duets may be
                      play'd by a guitar and violin. (London: Robert
                      Bremner).
                         RISM A/I: DK Sa.

(Mich/1698-MilC/1622[1])   Appendix II

MICHELI, Antoniodi

Mich/1698   *La nuova chitarra.* (Palermo).
                        Kirkendale: US Wc.

MILÁN, Luys [Luis]

MilL/1535   *Libro de musica de vihuela de mano, intitulado El
                        maestro. El qual trahe el mesmo estilo y orden
                        que un maestro traheria con un discipulo princi-
                        piante.* (Valencia: Francisco Diaz Romano,
                        [Kolophon: 1536]).
                           RISM A/I: C Tu. D-ddr LEm (inc.). E Bc, Mn
                        (2 ex.). F Pc, Pn (inc.). GB Lbm. I PAc, Tn.
                        NL DHgm. US Cn (inc., with complete photocopy).
                        Comments: Music composed for vihuela.

MilL/ME1535[1]   = MilL/1535 BreitkopfHärtel (1902, ed. by Conde de
                        Morphy).

MilL/ME1535[2]   = MilL/1535 CEstHist (1923, ed. by E. Martínez
                        Torner).

MilL/ME1535[3]   = MilL/1535 BreitkopfHärtel (1929, ed. by Leo
                        Schrade).

MilL/ME1535[4]   = MilL/1535 ZERBONI (1965, Italian and English
                        text, 2 v.).

MilL/ME1535[5]   = MilL/1535 OLMS (1967).

MilL/ME1535[6]   = MilL/1535 PennaStUniv (1971, ed. by Charles
                        Jacobs).

MilL/ME1535[7]   = MilL/1535 MINKOFF (1975).

MilL/ME1535[8]   = MilL/1535 HOFMEISTER (ca. 1975).

MILANUZZI, Carlo

MilC/1622[1]   *Primo scherzo delle ariose vaghezze, commode da
                        cantarsi a voce sola nel clavicembalo, chitar-
                        rone, arpa doppia, & altro simile stromenti, con
                        le littere dell' alfabetto, con l'intavolatura,
                        e con la scala di musica per la chitarra alla
                        spagnola ... opera settima.* (Venezia: Bartolomeo
                        Magni).
                           RISM A/I: D-brd Hs. I Bc.

Appendix II   (MilC/1622²-MilC/1635)

MilC/1622²   *Secondo scherzo delle ariose vaghezze, commode
                    da cantarsi a voce sola vel clavicembalo, chitar-
                    rone, arpa doppia, & altro simile stromento, con
                    le littere dell' alfabetto, con l'intavolatura,
                    e con la scala di musica per la chitarra alla
                    spagnola ... aggiontovi ... alcune sonate facili
                    ... opera ottava.* (Venezia: Alessandro Vincenti).
                      RISM A/I: I Mc.

MilC/1625   = MilC/1622²
                      RISM A/I: I Bc.

MilC/1623   *Terzo scherzo delle ariose vaghezze commode da
                    cantarsi a voce sola nel clavicembalo, chitar-
                    rone, arpa doppia, & altro simile stromento ...
                    con l'aggiunta nel fine di alcuni balletti,
                    saravende [!], spagnolette, gagliarde, follie,
                    ciaccone, & altre sonate ... opera nona.*
                    (Venezia: Alessandro Vincenti).
                      RISM A/I: D-brd Hs. I Mc.

MilC/1624   *Quarto Scherzo, op. 11.* (Venezia).
                      Wolf: D-brd Hs.

MilC/1628   *Sesto libro delle ariose vaghezze, comode da
                    cantarsi a voce sola nel clavicembalo, chitar-
                    rone, o altro simile stromento, con le lettere
                    dell' alfabetto per la chitarra alla spagnola
                    ... opera decimaquinta.* (Venezia: Alessandro
                    Vincenti).
                      RISM A/I: I Bc.

MilC/1630   *Settimo libro delle ariose vaghezze, comode da
                    cantarsi a voce sola, con le lettere dell' alfa-
                    betto per la chitarra alla spagnola, aggiuntavi
                    un' arietta a due voci con sinfonie di due
                    violini, se piace ... opera decimasettima.*
                    (Venezia: Alessandro Vincenti).
                      RISM A/I: I Bc.
                      Comments: Wolf cites the title as *Settimo
                      scherzo.*

MilC/1634   = Vinc/1634
                      Comments: Contains two works by Milanuzzi.

MilC/1635   *Ottavo libro delle ariose vaghezze, comode da
                    cantarsi a voce sola nel clavicembalo, chitar-
                    rone, o altro simile stromento ... opera decima
                    ottava.* (Venezia: Alessandro Vincenti).
                      RISM A/I: I Bc.
                      Comments: Wolf cites the title as *Ottavo
                      scherzo.*

(MilC/1643-Mill/1631[1])   Appendix II

MilC/1643   *Nono libro delle ariose vaghezze, commode da*
                     cantarsi a una, e due voci nel clavicembalo,
                     chitarrone, o altro simile stromento, con le
                     lettere dell' alfabetto per la chitarra alla
                     spagnola ... opera vigesima. (Venezia: Ales-
                     sandro Vincenti).
                     RISM A/I: PL Kj.

MILLIONI [MILIONI], Pietro

Mill/1627[1]   *Prima scielta di villanelle accomodate con*
                     l'intavolatura per cantare sopra la chitarra
                     spagnola. (Roma: Guglielmo Facciotti).
                     RISM A/I: I Bc.

Mill/1627[2]   *Prima impressione del quinto libro d'intavola-*
                     tura di chitarra spagnola ... con una regola
                     generale con la quale si può l'imparar' a
                     sonare ogni sorte di sonate con repicchi.
                     (Roma: Guglielmo Facciotti).
                     RISM A/I: I Bc.

Mill/1627[3]   *Quarta impressione del primo, secondo et terzo*
                     libro d'intavolatura ... sopra il quale ciascuna
                     da se medesimo puo l'imparare a sonare di chi-
                     tarra spagnola, accordare ... (Roma: Guglielmo
                     Facciotti).
                     RISM A/I: F Pn. I Bc.

Mill/1627[4]   *Seconda impressione del quarto libro d'intavola-*
                     tura di chitarra spagnola ... con una aggiunta di
                     molte sonate, et anco una regola generale con la
                     quale si può l'imparar' a sonare ogni sorte di
                     sonate con trilli. (Roma: Guglielmo Facciotti).
                     RISM A/I: I Bc.

Mill/1635[1]   = Mill/1627[4] *... Novamente ristampato ... con*
                     l'accrescimento di molte sonate curiose. (Roma:
                     Paolo Masotti).
                     RISM A/I: I Bc (inc.).

Mill/1631[1]   *Corona del primo, secondo, e terzo libro d'inta-*
                     volatura di chitarra spagnola di Pietro Millioni
                     ... Una regola per imparar' il modo d'accordare
                     dodici chitarre, per poterle sonare insieme in
                     concerto ciascheduna per differente chiave, overo
                     lettera; et anco l'alfabeto et accordatura per il
                     chitarrino, overo ghitarre italiana. (Milano:
                     Filippo Ghidolfi; G.B. Cerri & C. Ferrandi).
                     RISM B VI: F Pthibault.

                                    270

Appendix II $(Mill/1631^2-Mill/1652)$

Mill/1631^2 = Mill/1631^1 *Nuovamente stampata* ... (Roma: G.
                        Facciotti).
                            RISM A/I: I Rv. US Wcm.

Mill/1635^2 = Mill/1631^1 ... *et ristampata in Torino* ...
                            RISM A/I: I Tn.

Mill/1661   *Nuova corona d'intavolatura di chitarra spagnola*
                        novamente ristampata secondo il vero originale
                        ... *con alcune sonate, e passeggiate nuove* ...
                        tra le quali vi s'è anco aggiunto la Siciliana,
                        e le Letanie de' santi con l'intavolatura messe
                        spezzatamente. (Roma: erede del Mancini).
                            RISM A/I: I Bc.
                            Comments: Kirkendale indicates that Mill/1661
                            and Mill/1676 are plagiarisms of Pico/1608.

Mill/1676   = Mill/1661
                            Comments: See *comments* for Mill/1661.

MILLIONI, Pietro; MONTE, Lodovico (Joint Authorship)

Mill/[ca1627]   *Vero e facil modo d'imparare a sonare, et accor-*
                        dare da se medesimo la Chitarra spagnola, non
                        solo con l'Alfabeto, et accordatura ordinarii,
                        ma anco con un'altro Alfabeto, et accordatura
                        straordinarii, nuovamente inventati da P. Mil-
                        lioni et Lodovico Monte ... (Venezia: Angelo
                        Salvadori).
                            RISM B VI: NL DHgm.

Mill/1637   = Mill/[ca1627] *Et di nuovo ristampato, da me*
                        Lodovico Monte bolognese. (Roma, Macerata:
                        eredi Salvioni e Agostino Grisei).
                            RISM B VI: GB Lbm.

Mill/1644   = Mill/[ca1627] (Venezia: F. Vieceri).
                            RISM B VI: I Bc. US BE (inc.).

Mill/1647   = Mill/[ca1627] (Roma e Macerata: A. Grisei).
                            RISM B VI: I Bc.

Mill/ME1647   = Mill/1647 FORNI ([1977]).

Mill/1652   = Mill/[ca1627] (Venezia: Giacomo Bortoli).
                            RISM B VI: I Bc.

(Mill/1659-Ming/ME1754)   Appendix II

Mill/1659   = Mill/[ca1627] (Venezia: G. Batti).
                        RISM B VI: CS Ps.

Mill/1666   = Mill/[ca1627] (Venezia: C. Bortoli).
                        RISM B VI: F Pthibault.

Mill/1673[1]   = Mill/[ca1627] (Venezia: G. Didini).
                        RISM B VI: I Bc, Vnm.

Mill/1673[2]   = Mill/[ca1627] (Venezia: Macerata, Piccini).
                        RISM B VI: D HVl.

Mill/1678   = Mill/[ca1627] (Venezia: Giacomo Zini).
                        RISM B VI: GB Lbm (2 ex.). I Bc, MOe. US Wcm.

Mill/1684   = Mill/[ca1627] (Venezia: G. Zini).
                        RISM B VI: I Bc. US Wcm.

Mill/1737   = Mill/[ca1627] (Venezia: D. Louisa).
                        RISM B VI: F Pc.

Mill/ND   = MonL/ND
                        Comments: Contains works by Milioni.

MINGUET E YROL, Pablo

Ming/1774   *Academia Musical de los instrumentos que explica
                   Pablo Minguet en sus Tratados, los quales en-
                   señan el nuevo estilo de tãnerlos por musica y
                   cifra con perfeccion. Reglas y advertencias gene-
                   rales que enseñan el modo de tañer todos los in-
                   strumentos mejores y mas usuales como son la
                   Guitarra, Tiple, Vandola, Cythara, Clavicordio,
                   Organo, Harpa, Psalterio, Bandurria, Violin,
                   Flauta Travesera, Flauta Dulce y las Flautilla
                   con varios tañidos, danzas, contradanzas y otras
                   cosas semejantes, demonstradas y figuradas en
                   diferentes Laminas finas por Musica y cifra,
                   al estilo Castellano, Italiano, Catalàn y Francès
                   paraque qualquier Aficionado las pueda comprehen-
                   der con mucha facilidad y sin Maestro: con una
                   breve explicacion de como el Autor los aprendiò,
                   que està al bolver de esta hoja.* (Madrid: Joaquin
                   Ibarra).
                        RISM B VI: D WI. E Bc, Bd, Mn. F Pc. GB Lbm.
                        US Cn (inc.), NYp (partie I-V), Wcm. (Six fas-
                        cicles, three of which are dated 1752, 1754,
                        and 1774, each with a particular title).

Ming/ME1754   = Ming/1774 MINKOFF (the date 1754 on the MINKOFF
                        edition indicates the 1754 fascicle).

Appendix II   (Moli/ND-Monz/ND)

MOLINO, Valentino

Moli/ND   *Grand trio concertant [C] pour violon, alto et*
                       guitare ... oeuvre 10me. (Torino: les frères
                       Reycend & Co., No. 15).
                          RISM A/I: I Nc.

MONTE, Lodovico

MonL/ND   *Vago fior di virtù dove si contiene il vero modo*
                       per sonare la chitarriglia spagnuola, con sonate
                       facili per principianti, et per chi sona bene
                       sonate non più viste, raccolte da me Lodovico
                       Monte bolognese dalla Chitarriglia. (Venezia:
                       A. Salvadori).
                          RISM B I: I Bc.
                          Comments: Contains works by P. Milioni, Santino
                          da Parma (4), Todeschino, Anon (18).

MonL/[ca1627]   = Mill/[ca1627]
                          Comments: Joint authorship of Millioni and
                          Monte. See also entries following Mill/[ca1627].

MONTESARDO, Girolamo

MonG/1606   *Nuova inventione d'intavolatura per sonare i*
                       balletti sopra la chitarra spagnuola, senza
                       numeri e note. (Firenze: Christofano Marescotti).
                          RISM A/I: A Wgm. I Bc.

MonG/1612   *I lieti giorni di Napoli, concertini italiani in*
                       aria spagnuola a due, e tre voci con la [!]
                       lettere dell' alfabeto per la chitarra; madri-
                       galetti, et arie gravi passagiate a una, e due
                       voci per cantare alla tiorba, gravecimbalo, arpa
                       doppia, et altri istrumenti ... opera XI. (Napoli:
                       Giovanni Battista Gargano & Lucrezio Nucci).
                          RISM A/I: GB Ge.

MONZINO, Giacomo

Monz/ND   *Divertimenti per chitarra francese ... op. a*
                       14. a. (Milano: Antonio Monzino).
                          RISM A/I: I VEas.

(More/[ca1775]–Morl/1552²)   Appendix II

MORELLI

More/[ca1775]   = Anon/[ca1775]
                         Comments: Contains works by Morelli.

More/[ca1790]   = Anon/[ca1790]
                         Comments: Contains works by Morelli.

MORETTI, Federico

MorF/1799   *Principios para tocar la guitarra de seis ordenes.*
                     Precedidos de los elementos generales de la musica
                     ... por ... Federico Moretti ... I [-II] pt.
                     (Madrid: por Josef Rico).
                         RISM B VI: E Mn, Zsc. GB Lbm. US NH, NYp.
                         Comments: Contains music for six-course guitar.

MorF/ME1799   = MorF/1799 TECLA

MorF/ND¹   *Principi per la chitarra composti dal dilettante*
                     sig.ʳ D. Federico Moretti. (Napoli: Luigi
                     Marescalchi).
                         RISM B VI: I Bc.

MorF/ND²   = Gist/ND
                         Comments: Contains works by Moretti.

MORLAYE, Guillaume

Morl/[1550]   *Guillaume Morlaye. Tabulature de guiterne où sont*
                     chansons, gaillardes, pavanes, bransles, alle-
                     mandes, fantaisies, etc. (Paris: Michel Fezandat).
                         Brown: Now lost.

Morl/1552¹   *LE PREMIER LIVRE DE CHANSONS, GAILLARDES,*
                     PAVANNES, Bransles, Almandes, Fantaisies,
                     reduictz en tabulature de Guiterne par Maistre
                     Guillaume Morlaye joueur de Lut. [Cut of a guitar
                     lying on an open book] A PARIS. De l'Imprimerie
                     de Robert GranJon & Michel Fezandat, au Mont S.
                     Hylaire, à l'Enseigne des Grandz Jons. 1552.
                     Avec privilege du Roy.
                         Brown: CH SGv.
                         Comments: Music composed for four-course
                     guitar.

Morl/1552²   *QUATRIESME LIVRE CONTENANT PLUSIEURS FANTASIES,*
                     Chansons, Gaillardes, Paduanes, Bransles, re-
                     duictes en Tabulature de Guyterne, & au jeu de
                     la Cistre, par Maistre Guillaume Morlaye, & autres

274

Appendix II   (Morl/1553-Muda/ME1546[6])

bons autheurs. [Cut of a guitar lying on an open
book] A PARIS, De l'imprimerie de Michel Fezandat, au mont sainct Hylaire, a l'hostel d'Albret,
1552. Avec privilege du Roy, pour dix ans.
    Brown: CH SGv.
    Comments: Music composed for four-course
guitar.

Morl/1553

LE SECOND LIVRE DE CHANSONS, GAILLARDES, PADUANES,
Bransles, Almandes, Fantasies, reduictz en tabulature de Guiterne, par maistre Guillaume Morlaye
joueur de Leut. [Cut of a guitar lying on an open
book] A PARIS. De l'imprimerie de Michel Fezandat,
au mont sainct Hilaire en l'hostel d'Albret. 1553.
Avec privilege du Roy, pour dix ans.
    Brown: CH SGv.
    Comments: Music composed for four-course
guitar.

MUDARRA, Alonso

Muda/1546

Tres libros de musica en cifras para vihuela, en
el primero ay musica facil y dificil en fantasias:
y composturas: y pavanas: y gallardas: y algunas
fantasias para guitarra. El segundo trata de los
ocho tonos (o modos) tiene muchas fantasias por
diversas partes: y composturas glosadas. El ter-
cero es de musica para cantada y tañida. Tiene
motetes, psalmos, romances, canciones, sonettos
en castellano: y italiano versos en latin. Villan-
zicos. (Sevilla: Juan de León).
    RISM A/I: E E, Mn.
    Comments: Music composed for vihuela and four-
course guitar.

Muda/ME1546[1]

= Muda/1546 BreitkopfHärtel (1902, ed. by Conde de
Morphy).

Muda/ME1546[2]

= Muda/1546 CEstHist (1923, ed. by E. Martínez
Torner).

Muda/ME1546[3]

= Muda/1546 InstEspMusic (1949, ed. by Emilio
Pujol).

Muda/ME1546[4]

= Muda/1546 HOFMEISTER

Muda/ME1546[5]

= Muda/1546 BÄRENREITER (1980).

Muda/ME1546[6]

= Muda/1546 MINKOFF

275

(Murc/1714-Narv/ME1538[7])   Appendix II

MURCIA, Santiago de

Murc/1714   *Resumen de acompañar la parte con la guitarra*
                         comprendiendo en el todo lo que conduze para
                         este fin: en donde el aficionado hallara dis-
                         sueltas por diferentes partes del instrumento,
                         todo género de posturas, y ligaduras, en los
                         siete signos Naturales y accidentales ... Por
                         Santiago de Murcia, Mro. de guitarra de la
                         Reyna ... ([Madrid]).
                            RISM B VI: E Mn. US Cn, LA.

Murc/ME1714[1]   = Murc/1714 Entry 365 (1975, ed. by Elena M.
                         Lowenfeld, selected compositions).

Murc/ME1714[2]   = Murc/1714 BÄRENREITER (1980).

NARVÁEZ, Luis de

Narv/1538   *Los seys libros del Delphín de música de cifras*
                         para tañer vihuela [6 vol.]. (Valladolid: Diego
                         Hernandez de Cordova).
                            RISM A/I: E Mn (inc.). GB Lbl. US Wc.
                            Comments: Music composed for vihuela.

Narv/1546[1]   = Phal/1546[1]
                            Comments: See *comments* for Phal/1546[1].

Narv/1546[2]   = Phal/1546[2]
                            Comments: See *comments* for Phal/1546[2].

Narv/1568   = Phal/1568
                            Comments: See *comments* for Phal/1568.

Narv/ME1538[1]   = Narv/1538 BreitkopfHärtel (1902, ed. by Conde de
                         Morphy).

Narv/ME1538[2]   = Narv/1538 CEstHist (1923, ed. by E. Martínez
                         Torner).

Narv/ME1538[3]   = Narv/1538 InstEspMusic (1945, ed. by Emilio
                         Pujol).

Narv/ME1538[4]   = Narv/1538 HOFMEISTER (1965).

Narv/ME1538[5]   = Narv/1538 InstEspMusic (1971, ed. by Emilio
                         Pujol).

Narv/ME1538[6]   = Narv/1538 UMusicEsp (1971).

Narv/ME1538[7]   = Narv/1538 MINKOFF (1980).

Appendix II   (Nive/1666-Pell/ME1650^2)

NIVERS, Guillaume-Gabriel

Nive/1666   *Méthode facile pour apprendre à chanter la*
                       musique. Par un maître célèbre de Paris.
                       (Paris: Robert Ballard).
                           RISM B VI: F Pn. GB DRc. I Bc.

Nive/1670   = Nive/1666 *Second édition.*
                           RISM B VI: F Pc.

Nive/1696   = Nive/1666
                           RISM B VI: B Br. GB DRc.
                           Comments: No additional information is given on
                           this edition. It is also attributed to Charles
                           Lemaire.

Nive/1702   = Nive/1666 (Paris: C. Ballard).
                           RISM B VI: F Pthibault.

PAIXAÕ RIBEIRO, Manoel da

Paix/1789   *Nova arte de viola ... divida em duas partes ...*
                       com estampas das posturas ... e com alguns minu-
                       ettes, e modinhas por musica, e por cifra.
                       (Coimbra: "na Real Officina da Universidade").
                           RISM A/I: C Tu. D-ddr Bds. E Mn. F Pc. GB Lbl
                           (2 ex.), Ouf. US AA, NH, NYp, R, Wc.

PARRY, J.

Parr/1761   *A collection of Welsh, English & Scotch airs with*
                       new variations, also four new lessons for the
                       harp or harpsichord ... by J. Parry. To which are
                       added twelve airs for the guittar. (London: the
                       author and J. Johnson).
                           RISM B II: GB DU. US CAh, LA, Wc.

Parr/[ca1762]   = Parr/1761 (London: J. Johnson).
                           RISM B II: GB Lbm. US CAh, NYp.

PELLEGRINI, Domenico

Pell/1650   *Armoniosi concerti sopra la chitarra spagnuola.*
                      (Bologna: Giacomo Monti).
                          RISM A/I: F Pc (2 ex.). I Bc, Tn. US BE.

Pell/ME1650^1 = Pell/1650 S.P.E.S. (1978).

Pell/ME1650^2 = Pell/1650 MINKOFF

(Peso/[1648]-Peso/ND[2])   Appendix II

PESORI, Steffano

Peso/[1648]   *Galeria musicale ... compartita in diversi*
                   scherzi di chitarriglia ... parte battute e
                   parte sminuite; con un discorso utile, e curio-
                   sissimo alla virtuosa gioventù. (Verona: G.B.
                   Merli & fratelli).
                       RISM A/I: I Bc.
                       Comments: Wolf incorrectly cites the composer
                       as Pisari. *Kirkendale* states that the dedica-
                       tion of this otherwise undated work gives the
                       date 4 Luglio 1648.

Peso/ME[1648]   = Peso/[1648] S.P.E.S.

Peso/[1648/49]   *Lo scrigno armonico. Opera seconda ... ove si*
                   rinchiudono vaghissime danze, & ariette al modo
                   italiano, spagnolo, e francese; per suonare in
                   concerto con basso, violino, manacordo, & altri
                   instrumenti: et molte vaghissime villanelle, con
                   l'intavolatura della chitarra spagnola. (s.l.,
                   s.n.).
                       RISM A/I: GB Lbl. I Bc.
                       Comments: According to *Kirkendale*, the preface
                       of this work indicates that it was published a
                       few months after Peso/[1648].

Peso/ME[1640?]   = Peso/[1648/49] S.P.E.S.

Peso/[1650?]   *Toccate di chitarriglia, parte terza ... ove con*
                   cinque bellissimi ordini descritta si vede una
                   facilissima regola per apprendere il modo di
                   suonare la chitarriglia di Spagna. (Verona:
                   Andrea & fratelli Rossi).
                       RISM A/I: I Vnm.

Peso/ME[1650?]   = Peso/[1650?] S.P.E.S.

Peso/ND[1]   *I concerti armonici di chitarriglia ... ridotti*
                   in cinque beliss. ordini. (Verona: Andrea & fra-
                   telli Rossi).
                       RISM A/I: GB Lbl.

Peso/ND[2]   *Ricreationi armoniche overo toccate di chit-*
                   tariglia ... ove con bellissimo ordine descritto
                   si vede il vero modo per sonare ad uso moderno
                   la chittariglia di Spagna. (s.l., s.n.).
                       RISM A/I: I Bc.

Appendix II   (Phal/1546[1]-Phal/1568)

PHALÈSE, Pierre

NOTE: Phal/1570 and Phal/1573 were published in conjunction with Jean BELLÈRE.

Phal/1546[1]

Des chansons reduictz en TabulatuRE DE LUC A TROIS ET QUATRE PARTIES LIVRE DEUXIEME. [Cut of ten performing musicians] A LOUVAIN Par Piere Phaleys libraire. Lan de Grace M.D.XLVI.
    Brown: GB Lbmh.
    Comments: Ward (entry 191, p. 383-84) indicates that works by Narvaez appear in lute tabulature in this publication. Concordances are cited.

Phal/1546[2]

Carminum pro Testudine Liber IIII. IN QUO CONTINENTUR EXCELLENTISSIMA carmina, dicta Paduana & Galiarda, composita per Franciscum Mediolanensem: & Petrum Paulum Mediolanensem, ac alios artifices in hac arte praestantissimos. [Cut of ten performing musicians] LOVANII Apud PETRUM PHALESIUM Bibliopolam juratum. Anno Domini M.D.XLVI. Cum gratia & privilegio ad triennium.
    Brown: A Wn. GB Lbmh.
    Comments: Ward (entry 191, p. 384) indicates that this work, published under a Latin title, contains the same music as Phal/1546[1].

Phal/1568

LUCULENTUM THEATRUM MUSICUM, IN QUO (DEMPTIS VETUSTATE TRITIS CANTIONIBUS) SELECTISSIMA OPTIMORUM QUORUMLIBET AUTORUM, AC EXCELLENtissimorum artificum tum veterum, tum praecipuè recentiorum carmina, maiore quam unquam diligentia & industria expressa, oculis proponuntur. Et primo ordine continentur αὐτόματα quae Fantasiae dicuntur, Secundo Cantilenae quatuor & quinque Vocum. Postea Carmina difficiliora quae Muteta appellantur, eaque quatuor, quinque & sex Vocum. Deinde succedunt Carmina longe elegantissima duabus Testudinibus ludenda. Postremo habes & eius generis Carmina quae tum festivitate, tum facilitate sui discentibus, primo maximè satisfacient ut sunt Passomezo, Gailliardes, Branles etc. [Cut of ten performing musicians] LOVANII. Ex Typographia Petri Phalesii Bibliopolae Iurati. ANNO M.D.LXVIII.
    Brown: A Wn. D ROu. GB Ob. NL DHgm.
    Comments: Ward (entry 191, p. 384) indicates

(Phal/1570–Phil/ND³)   Appendix II

that this publication contains one fantasia by
Narvaez. Concordances are cited.

Phal/1570   *Selectissima elegantissimaque, gallica, italica
                   et latina in guiterna ludenda carmina, quibus
                   adduntur et fantasiae, passomezi, saltarelli,
                   galliardi, almandes, branles et similia, ex
                   optimis elegantissimisque collecta et iam cum
                   omni diligentia recens impressa. His accessit
                   luculenta quaedam & perutilis institutio qua
                   quisque citra alicuius subsidium artem facillimè
                   percipiet.* (Louvain: P. Phalèse; Antwerpen:
                   J. Bellère).
                        RISM B I: D ROu (2 ex.).
                        Comments: Contains plagiarisms of works pre-
                        viously published by Adrian Le Roy. See
                        Heartz (entry 229) for an explanation of the
                        relationship between LeRo/[1551][1] and this
                        work.

Phal/ME1570   = Phal/1570 SCHOTT (1969, ed. by F.J. Giesbert.
                   Published under the title *Flandrisches Gitarren-
                   buch*).

Phal/1573   *Selectissima carmina ludenda in Quinterna, cum
                   tripudis & institutione ad arte in eandem.
                   Lovanii apud Petrum Pha[lesiu]s & Antverp.apud
                   Bellerum.*
                        Brown: Now lost; actual existence questioned.

PHILLIS, Jean Baptiste

Phil/ND[1]   *Ah! vous dirai-je Maman. Avec 12 variations
                   pour la guittare.* (Paris: Imbault).
                        RISM A/I: D-brd DÜk.

Phil/ND[2]   *Étude nouvelle pour la guitare ou lyre dans les
                   tons les plus usités, majeurs et mineurs, ou
                   l'on démontre les difficultés, les agréments et
                   les positions du démanchement.* (Paris: Pleyel,
                   No. 203).
                        RISM A/I: DK Kk.

Phil/ND[3]   *Nouvelle méthode pour la lyre ou guitarre à six
                   cordes ... oeuvre 6.* (Paris: Pleyel, No. 435).
                        RISM A/I: I Mc.
                        Cox: F Pn. US U (Film).
                        Comments: Music composed for six-string guitar
                        and lyre.

Appendix II   (Pica/1752-PisD/1552)

PICA DA ROCHA, João Leite

Pica/1752 *Lican instrumental da viola Portugueza, ou de ninfas, de cinco ordens.* (Lisbon).
 Danner: P Pm.
 Comments: Danner's "Update...", p. 35 notes that Ronald Purcell confirmed the existence of this publication.

PICO, Foriano

Pico/1608 *Nuova scelta di sonate per la chitarra spagnola ... con alcune sonate e passegiate non più poste alla stampa, tutte curiose tra le quali vi s'è aggiunto la Siciliana e le letanie de'santi, con l'intavolature messe spezzatamente, e la Romanella.* (Roma: Giovanni-Francesco Paci).
 RISM A/I: F Pn. I Nn.
 Danner: I Bc, Nn. F Pn.
 Comments: Kirkendale indicates that Mill/1661 and Mill/1676 are plagiarisms of Pico/1608 and Pico/1609. *Kirkendale* and *Danner*, in conflict with *RISM*, cite Naples as the place of publication of the 1608 edition; the 1609 edition, not listed in *RISM* or *Wolf*, is listed as a Rome edition in *Kirkendale. Kirkendale* states that *Wolf* incorrectly cites Francesco Pari, 1628 for the Paci, 1608 edition. However, MINKOFF facsimile edition (Pico/ME1628) identifies the original edition as Naples: F. Pace, 1628, not 1608.

Pico/1609 = Pico/1608 (Rome).
 Kirkendale: F Pn. I Pn.
 Comments: See *comments* for Pico/1608.

Pico/ME1628 = Pico/1608 (Naples). MINKOFF

PISADOR, Diego

PisD/1552 *Libro de musica de vihuela, agora nuevamente compuesto por Diego Pisador, vezino de la ciudad de Salamanca, dirigido al muy alto y muy poderoso señor don Philippe principe de Espana ...* (Salamanca: D. Pisador).
 RISM B I: E E, Mn. F Pn. GB Lbl. US BE, R.
 Comments: Contains works by J. Basurto (2), M. Flecha, N. Gombert (3), Josquin (13), C. Morales, J. Mouton, J. Vasquez (3), A. Willaert (2). Music composed for vihuela.

(PisD/ME1552[1]-Porr/[1785])   Appendix II

PisD/ME1552[1]   = PisD/1552 BreitkopfHärtel (1902, ed. by Conde de
                        Morphy).

PisD/ME1552[2]   = PisD/1552 CEstHist (1923, ed. by E. Martínez
                        Torner).

PisD/ME1552[3]   = PisD/1552 MINKOFF (1973).

PLAYFORD, John

Play/1652   *A booke of new lessons for the cittern and
                      gittern.* (London).
                          Danner: GB Gu.
                          Comments: Contains music for four-course
                      guitar.

PLEYEL, Ignace

Pley/1788   = Porr/1788
                          Comments: Contains works by Pleyel.

Pley/ND[1]   *Six sonatines per [!] la guitarre avec accom-
                      pagnement d'un violon.* (Wien: Johann Cappi,
                      No. 986).
                          RISM A/I: CS Pnm.

Pley/ND[2]   *Duettino [C] für flöte oder violin und ghitar [!].*
                      (Wien: Pietro Mechetti q^m Carlo, No. 202).
                          RISM A/I: DK A (with price-tag: Copenhagen,
                      C.C. Lose).

Pley/[ca1800][1]   = Anon/[ca1800][1]
                          Comments: Contains works by Pleyel.

Pley/[1802]   *Six sonatines [G, D, A, G, C, G] pour la guitarre
                      avec accompagnement d'un violon.* (Leipzig: Breit-
                      kopf & Härtel, No. 96).
                          RISM A/I: A Wst. CH BE1. I CDO. US IObenton.

PORRO, Pierre-Jean

Porr/[1785]   *Nouvelles étrennes de guitarre ou recueil des
                      plus jolies romances et couplets qui aient paru
                      dans l'année 1784 suivis d'une sonate et de plu-
                      sieurs pièces pour la guitarre seule, mis en
                      musique et arrangés expressément pour cet instru-
                      ment ... par M. Porro. Oeuvre IV ...* (Paris:
                      Baillon).
                          RISM B II: F Pn. US NYp.

Appendix II   (Porr/ME[1785]-Riba/ME1677)

> *Comments:* Contains works by Grétry, Lalleman,
> J.P.E. Martini, de Mayer, P. Porro, Anon.

Porr/ME[1785]   = Porr/[1785] S.P.E.S. (*Opere scelte*, fascicle b).

Porr/1788   *Journal de guitarre, ou choix d'airs nouveaux*
                     de tous les caractères avec préludes, accom-
                     pagnements, airs variés, &c ... Pincé et doigté
                     marqués pour l'instruction ... par Mr. Porro ...
                     12 cahiers et les étrennes de guitarre ...
                     (Paris: Porro).
                     > *RISM B II:* F Pc (43p. out of 85p.). US NYp.
                     > *Comments:* Contains works by Bertoni, Bonesi,
                     > Cambini, Champein, Dalayrac, Desaugiers, M.
                     > Foignet, Grétry, J. Haydn, Hoffman, Kozeluch,
                     > Martini, Mengozzi, Pleyel, Porro, Propiac,
                     > J.J. Rousseau, Sacchini.

Porr/ME1788   = Porr/1788 S.P.E.S. (*Opere scelte*, fascicle c).

Porr/ND   *Collection de préludes et caprices dans tous les*
                     tons pour l'étude de la guitare. (Paris: auteur).
                     > *RISM A/I:* B Lc. F Pn.

Porr/ME/ND   = Porr/ND S.P.E.S. (*Opera scelte*, fascicle d).

PRIETO, P. F. Victor

Prie/1799   = Abre/1799
                     > *Comments:* Joint authorship (Abreu and Prieto).
                     > Prieto composed the divertimentos for this
                     > work.

RIBAYAZ, Lucas Ruiz de

Riba/1672   *Luz y norte musical para caminar por las cifras*
                     de la guitarra española, y arpa, tañer, y cantar
                     á compás por canto de organo; y breve explicacion
                     del arte, con preceptos faciles, indubitables, y
                     explicados con claras reglas por teorica, y
                     practica. Compuesto por D. Lucas Ruiz de Ribayaz.
                     (Madrid: Melchor Alvarez).
                     > *RISM B VI:* GB Lbm.

Riba/1677   = Riba/1672
                     > *RISM B VI:* B Br. D B. E Mmc, Mn (3 ex.). F Pc
                     > (2 ex.). GB Lbm, Lcm. US Cn, NYhs, NYp, SFs,
                     > Wcm.

Riba/ME1677   = Riba/1677 MINKOFF (1972).

(Ricc/1677-Ront/1618)   Appendix II

RICCI, Giovanni Pietro

Ricc/1677   *Scuola d'intavolatura con la quale ciascuno senza*
                     maestro puo le imparare à suonare la chitarriglia
                     spagnuola, accordare, fare il trillo, il repicco,
                     trasmutar da una lettera all' altra corrispon-
                     denti ... (Roma: P. Moneta).
                         RISM B VI: F Pthibault. GB Lbm (47p. out of
                         64p.).

RITTER, Peter

Ritt/ND   *Notturno pour guitarre, flûte et alto.* (Mainz:
                     Bernhard Schotts Söhne, No. 1165).
                         RISM A/I: D-brd Mmb (contains: fl, vla,
                         guitarre; price-tag: Köln, Gebrüder Almenräder).

ROLLA, Alessandro

Roll/ND   *Tre duettini* [F, C, F] *per chitarra e violino.*
                     (Zürich: Johann Georg Nägeli).
                         RISM A/I: CH BEk.

ROMANO, Remigio (Compiler)

See [in order of appearance] Anon/1618[3], Anon/1622[1], Anon/1623[3],
Anon/1625.

RONCALLI, Ludovico

Ronc/1692   *Capricci armonici sopra la chitarra spagnola,*
                     Op. I. (Bergamo: Sebastian Casetti).
                         RISM A/I: D-brd MUs. F Pthibault. GB Lbl.
                         I Bc, BGc, Mb, Rc, Rsc.

Ronc/ME1692[1]   = Ronc/1692 EdChanterelle (1979).

Ronc/ME1692[2]   = Ronc/1692 S.P.E.S.

Ronc/ME1692[3]   = Ronc/1692 FORNI (1969).

Ronc/ME1692[4]   = Ronc/1692 BÄRENREITER (1979).

RONTANI, Raffaello

Ront/1618   *Le varie musiche a una, due e tre voci per can-*
                     tare nel cimbalo, ò in altri stromenti simili con

Appendix II   (Ront/1619-Rowb/[1568])

l'alfabeto per la chitarra spagnola. Libro
secondo, opera sesta. (Roma).
    Danner: I Rsc.
    Wolf: I Vnm. GB Lbl. I Rvat-capp. giulia.

Ront/1619   Le varie musiche ... a una et due voci, per cantare nel cimbalo, o in·altri stromenti simili,
con l'alfabeto per la chitarra in quelle più a
proposito per tale stromento. Libro terzo, opera
settima. (Roma: Luca Antonio Soldi).
    RISM A/I: GB Lbl. I Vnm.

Ront/1620   = Ront/1619 Libro 5. (Roma).
    Wolf: I Vnm. GB Lbm.

Ront/1622   = Ront/1619 Libro 6. (Roma).
    Wolf: I Vnm. GB Lbm.

Ront/1621[1]   = Anon/1621[1]
    Comments: Contains two works by Rontani.

Ront/1621[2]   = Anon/1621[2]
    Comments: Contains two works by Rontani.

Ront/1623   Le varie musiche a una, due, e tre voci, per
cantare nel cimbalo, o in altri stromenti simili,
con l'alfabeto per la chitarra spagnola in quelle
più a proposito per tale stromento. Libro primo.
(Roma: Antonio Poggioli, appresso Giovanni
Battista Robletti).
    RISM A/I: GB Lbl. I Vnm.

Ront/1625   Varie musiche a una e due voci ... per cantare
nel cimbalo e nella tiorba, con l'alfabeto della
chitarra spagnola in quelli più a proposito per
tale instromento. Libro quarto, opera ottava.
(Roma: Giovanni Battista Robletti).
    RISM A/I: I Rvat-capp. giulia.

ROWBOTHAM, James (Publisher)

Rowb/[1568]   The breffe and playne instruction to lerne to
play on the gyttron and also the Cetterne.
(London: James Rowbotham).
    Brown: Now lost.
    Comments: This work may be an English transla-
tion of LeRo/[1551][1]. See Heartz (entry 229)
for an explanation of the relationship between
the two works.

285

(Rubi/1799-Sabb/1641)   Appendix II

RUBIO, M. J.

Rubi/1799   *Metodo Facil De Guitarra Dedicado a Los Aficio-*
                     nados Por M.J. Rubio. Propiedad. Pr: 28 Rs.
                     Madrid Este Metodo ademas de los conocimientos
                     generales. contiene otras cosas, 24 piezas de
                     todo genero de baile.
                         Cox: E Mn. US U.
                         Comments: Music composed for six-course guitar.
                         Cox dates this work 1799.

RUIZ DE RIBAYAZ, Lucas

See RIBAYAZ, Lucas Ruiz de

RUSH, George

Rush/ND[1]   *XII Favourite lessons or airs for two guittars,*
                     ... opera 2d. (London: James Oswald).
                         RISM A/I: GB Lbl.
                         Comments: Tyler (entry 3, p. 109) dates this
                         work ca. 1755 and indicates that it contains
                         music for English guitar, a type of cittern.

Rush/ND[2]   *A first set of sonatas [C, C, C] for the guittar,*
                     with an accompanyment for another guittar or
                     violin. ([London]: author).
                         RISM A/I: GB Gm, Lbl.

Rush/[ca1800][1]   = Anon/[ca1800][1]
                         Comments: Contains works by G. Rush.

SABBATINI, Pietro Paolo

Sabb/1622   = ?Anon/1622
                         Comments: Contains works by P.P. Sabbatino,
                         possibly Pietro Paolo Sabbatini who began
                         publishing his own works in the same city
                         (Rome) eighteen years after this edition.

Sabb/1640   *Canzoni spirituali ad una, a due, et a tre voci,*
                     da cantarsi, e sonarsi sopra qualsivoglia istro-
                     mento, libro secondo, opera decimaterza. (Roma:
                     Ludovico Grignani).
                         RISM A/I: GB Lbl. I Rvat-capp. giulia.

Sabb/1641   *Varii capricci, e canzonette a una e tre voci da*
                     cantarsi sopra qualsivoglia istromento, con l'al-
                     fabeto della chittara spagnola ... libro settimo,

Appendix II   (Sabb/1650-SanM/1565)

                     opera decimaquarta. (Roma: Vincenzo Bianchi).
                       RISM A/I: GB Lbl.

Sabb/1650   *Prima scelta di villanelle a una voce delli dieci*
                 libri ... da cantare sopra a qualsivoglia instru-
                 mento, con l'alfabeto della chitarra spagnola.
                 (Roma: Vitale Mascardi).
                   RISM A/I: I Rdp.

Sabb/1652[1]   = Sabb/1650 ... *di nuovo ristampate, e corrette.*
                   RISM A/I: GB Lbl.

Sabb/1652[2]   *Prima scelta di villanelle a due voci ... da*
                 sonarsi in qualsivoglia instromento, con le
                 lettere accomodate alla chittara spagnola.
                 (Roma: Vitale Mascardi).
                   RISM A/I: GB Lbl. US Wc.

Sabb/165[2][3]   *Seconda scelta di villanelle a una voce delli*
                 dieci libri ... da cantare sopra a qualsivoglia
                 instrumento, con l'alfabeto della chitarra spa-
                 gnola ... di nuovo ristampate e corrette. (Roma:
                 Vitale Mascardi).
                   RISM A/I: GB Lbl.

SAN SEVERINO, Benedetto

SanS/1620   *Intavolatura facile delli passacalli, ciaccone,*
                 saravande, spagnolette, fulie, pavaniglie, pass'e
                 mezzi, correnti, & altre varie suonate composte,
                 & accommodate per la chitarra alla spagnuola ...
                 opera terza. (Milano: Filippo Lomazzo).
                   RISM A/I: GB Lbl.

SanS/1622   *Il primo libro d'intavolatura per la chitarra*
                 alla spagnuola, de passacalli, ciaccone, sara-
                 vande, spagnuolette, folie pavaniglie, pass'e-
                 mezzi, correnti, et altre varie suonate ... di
                 nuovo ristampato, con aggionta d'alcune canzonette
                 dal istesso autore ... opera terza. (Milano:
                 Filippo Lomazzo).
                   RISM A/I: GB Lbl. I Bc.

SANCTA MARIA, Tomaso de

SanM/1565   *Libro llamado, arte de tañer fantasia, assi para*
                 tecla como para vihuela, y todo instrumento, en

(SanM/ME1565-Sanz/ME1674²)   Appendix II

> *que se pudiere tañer a tres, y a quatro vozes, y
> a mas ... el qual por mandado del muy alto con-
> sejo real fue examinado, y aprovado por el emi-
> nente musico de Su Magestad Antonio de Cabeçon,
> y por Juan de Cabeçon, su hermano. Compuesto por
> el muy reverendo padre fray Thomas de Sancta
> Maria ... Parte I[-II].* (Valladolid: Francisco
> Fernandez de Cordova).
>> *RISM B VI:* D B, Rp. E Bu, E, Mmc. F CH, Pn.
>> GB Ge, Lbm. US Cn, CAh, R, Wcm.
>> *Comments:* Music composed for vihuela and key-
>> board. Although primarily a work for keyboard,
>> theoretical discussions may be applied to the
>> vihuela and other instruments.

SanM/ME1565   = SanM/1565 MINKOFF (1973).

SANTINO DA PARMA

SanP/ND   = MonL/ND
>> *Comments:* Contains four works by Santino da
>> Parma.

SANZ, Gaspar

Sanz/1674   *Instruccion de musica sobre la guitarra española,
                     y método de sus primeros rudimentos, hasta tañer-
                     la con destreza. Con dos laberintos ingeniosos,
                     variedad de sones, y dances de rasgueado, y pun-
                     teado, al estilo español, italiano, françès, y
                     inglès. Con un breve tratado para acompañar con
                     perfeccion, sobre la parte muy essencial para la
                     guitarra, arpa, y organo, resumido en doze reglas,
                     y exemplos los mas principales de contrapunto,
                     composicion ... Compuesto por el licenciado
                     Gaspar Sanz, aragones,... Libro primo [-tercero].*
                     (Zaragoza: herederos de Diego Dormer).
>> *RISM B VI:* D Mbs. E Bd, Mn. US Wcm.

Sanz/ME1674[1]   = Sanz/1674 InstFernCat (1952).

Sanz/ME1674[2]   = Sanz/1674 Linda Ragus, "A translation and tran-
                       scription of Gaspar Sanz' Instrucción de música

Appendix II   (Sanz/ME1674³-SchC/ND³)

> sobre la guitarra española." Unpublished M.A. thesis, University of California at San Diego (1965).

Sanz/ME1674³   = Sanz/1674 InstEspMusic (1966).

Sanz/ME1674⁴   = Sanz/1674 Entry 374 (1974, ed. by Jerrold A. Manns, 30 dances).

Sanz/ME1674⁵   = Sanz/1674 *(libro primero)*. Entry 376 (1976-77, ed. by Rodrigo de Zayas).

Sanz/ME1674⁶   = Sanz/1674 SCHOTT

Sanz/1697   = Sanz/1674
                    RISM B VI: B Br. CH Gu. D B. E Mlg, Mn (2 ex.). F Pc. GB Lbm. NL DHgm. US R.

Sanz/ME1697¹   = Sanz/1697 InstFernCat (1952).

Sanz/ME1697²   = Sanz/1697 MINKOFF (1976).

Sanz/ME1697³   = Sanz/1697 SCHOTT

SARTI

Sart/[1788]   = Laba/[1788]
                    Comments: Contains works by Sarti.

SCHEIDLER, Christian Gottlieb

SchC/ND¹   *Sonate [C, G] pour la guitarre ... Nᵒ ([hand-schriftlich:] 1-2).* (Mainz: Bernhard Schott, No. 199[-200]).
                    RISM A/I: S Skma.

SchC/ND²   *Duo pour guitarre et violon ... Nᵒ ([hand-schriftlich:] 1 [D], 2 [D]).* (Mainz: Bernhard Schotts Söhne, No. 225[-226]).
                    RISM A/I: D-brd B, MZsch (1, 2).

SchC/ND³   *Duo pour guitarre et violon ... Nᵒ II.* (Eltville: Georg Zulehner, No. 225).
                    RISM A/I: A Wn (guitarre, vl).

(Sche/ND-SchF/ND[1])   Appendix II

SCHEIDLER, J. F.

Sche/ND
Nouvelle méthode en français et en allemand pour apprendre la guitarre ou la lyre ... 1ère partie. (Bonn: N. Simrock, No. 385).
    RISM A/I: CH Bchristen. D-brd Tu.
    Cox: F Pc. US U (Film).

SCHLICK, Johann Conrad

Schl/ND
Recueil de petites pièces pour la guitarre ... cahier I [12 Lieder, 2 Sonatinen in F und C]. (Leipzig: Breitkopf & Härtel).
    RISM A/I: D-brd LÜh. D-ddr Bds.

SCHÖNIGER

Schö/ND
Variations [G] pour deux guitarres. (Bonn: N. Simrock, No. 394).
    RISM A/I: D-brd LB.

SCHULZ, Andreas

SchA/ND[1]
6 Walzer nach Sächsischer Art [F, F, d, G, G, C] für Guitarre, Violin, und Flöte ... 4tes Werk, IItes Heft. (Wien: Artaria & Co., No. 2252 ([Umschlag:] 2202).
    RISM A/I: CH Ff (guitarre).

SchA/ND[2]
Sei variazioni con finale d'un tema originale per la chitarra. (Wien: Jean Traeg).
    RISM A/I: D-brd Mbs.

SCHULZ [SCHULTZ], Johann Abraham Peter

SchJ/ND
Klage der Schäferinn. Für die Guitarre. (Hamburg: Rudolphus; Altona: Cranz, No. 551).
    RISM A/I: A Wst.

SCHUMAN, Friedrich Theodor

SchF/ND[1]
Thirty eight lessons, with an addition of six French & Italian songs, for the guittar ... opera Ist. (London: Michael Rauche & Co.).
    RISM A/I: EIRE Dn. GB Gm, Lbl.

Appendix II   (SchF/ND^2-Soto/1764)

SchF/ND^2 *A second set of [21] lessons for one and two*
                      guittars ... opera II. (London: J. Johnson).
                      RISM A/I: GB Lbl. S Skma. US Cn, IO, NYp.

SEVERI PERUGINO, Francesco

Seve/1622   = ?Anon/1622
                      Comments: Contains works by F. Severi, possibly
                      Francesco Severi Perugino who published his own
                      work in the same city (Rome) four years later.

Seve/1626   *Arie di Francesco Severi Perugino Cantor di N.S.*
                      a una, due, et tre voci Da Cantarsi, nel Chitar-
                      rone, Clavicembalo, & altri simili Instroment.
                      Con alcune Arie con l'Alfabeto per la Chitarra
                      alla Spagnola. Libro Primo Opera Seconda. (Roma:
                      Appresso Paolo Masotti).
                      Wolf: I BDG, formerly Oscar Chilesotti's lib-
                      rary.
                      Comments: Chilesotti (entry 269) gives infor-
                      mation on this work and a transcription of ten
                      compositions.

SFONDRINO, Giovanni Battista

Sfon/1637   *Trattenimento virtuoso disposto in leggiadrissime*
                      sonate per la chitarra. (Milano: Giorgio Rolla).
                      RISM A/I: I Fc.

SORS, F [ernando]

Sors/ND   = Gist/ND
                      Comments: Contains works by F. Sors. According
                      to Jeffery (entry 558, p. 15), Sors was active
                      as a composer of opera and guitar music before
                      1800, although no published works are known.
                      In his catalog of Sors' works, Jeffery indicates
                      that Sors' Op. 1 was published in London, ca.
                      1815 and not before 1813.

SOTOS, Andrés de

Soto/1764   *Arte para aprender con facilidad, y sin maestro,*
                      á templar y tañer rasgado la guitarra de cinco

(Stra/ND-Stra/ME[1768])   Appendix II

órdenes, ó cuerdas; y tambien la de cuatro ó seis
órdenes, llamadas guitarra española, bandurria y
vandola, y tambien el tiple. Demuéstrase con
grande claridad la formacion de los 12 puntos
naturales, y 12 b.mollados con láminas, y prin-
cipalmente se pone una tabla, que por ella se
puede cifrar cualquiera tono, tocarle y cantarle
por doce modos distintos, sacado de las mejores
obras y maestros: dispuesto, recopilado y aumen-
tado por Andrés de Sotos. (Madrid: imprenta de
Cruzada).
    RISM B VI: E Mn. GB Lbm. US NYp, R, Wcm.

STEFANI, Giovanni (Compiler)

See [in order of appearance] Anon/1618[1], Anon/1621[1], Anon/1623[1],
Anon/1626, Anon/1620, Anon/1622[2], Anon/1623[2].

STRAUBE, Rudolf

Stra/ND   *Lessons for two guittars with a thorough bass.*
                     (London: Michael Rauche).
                         RISM A/I: GB Lbl.
                         Comments: Tyler (entry 3, p. 109) indicates
                         that this work contains music for English
                         guitar, a type of cittern, and dates it ca.
                         1765.

Stra/[1768]   *Three Sonatas for the guittar, with accompany-
                     ments for the harpsichord or violoncello ...
                     With an addition of two sonatas for the guittar
                     accompanyd with the violin. Likewise a choice
                     collection of the most favourite English, Scotch
                     and Italian songs for one, and two guittars, of
                     different authors ... Also thirty two lessons by
                     several masters.* (London: for M. Rauche).
                         RISM B II: GB Lbm.
                         Comments: Tyler (entry 3, p. 109) indicates
                         that this publication contains music for English
                         guitar, a type of cittern. Contains works by
                         Gervasio, N. Piccini, Straube.

Stra/ME[1768]   = Stra/[1768] BÄRENREITER (1979).

Appendix II   (Tard/1634-Tiss/[ca1780])

TARDITI, Oratio

Tard/1634   = Vinc/1634
                        Comments: Contains two works by Tarditi.

Tard/1646   *Arie a voce sola di Oratio Tarditi per cantar*
                      nella spinetta, chitarrone è altro istrumento.
                      Con le lettere, & intavolatura per la chitarra
                      alla spagnola, racolte da Alessandro Vincenti ...
                      (Venezia: A. Vincenti).
                        RISM B I: NL DHgm.
                        Comments: Contains works by F.M. Melvi.

THACKRAY, Thomas

Thac/ND[1]   *Six lessons [C, F, C, C, F, C] for the guittar.*
                      (York: Thomas Haxby, for the author).
                        RISM A/I: GB Gm, Lbl.

Thac/ND[2]   = Thac/ND[1] (York: Longman & Broderip).
                        RISM A/I: S Skma.

Thac/ND[3]   *Six lessons for the guittar ... opera seconda.*
                      (London: author).
                        RISM A/I: GB Gm. US Dp.

Thac/ND[4]   *Twelve divertimenti [C, C, F, C, F, C, C, C, F,*
                      C, C, F] for two guittars or a guittar & violin
                      ... opera 3d. (London: Longman, Lukey & Co.).
                        RISM A/I: GB Lbl.

Thac/ND[5]   *12 divertissements pour deux guittars avec*
                      l'accompagnement d'un violon ou guittar 2me ...
                      (s.l., s.n.).
                        RISM A/I: CS Pnm (guitar I).

Thac/ND[6]   *A collection of forty four airs ... for one or*
                      two guittars. (London: John Johnston).
                        RISM A/I: GB Gm (inc.).

TISSIER

Tiss/[ca1780]   *IVè Recueil d'ariettes d'opéra comiques et autres*
                      avec accompagnement de guitarre et autres airs
                      connus par la guitare seule par Mr. Tissier ...
                      Oeuvre 8è ... (Paris: Le Duc).
                        RISM B II: B Bc.

(Tode/ND-ValE/1547)   Appendix II

TODESCHINO

Tode/ND   = MonL/ND
                         Comments: Contains works by Todeschino.

TRAEG, Andreas

Trae/ND[1]   *Différentes petites pièces faciles pour la gui-*
                       tarre seule ... oeuv. 6. (Wien: Jean Traeg,
                       No. 313).
                         RISM A/I: A Wgm.

Trae/ND[2]   *15 Variationen ,,Quant' e più bello" aus ,,La*
                       Molinara" [von Paisiello]. Guitarre (Sammlung
                       verschiedener Variationen, Nr. 6). (Wien:
                       Jean Traeg, No. 184).
                         RISM A/I: A Wst. PL WRu.

TROMBETTI, Agostino

Trom/1639   *Intavolatura di sonate, nuovamente tradotte sopra*
                      la chitarra spagnuola ... libro primo, et secondo.
                      (Bologna: N. Tebaldini).
                        RISM A/I: I Bc.

VALDAMBRINI, Ferdinando

ValF/1646   *Libro primo d'intavolatura di chitarra a cinque*
                      ordini. (Roma: s.n.)
                        RISM A/I: I Rsc.

ValF/1647   *Libro secondo d'intavolatura di chitarra a*
                      cinque ordini. (Roma: s.n.).
                        RISM A/I: I Rsc.

ValF/1648   *Il primo libro d'intavolatura della chitarra*
                      spagnuola con una regola facilissima per poter
                      imparare a sonare accordare, e far le lettere
                      di detta chitarra da se medesimo. (Roma).
                        Danner: No locations given.

VALDERRÁBANO, Enriquez de

ValE/1547   *Libro de musica de vihuela, intitulado Silva de*
                      sirenas. En el qual se hallara toda diversidad
                      de musica [7 vol.]. (Valladolid: Francisco
                      Fernandez de Cordova).
                        RISM A/I: A Wn. E Bu, Mn (2 ex.), VAc (inc.).

Appendix II   (ValE/ME1547[1]-VanE/ND[4])

GB Lbl. I MOe. US NYhsa.
Comments: Music composed for vihuela.

ValE/ME1547[1]   = ValE/1547 BreitkopfHärtel (1902, ed. by Conde de Morphy).

ValE/ME1547[2]   = ValE/1547 CEstHist (1923, ed. by E. Martínez Torner).

ValE/ME1547[3]   = ValE/1547 InstEspMusic (1965, ed. by Emilio Pujol).

ValE/ME1547[4]   = ValE/1547 MINKOFF

VALVASENZI, Lazaro

Valv/1634   *Secondo giardino d'amorosi fiori, cioe arie a voce sola accomodate per cantarsi nel clavi-cembalo, tiorba, chitarrone, ouero altro simile instromento con l'alfabeto & intavolatura per la chitarra spag., opera ottava.* (Venezia: Bartolomeo Magni).
                  RISM A/I: GB Och.

VAN EYK, Jan Jacob

VanE/ND[1]   *VI Variazioni [C] per la chitarra con violino o flauto e viola obligata.* (Wien: Artaria & Co., No. 1759).
                  RISM A/I: A Wst, M.

VanE/ND[2]   *VI Variations [G] sur le thème: Nel cor più non mi sento, pour violon ou flûte et pianoforte ou guitarre ... oe. 42.* (Leipzig: Ambrosius Kühnel, No. 853).
                  RISM A/I: A Wgm, Wst.

VanE/ND[3]   *Six [=Douze] petites pieces [F, C, C, C, C, C (F, C, F, C, C, C)] pour piano-forte, & guitarre ... liv. I (II).* (Bonn: Nikolaus Simrock, No. 528[529]).
                  RISM A/I: D-brd LB (bk. I: pf; bk. II: pf inc., guitarre), Mbs.

VanE/ND[4]   *VIII. Petites pieces tres faciles pour le forte piano ed guitarre.* (Wien: Tranquillo Mollo).
                  RISM A/I: CS Bm (pf).

(VenH/1557-VidB/ND²)   Appendix II

VENEGAS DE HENESTROSA, Luys

VenH/1557   *Libro de cifra nueva para tecla, arpa, y vihuela,*
                      en el qual se enseña brevemente cantar el canto
                      llano y canto de organo, y algunos avisos para
                      contrapunto. (Alcalá: Ioan de Brocar).
                          RISM A/I: E Mn (2 ex.).
                          Comments: Music composed for vihuela, keyboard,
                          harp. Ward (entry 191, p. 383) indicates that
                          compositions by Narvaez are quoted literally
                          and are parodied in this publication. Ward
                          also cites concordances.

VenH/ME1557   = VenH/1557 InstEspMusic (1944, ed. by Higinio
                      Anglés).

VENERI, Gregorio

VenG/1621   *Li varii scherzi ... a una, due e tre voci per*
                      cantare nel cimbalo, o in altri stromenti simili
                      con l'alfabeto per la chitarra in quelle piu a
                      proposito per tale stromento, libro primo, opera
                      quinta. (Roma: Luca Antonio Soldi).
                          RISM A/I: GB Lbl.

VIDAL, B.

VidB/1776   *Les soirées espagnoles ou choix d'ariettes*
                      d'opéra comiques et autres avec accompagnement
                      de guitarre, menuets et allemandes par Mr. Vidal.
                      (Paris: Boüin).
                          RISM A/I: CH Zz (inc.). F Pc (inc.).

VidB/1786-87   *Journal de guitarre composée de sonates, de*
                      pièces d'airs arrangés d'ariettes et romances
                      avec accompagnement de guitarre et violon ad
                      libitum séparés du journal ... par Mr. Vidal.
                      (Paris: auteur).
                          RISM A/I: CH Bu (2e année). F Pc (2e année
                          [inc.]).

VidB/ND¹   [arrangement]: *Pot-pourri en trio concertant*
                      pour guitarre et deux violons. (Paris: auteur).
                          RISM A/I: F Pn.

VidB/ND²   *Recueil d'ariettes, d'opéra comiques, et autres*
                      ... avec accompagnement de guitare, plusieurs
                      airs variés, et trois duo pour guitare et vio-
                      lon, ou deux guitarre. (Paris: aux adresses
                      ordinaires; Rouen: Briere Luttier).

Appendix II   (VidB/ND³-Visé/[1682])

> *RISM A/I:* CH N.

VidB/ND³
> [*Vᵉ*] *Recueil de petits airs variés pour la guitare.* (Paris: auteur).
> *RISM A/I:* F Pn.

VidB/ND⁴
> *Recueil de pièces et airs variés, suites des premières leçons nouvellement composées pour la guitare.* (Paris: Decombe, No. 163).
> *RISM A/I:* F Pc.

VidB/ND⁵
> *Six sonates pour la guitarre avec accompagnement de violon ... IVème oeuvre de sonate.* (Paris: auteur).
> *RISM A/I:* F Pn.

VidB/ND⁶
> *Six duos concertants pour guitarre et violon ... VIIᵉ oeuvre de duos.* (Paris: Imbault, gravés par Mme Chaume).
> *RISM A/I:* F Pc (guitar).

VidB/ND⁷
> [Doubtful attribution] *Collection of easy pieces for the guitar.* (London: Vidal).
> *RISM A/I:* CS Pnm.

VINCENTI, Alessandro (Editor)

Vinc/1634
> *Arie di diversi raccolte da Alessandro Vincenti commode da cantarsi nel clavicembalo chitarrone, et altro simile stromento, con le lettere dell' alfabetto per la chitarra spagnola.* (Venezia: A. Vincenti).
> *RISM B I:* I Rsc.
> *Comments:* Contains works by G.P. Bert (2), C. Milanuzzi (2), Tarditi (2).

VIRCHI [TARGHETTA], Paolo

Virc/1574
> *Il primo libro di tabolatura di citthara di ricercari madrigali canzoni napolitane et saltarelli.* (Venezia: erede di Girolamo Scotto).
> *RISM A/I:* A Wn.

VISÉE, Robert de

Visé/[1682]
> *Livre de guittarre, dédié au Roy.* (Paris: Bonneuil, Nicolas Cheron, gravé par Hierosme Bonneuil).
> *RISM A/I:* F Pn. GB Lbl.

(Visé/ME[1682][1]-Weid/ND)   Appendix II

Visé/ME[1682][1]   = Visé/[1682] HEUGEL (1969, ed. by Robert Strizich.
                        Published under the title *Oeuvres complètes pour
                        guitare*).

Visé/ME[1682][2]   = Visé/[1682] SCHOTT ([1971], ed. by F.J. Giesbert.
                        Published under the title *Gitarrenbuch*).
                           Comments: The Suite in G major is omitted from
                           the edition.

Visé/ME[1682][3]   = Visé/[1682] MINKOFF (1973).

Visé/1686   *Livre de pièces pour la guittarre.* (Paris: Bon-
                        neuil, A. Letteguine, gravé par Bonneuil).
                           RISM A/I: F Pn (2 ex.).

Visé/ME1686[1]   = Visé/1686 SCHOTT ([ca. 1969], ed. by F.J. Gies-
                        bert. Published under the title *Gitarrenstucke*).

Visé/ME1686[2]   = Visé/1686 HEUGEL (1969, ed. by Robert Strizich.
                        Published under the title *Oeuvres complètes pour
                        guitare*).

Visé/ME1686[3]   = Visé/1686 MINKOFF (1973).

Visé/1689   = Visé/1686
                           Danner: No locations cited. *Fétis* indicates
                           that Corbetta published this third book.

VITALI, Filippo

Vita/1620   *Musiche ... a una, due e tre voci per cantare nel
                        cimbalo o in altri stromenti simili con l'alfa-
                        beto per la chitarra in quelle piu a proposito
                        per tale stromento, libro terzo.* (Roma: Luca
                        Antonio Soldi).
                           RISM A/I: F Pc. US Cn.

Vita/1622   *[15] Arie a 1.2.3. voci da cantarsi nel chitar-
                        rone, chitarra spagnuola & altri stromenti,
                        libro quarto.* (Venezia: stampa del Gardano).
                           RISM A/I: GB Lbl. PL WRu.

WEIDEMAN [WEIDEMANN], Karl Friedrich [Charles Frederick]

Weid/ND   *Weideman's favorite minuet, for the harpsichord,
                        two german flutes or two guittars.* (s.l., s.n.).
                           RISM A/I: GB Er, Lbl.

Appendix II   (Weid/[ca1775]-Yate/ND)

Weid/[ca1775]   = Anon/[ca1775]
                        Comments: Contains works by Weideman.

WILLIMANN [WILLMANN], Eduard A.

Will/ND[1]   *Auswahl von Liedern mit Begleitung der Guitarre*
                     von E.A. Willimann. (Wien: Hoffmeister & Co.;
                     Leipzig: im musikalischen Bureau, No. 96).
                        RISM A/I: D-brd LÜh.

Will/ND[2]   *Mein Herr Bauer, grossen Dank. Antwort des Malers*
                     an den Bauer. Gegenstück zur Arie: der Bauer und
                     der Maler. Componirt für's Forte-Piano. (Hamburg:
                     Johann August Böhme).
                        RISM A/I: D-brd Hmb. D-ddr Bds.

Will/ND[3]   = Will/ND[2] ... *Componirt für Gitarre und Forte-*
                     Piano. (s.l., s.n.).
                        RISM A/I: D-brd W.

WINTER, Peter von

Wint/ND   *Variationen ... über ein Thema von Caraffa ...*
                     für 2 Guitarren mit Hinweglassung der Worte
                     eingerichtet von Anton Diabelli. (Wien: Cappi
                     & Diabelli, No. 708).
                        RISM A/I: A Wn.

WRANITZKY, Anton

Wran/ND   *VI Variations concertantes sur un thème originale*
                     pour violon et guitarre. (Wien: Anton Paterno,
                     No. 503).
                        RISM A/I: A Wgm.

XIMENES, Antonio

Xime/ND   *Trois trios pour guitarre, violon et basse ...*
                     oeuvre 1er. (Paris: Vidal, gravés par Mlle
                     Michaud).
                        RISM A/I: F Pc, Pn.

YATES, William

Yate/ND   *A collection of moral songs or hymns for a voice,*
                     harpsichord and guitar. (London: Thompson & sons).
                        RISM A/I: GB CDp, Lbl.

(Zuck/ND-Anon/1648)   Appendix II

ZUCKERT, John Frederick (Johann Friedrich)

Zuck/ND
Six sonatas or solos for the guittar and bass ...
opera seconda. (London: author, Sarah Philips).
  RISM A/I: GB LEc.
  Comments: Tyler (entry 3, p. 109) indicates
  that this work was published in 1759 and contains music for English guitar, a type of
  cittern.

ANONYMOUS

Anon/1602
Secondo libro d'intavolatura di citara, nel quale
si contengono varie et diverse sorti di Balli.
Raccolti da diversi autori et nuovamente
stampati. (Venezia: G. Vincenti).
  RISM B I: I Bc.

Anon/1618[1]
Affetti amorosi canzonette ad una voce sola poste
in musica da diversi con la parte del basso, & le
lettere dell' alfabetto per la chittarra alla
spagnola raccolte de Giovanni Stefani con tre
arie siciliane, et due vilanelle spagnole.
(Venezia: G. Vincenti).
  RISM B I: I Bc.
  Comments: Contains thirty-five anonymous works.

Anon/1621[1]
= Anon/1618[1] *Novamente in questa terza impressione*
ristampate.
  RISM B I: I Bc. US Wc.

Anon/1623[1]
= Anon/1618[1] *Novamente in questa quarta impressione*
ristampate.
  RISM B I: I Bc.

Anon/1626
= Anon/1618[1] *Novamente in questa quarta impressione*
ristampate.
  RISM B I: I Bc.

Anon/1618[2]
Il primo libro d'intavolatura della chitarra
spagnuola con una regola facilissima per poter'
imparare à sonare, accordare e far le lettere à
detta chitarra da se medesimo. Composto e dato
in luce da incerto autore. Et in detto libro si
contengono anco molte sonate passagiate non più
da altri dati in luce. (Roma: Catalani).
  RISM B I: I Rsc.

Anon/1648
= Anon/1618[2]
  Kirkendale: I Rsc.

300

Appendix II   (Anon/1618[3]-Anon/1622[3])

Anon/1618[3]   *Prima raccolta di bellissime canzonette musicale,*
                     e moderne, di auttori gravissimi nella poesia, &
                     nella musica. Per il sig. Remigio Romano.
                     ([Vicenza?]: A. Salvadori).
                         RISM B I: GB Lbm.
                         Comments: Contains anonymous works only.

Anon/1622[1]   = Anon/1618[3]
                         RISM B I: US R.

Anon/1620   *Scherzi amorosi canzonette ad una voce sola poste*
                     in musica da diversi, e raccolte da Giovanni
                     Stefani con le lettere dell' alfabeto per la chi-
                     tarra alla spagnuola. Dedicati all' ill^{mo} sig.
                     Filippo Musotti mio signore e patron osserv.^{mo}.
                     Libro secondo novamente corretti et ristampati.
                     (Venezia: Al. Vincenti).
                         RISM B I: I Mc.
                         Comments: Contains twenty-five anonymous works.

Anon/1622[2]   = Anon/1620 *Libro secondo novamente corretti et*
                     ristampati.
                         RISM B I: I Bc.

Anon/1621[2]   *Giardino musicale di varii eccellenti autori,*
                     dove si contengono sonetti, arie, et vilanelle,
                     à una, e due voci, per cantare con il cimbalo,
                     et altri stromenti simili, con l'alphabeto per la
                     chitarra spagnola, in quelle più à proposito.
                     Dedicate al molt'illustre, e reverendiss. sig. il
                     sig. Paolo Quagliati. (Roma: G.B. Robletti).
                         RISM B I: I Rvat (lacks p. 5-6; 19-20).
                         Comments: Contains works by A. Antonelli, G.B.
                         Boschetti (3), O. Catalani (6), F. Cerasolo (2),
                         A. Costantini (2), G. Frescobaldi (3), S. Landi,
                         R. Rontani (2).

Anon/1621[3]   *Raccolta de varii concerti musicali a una et due*
                     voci. De diversi eccellentissimi autori. Per can-
                     tare nel cimbalo & altri stromenti simili, con
                     l'alfabeto per la chitarra spagnuola, in quelle
                     più à proposito ... (Roma: G.B. Robletti).
                         RISM B I: NL DHgm.
                         Comments: Contains works by A. Antonelli (2),
                         O. Catalani, G. Cenci (2), S. Landi, I. Macchia-
                         velli, D. Mazzacchi (2), P. Mutii, G.B. Nanino,
                         R. Rontani (2), Anon.

Anon/1622[3]   *Vezzosetti fiori di varii eccellenti autori, cioe,*
                     madrigali, ottava dialoghi, arie, et villanelle, a
                     una, e due voci. Da cantarsi con il cembalo, tior-
                     ba, chitarra spagnola, &c. (Roma: G.B. Robletti).

301

(Anon/1623²-Anon/1657)   Appendix II

> *RISM B I:* GB Lbm.
> *Comments:* Contains works by N. Borboni (2), A.
> Constantini, A. Granata, F. Grapuccioli, P.
> Mutii (2), G.G. Porro, P.P. Sabbatino, F.
> Severi, G.A. Todini (2), H. Torscianello.

Anon/1623²
> *Concerti amorosi. Terza parte delle canzonette*
> *in musica raccolte da Giovanni Stefano novamente*
> *ristampate et corrette ...* (Venezia: A. Vincenti).
> *RISM B I:* I Bc, Mc (inc.).
> *Comments:* Contains thirty-seven anonymous works.

Anon/1623³
> *Nuova raccolta di bellissimi canzonette musicali,*
> *e moderne, di auttori gravissimi nella poesia, &*
> *nella musica. Per il. sig. Remigio Romano. Parte*
> *quarta ...* (Venezia: A. Salvadori).
> *RISM B I:* GB Lbm. US R.
> *Comments:* Contains anonymous works only.

Anon/1625¹   = Anon/1623³
> *RISM B I:* US R.

Anon/1625²
> *Prima [-quarta] raccolta di bellissime canzonette*
> *musicali, e moderne, di autori gravissimi nella*
> *poesia, & nella musica. Per il sig. Remigio*
> *Romano.* (Pavia: G.B. de Rossi).
> *RISM B I:* F Pc. GB Lbm.
> *Comments:* Contains anonymous works only.

Anon/1645
> *Conserto vago di balletti, volte, Corrente et*
> *gagliarde, con la loro canzone alla Franzese*
> *nuovamente pôsti in luce per sonare con liuto,*
> *tiorba et chitarrino à quatro corde alla Napoli-*
> *tana insieme, ô soli ad arbitrio ... Composti da*
> *buono, mâ incerto auttore. Libro primo.* (Rome).
> *Danner:* I Bc.

Anon/1646
> *Intavolatura di chitarra e chitarriglia con le*
> *piu necessarie e facili suonate a chi si diletta*
> *di tal professione havute da duo eccellenti pro-*
> *fessori e dedicate all' ill.ᵐᵒ signore il sig.*
> *Bartolomeo Bolognini.* (Bologna: G. Monti).
> *RISM B I:* I Bc.
> *Comments:* Contains fifty-eight anonymous
> works.

Anon/1657
> *Canzonette spirituali, e morali, che si cantano*
> *nell' Oratorio di Chiavenna, eretto sotto la*
> *protettione di S. Filippo Neri. Accomodate per*
> *cantar à 1. 2. 3. voci come più piace, con le*
> *lettere della chitarra sopra arie communi e nuove*
> *date in luce per trattenimento spirituale d'ogni*

302

Appendix II   (Anon/1659-Anon/[ca1760]³)

persona. (Milano: C.F. Rolla).
   RISM B I: GB Ge. I REm.
   Comments: Contains works by T. Merula and
   seventy-two anonymous works.

Anon/1659   *Nuove canzonette musicali de diversi auttori.*
                           (Venezia: Giacomo Batti).
                              Wolf: No locations cited.

Anon/[ca1750]¹   *The Compleat tutor for the guittar, containing
                           the best and easiest instructions for learners
                           to obtain a proficiency, to which are added a
                           choice collection of the most celebrated Italian,
                           English & Scotch tunes, curiously adapted to that
                           instrument.* (London: C. & S. Thompson).
                              RISM B II: PL GD. US NYp.
                              Comments: Tyler (entry 3, p. 109) indicates
                              that this work contains music for English
                              guitar, a type of cittern.

Anon/[1755]   = Anon/[ca1750]¹ (London: J. Johnson).
                        RISM B II: EIRE Dn. GB Gm (inc.), Lbm. US Bp.
                        Comments: Contains works by Felton, Händel,
                        Oswald.

Anon/[ca1760]¹   = Anon/[ca1750]¹ (London: Thompson & Son).
                        RISM B II: GB Du, Gm (inc.).

Anon/[ca1760]²   = Anon/[ca1750]¹ *With two scales shewing the method
                        of playing in the keys of C. and G.: to which is
                        added eighteen favourite songs adapted for that
                        instrument. Book 1st [-2nd].* (London: J. Oswald).
                        RISM B II: GB Lbm.
                        Comments: Contains works by Händel, Hasse, J.
                        Oswald, Anon. Book 2nd is entitled "The pocket
                        companion for the guittar containing a favourite
                        collection of the best Italian, French, English
                        and Scotch songs ...".

Anon/[ca1750]²   *The Ladies' pocket guide or the compleat tutor
                           for the guittar, containing easy rules for
                           learners ... with a choice collection of the most
                           favourite airs ...* (London: D. Rutherford).
                              RISM B II: D Hs. GB Cpl, CDp, Lbm.
                              Comments: Contains works by Corelli, Grano,
                              Händel, Snow. Tyler (entry 3, p. 109) indicates
                              that this work contains music for English gui-
                              tar, a type of cittern.

Anon/[ca1760]³   *Méthode pour apprendre à jouer de la guitarre
                           par Don *** * (Paris: Le Menu; Madrid: J. Guerrero).
                              RISM B VI: US Wcm.

303

(Anon/[ca1770]-Anon/ND[1])   Appendix II

Anon/[ca1770]   *Compleat instructions for the guitar, containing*
                     the most modern directions, with proper examples
                     for learners to obtain a speedy proficiency,
                     corrected by the most eminent masters. To which
                     is added a collection of favourite minuets,
                     marches, songs &c. adapted purposely for that
                     instrument. (London: J. Longman & C⁰).
                         RISM B II: US Wc.

Anon/[ca1775]   *A pocket book for the guitar.* (London: Longman,
                     Lukey and Broderip).
                         RISM B II: GB Lbm.
                         Comments: Contains works by M. Arne, T.A. Arne,
                         C. Dibdin, Händel, Humphrys, Martini, P.A.
                         Monsigny, Morelli, Stanley, Weideman.

Anon/[ca1785]   *Bland's first collection of twenty four airs,*
                     marches, minuets, &c. Twelve for one, & twelve
                     for two guitars or a guitar and violin, composed
                     by the best masters. (London: J. Bland).
                         RISM B II: GB Lbm.

Anon/[ca1790]   *Complete instructions for the guittar containing*
                     the most useful directions & examples for learn-
                     ers to obtain a speedy proficiency. To which is
                     added a choice collection of favourite airs,
                     minuets, marches, songs &c. properly adapted
                     for that instrument ... (London: J. Preston).
                         RISM B II: GB Lbm (2 ex.). US NH, Wc.
                         Comments: Contains works by Giordani, Martini,
                         Morelli.

Anon/[ca1800][1]   *Elegant extracts for the guittar, consisting of*
                     the most celebrated songs sung at the publick
                     gardens, and from the latest operas and enter-
                     tainments, canzonets, rondos, airs with varia-
                     tions, allemands, dances, &c. composed and pro-
                     perly adapted for that instrument by the most
                     eminent masters. (London: J. Preston).
                         RISM B II: GB Gm (v. 2), Lbm.
                         Comments: Contains works by Dr. Arne, Arnold,
                         C. Bossi, Dibdin, Giordani, Haydn, Hook, Kotz-
                         wara, Nicolai, Pleyel, W. Reeve, Rouget de
                         Lisle, G. Rush, Storace, J. Wanhal.

Anon/[ca1800][2]   *Méthode pour jouer de la guitarre.* (Paris).
                         RISM B VI: F Pc.

Anon/ND[1]   *Il vero modo per imparare sonare la chitarriglia*
                     spagnuola con sonate nuove e facili per princi-
                     pianti raccolte da diversi. (Perugia: per il
                     Cost[a]ntini).

                                304

Appendix II   (Anon/ND^2)

        Wolf: No locations cited.

Anon/ND^2 = MonL/ND
        Comments: Contains eighteen anonymous works.

Chronological List

A number placed after a name indicates the number of works published in that year.

A number preceded by ME indicates the number of modern editions of that work.

1535	Milán 1, ME 8	156?	Gorlier 1
1538	Narváez 1, ME 7	1570	Phalèse 1, ME 1
1546	Mudarra 1, ME 6	1573	Phalèse 1
	Narváez 2		
	Phalèse 2	1574	Virchi 1
1547	Valderrábano 1, ME 4	1576	Daza 1, ME 4
1549	Barberis 1	1578	Cabeçon 1, ME 1
			Le Roy 1
1550	Morlaye 1		
		1586	Amat 1
1551	Gorlier 1, ME 1		
	Le Roy 2, ME 1	158?	Giuliani, [G.] 1
1552	Le Roy 1, ME 1	1596	Amat 1
	Morlaye 2		
	Pisador 1, ME 3	1602	Anon 1
1553	Brayssing 1	1606	Montesardo 1
	Le Roy 1, ME 1		
	Morlaye 1	1608	Pico 1
1554	Fuenllana 1, ME 4	1609	Pico 1
	Le Roy 1, ME 1		
		1610	Kapsberger 1
1555	Le Roy 1, ME 1		
		1612	Kapsberger 1
1557	Venegas de Henestrosa 1, ME 1		Montesardo 1
1564	Fuenllana 1	1614	Marinoni 1
1565	Sancta Maria 1, ME 1	1616	Aragona 1
			Corradi 1
1568	Narváez 1		Falconieri 1
	Phalèse 1		
	Rowbotham 1		

Appendix II   (1618-1638)

1618   Corradi 1
        Giaccio 1
        Rontani 1
        Anon 3

1619   Falconieri 2
        Kapsberger 2
        Rontani 1

1620   Colonna 2
        Landi 1
        Rontani 1
        San Severino 1
        Vitali 1
        Anon 1

1621   India 1
        Landi 2
        Rontani 2
        Veneri 1
        Anon 3

1622   Milanuzzi 2
        Rontani 1
        Sabbatini 1
        San Severino 1
        Severi 1
        Vitali 1
        Anon 3

1623   Colonna 1
        Ferrari 1
        Ghizzolo 1
        Giamberti 1
        India 1
        Kapsberger 1
        Milanuzzi 1
        Rontani 1
        Anon 3

1624   Aranies 1
        Berti 1
        Milanuzzi 1

1625   Milanuzzi 1
        Rontani 1
        Anon 2

1626   Amat 1
        Briçeño 1, ME 1
        Grandi 1
        Severi 1
        Anon 1

1627   Abbatessa 1
        Amat 1, ME 1
        Berti 1
        Colonna 1
        Costanzo 1
        Fasolo 1
        Millioni 5
        Monte 1

1628   Crivellati 1
        Fasolo 1
        Milanuzzi 1
        Pico ME 1

1629   Foscarini 1
        Grandi 1

1630   Milanuzzi 1

1631   Millioni 2

1633   Camarella 1

1634   Berti 1
        Milanuzzi 1
        Tarditi 1
        Valvasenzi 1
        Vincenti 1

1635   Abbatessa 1
        Milanuzzi 1
        Millioni 2

1637   Abbatessa 1
        Colonna 1, ME 1
        Landi 1
        Millioni 1
        Sfondrino 1

1638   Bartolomeo 1

(1639-1674)   Appendix II

1639   Amat 1
        Corbetta 1
        Trombetti 1

1640   Bartolotti 1
        Busatti 1
        Carbonchi 1, ME 1
        Doizi de Velasco 1
        Foscarini 2, ME 1
        Pesori ME 1
        Sabbatini 1

1641   Sabbatini 1

1643   Carbonchi 1, ME 1
        Corbetta 1, ME 1
        Milanuzzi 1

1644   Busatti 1
        Calvi 1
        Millioni 1

1645   Doizi de Velasco 1
        Anon 1

1646   Calvi 1, ME 1
        Granata 1, ME 2
        Tarditi 1
        Valdambrini 1
        Anon 1

1647   Millioni 1, ME 1
        Valdambrini 1

1648   Corbetta 1
        Marchetti 1
        Pesori 1, ME 1
        Valdambrini 1
        Anon 1

1648/   Pesori 1
  49

1650   Pellegrini 1, ME 2
        Pesori 1, ME 1
        Sabbatini 1

1651   Granata 1

1652   Abbatessa 1
        Millioni 1
        Playford 1
        Sabbatini 3

1653   Banfi 1

1655   Marini 1

1657   Anon 1

1659   Granata 1, ME 1
        Millioni 1
        Anon 1

1660   Marchetti 1, ME 1

Post-   Marchetti 1
1660

1661   Millioni 1

1663   Bottazzari 1, ME 1
        Martin 1

1666   Millioni 1
        Nivers 1

166?   Marchetti 1

1670   Coriandoli 1
        Nivers 1

1671   Carré 1, ME 1
        Corbetta 1, ME 1
        La Grange 1

1672   Ribayaz 1

1673   Corbetta 1
        Millioni 2

1674   Asioli 1, ME 1
        Corbetta 1, ME 1
        Granata 1, ME 1
        Sanz 1, ME 6

309

Appendix II   (1676-1770)

1676	Asioli 1 Médard 1 Millioni 1	1717	Campion 1
1677	Corbetta 1 Ribayaz 1, ME 1 Ricci 1	1730	Campion 1, ME 1
		1732	Majer 1
1678	Millioni 1	1734	Campion 1
1680	Granata 1 Grenerin 1, ME 1 Matteis 1	1737	Millioni 1
		1741	Majer 1
		1745	Amat 1
1682	Matteis 1, ME 1 Visée 1, ME 3	1750	Amat 1 Anon 2
1684	Granata 1 Millioni 1	1752	Pica da Rocha 1
1686	Visée 1, ME 3	1754	Minguet e Yrol ME 1
		1755	Anon 1
1688	Busatti 1 Derosier 1	1758	Amat 1 Bremner 1
1689	Kremberg 1 Visée 1	1760	Anon 3
1690	Derosier 1, ME 1	1761	Amat ME 1 Merchi ME 1 Parry 1
1692	Roncalli 1, ME 4		
1694	Guerau 1, ME 2	1762	Parry 1
1696	Derosier 1 Nivers 1	1764	Lagarde 5 Sotos 1
1697	Sanz 1, ME 3	1765	Amat 1 Asuni 1
1698	Micheli 1	1766	Merchi 1
1699	Derosier 2	1768	Merchi 1 Straube 1, ME 1
1702	Nivers 1		
1705	Campion 1, ME 1	1769	Merchi 1
1714	Murcia 1, ME 2	1770	Bouleron 1 Merchi 1 Anon 1
1716	Campion 1, ME 1		

(1773-ND)   Appendix II

1773   Bailleux 1, ME 1   1799   Abreu 1
         Lemoine ME 1   Ferandiere 1, ME 1
                                          Moretti 1, ME 1
1774   Minguet e Yrol 1   Prieto 1
                                          Rubio 1
1775   Martini 1
         Morelli 1   1800   Gatayes 1
         Weideman 1   Giordani 1
         Anon 1   Pleyel 1
                                          Rush 1
1776   Vidal 1   Anon 2

1777   Merchi ME 1   1802   Pleyel 1

1780   Ballesteros 1   ND   Abbatessa 1
         Merchi 1   Albanese 2
         Tissier 1   Amat 1
                                         Amon 4
1781   Baillon 1, ME 1   Aubert 1
                                         Bartolotti 1
1785   Asuni 1   Boecklin 1
         Martini 1   Brand 1
         Porro 1, ME 1   Bremner 1
         Anon 1   Calegari 5
                                         Canobbio 1
1786   Albanèse 1   Carter 1
         Alberti 1   Castro 3
                                         Cherbourg 1
1786-   Vidal 1   Cimarosa 1
  87   Corbetta 2
                                         Corrette 1
1788   Labarre 1   Dalayrac 3
         Martini 1   Delver 1
         Pleyel 1   Dibdin 1
         Porro 1, ME 1   Doisy-Lintant 15
         Sarti 1   Eppinger 2
                                         Foscarini 2
1789   Paixaõ Ribeiro 1   Gaude 1
                                         Gistau 1
1790   Giordani 1   Giuliani, G.F. 1
         Martini 1   Göpfert 6
         Morelli 1   Gragnani 4
         Anon 1   Granata 1
                                         Huber 1
1795   Chabran 1   Keck 1
         Guichard 1   Kraus 1
         Light 1   Lemoine 3, ME 1
                                         L'Hoyer 8
1796   Vidal 1   Losy 1, ME 1
                                         Martín y Soler 1

Appendix II

(ND)

Merchi 11, ME 5
Millioni 1
Molino 1
Monte 1
Monzino 1
Moretti 2
Pesori 2
Phillis 3
Pleyel 2
Porro 1, ME 1
Ritter 1
Rolla 1
Rush 2
Santino da Parma 1
Scheidler, C.G. 3
Scheidler, J.F. 1
Schlick 1
Schöniger 1

Schulz, A. 2
Schulz, J.A.P. 1
Schuman 2
Sors 1
Straube 1
Thackray 6
Todeschino 1
Traeg 2
Van Eyk 4
Vidal 7
Weideman 1
Willimann 3
Winter 1
Wranitzky 1
Ximenes 1
Yates 1
Zuckert 1
Anon 2

How to Use the Index

Authors	Names of authors, editors, compilers, and reviewers are printed in bold face type.
Subjects	Names of individuals who are subjects are printed in elite type, as are all other subjects.
Titles (composer)	Titles of books and large musical works are printed in italics. The name of the composer or author appears enclosed in parentheses after the title.
"Titles" (composer)	Titles of small musical works appear in elite type and are enclosed in quotation marks. The name of the composer appears enclosed in parentheses after the title.

NUMBERS

100	Entry numbers of literature in the bibliography are in bold face type.
100	Page numbers are in elite type.
100	The number of an entry of which the author is a reviewer appears in italic type.

The Index

Abbatessa, Giovanni
Battista 229, 307-08,
310; 294
Ablóniz, Miguel 834
Abreu, Antonio 229,
283, 310; 266
Abreu, Sergio and
Eduardo (duo) 632
accompaniment 60; 37,
408
Berlioz, Hector 435,
438
ensemble 223; 5, 286,
466, 512, 803
keyboard and guitar
1; 38-41
Sor, Fernando 570
voice and guitar (*al-
fabeto* notation) 223,
229, 234-35, 237,
250-51, 268, 291,
301; 3
voice and guitar 223,
233, 236, 240, 248,
251, 257-58; 3, 5, 71,
135, 269, 286, 395,
496, 501, 529, 531-34,
586-87, 656, 673, 701,
709
Achillini, Giov.
Filoteo 878
"Acoustical properties
of complex cavities.
Prediction and mea-
surements of reso-
nance properties of
violin-shaped and
guitar-shaped cavi-
ties 1016
acoustics 188; 648,
970, 1016-30
Adame, Rafael 80
Adams, Henry 747, 855,
866, 868, 870, 953,
982, 995; *35, 45*

Agafoschin, Peter *See*
Agafosyn, Peter
Agafosyn [Agafoschin],
Peter 103, 108
Agostino, P. 251
Aguado, Dionisio 414

Aguado, Dionisio 96;
32, 110, 401, 410, 412,
415-23, 568, 633, 810,
814, 943
Aguiree, Ricardo xx
Agutter 326
Aimon, Pamphile Leopold
François 590
"1er Air varié", op. 21
(Giulio Regondi) 524
"2eme Air varié", op.
22 (Giulio Regondi)
524
airs 232-33, 236, 240,
243-44, 247, 250, 252,
259, 261, 266-67, 277,
283, 286, 293, 297, 304
Aksenow, S.N. 99
Aksjonow, Siemion 102
Alba, Duchess of 544
Albanèse, Egidio
Giuseppe Ignazio 230,
267, 310
Albéniz, Isaac 405
Alberti, Francesco 230,
310
Alcázar, Miguel 724
Alessio, Gregory d'
132, 890, 896
Alexandrow, N.I. 99
alfabeto 229, 232, 234,
239, 243, 247, 250-51,
254-56, 264, 268-71,
273, 285-87, 291, 295-
96, 298, 300-01; 3
Alfonso, Licentiate
Sebastian 375
Alfonso, Nicolás 21
Alfonson, Francisco 21
"Alias" (Goffredo
Petrassi) 719
Allemande 304
Corbetta, Francesco
348
Doisy-Lintant,
Charles 247
Le Roy, Adrian 260
Morlaye, Guillaume
274-75
Phalèse, Pierre
279

314

Index   A-

Vidal, B. 296
Visée, Robert de 382
*Allgemeine musikalische
Zeitung (AMZ)* 413,
526-28
Almeida, Laurindo 639,
649
Alonso, Felipe 21
Alonso y Castillo,
Mariano 21
"L'Alouette" (Brayss-
ing) 236
Alsina, José 21
alto (viola) 235, 245-
46, 252, 273, 284
Alvarado, A. 983
Alver, Alfred W. 392,
505
Amat, Juan Carlos [Joan
Carles] xx, 36, 230-
31, 306-07, 309; 21,
271, 289, 291, 330-31
America (United States)
general 20
late 18th-early 20th
c. 10
status, early 20th c.
guitar 48
string manufacturing
1031
The American guild of
banjoists, mandolin-
ists, and guitarists
124-29
"The American guild of
banjoists, mandolin-
ists, and guitarists.
Preamble" 124
The American Guitar
Society 130
Ametller Cabrer, Narci-
so de 21
Amon, Johann Andreas
231-32, 310
Anderson, Peter 544,
770
"Andrés Segovia. Cele-
brated guitarist" 771
"Andrés Segovia - Gold-
en Jubilee. Fifty
years of concertizing

in the United States"
772
Andriessen, Jurriaan
xxiii
Angel, Miguel 720
Angel, Nico 869
angelica 257; 2, 260
Anglès, Higini 296; 223
Anido, Maria Luisa 650-
53
"Annie Laurie" (E.
Blessner) 135
"Antique guitars are
going for a song" 923
Antoine ("Gatayes"),
Guillaume Pierre 592
Antonelli, A. 301
"Antonio Lauro in con-
versation with Sue
McCreadie" 867
Apel, Willi xix; 167
Appleby, Wilfrid M. 71,
152, 448, 545-46, 835,
895; *37, 51*
Aragona, Paolo d' 232,
306
Arañes [Aranies], Juan
232, 307; 289
Aranjo, Mozart 64
Arcas Lacal, Julián
Gavino 32, 110, 424-
26
archlute 2
Arcos, Duque of 35
Argentina 15, 188; 45,
56-62, 946
Argento, Dominick 654-
56
*Letters from compo-
sers* 655-56
aria 362
Aria brand guitars 1012
aria di fiorenza 60;
280
arie [Arien] 234-35,
237-38, 240, 244, 248,
250, 254, 256, 258,
265, 273, 300-01
ariettes 230, 236, 248,
293, 296

A-B

*Armoniosi concerti
sopra chitarra spag-
nuola* (Domenico Pell-
egrini) 369
Arne, Dr. 304
Arne, M. 304
Arne, T.A. 304
Arnold 304
Arnold, Johann Gott-
fried 593
arpa [arpa doppia] 237,
251, 255, 272, 288, 296
see also harp
Artzt, Alice 372, 738,
775
Artzt, Alice 852-54
Asaflev, B. 108
Asioli, Francesco 232,
308; 253
Assimakopoulos, Evange-
los *See* Athenian Gui-
tar Duo
Asuni, Ghillini di 232-
33, 309-10
Ateneo (in Madrid) 787,
796
Athenian guitar duo
632, 739
Aubert, Pierre François
Olivier 233, 310
Augustine, Albert (gui-
tar strings) 1032
Augustine, Rose L. 748
Australia 1017
Austria 188; 254, 413
Viennese instrument
making 947
Avshalomov, Jacob xxiii
Azkoul, Jihad 678
Azpiazu, José de 6, 250
Azpiazu, José de 21

Bach, Johann Sebastien
xxii; 656, 865, 1034
Bachmann, Otto 916
Bacon, Frederick J.
141, 146
Badessa *See* Abbatessa,
Giovanni Battista
bagpipe 403
bailes 217

Bailleux, Antoine 233,
309; 398
Baillon, Pierre-Joseph
233, 309
Baines, Anthony
(trans.) xvi
Bakus, Gerald J. 7
Bal [y Gay], José xix;
193, 224
Balada, Juan Ruano 657
Balaguer, Rafael 823
ballad 200, 242
Ballard, Robert 160,
229-30
Ballesteros, Antonio
233, 309
balletti 269, 302
Ballo del Gran Duca
(alternative name for
Aria di fiorenza) 60;
280
bandurria 272, 292; 166
Banfi, Giulio 234, 308
banjo 124
Banks, Benjamin 932
Barberis, Melchior de
xvi, 234, 306; 161,
208
*Opera intitolata con-
tina* ... 208
Barbero, Marcello 958,
1012
Barbosa-Lima, Carlos
63, 90
Barbour, James Murray
153
Barcelona (Spain) 955
Bargalló, Miguel Más
109
Barrios Mangoré,
Agustín Pio 66, 78,
643, 657-61
Humoresca 657
Romanza 657
Preludio Saudade
661
Barrueco, Manuel 855
Barta, Lubor 67
Barth, M. 878
Bartolomeo, de Selma e
Salaverde 234, 307

316

Index   B-

Bartolotti, Angiolo
   Michele 234, 307, 310
bass 300
basse 299
basse de viole 245
basso 253-54, 278
basso continuo 60, 234,
   238-39, 243-45, 254,
   258, 265; 3, 289, 292,
   362 *See also* figured
   bass and thorough-
   bass
basso, la parte de 232
basson 252
Basurto 244, 281
Bateman, William O.
   112, 141
Bathioli, Franz 499
Baumbach, Friedrich
   August 594
Beck, Sydney 871
Becker, Gunther xxiii
"Becqueriana" (Emilio
   Pujol) 753
Beethoven, Ludwig von
   30, 404, 476
Behlen, H. & Bros.,
   Inc. 999
Belgium 35
Bella, Stéphano de 884
Bellère, Jean xvi, 36,
   279-80; 160
Bellow, Alexander 59,
   177; 8, 369, 997
Bellow, Alexander 662
Benjamin, Gerald R. 674
Benton, Rita xxii, 226

"La Beolca" (Colonna)
   241
Beran, Alois 91-92
Berg, Alban 642
Bergonzi 903
Berlin (Germany) 558,
   707
Berlioz, Hector 428-33
Berlioz, Hector 96; 30,
   396, 434-39, 515, 642
Bermudo, Juan 209-12
Bermudo, Juan xvi-
   xviii, xx, 35-36; 153,

159, 165, 168-69, 179,
   197, 213-14, 228, 875
Bernabé, Paulino 959
Berner, A. 1000
Berner, Alfred 168
Berti, Giovanni Pietro
   234-35, 297, 307
Bertoni 283
Biberian, Gilbert 775
Biberian, Gilbert 643
Biblioteca nacional
   (Mexico) 83
Bickford, Vahdah Olcott
   112, 463
Bickford, Vahdah Olcott
   130, 663-64
Bickford, Zarh M. 130
Bickford, Zarh M. 112
Biedermeier period
   38-41
"Biography of a classi-
   cal guitarist. Anido
   Gonzales Isabel Maria
   Luisa" 650
"Biography of a compo-
   ser. Federico Moreno
   Torroba" 830
"Biography of a guitar-
   ist. Julian Bream"
   666
"Biography of a luthi-
   er. Domingo Esteso
   Lopez" 964
Birnbach, Henry August
   595
Blantchor, Francis 134
Blessner, E.
   "Annie Laurie" 135
Blümml, Emil Karl 936
Blum, Carl Ludwig 596
Blume, Friedrich xxvi
Bobri, Vladimir 63,
   773, 775, 795, 896,
   1033
Bobri, Vladimir 133,
   836, 890
Bobrowicz, Jan Nepomu-
   can [Jean Nepomucene
   de] 87, 597
Bobzin, Charles 1031

317

B-   Index

Boccherini, Luigi 96;
440-44, 508
Bodleian Museum of
    Oxford University
    924
Boecklin, Franz Fried-
    rich Siegmund August
    von 235, 310
Böhm, Joseph 499
Boetticher, Wolfgang
19
Bohr, Heinrich 415
Boileau, S. 244
bolero (Fernando Car-
    ulli) 451
Bologna (Italy) 360
Bolzmann, Franziska
499
Bonanni, Filippo 295-
96
Bone, Philip J. xxi,
96; 51, 416, 440, 445,
450, 454, 464, 469,
470, 485, 494, 506-07,
522-23, 590-628, 924
Bone, Philip J. 548
Bonesi 283
Boom, Jan van 598
Borboni, N. 302
Bortolazzi, Bartolomeo
499, 599
Boschetti, G.B. 301
Bosman, Lance 67, 194,
241, 547, 713, 721,
768, 852, 864
Bossi, C. 304
Boston (American Guild
    of Banjoists, Mando-
    linists, and Guitar-
    ists) 127
Botet, Maria Emma 471
Bottari, Ferdinando
924
Bottazzari, Giovanni
235, 308
Bouchet, Robert 960
Bouleron 235, 309
Boulez, Pierre xxiii;
642, 665, 803
    Domaines 665
    Eclat 665

Le Marteau sans
    maitre 665
Pli selon pli 665
Boulley, Aubery du 600
Bourree
    by Robert de Visée
    385
Boyd, Liona 856
Brabec, Lubomír 67
Brand, Aloys Carl
235, 310
Brandon, George 133
bransles [branles]
260, 274-75, 279-80
Braque, George 873,
882, 890
Brayssing, Gregor xvi,
36, 236, 306
Brazil 1; 63-66, 77
Brazilian folk tunes
    (Heitor Villa-Lobos)
    837
Brazilian Song (canção)
    (Francisco Mignone)
    63
Bream, Julian 775
Bream, Julian 30, 639,
666-70, 686, 775
Bremner, Robert 236,
309-10
Breukers, El 857, 859
Briceño, Luis de 236,
307; 271, 289, 291,
332-34
Bridge, Sir Frederick
319
A briefe and plaine
    instruction (James
    Rowbotham) 229
Britten, Benjamin 634,
642, 655, 671-73
    Nocturnal 671-72
    Songs from the Chi-
    nese 655, 673
Broca, José 109-10
Brommelle, Norman 1000
Brondi, Maria Rita 9
Brosnac, D. 1001
Brossard, Sébastien de
297-98

318

Index   B-C

Brossard, Sébastien de
308
Brouwer, Leo 78, 643,
857
    "Metafora del amor"
    857
    "Hommage a Lenin" 857
Brown, Howard Mayer
xxiv, 224, 230, 250,
252, 259-61, 274-75,
279-80, 285
Browne, Rosalind 133
Brussels (Belgium) 100
Buchner, Alexander 897-
98
Buckley, W. 112
Buek, Fritz 10, 715,
806
Buek, M. 940
Buenos Aires 61-62
Buonanni, Filippo *See*
    Bonanni, Filippo
Burleson, Spencer 646
Burtnieks, Janis A.
386, 472, 548, 774
Busatti, Cherubino 236,
307-09
Button, Stuart W. 72

C., H. de *775*
C., M.G. 760
Cabezón [Cabeçon],
    Antonio
        *Obras de musi-
        ca* 36, 223,
        237, 287, 306;
        167, 215, 246
        "Tres 'sobre
        el cantollano
        de la alta"
        216
Calabria (Italy)
268
Caldersmith, Gra-
    ham 961, 1017
Calegari, Frances-
    co 237, 310
Call, Leonard von
454-56, 499
Calvi, Carlo 237-
38, 308

Camarella, Giovan-
    ni Battista 238,
    307, 309
Cambini 283
Campion, François
238-39; 252-53
canarios 60; 282
canciones 275; 217
"Canhoto", Ameri-
    co Jacomino
    [João] 64, 66
Cano, Antonio 110
Cano Tamayo, Manu-
    el 954
Canobbio, Carlo
239, 310
cantade 234-35,
254
cantate 243, 248
canzonette 60,
229, 232, 241,
251, 286-87,
300-02, 304; 269
canzone alla Fran-
    zese 302
canzoni 234, 297
Caprani, A. 11
Capron, Henry 120
*24 Caprichos de
    Goya* (Mario Cas-
    telnuovo-Tedes-
    co) 682
Caravaggio 878
Carbonchi, Antonio
239, 307-08
Carcassi, Matteo
96; 13, 395, 401,
412, 445-47, 810
Carfagna, Carlo
11, 73
Carfagna, Carlo
1038
Carlevaro, Abel
66, 678
Carr, Benjamin 136
    "Dead march and
    monody" 136
Carré Sieur de la
    Grange, Antoine 239,
    308; 255, 291

319

C-

Carrillo-Trujillo,
Julián Antonio 188;
79-80, 674-77
Carter, Charles Thomas
239-40, 310
Carter, Robert 120
Carulli, Fernando 96;
13, 395, 401, 412, 448-
53, 467, 567
Casanova, Maria Julia
549
Casanovas, Joaquín 109
Castellacci, Luigi 601
Castelnuovo-Tedesco,
Mario 38-41, 634,
643, 679-84
Castro 240, 310
Catalani, O. 301
"Caterete" (Oliveira
Queiróz) 63
Cateura, Baldomero 109
Cavalieri 280
cavatina 244
Ceballos 244
Cellier, Jacques 291
Cenci, G. 301
Cerasolo, F. 301
Cerone, D.P.
   El Melopeo 197, 256
Cerreto, Scipione 299-
300
Cerreto, Scipione 165
Cerutti, Silvio 751,
762, 784, 860
Cervantes, Miguel de
36; 217-20, 330
cetterne 285
Chabran, Francesco 240,
310
chaconne 276, 281
Chambonnières, Jacques-
Champion de 878
Champein 283
"Le changement du
Spectre et du timbre
de la guitare du a la
qualité differente du
bois de la table de
resonance" 1018
chanson, French 36,
236, 260-61, 273-74,

289; 202 *See also*
French song
Charles, Sydney Robin-
son xxiii
Charles II of England
258, 338, 343, 347
Charleston (West Vir-
ginia) 121
Charnassé, Hélène 12,
285, 332
Charpentier, Marc-
Antoine 882
Chase, Gilbert 15, 36;
154-55
Chavarri, Lopez 808
Chavez, Carlos 722
Chavez, Carlos 80
Cherbourg, Mlle 240,
310
chiacone 241
Chiesa, Ruggero 749,
804
Chiesa, Ruggero 718,
858, 860, 863
Chilesotti, Oscar xxi,
290; 252-53, 269, 379
Chilesotti, Oscar 685
chitarra battente 36;
166, 267-68, 397, 896,
925, 928
chitarra napolitana
307
"Una chitarra quarti-
tonale" 1037
chitarriglia [chittar-
riglia] 237-38, 253-
54, 273, 278-79,
284, 302; 166
chitarrino 270, 302;
166
chitarrone [chitarone]
234-35, 237, 243, 250,
254-56, 268-70, 293,
295, 297-98; 2
chiterna 320
Chopin, Frederic 30,
656
"Chôro" (Heitor Villa-
Lobos) 834-35, 837
Choron, Alexander
Etienne 483

Index   C-

Chrichton, Ronald 689
Christensen, Ove 1019
"Christian Gottlieb
    Scheidler (ca. 1752-
    1815)" 526
Christoforo ab Andlaw,
    Sig^r Cav. Fra 256
"The chronicle" 131
ciaccona 60, 269, 287;
271, 277, 284
ciacones 335
Cimarosa, Domenico
240, 310
cimbalo 229, 250-51,
284-85, 296, 298
Cimma, Pier Luigi 668
cistre 274; 12
citole xv
cittern
    four-course French
    160
    English guitar 223-
    24, 236, 262, 286,
    292, 300, 303; 929
Ciurlo, E. Fausto
1002, 1038
clarinetto 253
Clark, Matthew 1; 13
Claudius, Carl xxi
clavecin 257
clavicembalo 234-35,
237, 243, 250, 254-55,
268-70, 295, 297
clavicordio 272
Clementi, Orazio 335
Clinton, George 775-77,
960, 980, 988, 991
Coelho, Olga 64, 723
Cohen, Albert 286
colachons xvi
"Collection of guitars"
925
"Collectors' pieces"
998
Colombia 77
Colonna, Giovanni
    Ambrosio 240, 307;
    271, 294
"Come Heavy Sleep"
    (John Dowland) 671-
    72

Company, Alvaro 647
concerti 232
concertina 413
concerto (guitar with
    orchestra) 11, 760,
    762
    Giuliani 477, 482,
    484
Concierto de Aranjuez
    (Joaquin Rodrigo)
    760, 764-65, 767
"Conde Claros" (Luis de
    Narváez) 241
Cone, Michael 962
Constantini, A. 302
"Constitution and by-
    laws of the American
    Guild of Banjoists,
    Mandolinists and
    Guitarists" 125
"Contemporary guitarist
    no. 4" (Alexander
    Bellow) 662
"Contemporary guitarist
    no. 5" (Maria Luisa
    Anido) 651
continuo *See* basso con-
    tinuo
Contreras, Segundo N.
14, 56-58
"A Conversation. Julian
    Bream - Malcolm Wel-
    ler" 667
"A conversation with
    Michael Cone" 962
Cook, Frederick xvi,
35; 169-72, 907
Cooper, Colin 775
Cooper, David Edwin
xxiv
Coover, James 187
Coques, Gonzales 878
Corbera, Franciscus
242; 341
Corbetta, Francesco
241-42, 298, 307-08;
252-53, 255, 258-59,
265, 291, 335-48, 359
Corelli 303
Coriandoli, Francesco
243, 308

321

Corradi, Flamminio 243, 306

Corrêa de Azevedo, Luis-Hector 65

correnti [corrente] 234, 241, 243, 248, 287, 302

Corrette, Michael 243, 310

Cortés, Narciso Alonso 243

Costa, Onorato da 499

Costa Rica 77

Costantini, A. 301

Costanzo, Fabrizio 243, 307; 294

Coste, Napoleon 412, 457-62, 559-60

Cotillions (Francis Blantchor) 134

"Courante" (Robert de Visée) 383

de Courcy 513

Coutagne, Henry 908

Covarruvias Orozco, Sebastien de 301

Covarruvias Orozco, Sebastien de xvii-xviii; 302

Cox, Paul xxi-xxiv, 36, 224, 246, 259, 262, 280, 286, 290; 393-94

Crecquillon 244

Crivellati, Domenico 243, 307

Crocket, Jim 778

Crocket, Jim 788

Cuarteto, Dona-Dio 84

Cuba 857

Cubist art 892

Cumpiano, William 1020-21

Cythara 272

Czechoslovakia 15; 67

Dagoty, Gouache de Gauthier *See* Gauthier Dagoty, Gouache de

Dalayrac, Nicolas-Marie 244, 283, 310

"Dalle antiche cronache" 491

Damas, Tomás 109-10

Danner, Peter xxvi, 224, 226; 114-16, 134, 151, 173, 287, 337, 355, 357, 451, 488, 529; *8, 20*

Danner, Peter xxiv, xxvi, 230-31, 237-38, 242, 247-48, 263, 265, 267, 281-82, 285, 294, 298, 302; 356

Daumier, Honoré 885

Daza, Esteban xvi, 35, 244, 306; 192, 221-22

De inventione et usu musicae (Tinctoris) xvi

"Dead march and monody" (Benjamin Carr) 136

Debussy, Claude-Achille 30, 656, 689-91, 693-94

Parfums de la nuit 691

La Soirée dans Grenade 691, 693

Decker-Schenk [Dekker-Schenk], J[ohann] F. 98, 102

Declaracion de instrumentos (Juan Bermudo) xvi-xviii; 175, 209-14

Degas, Hilaire Germain Edgar 177; 877

Dekker-Schenk, Johann *See* Decker-Schenk, J.F.

Dell'Ara, Mario 254, 434, 452, 550-51, 711

Della practica musica (Scipione Cerreto) 165

Delver, Friedrich 244, 310

Denis, Françoise-Emmanuelle 255

Denmark 15; 68-69

Index   D-

Denning, Darryl
174
Derosier, Nicolas 245,
309; 291
Des Prez, Josquin *See*
   Josquin des Prés
Desaugiers 283
Deutsch, Otto Erich 530
Deutsch, Otto Erich
533-35
"2eme Air varié", op.
   21 (Giulio Regondi)
   524
Devoto, Daniel 195, 333
Dezède 267
Diabelli, Anton 96,
299; 463-65, 483, 499
Diaz, Alirio 685, 775
Diaz, Alirio 859-60,
866
Diaz, Bartolomé 678
Dibdin, Charles 245,
304, 310
Dichler, Josef 38-41
Dickens, Fred T. 963
dictionaries
   General, of guitar-
   ists 51-55
   Italian guitarists
   and luthiers 73, 76
   Luthiers 903-05
Diderot, Denis 291,
875, 877, 882
Diesel, Nathanael 349-
51
diferencias [differen-
   cias] 36; 202, 215,
   241
dimitum leutum xviii
Djakow, J.I. 98
Dobson, Charles 160,
165
Doce canciones (Federi-
   co Moretti) 501
Dodgson, Stephen 38-41,
634, 643, 686-88
Doisy[-Lintant],
   Charles 245-47, 310;
   602

Doizi de Velasco,
   Nicolás xix, 247,
   307-08; 266, 289,
   291
Dominguez, F. 779
Domaines (Pierre
   Boulez) 665
domra 93
Dona-Dio 84
"Donna Diana" (Carl
   Maria von Weber) 589
Donneaud 246
doppelgitarre 413
Dorigny, Henri 740
Dorigny, Henri 632
Dorn, Charles James 112
Dorotea (Lope de Vega
   Carpio) xix
Dotzauer, Justus Johann
   F. 603
Dowland, John
   "Come Heavy Sleep"
   671-72
Douglas, Anthony G. 552
Drei Tentos für Gitarre
   (Hans Werner Henze)
   697-98
Dresden xx
Duarte, John xxvi; 632-
33, 679, 741-42, 775
Duarte, John 643
Duchamp, Gaston (pseud.
   of Jacques Villon)
   871
Duckles, Vincent xxii,
xxiv, 187
Dufourcq, Norbert 872
Duiffiproncart [Duiffo-
   proucart], G. 878, 908
Duni 267
duo (of guitars) 46,
136, 349, 480, 559-60,
632-33, 709
Dupuich, R. (pseud.)
   See Robert, Fissore
Dussek, Jan Ladislav
467 (piano performance)

323

E-F

eccossaises [eccosai-
sen] 231, 250
Eclat (Pierre Boulez)
665
"Editorial. A brief
history of the Ameri-
can Guild of Banjo-
ists, Mandolinists,
and Guitarists – What
the organization has
done in the interest
of the stringed in-
struments and what it
hopes to accomplish
in the future" 126
eight-string guitar
1034
Eitner, Robert xxiv,
224, 226, 231, 238,
242, 248
El Maestro (Luis Milan)
233-40
"El que quisiera
amando" (Fernando
Sor) 701
electric guitar 15, 646
Elizabethan guitar xv
Elliker, Calvin 473,
629
embellishments 287 *See
also* ornaments
"Emilio Pujol: a com-
plete list of works"
750
"An eminent guitarist"
(Madame Sidney Prat-
ten) 518
L'Encouragement, op. 34
(Fernando Sor) 559-60
England 15, 95
contemporary 635
Fernando Sor 556-58
Julián Arcas recitals
425
1600-1900 72
song and guitar, 19th
c. 71
string manufacturing
1031-32

English guitars 223-24,
236, 262, 286, 292,
300, 303
English songs 233, 266
enharmonic guitar 584-
85, 926
Eppinger, Heinrich 247,
310
"Escritura para guitar-
ra. Sistema antiguo"
203
Escudero, José Castro
333
Escuela musica xvii;
315-17
Espasa, Domingo Bonet
109
Espinel, Vicente xix-
xx; 352-53
Esteso Lopez, Domingo
964-66, 1012
"Etudes" (Heitor Villa-
Lobos) 837
etymology 158, 168,
191, 205
ciaccona 284
passacaglia 284
Eulenstein, Carl 604
Eusebio, Font y Moreso
553
Evans, Tom and Mary
xxi, 1, 60, 177; 15-16
Evers, Reinbert 221
"Explicación para tocar
la guitar de punte-
ado" (Juan Antonio
Vargas y Guzman) 378

Fabricio xvi, 35; 170
Falconieri, Andrea 247-
48, 306-07
"Falla's 'Homenaje pour
le tombeau de Claude
Debussy'. A master
lesson with Rey de la
Torre – taped in the
form of a conversa-
tion with Walter
Spalding, Sept. '76"
690

Index   F-

Falla, Manuel de
    *Homenaje pour le tom-
    beau de Claude
    Debussy* 689-94, 752
*The false consonances
    of musick* (Nicola
    Matteis) 363-64
falsobordone 60; 275
Falú, Eduardo 695
Famintsin, A.S. 93
fantasia [fantasie] 36,
    234, 236, 244, 260,
    274-75, 280, 287; 208,
    221, 226
*Fantasia para un gen-
    tilhombre* (Joaquin
    Rodrigo) 282, 763
fantasy 202
Farish, Margaret K.
    xxiii
Farrell, Susan Caust
    187
Farrell, Terrence 686,
    709; 858, 971
Fasolo 248, 307; 253,
    269
fedele 60; 275
Feldman, Morton xxiii
Felton 303
Fenton, Edward 888-89,
    893
Ferandière, Fernando
    248, 310; 266, 466
Fernandez, Francisco
    967
Fernândez, Oscar Lor-
    enzo 64
"Fernando Sor. Zwölf
    Regeln des Gitarren-
    spiels" 543
Ferrandière *See* Feran-
    dière, Fernando
Ferranti, Marco Aurelio
    Zani de 95; 96, 100,
    396, 467, 931
Ferranti, Sir Vincent
    de 931
Ferrara (Italy) xvi
Ferrari, Ascanio 256
Ferrari, G. 248, 250,
    307

Ferrari, Prof. Rómulo
    [Romolo] 472, 489,
    714
Ferrer Esteve, José
    109-10
Ferrer, Manuel Y. 112,
    137
    "Spanish mazurka,
    no. 2" 137
Fétis, [François] 95,
    224, 231, 298; 467
Fierro, Martín 60
figured bass 363-64 *See
    also* basso continuo
    and thorough bass
Fijt, Jan 878
Fink, Michael *558*
Finochelli, Francesco
    343
Fiorillo, Tiberio
    ("Scaramouche") 354
Fischer 96
Fischer, Hans 871
Fischhof, Josef *See*
    Fischof, Josef
Fischof, Josef 650
Fiset, C.F. 112
Fisk, Eliot 861-62
Fissore, Robert (R.
    Dupuich, pseud.) 903
Flac, Philippe 908
flamenco guitar 11, 15-
    16, 22
Flamminij, Sig^r Cavali-
    er Flamminio 255
*Flandrisches Gitarren-
    buch* 280
flauta dolce See flute
flauta traversa See
    flute
flautilla 272
flauto See flute
Flecha, M. 281
Fleta, Francisco Manuel
    969
Fleta, Ignacio 968
flöte See flute
flute xxv, 244, 252-53,
    256, 272, 282, 284,
    290, 295

Index   F-G

flute, German 239, 245,
298
Foden, William 112,
114, 138-47, 715
Foignet, M. 283
folia 36, 60; 194, 270,
273-76
"Folia de Espania,
   Variations sur"
   (Manuel Ponce) 271
folie pavaniglie 286
Les Folies d'Espagne
   (Federico Moretti)
   500
Folios for guitar (Toru
   Takemitsu) 697, 803
folk music
   Iberian 155
   Mexican 722-23
folklore 22
follie 241, 269
Ford, Charles 989; *51*
Ford, John 675-77
"Foreign guitar makers
   and English music
   sellers" 926
Fortea, Daniel 109
fortepiano [forte
   piano] 244, 295, 299;
   38-41
Fortune, Nigel 307
Foscarini, Giovanni
   Paolo 249, 307, 310,
   271, 294, 355-56
Fox, Charles Warren 36;
204
Fraenkel, Gottfried S.
175
France 15, 36, 59, 188;
10, 162, 255, 286, 387,
398, 407, 411, 556-58,
884-86, 910, 948-49
"Francisco Tárrega: a
complete list of works"
807
"Francisco Tárrega se-
gún..." 808
Fragonard, Jean Honore
878
Frank, Mortimer 136
Franklin, Benjamin 120

Frary, Peter Kun xxii
French song 232-33,
289
Frescobaldi, Girolamo
301; 271
frescos 875
Froese, Reinhard 671
Fromlich, Yane 885
Frosoli, Patrizia 937
frottola 36; 202
Fuenllana, Miguel de
xvi, xx, 35, 249-50,
306; 161, 175, 192,
197, 200-01, 204,
223-27, 245
Fürstenau, Anton Bern-
hard 606
Fürstenau, Caspar 606
Fuertes, Mariano Sor-
   iano *See* Soriano
   Fuertes, Mariano
Füssl, Karl Heinz
xxiii
fulie 287
Fux, Matthias 898

Gábry, György 899
Gärtner, Karl von 499
gagliarde 241, 269, 302
302 *See also* gaillardes
   [gailliardes] and
   galiarda
Gaglione, Ferdinando
xxi; 397
gaillardes [gailliard-
   es] 260, 274-75, 280
galiarda 279
Gallot, Henry François
   de [Gallot D'I] 255,
   357-59
gambling rackets (of F.
   Corbetta) 343
Gangi, M. 73
Gansbacher, John 607
Garcia, Enrique 109
Garcia, Hector 914
Garcia, Miguel 61
Garcia Castillo,
   Enrique 933

326

Index   G-

Garcia de Baigorri,
   Maria Antonia 17
Gardeton, Cesar xxv;
387
Garnier, Jean 872
Garnsey, Sylvia 363
Gatayes, Guillaume
   Pierre Antonio
   [Antoine] 250, 310;
   395, 592
gaucho 57-58, 60
Gaude, F. 250, 310
Gauthier Dagoty,
   Gouache de 872
Gavaldá, Miguel Querol
217
Gavoty, Bernard 780-81
Gelas, [Lucien] 457
Gelatt, Roland 872
"George C. Krick" 149
Gérard, Marguerite 874
Gerhard, Roberto xxiii
Germany 15, 188; 10,
42, 254, 402-03, 413,
455, 827, 918-21, 934,
944, 950, 1031
Gervasio 292
Ghiglia, Oscar 863
Ghillini di Asuni *See*
   Asuni, Ghillini di
ghittar 329
Ghizzolo, Giovanni 250,
307
Giaccio, Orazio 251,
307
Giamberti, Gioseppe
251, 307
Gianoli, L. 873
Gibb, William 900
Giertz, Martin 18
Giesbert, F.J. 298
Giga (Santiago de
   Murcia) 368
Gigue (Robert de Visée)
385
Gilardino, Angelo 137;
634-38, 853
Gilbert, Alice 955
Gill, Donald xvi; 288,
326-27, 358

Gill, Louis 133
Gillot, Claude 882
Gilmore, George xxii
Giordani 251, 304, 310
Giordano, M. 74, 458
Giornale del Regno
   delle Due Sicilie
      Death notice of
      Mauro Giuliani 479
Gistau, S. Castro de
251, 310
"Gitarre" 19
gittar 319
gittern 152
"Giuliani" xv; 468
Giuliani, Giovanni
   Francesco 251, 310
Giuliani, [Girolamo]
252, 306
Giuliani, Mauro 96;
13, 386, 388-89, 400,
402, 410, 412-13, 468-
84, 499, 516, 547, 564,
613, 618, 631
Giuliani-Giulielmi,
   Emilia 499
Giulianiad xxvi, 95;
386
Giusti, George 928
Giustiniani, Vincenzo
303-06
Giustiniani, Vincenzo
307
Gladstone, Ralph J. 836
Gluck 266
Godwin, Joscelyn 927
Göpfert, Carl Andreas
252, 310
Goethe
   Erlkönig (Franz
   Schubert) 529
Gollmick, Carl 608
Gombert, N. 281
Gombosi, Otto 270
Gomez-Santos, Marino
761
Gorlier, Simon xvi, 36,
252, 306; 161
Gorner, Peter 783

G-   Index

Goya y Lucientes,
    Francisco José de
    177; 682, 871-73,
    881, 888-89
Graeffer, Antoine 609
Gragnani, Felipe 253,
    310
Grammont, Count 338
Granada (Spain) 111,
    954
Granadan guitar makers
    957
Granados (y Campina),
    Enrique 405
Granata, Giovanni
    Battista 253, 302,
    309-10; 360
"Grand septuor"
    (Goffredo Petrassi)
    719
"Grand solo", op. 14
    (Fernando Sor) 581
Grandi, Alessandro 254,
    307
Grano 303
Grapuccioli, F. 302
Grassineau, James 308-
09
gravecimbalo 273
Great Britain *See*
    England
Grebe, Maria Ester 176
Greene, Thomas E. 177
Grénerin, Henri 254,
    309; 255, 334
Grétry 235, 267, 283
Grial, Hugo de 79
Grunfeld, Frederic V.
    177; 20, 395, 886-87
Guadagnini 903
Guarnieri, M.C. 66
Guerau, Francisco 254-
55, 309; 293, 361
"La Guerre" (Brayssing)
236
Guerrero, Francisco
244; 289
Guichard, L. 255, 310
Guidonian hexachord
    system 177

Guild *See* Guitar Soci-
    eties and Clubs
guitar - variant forms
    chitarra battente
    xxvi; 166, 267-68,
    397, 896, 925, 928
    chitarra napolitano
    307
    chitarriglia 166
    chitarrino 166
    chitarrone 2
    chiterna 320
    doppelgitarre 413
    eight-string guitar
    xxvi, 188; 1034
    electric guitar 15,
    646
    English guitar *See*
        cittern
    enharmonic guitar
    584-85, 926
    ghittar 329
    ghiterna xviii
    ghiterra xviii
    gittar 319
    gittern 152
    guitar-tirol 928
    guitare en bateau 267
    guitar
    guiterne 229
    guiterre 229
    harp guitar 928
    lyra guitar 402
    microtonal guitar
    xxvi, 188; 1037-39
    quarter-tone guitar
        See microtonal
        guitar
    quinterna 320
    Russian guitar xxvi;
    90, 928
    ten-string guitar
    xxvi, 188; 847-51,
    1035-36
    terz guitar xxvi;
    629-31, 803, 896
    theorbo guitar 896
    violão 65
Guitar Foundation of
    America xxiv, xxvii

328

G-H

Guitar Societies and
 Clubs
   The American Guild
   of Banjoists, Man-
   dolinists, and
   Guitarists 124-29
   The American Guitar
   Society 130
   International
   Guitar Club 409
   Leipzig Guitar Club
   42, 409
   List of Societies
   66
   Society of the
   Classic Guitar 131-
   33, 554
"Guitar gallery" 874
"Guitar history" 932
"Guitar in Mexico" 80
"Guitar music. Pedrell
 and Petrassi" 717
"Guitar music. The art-
 istry of Miguel
 Llobet (1878-1938)"
 703
Guitar Player Magazine,
 editors 639
Guitar Review Editors
554, 928
guitar-tirol 928
guitare en bateau 267
"Guitarras y guitarrer-
 ros" 965, 974, 978,
 984
guitarrilla xvii
"Guitarristas célebras;
 fichas biográficas 21
guiterne 229
guiterre 229
guitterne 229
Gulièn-Sor, Madame 578
Guzman, Juan Antonio
 Vargas Y See Vargas Y
 Guzman, Juan Antonio
Guzman, Luis de xvii;
228
gyttron 284

Haas, Robert 465, 587,
769
Haemmerling, Konrad
 (Moreck, Curt,
 pseud.) 881
Händel 303-04
Haines, Daniel 1022
Haines, Daniel 970
Haley, George 352
Hall, Monica J.L. 178,
330
Hamburg (Germany) 939
Hamilton, Anthony 338
Harder, August 610
Hardie, Colin 775
harmonics 648
   Berlioz, Hector 428-
   33
harmonium 1025
harp [harpa, harpe]
257, 272, 277, 296; 12
harp guitar 928
harpsichord 239, 245,
277, 292, 298-99; 38-41
Harris, David 1034
Harris, John 555
Harrison, Frank 875
Harrison, Frank M. 521
Haskins, H. Wolcott 396
Hasse 303
Haug, Hans 38-41
Haupt, Helga 947
Hauser, Hermann 971-73,
1012, 1032
Haward, Lawrence 891
Hayden, William 148
Haydn, J. 304
Haydn, Franz Joseph 283
   use of folk instru-
   ments 403
Haywood, Charles 218
Heartz, Daniel xv, 259,
280, 285; 160-61, 229
Heck, Thomas xxi,
xxiii, 36, 95; 44, 75,
135, 267, 397-99, 474-
80, 486, 531-34, 809;
8, 20, 35, 43, 53
Heitland, Winfried 913
Held, Ignatz 102

329

H-I   Index

Hellwig, Friedemann 909

Hellwig, Günther 938-39

Henestrosa, Luys
   Venegas de *See*
   Venegas de Henestro-
   sa, Luys

Henke, Matthias 435

Henze, Bruno xix, xxi,
xxiii; 400

Henze, Hans Werner 634,
655, 670, 696-99

Hernandez, Sobrinos de
   Santos 974, 1012

hexachord system
   (Guidonian) 177

Heyer, Anna Harriet
xxiii

Hickmann, Hans 19

Higbee, Dale *20*

Higham, Peter 680-81

Himmel, Friedrich
   Heinrich 611

Hindemith, Paul
   *Music for three
   guitars* 700

Hipkins, Alfred James
900

"History and design of
   stringed instruments.
   A new look" 977

Hoffman 283

Hofmeester [Hofmeis-
   ter], Theodorus M.
   Jr. 137; 810, 941

Hofmeester [Hofmeis-
   ter], Theodorus M.
   Jr. 942

Hofmeister, Friedrich
xxv

Höhne, Erich 876

Holland 857

Holland, Justin 112

"Homenaje 'Le Tombeau
   de Claude Debussy'"
   689-91, 693-94

"Home sweet home"
   (Francis Weiland) 151

"Hommage a Lenin" (Leo
   Brouwer) 857

Honegger, Marc 244-45

Hook 304

Hoorickx, Fr. Reinhard
   van 535

Hopkinson, Francis 120

Horetzky [Horetzsky],
   Felix 95; 87, 468,
   485-87

Horniman Museum
   (London, England) 895

Hoskins, Arthur C. 141

Howell, Almonte 256

Howell, Almonte C., Jr.
317

Huber, J. 22

Huber, J.N. 255, 310

Hudson, Richard 249;
196, 257, 271-79

Huel 903

Huerta, A.F. 115

Huerta, Don F. 612

Huerta, Trinidad 110

Huffman-Blain Stearns,
   Roland 1

Hughes, John 215

Hulinzký, Thomas A. 898

Hultberg, Warren Earle
246, 248

Humanism 182

Hummel, Johann Nepomuk
96; 388, 473, 483, 613

Humoresca (Barrios
   Manjoré) 657

Humphrys 304

Hurdy-gurdy 403

Hutchinson, Loving 247

Huttig, H.E. II 417,
715, 1003

hymns 299

"I do not like the gui-
   tar! Being an exami-
   nation of the objec-
   tions raised against
   that instrument" 388

Ibanez, Salvador 976

"Iberian folk music"
155

Iglesia de la Compañía
   de Jesús (Quito,
   Ecuador) 907

Index   I-J

"Incontri. Colloquio
    con Alice Artzt" 853
"Incontri. Colloquio
    con Emilio Pujol" 751
"Incontri. Colloquio
    con Julian Bream" 668
"Incontri. Incontro con
    Federico Moreno Tor-
    roba di Griselda
    Ponce de Léon" 831
"Incontri. Intervista a
    Goffredo Petrassi"
    718

"Incontri. Intervista a
    Hans Werner Henze"
    696
"Incontri. Intervista a
    Oscar Ghiglia" 863
"Incontri. Intervista
    ad Alexander Tansman
    di Ruggero Chiesa"
    804
"Incontri. Intervista
    ad Alirio Diaz" 860
"Incontri. Intervista
    ad Andrés Segovia"
    784
"Incontri. [Joaquin
    Rodrigo]" 762
"Increasing popularity
    of the guitar" 117
India, Sigismondo (D')
    255, 309
"*Instructions to my
    daughter for playing
    on the enharmonic
    guitar*, by a member
    of the University of
    Cambridge. Goulding
    and D'Almaine" 584
International Guitar
    Club 42, 409
"Interview: Artzt" 854
"Interview: David
    Rubio" 990
"Interview: Manuel
    Rodriguez" 987
"An interview with
    Daniel Haines" 970

"An interview with
    Fred T. Dickens" 963
"An interview with
    Richard Schneider –
    the origins of the
    Kasha design are dis-
    cussed" 993
"Introducing Dominick
    Argento" 654
"Introduction et
    Caprice", op. 23
    (Giulio Regondi) 524
Irvine, Kip 763
Isakow, Peter 103
Isbin, Sharon 864
Isekov, Peter 108
Italian song 36, 232-
33, 266, 290, 292; 202
Italy 15, 36, 59
    Calabria 268
    Dictionaries of gui-
    tarists 73, 76
    early guitar 3
    eighteenth c. 254
    general 10
    Giuliani in 476
    Ricordi house of
    publishing 75
    Sardinia 74
    string industry 1031
    tablature 4
    twentieth c. 636
Ito, Ako 632
Ivan Carlos *See* Amat,
    Juan Carlos
Ivanov 94
Iwanow-Kramskoj,
    Aleksandr 103

Jacobs, Charles 179,
234
Jacobs, Walter 112
Jacquemart-André, Musée
    (Institut de France)
    912
Jaffee, Michael 837
Jahnel, F. 1004
Jakovlev 1025
Jambou, Louis 197
Janequin 252

J-K-L   Index

Jankovski 1025
Janon, Charles de 112
Jansen, C.W.F. 112
Japan 797, 802
Jape, Mijndert xxii
Jazz 11, 22
"The jealous extre-
    maduran" (Miguel de
    Cervantes) 330
Jeffery, Brian 291;
418-19, 501, 556-60,
724
Jeffery, Brian 701
Jenkins, Jean 187
Jensen, Richard d'A.
357, 691
Jesuit missions (Para-
    guay) 58
Jimenez, Salvador 847
Jobin, Bernard 878
Josquin des Prés 281;
244-45
Jovius, Paulus 228
Don Juan of Austria 373
"Julián de Arcas" 424
Juriew, Wasil 103

Kagel, Maricio 647
Kamimoto, Hideo 1005
Kammermusik 1958 (Hans
    Werner Henze) 655,
    698
Kapsberger, Johannes
    Hieronymus 255-56,
    306-07
Kasha, Michael 23
Kasha, Michael 962,
977, 993-94
Keck, P.L. 256, 310
Keim, Betty 692
Keith, Richard 258, 339
Kelly, Christine Kuehn
838
Kendall, Alan 877
Kennard, Deric 259, 340
Kerll, Johann Kaspar
271
Kessner, Daniel 697
Keyboard 1, 36, 223,
288; 38-41, 167, 190,

214-15, 249, 251, 271,
280
Kiev 101
Kinsky, Georg 536, 878-
80
Kircher, Athanasius 326
Kirkendale, Warren
xxiv, 225-26, 229, 249,
268, 271, 278, 281,
300; 280
Kirkpatrick, Ralph 861
Kirsch, Dieter 36; 156
Kitchener, W.J. 401
Kitchener, W.J. 129
Klingenbrunner, Wilhelm
499
Klinger, J.A. 98
Kmoch, Vladimir 509
Kmoch, Vladimir 513
Koczirz, Adolf xix,
xxi; 24, 208, 225, 260,
335, 362, 373, 402,
466, 481
Körner, [(Karl)
    Theodor] 950
Kohno 961
Kolon, V. 453
Kotonski, Wlodzimierz
xxiii
Kotzwara 304
Kozeluch 283
Kozinn, Allan 701, 752-
53, 785, 848, 861
Kucera 67
Kuffner, Joseph 614
Kramer 493
Kraus, J. 256, 310
Kreidler, Dieter *773*
Kremberg, Jacob 256-59,
309; 42, 362, 878
Kreutzer, Joseph 488
Krick, George 142-44,
510, 537
Krick, George 112, 149

Labarre, Trille 257,
310
Lach, R. *55*
Laconi 341

332

Index   L-

Lacote, René François
903, 926, 931

Lagarde, Pierre (de)
257-58, 309

Lagoya, Alexander 633,
645, 739, 742-44 *See
also* Ida Presti

La Grange, de 258, 308

Lalleman 283

lamentation 36; 202

Lancret, Micolas 881

Landi, Stefano 258,
301, 307

Langlois, Vincent M.
871

Lansing, Geo. L. 129

Laprevotte 903

Larmessin 882

Latin America 15; 15,
27, 77-78, 82, 176, 855

La Tour, Francesco 326

laud 302 *See also* lute

Laurens, Henri 871

Lauro, Antonio 78, 866-
67

Lauthe *See* lute

lauto *See* lute

Lawrence, Catherine
743, 856, 865

Lear, Edward (poet) 30

Lebedeff, W.P. 98

Lebiediew, Wasil 102

Leckie, Walter J. 702

Ledhuye, Adolphe 420

Leeb, Hermann 137; 786

Legnani, Luigi 413,
489-92, 499, 515

Legouvé, Ernest 436-37

Leipzig guitar club 42,
409

Leisner, David 698

Lemaire, Charles 277

Lemoine, Antoine M.
258-59, 310; 398, 615

Le Nain, Antoine 872

Léon, Griselda Ponce de
831

Léonard 257

Lesure, François xxv,
225; 162, 230, 328,
334, 910

Lerida (Spain) 754

Le Roy, Adrian xvi, 36,
259-61, 280, 306; 160-
61, 163, 229-30

Letters from composers
(Dominick Argento)
655-56

Lewis, John xxiii

LEWIS LUTHIER SUPPLIES
1006

L'Hoyer, Antoine de
261-62, 310

Libbert, Jürgen 25,
456, 493

*Libro de musica de
vihuela* (Pisador)
xvi; 175

*Libro de musica de
vihuela, intitulado
Silva de sirenas*
(Valderrábano) xvi

*Libro de musica en
cifras para vihuela,
intitulado el Parnaso*
(Daza) xvi

*Libro de musica para
vihuela, intitulado
Orphenica lyra*
(Fuenllana) xvi

Lichtenwanger, William
(comp.) 187

Lied (Franz Schubert)
531-34

Lieder (Carl Maria von
Weber) 586-87

Lidel, Joseph (cellist)
413

Light, Edward 262, 310

Lindley, Mark 235

Lintant, C. 616

Lipscomb, Pamela 356

lithography 177; 885-
87

liuto 302 *See also* lute

Llobet, Miguel 811-12

Llobet, Miguel 137;
109, 638, 653, 690,
694, 703-10, 786, 808,
814, 829

Lockwood, Lewis xvi

Lolikoff, A.K. 98

L-M

London (England)
early 19th c. music
sellers 926
Fernando Sor 555, 558
Giulio Regondi 413
Mauro Giuliani 472
Lope de Vega Carpio
xix
Lopez xvi, 35
López 170
Lopez, Antonio 813
Lorca, Antonio 978
Lorca, Federico García
711-12
Lorente 256
Lorimer, Michael 839
Losy, Jan Antonín 262,
310
Lotz, Kornélia 899
Louis XIV 258
Lowenfeld, Elena M.
276; 365-66
"Lucas Ruiz de Ribayaz"
370
Lütgendorff, Willibald
Leo, Freiherr von 904
Luse, Marvin W. Jr. 725
lute xv-xvi, 36, 224,
226, 234, 257; 1-2, 9,
12, 34-35, 45, 47, 49,
55, 154, 156, 159, 167,
173-74, 183, 186, 189-
91, 199, 208, 234, 253,
260, 263, 302, 328-29,
527-28, 803, 901(Arabic
lute), 904, 906, 990,
1004, 1034 *See also*
laud, luth
lute construction (lute
making) 990-92, 1004
lutenists 73, 76, 191
luth 238, 245; *See also*
lute
luthiers 73, 76, 904-
05, 908
Luz y norte musicale
(Lucas Ruiz de Ri-
bayaz)370-71
Lyon (France)
16th c. luthiers
908

Lyons, David Bruce 349-
50
lyra xviii
lyra guitar 402
lyre 240, 246, 250, 259,
280, 290; 397
lyric drama (Spanish)
155

"Macarena" (Andrés
Segovia) 791
Maccaferri, Mario 775
Macchiavelli, I. 301
Mace, Thomas 32
Machabey, Armand 281
Machado 712
Mackévitch, M.V.-P. 561
"Madame Giulia Pelzer,
mandolin and guitar
artiste, of London,
England" 519
Maderna, Bruno xxiii
Madrid (Spain) 915, 955
"Madrid School of
guitar makers" 985
madrigaletti 273
madrigali 234, 238, 297
El Maestro (Luis Milan)
xvi; 233-40
The Magic Flute (Moz-
art-Sor variations)
547
Magnien, Victor 617
Magula, George 482
Mahling, Christoph-
Hellmut 403
Mairants, Ivor 775,
956, 959, 968, 986;
15, 794
Maillard, J. 244
Majer, Joseph Friedrich
Bernhard Caspar 262-
63, 309
Makarow [Makarov, Mak-
aroff], Nicolai
Petrovich 95-96
Makarow [Makarov, Mak-
aroff], Nicolai
Petrovich 100-02

Index   M-

"Making a classical
   guitar - José Oribe"
   979
Malipiero, Riccardo
   xxiii
"Man with a guitar.
   Julian Bream. A self-
   portrait, with music"
   669
manacordo 278
mandola 2, 166
mandolin 51, 118, 124,
   149, 403, 507, 769
mandolinists *See* Amer-
   ican Guild of Banjo-
   ists, Mandolinists,
   and Guitarists
"The mandolin and gui-
   tar" 118
mandora xv
mandores xvi
Manelli [Mannelli],
   Francesco 248
Manet, Edouard 871, 874
Manet, Eugène 882
Manifold, J.S. 219
Manjón, Antonio Jiménez
   109
Manns, Jerrold (Allen)
   289; 374; *43*
manufacturers (of gui-
   tars) 187
máquina *See* tripódison
marche 231-32
Marchetti, Tommaso 263,
   308
Marcos, Maria Lívia São
   66
Marcos, Juan José Rey
   xvi; 180
Marcus, Robert Samuel 289
Marcuse, Sibyl 26
Marini, Biagio 264, 308
Marinoni, Girolamo 264,
   306
Markow, W.J. 99
Marlow, Janet 1035
Marriott, David F. 647,
   802
Marsh, William Sewall
   109

Le marteau sans maître
   (Pierre Boulez) 665
Martin, Christian Fred-
   erick 934
Martin, François 264,
   308
Martin, Frank 634, 713
Martín y Soler, Vicente
   264, 310
Martini 264, 283, 304,
   310
Martini, Padre J.B. 30
Mascherpa, G. 873
Maschkewitsch [Masche-
   witz], W.P. 97-100
Maskewic, Vladimir 103
Mason, Barry 200
Massys, J. 897
Matiegka, Wenzel[slaus
   Thomas] 493, 499,
   535-37, 539
Matisse, Henri 177; 874
Matsuda 775
Matteis, Nicola 265,
   309; 3, 318, 363-64
Mauerhofer, Alois 455
Maugin, J.C. 917
Maxson, Gloria (trans.)
   712
Mayer, de 283
Mayseder, Joseph 618
Mazzacchi, D. 301
McBride, Robert xxiii
McCreadie, Sue 670
McCreadie, Sue 867
McLeod, Donald 1007
Médard, Remy 265, 308;
   255
Meijering, Cord 693
Meissonnier, Antoine
   619
Meissonnier ("Le
   Jeune"), Joseph 395,
   619
El Melopeo (D.P.
   Cerone) 197, 256
melophone 413
Melvi, F.M. 293

335

M-   Index

"A memorable day for Boston. The launching of the Guild and the holding of a festival" 127

Mendez, G[uillermo] F[lores] 726-27, 951

Mendl, Franz 499

Mendoza xvi, 35; 170

Mengozzi 283

menuets 230, 233, 240, 247, 296 *See also* minuets

Merchi, Giacomo 265-67, 309-11; 620

Mereaux 267

Mersenne, Marin 310-12

Mersenne, Marin 313-14, 326

Mertz, Johann Kaspar 494-97, 499

Mertz, Josephine, née Plantin 495

Merula, T. 303

Messaien, Olivier 803

"Mestiça" (Anon.) 63

"Metafora del amor" (Brouwer) 857

Metropolitan Museum of Art (New York) 925, 928

Mexia, Pero 228

Mexican 79, 84, 377-78, 722-23 *See also* Mexico

Mexico 15, 188; 77, 80-83, 176, 728, 734, 951-52 *See also* Mexican

Meyer, Jürgen 1023-24

Micheli, Antoniodi 267, 308

microtonal guitar xxvi; 1037-39

Mignone, Francisco 63, 66

"Miguel Soles Llobet" 704

Milan, Luis 231-32, 236

Milan, Luis xvi, xviii, 35-36, 268, 306; 13, 159, 167, 192, 197, 201, 207, 233-35, 237-40

Milanuzzi, Carlo 268-70, 297, 307-10; 271, 294

Miller, Carl 672; *8, 15, 20, 35*

Milliot, S. 948

Mills, John 775

Miller, J.M. 495

Millet, Luis 808

Millioni, Pietro 269-72, 306-08, 310; 271, 294

Minguet y Yrol, Pablo 272, 309-10; 289, 878

minuets 232, 276, 303

Minutier Central des notaires de Paris, Archives nationales 910

Mirimonde, A.P. de 884, 894

Mitjana, Rafael 427

modality (mode) 176, 244-45, 272

mode *See* modality

Modena (Italy) 492

Moffatt, Peter 775

Molino, Valentino 273, 311

Molitor, Simon 402, 408, 498-99
    description of a lyra guitar 402

"La Molinara" 294

Molino, Don François 621

Möller, Dirk 682

Monagne, Victor 808

Monsigny 235, 267, 304

Montanos 256

Monte, Lodovico 273, 307, 311; 294

Montesardo, Girolamo 273, 306; 271, 279-80, 284, 291, 294

Monzino, Giacomo 273, 311

Moraes Sarmento, Olga de 844

Morales, C. 281

Moramarco, Luigi 133

Index

Moreck, Curt (pseud.)
  See Haemmerling,
  Konrad
Morelli 273, 303, 310
Moreno-Torroba, Fed-
  erico 643
morescha 248
Moretti, Federico 251,
274, 310-11; 61, 500-02
  Doce Canciones 501
  "Les Folies d'Espag-
  ne" 500
Morkow, Ladislaus 102
Morlaye, Guillaume xvi,
36, 274-75, 306; 161
Morphy, Conde de
  [Guillermo] xix, xxi,
  244, 275-76, 295; 716
Morris, Charles 129
Moschelles [Moscheles],
  Ignaz 388, 622
Moscow (Russia) 558
Moser, Wolf xxii, 96;
110, 213, 237, 438,
562-63
motetes 244, 275
motetti 234, 264
Mouton, J. 234, 281
Moutron xxi
Mozart, Wolfgang
  Amadeus 547
Mozzani, Luigi 636,
714-15
Mudarra, Alonso xvi,
35, 275, 306; 161, 173,
192, 194, 197, 201, 245
Muñoz, Ricardo 27, 59
Muñoz, Ricardo 808
Munrow, David 157
Murcia, Santiago de
276, 309; 266, 289,
293, 365-68
  "Giga" 368
  Passacalles y obras
  367
  *Resumen de
  acompañar la parte
  con la guitarra*
  365-66
  "Sarabande" 368

Murphy, M. 261
Murphy, Sylvia 28,
290-91
Murr, Emma 145
Murray, D. 952
Museums 9
  Bodleian Museum of
  Oxford University
  924
  Horniman Museum
  (London, England)
  895
  Metropolitan Museum
  of Art (New York,
  N.Y.)925, 928
  Musée Jacquemart-
  André, Institut de
  France 912
  Museo Stradivariano
  (Cremona, Italy)
  937
*Music for three
  guitars* (Paul Hinde-
  mith) 700
"Música en la antigue-
  dad. Luis Milan" 233
musica ficta 36; 204,
246-47
musical forms
  allemande 348, 382
  aria 362
  aria di fiorenza 280
  ballo del Gran
  Duca 280
  bourree 385
  chaconne 276, 281
  ciaccona 271, 277,
  284, 335 (ciacones)
  courante 383
  fantasia 208, 221, 226
  fantasy 202
  folia 194, 270, 273-
  76
  passacaglio [passa-
  caglia] 271, 276-78,
  284, 335, 373
  passacaille 281, 348,
  380

337

M-N-O   Index

prelude [preludio] 147,
348, 373, 382, 661,
724, 834, 837, 839,
842, 846
romance 193, 195, 200,
202, 217, 225, 473
romanesca 194
sarabande 276, 368,
383
sonata 551, 725
tarantella 58, 198
zarabanda 279
zarabande francese 279
zarazuela 283
*Musicalische Gemüths-
Ergökung oder Arien*
(Jakob Kremberg) 42,
362, 878
Mutii, P. 301-02
Myers, Joan 181

N. 564
Nanino, G.B. 251, 300
Naples (Italy) xx, xxi
Napolitane 296
Narváez, Luis de xvi, 35,
224, 276, 279-80, 296,
306; 170, 180, 188, 192,
194, 241-42, 245
"Conde claros" 241
"Passeavase el Rey
Moro" 242
Nassarre [Nassare], Pablo
de xvi; 256, 266, 317
Naumann, Johann Gottlieb
xx-xxi
Nava, Antonio Maria 75,
395
Navarro 244
Nelson, Martha 29, 63,
198, 205, 282, 896
Neri, S. Filippo 302
Newcomb, A.H. 446
New York (N.Y.)
Concert life 121
early 20th c., guitar
popularity 118
Ida Presti in 738
Nichols, George 30
Nickel, Heinz 163, 901
Nicola, Isaac 31, 652

Nicolai 303
Nielsen, Karen Dusen
Dusgaard *18*
Nivers, Guillaume-
Gabriel 277, 308-09
Nocturnal (Benjamin
Britten) 671-72
Nogueira, A.T. 66
Nordau, Max 787
North, Roger 318
Novelas Ejemplares
(Miguel de Cervantes)
219
"Nunc" (Goffredo
Petrassi) 719
Nupen, Christopher 770,
775, 777

Oberleitner, Andrew 623
["The obituary and epi-
taph of Francisque
Corbet"] 336
"Obituary notice" (Man-
uel Ponce) 728
Obras de música (Anton-
io de Cabezón) 167
Obrecht, Jas 1
Obrovská, Jana 67
"On the comparative mer-
its of the piano-forte
and guitar, as an ac-
companiment to the
voice" 390
"On the capabilities of
the guitar" 389
Odell, Herbert F. 112,
129
Olsen, Poul Rovsing
xxiii
opera
arrangements for
guitar 399
Sors, F. 291
Opera intitolata contina
(Melchior de Barberis)
208
Ophee, Matanya 137;441,
483, 496, 630-31, 814,
942-43
Ordonez, P. 244

338

Index   O-P

Orel, Alfred 404
organo 272, 288
organs 215
Oribe, José 788
 Oribe, José 979
"The original classic
    guitar" 378
ornamentation 60; 293,
373 *See also* embellish-
    ments
Orozco, Juan 980
Orozco, Sebastien de
    Covarrubias *See*
    Covarrubias Orozco,
    Sebastien de
orpharion 2
Orphénica Lyra (Miguel
    de Fuenllana) xvi,
    249; 175, 197, 223-27
ostinato basses 194
Oswald, J. 303
Otero, Corazon 81, 729
Otero, Diego Vásquez xx
Otto, Jakob August xix,
xxi; 918-21
Otto, Jakob August 42,
950
Oudry, Jean-Baptiste
876
Overholtzer, Arthur E.
1008

Paez, Francisco xvi,
35; 170
"Paganini - guitarist"
503
Paganini, Nicolò 96; 30,
413, 503-17
"Paganini. Violinist and
    guitarist" 504
Page, Christopher xvi
Pages (guitar maker) 935
Paisiello 233, 294
Paixaõ Ribeiro, Manoel
    da 277, 310
Panama 77
pandora 2
Panin, Peter 108
Panocchieschi de Conti
    d'Elci, Signor Marcel-
    lo 256

Panormo, Louis 903, 931,
935
Paracho (Mexico) 952
Paraguay 15; 58, 77,
85
Parfums de la nuit
    (Claude Debussy) 691
Pari, Francesco 281
Paris (France) 251
    construction in, 18th
    c. 948
    construction in, 16th
    c. 910
    early 19th c. 411,
    413, 435
    Segovia and Villa-
    Lobos in 844
Parison, Mr. 235
parody technique 188,
190
El Parnaso (Esteban
    Daza) xvi, 244; 221-
    22
Parry, J. 277, 309
passacaglio [passa-
    caglia] 60, 277, 309;
    271, 276-78, 284,
    335, 373
passacaille [passacalli,
    passacailli] 241, 287;
    281, 348, 380
Passacalles y obras
    (Santiago de Murcia)
    367
"Passeavase el Rey Moro"
    (Luis Narváez) 242
pass'emezi 241, 287 *See
    also* passomezo
Passereau 234
passomezo 279-80
Partee, Clarence L. 112
Paterson, John 994
"Pater Noster" (Pisa-
    dor-Willaert) 246
pavan [paduana] 36,
274-75, 279; 199, 202,
240
pavanes 260
Pavlakis, Christopher
187
Paz 712

339

P- Index

payadores (gaucho) 60
Payer, Hieronimus 624
pedagogy 1, 35, 50,
119, 122, 150, 393-94,
420, 466, 562, 678,
773, 810, 814, 818, 827
Pedraza, Bermudez de
228
Pedrell, Carlos 717
Pedrell, Felipe xxi;
283
Pedrell, Felipe 644,
716, 808, 829
Peel, Douglas 405, 511,
789
Pellegrini, Domenico
  *Armoniosi concerti
  sopra la chitarra
  spagnuola* 277, 308;
  369
Pelzer, Ferdinand 95;
391, 520
Pelzer, Giulia 519-20
peñazuela (16th c.
  capotasto) 169
Pennington, Neil
  (Douglas) 367, 442
Pepys, Samuel 319
Pereira, Mark xxii
periodicals
  European and American
  386
  German 55
  Giulianiad 386, 520
  *Revue et Gazette
  Musicale* 567
Perott, Boris A. 101,
790
Perronet, General T.
  See Thompson, General
  T. Perronet
Peru 15; 86
Pesori, Steffano 278-
79, 308, 311
Petrassi, Goffredo 717-
19
  "Alias" 719
  "Grand septuor" 719
  "Nunc" 719
  "Seconda-serenata
  trio" 719

Pettine, Giuseppe 146
Pettine, Giuseppe 141
Pettoletti, Pietro 98,
102
Phalèse, Pierre xvi,
36, 224, 259, 276, 279-
80, 306; 160
Philadelphia (Pennsyl-
  vania)
  concert life 121
Philidor 235
Phillis, Jean Baptiste
280, 311
pianoforte xxv, 231-32,
239, 244, 295; 38-41,
390, 467, 533-34, 692
  performance by Dussek
  467
Pica da Rocha 281, 309
Picart, Etienne 878
Picasso, Pablo 177;
882, 890-92
Picchianti, Luigi 625
Piccini 267, 292
Pick, Richard 150
Pico, Foriano 281, 306-
07; 271, 294
Pierre, Constant 949
Pietrobono xvi
Pimentel, Lorenzo 914,
981
Pincherle, Marc 730,
882
Pinel, Germain 334
"Pinnell completes
  dissertation" 345
Pinnell, Richard 241;
262, 342-45, 359, 368;
558
Pinturicchio, Bernar-
  dino 881
Pique, Eduard 499
Pirastro 1032
Pisador, Diego xvi, 35,
281-82, 306; 175, 192,
204, 243-47
pitch 189
Playford, John 282, 308

340

Index   P-

Pleyel, Ignace 282-83,
304, 311
   letters from Hector
   Berlioz 443
Pli selon ple (Pierre
Boulez) 665
poetry 30, 57, 195,
333, 386, 711-12, 924
Poglietti, Alessandro
271
Polanco, Arismendi 133
Poland 15; 87-88
Pollet, Charles Fran-
   çois Alexander 626
Pollet, Jean Joseph
   Benoit 626
Pollet, L.M. 626
Polupajenko, M.W. 98
Pomponio-Martinez duo
633
Pon, Juan Nogués 109
Ponce, Manuel M. 13,
38-41, 79-81, 643, 670,
720-37, 776
   Sonata III 725
   "Variations sur Folia
   de Espania" 721
Pons 903
Pope (Conant), Isabel
182, 353
Popow, Arsenij 103
Porro, Pierre-Jean 282-
83, 302, 311
Porta, A. 754
Porta, Francesco 256
"Portrait issue" 641
Portrait issues
   Guitar News 138; 640
   Guitar Review 138;
   641
"[Portraits of contem-
   porary guitarists and
   composers]" 640
Portugal xv, 15; 89,
254
Portuguese musicians
191
Poselli, Franco 427,
502
Poulton, Diane 36; 183-
84, 199, 249, 302, 911

Powróźniak, Józef 52-
53, 87, 102-03, 487; *3*
Della practica musica
   (Scipione Cerreto) 165
Praetorius, Michael
320-25
Praetorius, Michael
165, 168
Prat, Domingo 54, 775
Prat, Domingo 425, 427,
702, 810, 814
Pratten, Madame Sidney
   (Catherine Josepha)
   30, 488, 518, 520-21
Prefumo, Danilo 512-13
Preludes
   Corbetta, Francesco
   348
   Foden, William "Pre-
   ludes" 147
   Le Roy, Adrian 260
   Merchi, Giacomo 266-
   67
   Ponce, Manuel M. "24
   Preludes" 724
   Villa-Lobos, Heitor
   834, 837, 839, 843,
   846
   Visée, Robert de 382
Preludio o Capricho
arpeado (Sanz) 373
Preludio Saudade (1938)
   (Barrios Mangoré) 661
"1er Air varié", op. 21
   (Giulio Regondi) 524
Prés, Josquin des *See*
Josquin des Prés
"The President's cor-
   ner. The first plan
   for a Guild" 128
Presti, Ida 633, 645,
738-46
"Presti + Lagoya + two
   guitars" 744
Prieto, Víctor 229,
283, 310; 266
Prosperi, Carlo xxiii
Propiac 283
Provost, Richard 263,
346, 687
Prud'homme, Brian 380

P-Q-R   Index

Prusik, Karl 498
Prynne, Michael 912
psalmos 275
psalterio 272
pseaulmes 260
"Public concerts" 391
Publishing
  Le Roy and Ballard
  230
  Paris, 16th c. 161-62
  Venegas de Henestro-
  sa, Luys 251
Pujet, François 873,
878
Pujol, Emilio 1, 36,
275-76, 295; 32-33, 89,
158, 203, 206, 716,
815-21
Pujol, Emilio 137; 427,
645, 702, 747-59, 786,
808, 810, 814, 829
  "Becqueriana" 753
punteado xvii, 60
Purcell, Ronald C.
xxiv, 137, 244, 281;
137, 222, 406, 663,
683, 755
Pythagorean fretting
188; 906
Pythagorian theory 1020

quarter-tone guitar
1037-39
quartet
  Cuarteto Dona-Dio 84
  Giuliani, Mauro 484
  Paganini, Niccolò
  509, 513, 516
  Schubert, Franz 493,
  530, 535-40
Quatre pièces brèves
  (Frank Martin) 713
Queiróz, José de
  Oliveira
    "Caterete" 63
Quensel, A. 884
Quine, Hector 686
quinterna 320
Quito (Ecuador) 907

Radke, H. 514
Radole, Giuseppe 1; 34
Ragossnig, Konrad 1,
177; 35
Ragus, Linda 288
Raimondi, Marc-Antoine
177; 872
*Ramillete de Flores, O
  Colección de Varias
  Cosas Curiosas* xvi,
  35; 170, 180
Ramirez, José 796, 956,
961-62, 982-86, 1036
Randolph, Laurie 775
rasgueado [rasguado]
xxvii, 60
Rasmussen, Knud 351
Ratliff, Neil xxv
Ravel, Maurice 691
Raygada, Carlos 731
"Real Time Analyzer"
  (experimentation)
  1029
recitals 95
  Llobet, Miguel (April
  1916) 710
  Paris (1829-1839) 411
  Programs 47, 116,
  121, 131, 491-92,
  659, 707, 709, 749,
  755-56, 809, 815,
  870
  Reviews 141, 391,
  413, 425, 527-28,
  556-57, 582, 707,
  755, 799
  Segovia, Andrés 772
  Tárrega, Francisco
  (1904) 824
Reeve, W. 304
Regondi, Giulio 401,
413, 499, 522-25
  "ler Air varié",
  op. 21 524
  "2eme Air varie",
  op. 22 524
  "Introduction et
  Caprice", op. 23 524
Reimer, Karel 67
Reinhard, Kurt 19

Index

reprisa 60; 278

Resumen de acompañar la parte con la guitarra (Santiago de Murcia) 365

"Return with us now. The *Soundboard*'s featured facsimile" 791

Reviews of literature on Ponce, Manuel 729 Sor's *Method* 567 *See also* reviews listed under individual entries

"Rèverie nocturne", op. 19 (Giulio Regondi) 524

Revue Musicale 690, 694

Rey de la Torre 690

Ribayaz, Lucas Ruiz de *See* Ruiz de Ribayaz, Lucas

Ribouillault, Danielle 407

Ricci, Giovanni Pietro 284, 309

Richafort, J. 244

Richter, John 836

Ricordi publishing firm (1808-1857) 75, 399

Riemann, Hugo 266

Riera, Juan 705, 750, 756

Rierra, Juan 566

RILM Abstracts of music literature (International Inventory of Music Literature) xxvii

Rimmer, Joan 875; *8*

Rimski-Korsakov, A.V. 1025

"Ring" Trilogy (Toru Takemitsu) 803

Rioja, Eusebio 957

Rischel, Thorwald [Thorvald] 68-69, 459

ritornello 60; 278

Ritter, Peter 284, 311

The Rizzio guitar 900

Robbins, Lance 914

Roberts, John 60, 111, 185, 228, 347, 354, 375, 421, 425, 567-68, 702, 706, 757, 775, 822-24; *51, 756*

Robledo, Josefina 66

Roch (method) 810, 814

Rodrigo, Joaquin 764-65

Rodrigo, Joaquin 282, 634, 643-44, 760-67

Rodriguez, Manuel 987

Roemer, Kammersänger 588

Rolla, Alessandro 284, 311

Romance 36, 236, 257, 259, 261, 266, 275, 282, 296; 193, 195, 200, 202, 217, 225 *La Sentinelle* 473

romanesca 36, 60; 194

Romanillos, José 426

Romanillos, José 988-89

Romano, Remigio 284, 301-02

"Romanza" (Barrios Mangoré) 657

Rombouts, Theodoor [Theodor] 875, 878

Romea, Alfredo 569

Romero family 868-69

Romero, Luis T. 112

Roncalli, Lodovico 284, 309; 253, 259

rondeau 247

rondo 237, 304

Rontani, Raffaello 284-85, 301, 307

Roth, Elizabeth E. 871

Rothschild, Germaine de 443

Rosetta, Giuseppe *Sonatine* 768

Rosier, Nicolas de *See* Derosier, Nicolas

Rossato, Daniela 490

Rossi, A. 570

Rossi, Luigi 271

R-S   Index

Rossini, Gioacchino
  "Zelmira", arranged
  for guitar 399
Rouget de Lisle 304
Rousseau 267, 283
Róveri, Ercole Remo 653
Rowbotham, James 285,
  306; 229
Rubio, David 990-92
Rubio, M.J. 286, 310
Ruiz de Ribayaz, Lucas
  283, 309; 266, 289,
  291, 293, 370-71
Rush, George 286, 304,
  311
Russia 15; 91-92, 97,
  100, 102, 107-08, 556-
  58, 561, 578 *See also*
  Soviet Union
Russian guitar xxvi;
  90, 93-95, 99
Russian guitarists 98
Ryckaert, David III 874

S., A.L. 524
S., K. 527
Sabbatini, Pietro Paolo
  286-87, 302, 307-08
Sacchini 283
"Sacrifice" (Toru
  Takemitsu) 803
Sadie, Stanley xxvi
Sagreras 814
Sainz de la Maza,
  Regino 36, 825
Sainz de la Maza,
  Regino 66, 109, 760,
  870
Salazar, Adolfo 220
Salazar, Adolfo 644
Salisbury Journal 932
saltarello 280, 297
"Salve Regina" 264
San Martino, Fr.
  Leonardo de 230
San Severino *See* San-
  severino, Benedetto
Sancho, Sebastian
  Caldentey 109

Sancta Maria, Thomas de
  36, 227, 287-88, 306;
  153, 248-49
Sandi, Luis 80
Sanseverino, Benedetto
  287, 307; 271, 291, 294
Santa Cruz 289
Santa Mariana de Jesús
  907
Santiago de Murcia *See*
  Murcia, Santiago de
Santino da Parma 273,
  288, 311
Santorsola, Guido 38-41
Santos, Turibio 840
Sanuy, Ignacio María
  758
Sanz, Gaspar xix, 288-
  89, 308-09; 194, 266,
  282, 289, 291, 293,
  341, 371-76, 763
São Marcos, Maria Livía
  66
Sarabande
  Baroque five-course
  guitar 60; 276
  Murcia, Santiago de
  368
  Visée, Robert de 383
Sarabia, Benito 109
saravende 269, 287
Sardinia (Italy) 74
Sarenko, W[asil] S. 99,
  102
Sarti 258, 289, 310
Sasser, William Gray
  571-72
Saunier 903
Savio, Isaías 66, 826
Scandinavian countries
  10
"Scaramouche" 354
Scarlatti, Vincenzo
  444, 577, 841, 967,
  976
Schaffer, John W. 842-
  43
Scheidler, Christian
  Gottlieb 289, 311;
  526-28

344

Index

S-

Scheidler, J.F. 290,
311
Scheit, Karl 972
Schenkerian theory 1;
843
Schertzer 96
scherzi 232, 241
Schick, Gottlieb 881
Schick, Otto 902
Schiller, Johann Chris-
toph Friedrich von
950
Schlager, Karlheinz 225
Schlick, Johann Conrad
296, 311
Schmid (l'aîné),
Bernhard 878
Schmid, Heinrich Kaspar
538
Schmid, Heinrich Kaspar
530
Schmitz, Eugen 264
Schneider, James 1039
Schneider, John 642-43,
1009
Schneider, Richard 993-
94
Schneider-Klement,
Albrecht 1010
Schönbach, Dieter xxiii
Schoenberg, Arnold
xxiii; 642, 769
    Serenade, op. 24 769
Schöniger 290, 311
Schotty 515
Schrade, Leo 238
Schrade, Leo 716
Schroth, Andreas 408
Schubert, Franz 96;
403, 493, 496, 529-40,
656
    "Erlkönig" 529
    letter, as the basis
    of a song in Domi-
    nick Argento's
    *Letters from compo-
    sers* 656
    Lieder 531-34
        Lied "Hänflings
        Liebeswerbung" 532

Lied "Nacht und
    Träume" 532
Quartet 493, 530,
535-40
"Ständchen" (tran-
scription by Johann
Kaspar Mertz) 496
use of folk instru-
ments 403
Schultz *See* Schulz,
    Johann Abraham Peter
Schulz 96
Schulz, Andreas 290,
311
Schulz [Schultz], Jo-
hann Abraham Peter
290, 311
Schulz, Leonard 499
Schüsse, Erich 573
Schuman, Friedrich
Theodor 290-91, 311
Schuster, Friedrich 950
Schwarz-Reiflingen,
Erwin xxi; 70, 409,
460-61, 515, 539-40,
574-75 589, 700,
707-08, 759, 792,
827, 902, 944
Sclar, Joyce Rohr 655-
56, 673
Sczepanowski, Stan-
islaus 627, 931
Searle, Humphrey xxiii
"The seasons of the
year, in four solo
sonatas for chitarra
francese" (Antonio
Nava) 75
Sebastian, Felix de
Santos 109
"Seconda-serenata
trio" (Goffredo
Petrassi) 719
Segerman, Ephraim 160;
3
Segovia, Andrés 732,
745, 793-97, 844, 973,
1032-33

Segovia, Andrés 137;
47, 64, 410, 419, 638-
39, 644, 668, 683,
724, 733, 761, 770-92,
798-801, 804, 831,
860, 890
Segovia, Andrés Jr.
772
seguidillas 236
Seiber, Mátyás xxiii
*Selectissima elegant-
issimaque* (Pierre
Phalèse) 229
Sellas, Georgius 898
Sensier, Peter 36; 82,
85, 186, 658, 695,
849, 929, 935, 945-46
Serenade, op. 24 (Ar-
nold Schoenberg) 769
Severi Perugino,
Francesco 291, 302,
307; 269
Sfondrino, Giovanni
Battista 291, 307
Shahn, Ben 877
Shaker table (experi-
mentation) 1030
Sharpe, A.P. xxi; 37,
1011
Shearer, Aaron 119
Shelley, Percy Bysshe
924
Sherry, James 746, 869,
966, 969, 975, 1036
Shomura, Kiyoshi 802-03
Shore 326
Shulfer, Glen 484
Sicca, Mario 1; 38-41
Sichra [Sychra], A.O.
99, 101-02
Siegel, Samuel 129
Sigurbjörnsson,
Thorkell xxiii
Silva, Jesus 733
Silva, José Fernandez
899
Simões, Ronoel 66
Simplicio, Francisco
109, 933
Simpson, Clinton 120

Simpson, Glenda 200
sinfonie 243
sister tanbur 1004
Slavski, Vladimir 108
Sloane, Irving 1012-13
Slonimsky, Nicholas 77
Smith, Carleton Sprague
734
Smith-Brindle, Reginald
643
Snow 303
Snitzler, Larry 850
Societies *See* Guitar
Societies and Clubs
Society of the Classic
Guitar 131-33, 554
Soirée dans Grenade
(Claude Debussy) 691,
693
Sokolowski, Marek
Konrad 87
Sokolowski, M.L. 100
Solerti, Angelo 306
Solowiow, Alexander 102
"Some officers of the
Guild" 129
sonata [sonate, sonet-
tos] 230, 232, 235,
239, 241, 243, 246,
252-54, 257, 261,
264, 269, 271, 275,
281-82, 286, 292,
300
Sor, Fernando 551
"Sonata III" (Manuel
Ponce) 725
sonate ricercate 243
Sonatine (Giuseppe
Rosetta) 768
sonetos 244
"12 Songs for guitar"
(Toru Takemitsu) 803
Songs from the Chinese
(Benjamin Britten)
655, 673
"Sonido Trece" (Julián
Carrillo's Micro-
tonal system) 674-77
Sonneck, Oscar G. xxv;
121

346

Index   S-

Sopeña, Federico 644
Sor [Sors], Fernando
96, 251, 291, 311; 13,
32, 400-01, 405-06,
410, 412, 419-21, 460,
473, 498, 541-83, 633,
710, 810, 926, 935
"Sor" 541
Soriano Fuertes, Mari-
ano 427
"[Sor's obituary]" 542
Sorriso, Marino 268
Soto, Luis de 808
Sotos, André de 291-
92, 309; 266, 289
South American folk
music 860
Soviet Union 103 *See
also* Russia
"La Spagne" (tenor
melody/Cabezón) 216
spagnolette 269, 287
Spain 15, 35, 59
    construction 188;
    953-57
    early guitar xv,
    xvii; 3
    general 155
    Granada (Spain) 111
    Segovia, Andrés 796
    tablature 4
    18th c. 254
    18th-20th c. 10
    19th-20th c. 109-11
Spalding, Dolber B.
794
Spalding, Walter 216,
735
Spalding, Walter 690,
962
"Spanish mazurka, no.
2" (Manuel Y. Ferrer)
137
Spies, Warner 892
Spinetta 258, 293
Squire Lottery (alias
of Francesco Cor-
betta) 343
Stadlman, Michael
Ignatius xxi

Stakhovich, M.A. 104
Stanley 304
"Stanza I" (Toru
Takemitsu) 803
Starkie, Walter xix
Staufer, Johann Georg
934, 936
Stefani, Giovanni
(comp.) 292, 300-02
Stravinsky, Igor 642
steel-string acoustic
guitar 15
Stegemann, Michael 435
Stetson, Karl A. 1026
Stevenson, Janis M.
254; 361
Stevenson, Robert 83,
86, 214, 377
Stevenson, Robert Lewis
(poet) 30
Stewart, Jimmy 422,
447, 462, 684, 736,
766, 798, 805, 828,
845
Stockmann, J.M. 98
Stockhausen, Karlheinz
642
Stoll, Franz de Paula
413, 499
Stone, Tom 1009, 1020
Storace, [Bernardo]
304; 271
Stover, Richard (D.)
78, 659-61
St. Petersburg (Russia)
Fernando Sor in 558
Stradivarius, Antonio
288, 900, 937
Stratton, Stephen S.
513
Straube, Rudolf 292,
309, 311
strings, guitar 188;
1031-33
Strizich, Robert 298;
265, 292-93, 371
Subira, José 164
Subira, José 427
Suite Brasilienne
(Heitor Villa-Lobos)
834

347

S-T   Index

*Suite populaire bresi-
lienne* (Heitor Villa-
Lobos) 837
Suite in d minor
(Robert de Visée)
298; 380-85
Sussex, Duke of 544
"Suoni notturni"
(Goffredo Petrassi)
719
Switzerland 413
Sychra, A.O. *See* Sichra
Sichra, A.O.
Symphony 9
Syntagma musicum (Mich-
ael Praetorius) 165
Szczepanowski, Stanslaw
Prus 87

Takemitsu, Toru 697,
802-03
"Folios" for guitar
697, 803
"Ring" trilogy 803
"Sacrifice" 803
"12 Songs for guitar"
803
"Stanza I" 803
"Valeria" 803
Talbot 291, 326
Tamayo, Manuel Cano *See*
Cano Tamayo, Manuel
Tandler, Franz 499
Tanno, John C. 84, 122,
147, 150, 410, 648,
981, 996, 1014
Tanno, John W. xxiv;
981, 1027; *53*
Tansman, Alexander 634,
804-05
Tappert, W. xxi; 42
tarantella 36, 60; 29,
58, 198
Tarditi, Oratio 293,
297, 307-08
Tárrega, Francisco
xxii, xxvii, 96, 137;
14, 32, 36, 110, 410,
638, 645, 653, 702,
708, 747, 751-52, 754,
756-57, 796, 806-29

"Tárrega als Mensch und
Künstler im Urteil
seiner Zeitgenossen"
829
Tatay, Vicente 995-96
Taunay, N.A. 872
Technique
ca. 1770-1850 xxiv;
393-94
Aguado, Dionisio 419-
20, 423
Berlioz, Hector 428-
33
Carlevaro, Abel 678
Ferandière, Fernando
466
France, early 19th c.
407
general 11, 33
iconography 177
Lagoya, Alexander 743
nail vs. flesh 1; 32,
35
Segovia, Andrés 419,
773
Sor, Fernando 419,
543, 565, 568, 575
vihuela 158, 178,
181, 183-84, 225
Yepes, Narciso 850
tecla (keyboard) 237,
296
Tecla Editions 701
Teixeira, Patricio 64
Tello, Francisco José
Leon 266
Tempel, Hans 411, 576
temperament 153, 235,
1020
Tenebaum, Elias xxiii
Teniers le Jeune, David
872
ten-string guitar 847-
50, 1035-36
The Term Catalogues 242
terz guitar 95-96; 629-
31, 803, 896
Terzi, Benvenuto 76

348

Index

T-

Tesoro de la lengua castellana o española (Covarrubias Orozco) xvii; 301

Teti, Giuseppi 1037-38

Thackray, Thomas 293, 311

Theatre
  17th & 18th c.
  Spanish 60; 283, 289
  Spanish lyric drama 155

theorbo [théorbe] 238, 245; 2

theorbo guitar 896

theorboists 73

Thibault, G. 230, 1000

Thomajan, P.K. *794*

Thompson, General T. Perronet 584-85, 926, 1020

thorough-bass 292; 365-66 *See also* basso continuo

Tielke, Joachim 877, 938-39

tiento 36; 197, 215

Tilmouth, Michael 329, 364

Tinctoris xvi, xviii

tiorba 273, 285, 295, 302

tiple 272, 292

Tissier 293, 309

Todeschino 273, 294, 311

Todini, G.A. 302

Töpfer, Karl 499

Tolly, Kevin 688

Tonazzi, Bruno 2, 516, 694, 709

Torner, E. Martínez 244, 275-76, 295

Torscianello, H. 302

Torres Jurado, Antonio de 256, 653, 747, 902, 929, 940-45, 962, 1003, 1012

Torroba, Federico Moreno 830-32

Tosca, Tomás Vicente 266

tourdions 260

Traeg, Andreas 294, 311

Traetta 232

Transcription methodology 36; 1-2, 5, 203-07, 234, 245-46, 263
  Of music by
    Corbetta, Francisco 344
    Daza, Esteban 222
    Guerau, Francisco 361
    Sanz, Gaspar 372, 376

Trend, J.B. xix; 239

Tres libros de musica en cifras para vihuela (Mudarra) xvi

"Tres 'sobre el cantollano de la alto" (Antonio Cabezón) 216

Trichet, Pierre 328

Trichet, Pierre 162, 291

trio (Wenzelslaus Matiegka) 535-37, 539-40

trios (Gallot D'I) 357

tripod *See* tripódison

trípode *See* tripódison

tripodion *See* tripódison

tripódison (invention of Dionisio Aguado) 414, 417, 421

Trombetti, Agostino 294, 308

Truhlar, Jan 67

tuning 285, 287-88, 291, 906

Turina, Joaquin 643, 833

Turnbull, Harvey xxi, 1, 60, 177; 43-44

Turner, William 329

"12 Songs for guitar" (Toru Takemitsu) 803

349

T-U-V   Index

24 Caprichos de Goya
   (Mario Castelnuovo -
   Tedesco) 682
Tyler, James xxiv, 60,
226, 236, 286, 292,
300, 303; 3, 160, 165-
66; *8*
Tyler, Thomas C.B. 497

United States 15; 112-
51 *See also* America
Upton, William Treat
xxv
Uruguay 15; 45
Usher, Terence 931
Usillos, Carlos 799

"Vahdah Olcott Bick-
   ford" 664
Vaillant, Jean xvi
Valdambrini, Ferdinan-
   do 294, 308
Valderrábano, Enríquez
   de xvi, 35, 294-95,
   306; 167, 188, 245,
   250
Valdez-Blain, Albert
   Sr. 123
"Valeria" (Toru Take-
   mitsu) 803
Valvasenzi, Lazaro 295,
307
Van der Meer, J.H. 1000
Van Eyk, Jan Jacob 295,
311
Vandola 230, 272, 292;
166, 330
Vannes, René 905
Vannes, René 985
variations
   chaconne 281
   Corbetta, Francesco
   348
   diferencias 202, 241
   folia 194
   "Folia de Espania"
   (Manuel Ponce) 721
   Giuliani, Mauro 477
   Kreutzer 488
   romanesca 194

La Sentinelle 473,
483
Sonatine, rondo
   (G. Rosetta) 768
Sor-Mozart Variations
547
"Variations sur Folia
   de Espania" (Manuel
   Ponce) 721
Vargas Y Guzman, Juan
   Antonio 377-78
Vasquez, J. 281
Vaudeville 266
Váya Pla, Vicente 767
Vechten, Carl van 710
Vega, Carlos 61-62, 800
Vega Carpio, Lope de
xix
Velasco, Nicolás Doizi
   de *See* Doizi de
   Velasco, Nicolás
Velasco, Venancio
   García 423
Velasquez, Diego 875,
881
Velazquez, Manuel 997
Venegas de Henestrosa,
   Luys 36, 223, 296,
   306; 216, 245, 251
Veneri, Gregorio 296,
307, 311
Venezuelan music 866
Vera, César 915
Vera, Fernando 915
Verdi, Giuseppe
   Otello, excerpt with
   guitar part 431-32
Verini, Philippo 546
Vernillat, France 12
*La vida del escudero
   Marcos de Obregón*
   (Vicente Espinel) 352
Vidal, B. 296-97, 310
Vidal, Mr. 120
Vidal, Robert J. 645
Vienna (Austria) 402-
04, 499
   construction in 947
   Giuliani in 474
   Schubert Lieder 533-34

350

Index

Viennese classical
  composers 403
Viennese guitar school
402, 404, 455, 474, 499
Viglietti, Cedar 45
vihuela de Flandes
xviii
vihuelists xvi
  Daza, Esteban xvi;
  192, 221-22
  Fuenllana, Miguel de
  xvi; 161, 175, 192,
  200-01, 204, 223-27,
  245
  Milan, Luis xvi; 13,
  159, 167, 192, 197,
  201, 207, 231-40
  Mudarra, Alonso xvi;
  161, 173, 192, 194,
  197, 201, 245
  Narváez, Luis de xvi;
  170, 180, 188, 192,
  194, 241-42, 245
  Pisador, Diego xvi;
  175, 192, 204, 243-
  47
  Valderrábano, Enrí-
  quez de xvi; 167,
  188, 245, 250
Villalar 244
Villalba Muñoz, Luis
227
Villa-Lobos, Heitor 737
Villa-Lobos, Heitor 64,
78, 634, 643, 804, 834-
46
  "Etudes" 837
  "Preludes" 843, 846
  Suite Brasilienne 834
  *Suite populaire bre-
  silienne* 837
villancico 36, 232,
275; 193, 195, 202
villanelle [vilanelle]
247, 255-56, 270, 278,
287, 300-01
villanescas 244
Villon, Jacques (Gaston
  Duchamp, pseud.) 871
Vinaccia, Antonius xxi

viola xviii, 247, 253,
294; 65, 191
viola di gamba 257
viola Portugueza 281
violão 65
violin xxv, 239, 245,
247, 253-54, 257, 265-
67, 269, 272, 278, 282,
284, 286, 290, 292-93,
295, 299 *See also*
  violon
violin notation 75
violin strings xx
violin technique
  Niccolò Paganini's,
  as compared to his
  guitar technique 515
violon 230-31, 233,
235, 239, 246, 257,
262, 273, 289, 296-97
violoncell [violon-
  celle, violoncello]
  231, 235, 246, 253,
  292
viols 901
Viñas Dias, José 109-10
Vincenti, Alessandro
235, 297, 307
Virchi [Targhetta],
  Paolo 297, 306
Visée, Robert de 297-
98, 309; 252-53, 255,
291, 379-85
Vistisen, Bo B. 1019
Vitali, Filippo 298,
307
Vogl, Hans 998
voix de ville 261
Volkonsky, Andrei xxiii
Vollmer, Tom *775*
Volman, Boris 578
Vol'man, Boris L'vovich
105-07
Vreedman 160

Wade, Graham 1; 46-47,
187, 201, 240, 381-85,
412, 579-81

W-X-Y-Z

Wager-Schneider, John 665, 699, 719, 803, 862 *See also* Schneider, John
Wagner, Frank 88, 108
Walker, Donald 775, 801
Walker, Thomas 284
Wallo, Joseph F. 1015
walses 235, 247 *See also* waltzes
Walter, E. 851
waltzes 231-32, 237, 250 *See also* walses
Wanhal, J. 304
Ward, John M. xvii, 35-36, 279, 290, 296; 188-91, 251
Warren, Eve 869
Warsaw (Poland) Fernando Sor in 558, 582
Washington, George 136
Watteau, Antoine 177; 878, 881, 891, 893-94
Weber, Carl Maria von 96; 586-89
Weber, Gottfried 628
Webern, Anton 642
Weckerlin, Jean Baptiste Theodore 906
Weideman [Weidemann], Karl Friedrich [Charles Frederick] 298-99, 304, 310-11
Weidlich, Joseph 294
Weiland, Francis 151
Weimar xx
Weiss, Sylvia Leopold 1034
Welford, Robert 1007
Weller, M.P.I. 883
Weller, Malcolm 992
Weller, Malcolm 667
Wettengel, Gustav Adolf 922
Whalen, Margaret 48
Whistling/Hofmeister, *Handbuch de Musikalischen Literaturen* xxv; 493, 529, 533-34

White, Timothy P. 1028-30
Willaert, Adrian 281; 246
Willee, Gerd 1010
"William Foden" 138-40
Williams, John 775
Williams, John 639, 686
Willier, Stephen A. xxiv, 226
Willimann [Willmann], Eduard A. 299, 311
Wilson, John 318
Winter, Peter von 299, 311
Witoszynskyi, Leo 49
Wolf, Alois 499
Wolf, Johannes xxiv, 225-26, 230, 238, 242, 245, 253-54, 269, 278, 281, 285, 291, 303, 305; 4, 5
Wolfe, Richard J. xxv
Wranitzky, Anton 299, 311
Wright, Lawrence xv
Wyssotzki, M.T. 99

Xarava y Bruna, Diego (Licentiate for Gaspar Sanz) 375
Ximenes, Antonio 299, 311

Yacopi, José 946
Yampol'sky, Izrail Markovič 517
Yates, William 299, 311
Yepes, Narciso 188; 847-51, 1035

Zabal, Fidel 133
Zadushevnaya Ispoved (Nicolai Petrovich Makaroff) 96
Zani de Ferranti, Marco Aurelio *See* Ferranti, Marco Aurelio Zani de
zarabanda 60; 279

Index   Z

zarabande francese 60,
241; 279
Zarate duo 633
zarazuela 60; 283
Zayas, Rodrigo de 36,
289; 159, 192, 202,
207, 242, 376, 915
Zeidel, Scott 348
Zoi, Liza *See* Athenian
  Guitar Duo
Zimmermann, F.M. 99
Zimmermann, Fiordor 102

Zuckert, John Frederick
  (Johann Friedrich)
  300, 311
Zurfluh, Jean 538
Zuth, Joseph xix, xxi;
24, 55, 413, 439, 499,
528
Zvengrowski, Steven
  Theodore 1; 50, 846
Zwolle (Holland)
  Alirio Diaz in 859